JFK

The Presidency of John F. Kennedy

HERBERT S. PARMET

Published by
The Dial Press
1 Dag Hammarskjold Plaza
New York, New York 10017

Library of Congress Cataloging in Publication Data

Parmet, Herbert S.
JFK, the presidency of John F. Kennedy.

1. Kennedy, John F. (John Fitzgerald), 1917-1963.
2. United States—Politics and government—1961-1963.
3. Presidents—United States—Biography. I. Title.
II. Title: J.F.K., the presidency of John F. Kennedy.
E842.P34 1983   973.922'092'4 [B]   82-24592
ISBN 0-385-27419-X

THE DIAL PRESS   NEW YORK

For Wendy and Ron
with love and admiration

Published by
The Dial Press
1 Dag Hammarskjold Plaza
New York, New York 10017

Library of Congress Cataloging in Publication Data

Parmet, Herbert S.
  JFK, the presidency of John F. Kennedy.

  1. Kennedy, John F. [John Fitzgerald], 1917–1963.
2. United States—Politics and government—1961–1963.
3. Presidents—United States—Biography. I. Title.
II. Title: J.F.K., the presidency of John F. Kennedy.
E842.P34 1983   973.922'092'4 [B]   82–14575
ISBN 0–385–27419–X

Contents

88808

Contents

Acknowledgments

This second and concluding volume of my biography of John F. Kennedy could not have been accomplished without the usual patient and gracious cooperation of the entire research staff of the John F. Kennedy Library at Columbia Point in Boston. The current work is further indebted to the research facilities and staffs of the Seeley G. Mudd Library at Princeton University; the Sterling Memorial Library at Yale; the Franklin D. Roosevelt Library at Hyde Park, New York; the Minnesota Historical Society at St. Paul; the Richard Russell Library at the University of Georgia at Athens; and the University of Arkansas at Fayetteville, where Samuel A. Sizer was especially courteous and helpful in leading me through the Fulbright Papers. At Austin, Texas, during an extended stay, I was the beneficiary of help from some very wonderful people: Nancy Smith, Linda Hanson, and Tina Lawson. As in the first volume, the holdings of the Oral History Research Office at Columbia University were invaluable.

My efforts were also greatly simplified by my ability to use the Wertheim Study of the New York Public Library and the services of the staffs of my two "home" libraries, at Queensborough Community College and the Graduate Center of The City University of New York.

A number of people were kind enough to provide special access to their private papers or restricted holdings at various repositories. They include Charles Bartlett, Edwin Bayley, Orren Beaty, Jr., Isaiah Berlin, Richard Bissell, William McCormick Blair, Bernard L. Boutin, Joseph Clark, Clark Clifford, Wilbur Cohen, Ralph Dungan, Myer Feldman, J. W. Fulbright, Edward Gullion, John Harllee, W. Averell Harriman, Brooks Hays, Walter W. Heller, Jacob Javits, U. Alexis Johnson, William Josephson, Philip M. Kaiser, Lyman B. Kirkpatrick, Jr., Marian N. Lewin, Edwin Martin, Earl Mazo, Newton Minow, Richard Neustadt, Paul H. Nitze, Chalmers Roberts, Charles Roberts, Pierre Salinger, John Sharon, Janet G. Travell, Marietta Tree, Roger Tubby, Joseph Tydings, Robert C. Weaver, Adam Yarmolinsky, and Paul Ziffren.

Many others granted me personal and telephone interviews, sometimes several, during the years devoted to my work on John F. Kennedy. Several desire to remain anonymous, but their cooperation is deeply appreciated. Others who contributed by making themselves available were Joseph W. Alsop, Robert B. Anderson, William Attwood, Robert G. Baker, Richard M. Bissell, Jr., Roger Blough, McGeorge Bundy, George G. Burkley, Clark Clifford, Chester V. Clifton, Michael DiSalle, Michael V. Forrestal, J. William Fulbright, David Garth, Arthur J. Goldberg, Richard N. Goodwin, Edmund Gullion, Kay Halle, Walter W. Heller, Ellis Hendrix, Fred Holborn, Hubert H. Humphrey, Walter Jenkins, Joseph E. Johnson, Lady Bird Johnson, Carl Kaysen, James Killian, Fletcher Knebel, Laura Bergquist Knebel, Robert W. Komer, Hans Kraus, James I. Loeb, Eugene McCarthy, George McGhee, Edwin M. Martin, Wilbur Mills, Lawrence F. O'Brien, Kenneth P. O'Donnell, Chalmers Roberts, Walt W. Rostow, Dean Rusk, Arthur Schlesinger, Jr., R. Sargent Shriver, George Smathers, Earl E. T. Smith, Theodore C. Sorensen, John Steele, Phillips Talbot, Janet G. Travell, William Walton, Robert C. Weaver, and Ralph Yarborough.

Several people were instrumental in helping to improve the quality of the final manuscript. Both Marie B. Hecht and Robert D. Parmet read drafts and helped to minimize errors. Douglas Stumpf of The Dial Press made substantial improvements from the original typescript. Dr. Jacqueline Aronson devoted much of her spare time to help prepare the final version for publication. As usual, however, responsibility for what appears in print remains with the author.

Herbert S. Parmet
Bayside, New York

JFK

1

"A Time for Greatness"

"Camelot" began with smoke from a defective rostrum and closed with a burst of gunfire in the street of an American city. So ended just over a thousand days of elegance, alluring prose, chivalrous masculinity, and drama. John F. Kennedy's widow, with a sophisticated realization of history's vagaries, begged a favorite journalist not to let her husband's story be left to the "bitter old men."[1]

No Kennedy mythologist tried to embellish that Inaugural setting because the gods had done the job. The youngest of America's elected presidents, never appearing more virile than at that moment, was replacing a worn general; the Democratic senator—a "consummate" politician —who had seen the war from South Pacific PT boats and the islands of Blackett Strait, was taking over from the Supreme Commander whose patriotism was convincingly stronger than his partisanship. The new and glamorous First Lady, of Bouvier–Auchincloss pedigree, from Miss Porter's, Vassar, and George Washington University, was succeeding the duteous sixty-four-year-old Army wife from Denver. No wonder the press marveled that the turnover showed no friction. It was far more cordial than when President-elect Eisenhower had come to call on Harry Truman eight years earlier.

The constitutional change came officially at noon, but the program itself got under way at 12:21, and even then there were a few snags. The eighty-five-year-old poet from New England, Robert Frost, tried to read lines written especially for the occasion, to commemorate the inauguration of the man who had departed from custom by inviting his participation. But the strong glare from the sun was too much for his eyes, so he substituted a poem he knew by heart. Those lines also seemed especially appropriate:

The land was ours before we were the land's.
Something we were withholding made us weak
Until we found out that it was ourselves
We were withholding from our land of living
And forthwith found salvation in surrender.[2]

Then Richard Cardinal Cushing experienced moments of anxiety. The clergyman closest to the Kennedy family, chosen as one of the four prelates to deliver an invocation, had a voice that already suffered from the twin disabilities of emphysema and asthma. But, as he began to speak, wisps of fine, blue smoke rose from the lectern. A mechanism used to elevate the stand had developed a short circuit. "Here's where I steal the show," the cardinal later remembered thinking. "If that smoke indicates a bomb and if the bomb explodes while I am praying, I'm going to land over on the Washington Monument."[3] Just then Eisenhower leaned over and whispered to Kennedy, "You must have a hot speech."[4] The plug was pulled, the incident passed, and the new President finally stepped forward.

He slipped off his coat, placed his hand on the family's Bible, the Douay Version—an English translation made for Roman Catholics in the sixteenth century—and faced Chief Justice Earl Warren. After Kennedy had repeated the oath of office, he delivered his address of 1,355 words, one of the briefest in all of American history (only President Washington's second was shorter). Those long since familiar with his Harvard accent, clipped voice, and expressive right hand, which chopped the air as he spoke, recognized Kennedy in his best campaign form.

Skepticism had been replaced by hope. And he was never more persuasive. His delivery was more certain, the words came out more deliberately and clearer than usual, and the crowd in the surrounding plaza, including the Kennedys seated behind him on the platform, ignored the twenty-two-degree cold. He knew they were with him, and his conviction produced the power to inspire.

It had seemed as though everybody wanted to share those moments, to contribute some of their own words and thoughts. "The main thing,"

Adlai Stevenson had suggested, after urging that the speech contain an "unequivocal commitment to disarmament," was to "create the impression of a new, bold, imaginative, purposeful leadership; to de-emphasize the bi-polar power struggle; and to emphasize the affirmative approaches to peace."[5] Walter Lippmann, when shown a draft, suggested that a reference to Russia as the "enemy" be replaced with the word *adversary*.[6] "This is pre-eminently a speech for those who will read it rather than those who will hear it," advised Ken Galbraith when he forwarded a draft he had put together with the help of Arthur Schlesinger, Jr., and Walt Whitman Rostow. "The immediate audience will not long remember. The readers will render the ultimate decision. So, rightly, I believe, I have made few concessions to your speaking style."[7] But John Kennedy was determined that this work, unlike much of what had appeared under his name, would be his own.[8]

Ted Sorensen's talent was nevertheless evident, and the words came easily from the new President's lips:

—*"We observe today not a victory of party but a celebration of freedom . . .*

—*"Let the word go forth from this time and place, to friend and foe alike, that the torch has been passed to a new generation of Americans —born in this century, tempered by war, disciplined by a hard and bitter peace, proud of our ancient heritage . . .*

—*"Let every nation know . . . that we shall pay any price, bear any burden, meet any hardship, support any friend, oppose any foe, to assure the survival and the success of liberty.*

—*"For only when our arms are sufficient beyond doubt can we be certain beyond doubt that they will never be employed. . . . [N]either can two great and powerful nations take comfort from our present course . . . both racing to alter that uncertain balance of terror that stays the hand of mankind's final war. So let us begin anew—Let us never negotiate out of fear. But let us never fear to negotiate.*

—*"All this will not be finished in the first one hundred days. Nor will it be finished in the first one thousand days, nor in the life of this Administration, nor even perhaps in our lifetime on this planet. But let us begin.*

—*"And so, my fellow Americans: ask not what your country can do for you—ask what you can do for your country."*[9]

For the long run, however, Galbraith's advice was on target. The next generation—"Kennedy's children"—all too often read his words as a summons leading to new, more bellicose cold-war objectives. One later historian charged that the speech was full of "swollen Cold War language" and that the "pompous phrasing" was too "alarming."[10] Proclamations of "a celebration of freedom" were the cloak for a new "manifest destiny," rhetoric more elegant but no less menacing than that which had come from America during the Eisenhower–Dulles years.

Had he lived to see how his history would be written, John Kennedy would neither have been shocked nor surprised. He had hired the experts, surrounding himself with more scholars than had been seen in the White House since Roosevelt's day. But all too often he viewed them with jaundiced doubts. It was easier to write than to make history. How convenient for them to forget in the years that followed the relief and expectations of the nation at the moment he took up the challenge!

And, when he did, there was hardly any dissent. "The fact is that he does have a mandate to solve our international problems by means of any device that will work," wrote Father John B. Sheerin in *Catholic World.*[11] "God," Barry Goldwater told newsman Jack Bell, "I'd like to be able to do what that boy did there."[12] From Arizona, Eleanor Roosevelt sent Kennedy her "gratitude" for the "sense of liberation & lift." She had read his words over and over, and she was "filled with thankfulness."[13] Stevenson called it "eloquent, inspiring—a great speech," while Harry Truman thought "it was just what the people should hear and live up to."[14] *The New Republic* hailed the Kennedy speech with a frontcover excerpt under the heading "Let Us Begin" and applauded it for advancing the "realistic proposition that the unifying forces in the world today are stronger than the divisive forces" and for opening "the door to new opportunities," which, it assumed, "have not been lost on Mr. Khrushchev."[15]

And so it went. Far from charging Kennedy with bellicosity, just about everybody praised his moderation. The speech was not only eloquent, wrote James Reston, "but moralistic and even religious," one that called for the transformation of "our national life, our relations with the Allies, and our relations with the Communists."[16]

Nor did the Russians themselves in any way anticipate the complaints of later American critics. Both nations promptly exchanged diplomatic messages that were remarkably warm and stressed the word *cooperation.*[17] Tass, the Soviet press agency, reported Kennedy's words without their usual editorial interpolations, and *Izvestia* even printed the full text.[18]

It was hoped, as the Kennedy campaign slogan had suggested, that it *was* "a time for greatness," and that expectation inspired the inaugural pageantry. If, privately, he was nervous, that mattered little to those who wanted to believe. The address completed, enthusiasms higher than ever, the band played "Hail to the Chief."

With Jacqueline, he rode in the open, bubble-top limousine, waved his hand, and smiled for most of the forty-five minutes that it took to reach the reviewing stand. And there he remained, long after the First Lady had given up, still greeting each governor who came by. The cameras showed the forty-one floats and seventy-two bands that embellished the eight-mile-long parade. Kennedy became especially animated with the approach of a thirty-two-ton PT boat with the number *109* on its side. Not until 6:15, after the sun had gone down and the temperature had dropped, did the last unit march by the stand in front of the White House. Robert F. Kennedy and his wife, Ethel, were still with him, and they all walked back to the mansion to relax before that evening's round of parties.

One of the members of the Inaugural Committee who had helped plan it all was Kay Halle, the Washington socialite, writer, and longtime friend of the Kennedy family. Kennedy's choice of Robert Frost to read a poem had inspired her to send invitations as special guests to prize winners in the arts, sciences, and humanities. One Nobel prize winner who could not attend was Ernest Hemingway, then hospitalized in the Mayo Clinic with high blood pressure and severe depression. In lieu of the trip to Washington, he decided to write a tribute.

Those sentences, written half a year before his suicide, were difficult for Hemingway. Several times during the process, he betrayed his agony by calling Halle just to talk. His wife, Mary, has explained that, as he wrote, "his pen hovered with a nervous uncertainty" and a "sense of urgency, futility, almost a smell of desperation oozed out of him." He labored for a week before he finally produced his tribute, which Halle then mounted in a souvenir scrapbook.

Several months after the inauguration, Halle finally showed the President her collection. "I had put little markers in places where I thought he'd be particularly interested," she recalled. He read so rapidly Halle thought he must have been skimming: she had forgotten his mastery of speed-reading.[19] When he reached Hemingway's words, he repeated them aloud:

Watching the inauguration from Rochester there was the happiness and the hope and the pride and how beautiful we thought Mrs. Kennedy was and then how deeply moving the inaugural address was. Watching on the screen I was sure our President would stand any of the heat to come as he had taken the cold of that day. Each day since I have renewed my faith and tried to understand the practical difficulties of governing he must face as they arise and admire the true courage he brings to them. It is a good thing to have a brave man as our President in times as tough as these are for our country and the world.[20]

Halle explained that Hemingway was the most troubled of all those invited to the swearing in. All those calls from Minnesota to Washington had shown his obvious agony, and, she said, she had been tempted to suggest a presidential telephone call as a way of lifting the writer's spirits. "Kay," the President told her, "you know that sometimes it's better not to try and play God."[21]

If, in that instance, Kennedy had not chosen to "play God," his appeal had nevertheless cast him in a role where he was doing exactly that for millions. His outward display of confidence was enhanced by the physical attractions of youth and glamour. That night, he was tireless. He went on and on. Jackie accompanied him to the massive ball at the District of Columbia Armory. Finally she tired and returned to the White House for the night, but he continued. At two in the morning he made his final visit, to the Georgetown home of columnist Joe Alsop, where he was also joined by two of his old friends, Flo and Earl E. T. Smith.[22] By 3:30 that morning, play was done, and it was time to "get America moving again."

On January 14, 1960, less than two weeks after declaring his presidential candidacy, the author of *Profiles in Courage* faced the National Press Club. He scorned the presidency of Dwight D. Eisenhower for its lack of leadership, and quoted from *King Lear:* "I will do such things,—What they are yet I know not,—but they shall be The wonders [*sic*] of the earth." His summons to responsibility and action tapped an impulse that wanted to counter what had been increasingly characterized as the inert state of American politics. Jack Kennedy, the senator from Massachusetts, proposed that the presidency be rebuilt by "a man who will formulate and fight for legislative policies, not by a casual bystander to the legislative process."

He said that the dangerous decade that lay ahead demanded "a real fighting mood in the White House," which, as in the time of strong presidents of the past, "must be in the center of moral leadership." John F. Kennedy, not yet forty-four, declared that "We will need in the sixties a President who is willing and able to summon his national constituency to its finest hour—to alert the people to our dangers and our opportunities—to demand of them the sacrifices that will be necessary."[23]

He had been brought up to believe that government was indeed a challenge, the highest calling for those equipped with the training and heritage. The failure to respond by those so charged had been disastrous once before in his lifetime. Now, as in the 1930s, when England had slept, the purpose was amply clear. Could a democracy survive in competition with totalitarian states? Could it produce leaders with the courage to risk popular displeasure, even if they had to tell the people what the people did not want to know? It was, then, up to decent men; however dangerous a place the world was, the risks were multiplied when men of goodwill and ability failed to respond.

In the early fall of 1946, he had addressed his former teachers and students at the Choate School. His word was circulated by the *Alumni Bulletin* as "Jack Kennedy's Challenge," a plea for independent preparatory schools to equip America with more political leadership.[24] It was a theme that he repeated over and over again with whatever variations audiences required. He insisted that courage involved the will to confront the coming "struggle between 'collectivism and capitalism.' "[25] Through the years Jack Kennedy's analysis became more sophisticated, his constituency more national and diverse, but the voice remained focused on the task of preserving democracy as a challenge to the courage of those whom Dixon Ryan Fox had called "the few, the rich, and the well-born."

"When the Executive fails to lead," he wrote in 1958, "it leaves a vacuum that the Legislative branch is ill-equipped to fill." He pointed to the failure "to develop courses of action to meet protracted competition with the Soviet Union." He charged the executive branch with having had a "failure of nerve," which had resulted in a technological lag that had produced a "missile gap" and blindness toward "the economic revolution that is sweeping through Asia, the Middle East, Africa, and Latin America." The key words were *challenges, vigorous, fight,* and the need for a President ready to "exercise the fullest powers of his office."[26]

Kennedy's publisher friend, Ben Bradlee, noted that he was fascinated by the "use and abuse of all power."[27] Chester Bowles, reminiscing after the short presidency had ended, observed that Kennedy went into politics "largely because he was interested in securing power, but once he was in public life and once he had become President, it seems to me that he moved steadily toward this broader concept of using power constructively."[28]

New Presidents and young lovers share a common delusion: They can reorder the world. Jack Kennedy and his youthful "band of brothers" had no such notion. Their milieu was too sophisticated for that, Kennedy himself too cynical about human nature. But they felt the sense of the political cycle, and, as Arthur Schlesinger, Jr., had argued that year, they knew the country was ready for them.

The general in the White House was, at best, benign. He smiled, soothed, and made as few waves as possible. He evaded controversy, finessed his way around the rough spots, and minimized the drama. He retained his cool, and his decade seemed deceptively placid. By 1960 his popularity had survived the inevitable setbacks and blunders. His hold on the American psyche was undimmed. Nobody argued that he could not have won another term if he were so disposed and there were no Twenty-second Amendment. But, although durable and faithful, he had also become worn, dull, unimaginative, languid, sexless; pure but anti-septic, uncreative and unprogressive. The fickle were ready to have their heads turned, and Kennedy rose at the right time.

He was young. He was elegant. Maturity, and improved health, had filled out his face, and he had never looked better. His sandy hair often seemed reddish, and his eyes were capable of projecting the gleam that gave his smile the incarnation of the Irish stereotype. When relaxed, he radiated the hint of a mischievous schoolboy with thoughts that were best kept private. After some fourteen years in public life, he had developed into a remarkably photogenic figure, and, with the electronic media also maturing, he was about to become the first picture star in the White House.

By the start of that year's Democratic National Convention in Los Angeles, after months of primaries, political trade-offs, and media that gladly contributed to making the most of JFK, Kennedy had the votes. Hubert Humphrey, disappointed at having been forced by defeat in West Virginia to withdraw his candidacy, confirmed that simple fact to Lyndon Johnson. The next morning's papers reported George Meany's statement that in no way would the majority leader be acceptable to organized labor. Four days before the balloting, then, Lyndon Johnson's brief, curious campaign for the presidential nomination was dead.

More confirmation came from his telephone conversation with Ross Barnett, the ultra-segregationist governor of Mississippi. Barnett was upset that a *Reader's Digest* article had termed Johnson's political philosophy as both liberal and conservative. No touch of liberalism would do, and that was enough to make him unacceptable. Johnson returned the phone to the receiver and said to an aide, "It's all over. It's going to be Kennedy by a landslide."[29]

On Wednesday, Governor LeRoy Collins of Florida gaveled the Democrats to order. Johnson was nominated by Sam Rayburn, the aging, legendary Texan. Almost two hours later, Orville Freeman, Minnesota's forty-two-year-old governor, came to the rostrum and described John F. Kennedy "as a man of devoted liberal principle" who would "bring courage and drive and dedication at a time when it is desperately

called for in America and the world." Then he added the thought that
Kennedy would help "lead us to a fruitful America, to a peaceful world
for mankind everywhere."[30]

Following tradition, Freeman had saved Kennedy's name for the end.
That triggered the circus that had become so much a part of presidential
nominating conventions. Pat Brown looked as ebullient as if he had just
fulfilled his own presidential dreams when he led the demonstrators
down the aisle. The band played "Happy Days Are Here Again" and
"Anchors Aweigh," striking a mood in tune with those so confident they
had the candidate able to live up to their campaign slogan, "A Time for
Greatness." From his rented hideaway apartment on the fringes of Hollywood, Jack Kennedy watched the scene on television. Whatever the
head count, he had not relaxed that day, having completed visits to seven
state caucuses. Nobody had a better grasp of the shape of the votes to
come, but he was not taking the results for granted.

Neither were the Stevensonians. Through eight Eisenhower years,
they had endured that "spell in the wilderness," and they feared
Kennedy's nomination would lead to more of the same: sterile conservatism, opportunism by pros more enchanted with power than progress;
another big money victory. With Johnson going nowhere, and Stu Symington's candidacy not amounting to very much, liberals could only
bank on Adlai. If the twice-defeated candidate couldn't make it now,
perhaps the whole thing no longer mattered. Truman had fired an anti-
Kennedy salvo and gone home in disgust; they could do the same.

At eight o'clock on the evening of the thirteenth, Eugene McCarthy
spoke for Stevenson and delivered one of the most eloquent and rousing
speeches ever heard at a presidential nominating convention, a performance so effective that it was almost immediately suspected to have been
a desperate last-minute attempt at siphoning off Kennedy votes.
"Power," he said, "is best exercised by those who are sought after. Do
not reject this man who made us proud to be called Democrats. Do not
reject this man who is not the favorite son of one state, but the favorite
son of fifty states and of every country on earth."[31]

That set off one of the great floor demonstrations of convention history. David Garth, then a TV producer, had worked with a team to put
it all together. Kennedy's people had controlled the convention, which
also gave them access to the balcony tickets. But when, as expected, they
put off actually taking their seats, Garth "kept sneaking people in and
filled up the balconies with Stevenson people. Then we had people left
over. They were milling around inside but not on the floor. And every
time a demonstration came up for Stu Symington or any other favorite

son, they didn't have enough people to fill out their own demonstration so our kids would join in, and so they got on the floor. So by the time we came on with the Stevenson demonstration, we ended up by having about five hundred extra people on the floor, plus having jammed the people in all those seats on the balcony."[32]

Frustrated by his repeated inability to end the uproar, Governor Collins ordered the house lights turned off. A single, powerful spotlight then swept through the darkened hall and dramatically highlighted the large American flag. Even that hardly helped. Not until twenty-five minutes later was Collins able to restore order and call for seconding speeches.[33]

Taking it all in from his North Rossmore Avenue apartment, Kennedy had feared the belated Stevenson drive as a potentially destructive storm. Earlier in the week ovations for both Eleanor Roosevelt and Stevenson had rekindled enthusiasm at the Memorial Sports Arena, and there were other demonstrations in the city. Unsettling rumors were heard about the Stevenson virus causing several delegations to abandon Kennedy for various favorite sons, all of whom could have had a possibly fatal effect on the chances of a first-ballot victory.

Some Stevensonians even convinced themselves that their man had an outside chance at winning. A Kennedy first-ballot failure might give Stevenson enough second-ballot strength to throw the convention wide open. Kennedy would inevitably begin to fade, and the convention would turn into a Stevenson–Johnson horse race with an uncertain number of Kennedyites drifting toward the Governor. A state-by-state breakdown taken by Stevenson's manager concluded that the scenario was reasonable.[34] "Those sort of things were of great concern," recalled Charles Spalding, one of Kennedy's closer friends. "How much strength would it have? Would it upset the apple cart? Would the delegates be swayed by a former idol?"[35] But when the storm passed, the Kennedy tower still stood.

As the delegations announced their votes, the futility of the stop-Kennedy drive became obvious. When Wisconsin's fifteen went for him, Kennedy was over the top. He immediately telephoned Jacqueline, whose pregnancy had kept her at Hyannis Port, and then sped the twelve miles to the Sports Arena with a police motorcycle escort. Johnson's press secretary, George Reedy, handed reporters a one-paragraph statement saying that the Texan had accepted Kennedy's nomination "with all my heart." Shortly before midnight in Los Angeles, Kennedy faced the shouting convention. He praised both Johnson and Symington, and pointedly ignored his unannounced rival. Few people were in the mood for a windy speech at that hour, and Kennedy briefly promised to carry the fight to "the people . . . and we shall win."[36]

Winning the nomination usually involves wooing the professionals. The pros had the final word; they were in control. During the 1970s much would be made of "outsiders" taking over the presidency. But in 1960, although the rules had yet to change, John Kennedy was a political "outsider." His accomplishment was made possible by the absence of a + powerful consensus for any single rival.

Hubert Humphrey took his candidacy seriously, and so did significant numbers of liberals. A veteran of the Americans for Democratic Action and a central figure of the celebrated civil rights floor fight that had ripped apart the 1948 convention, his progressive credentials carried none of the uncertainties attached to Kennedy's. His spirit combined liberalism and pragmatism, but, in 1960, neither liberals nor conservatives doubted where he stood.

At the age of forty-nine, having already tasted disappointment at the 1956 convention when Stevenson bypassed him as a running mate after Hubert thought he had had a firm commitment, he was ready to go all the way. But he had to convince the politicians by first convincing the voters, and that meant proving himself in the primaries. He fought hard, as Hubert always did, but he couldn't muster the material means needed for winning in the jet age. Academics, ADA intellectuals, and labor leaders were not enough to compensate for the politicians wary about lining up at his door. Conservatives resisted a man who was both New Dealish and for "nigger" equality. And he was hardly given much credibility as a candidate in the West Virginia primary when Senator Robert Byrd made clear that he was regarding Hubert as a stalking horse for Lyndon Baines Johnson.

Johnson, the majority leader, thought he could take it all without the primaries. With Humphrey's help, Kennedy would fall on his face. Possessing a southern base and powerful control over certain northern bailiwicks, the master of the Senate would come out on top. From Texas hill country, he was widely regarded as a sufficiently legitimate Southerner, and it was vital that someone with his credentials be at the helm because, as Jim Rowe warned his friend, "we're going to get in a hell of a mess on civil rights."[37] But, to Johnson, the Southern label was lethal. If Kennedy had his religion, Johnson had the burden of regionalism. Liberals would never accept him. Five years earlier, when he was but forty-seven, he had had a serious heart attack, and that also weighed against him.

Lyndon was an infuriating man. Maybe that was natural for a dynamo with both a need for power and wealth, and a thirst for manipulation. He was also a primitive. He railed and sulked at what he found others writing about him, and treated his associates, including the press, with alternating waves of effusiveness or brutality. Everything seemed to get under his skin, and he never quite knew how to handle it.[38]

Neither did he know what to do about a woman who connected with his sensitivities. She worked in his office and was usually part of the Johnson entourage. Later she married and left Lyndon's orbit. But, in 1960, his infatuation was no secret. The only question that divided those who knew both was how far it would move Johnson toward reordering his life. He was never casual about anything. At least one associate thinks he was sufficiently enchanted to consider leaving Lady Bird.

At that critical point a disruption of that sort would have meant political disaster. Perhaps that explains the tentative quality of his presidential "drive," the withholding of commitment, the appearance of desiring that events foreclose choices. One friend recalls that "in almost every campaign he ever ran, he got sick in the middle of it, almost a psychological thing. He tried some way to get out of it. And I would think there was a lot to that."[39]

Adlai Stevenson is usually portrayed as the Hamlet of the piece. His grand gesture at the 1956 convention of throwing to the delegates the choice of a running mate, thereby creating the Kennedy–Kefauver contest, probably contributed as much as anything else to that reputation. The perspective of years enables the move to be seen more accurately as a shrewd political and public-relations ploy. Adlai's 1960 role was also less mysterious than politic.

To Kennedy, of course, it was infuriating. "I've got it locked up," Jack told a Stevenson speechwriter, William Attwood. "Either he joins me or the hell with him."[40] Kennedy paid a visit to Stevenson's Libertyville home in May and found that the "Guv" would not budge, and so he left that session with obvious disappointment. He had heeded the advice of Stevenson's friends and had not dangled the State Department as a reward.[41] The Governor might take umbrage at the suggestion of a bargain, but neither was Kennedy crazy about having a secretary of state with the prima donna instincts of a John Foster Dulles.

Two days after that strained Libertyville meeting, Arthur Krock called Kennedy and remarked that Adlai was running hard for the nomination. "And how!" replied Kennedy.[42] Only to outsiders did he appear ambivalent. They heard his standard explanation about not intending to become a candidate, which was, of course, true in a technical sense, and he meant that up until the convention. He answered requests for his support by recalling promises to avoid endorsements, which was also technically true. Still, he was under the almost constant pressure from a trio of high-powered women: Eleanor Roosevelt, Mary Lasker, and Agnes Meyer. All argued that it was his duty to declare early. Mrs. Roosevelt was especially convinced that only a Stevenson–Kennedy ticket could keep Richard Nixon from reaching the White House.[43]

A small group of political insiders, however, most notably Senator A. S. "Mike" Monroney of Oklahoma and Monroney's astute aide, Tom Finney, were much more in tune with Stevenson's position and advised playing for a convention deadlock. At that point they calculated that the delegates would turn to their sentimental favorite for a third time. Monroney, Finney, John Sharon, and Jim Doyle, Stevenson's man in Wisconsin, went around the country trying to whip up a "draft Stevenson" movement.[44] In New York, Dave Garth and friends developed a volunteer organization that grew to six thousand people and twenty-one headquarters throughout the state.[45]

Stevenson's public detachment did not reflect his real mood. He expressed an obsessive feeling that the "country would be unsafe" in Nixon's hands. Attwood remembered that the Governor "just detested Nixon. He was the only man I ever heard him refer to as a son of a bitch. He was very careful with his language."[46] That kind of vehemence magnified the importance of the Democratic choice in the Governor's mind. It also suggests the thought that his passionate dread of a Nixon presidency and personal fear of failure may have been additional inhibitions.[47] If he could accept Kennedy, it was mostly as a far less threatening individual; put negatively, by far the lesser of two evils. "My difficulty is that I don't think he'd be a good President," Stevenson told Barbara Ward. "I do not feel that he's the right man for the job; I think he's too young; I don't think he fully understands the dimensions of the foreign affairs dilemma that are [sic] coming up; and I cannot in conscience throw my support to someone whom I do not really think is up to it. . . . I can't in conscience suddenly say, because I want to be secretary of state, 'Okay, I have changed my mind.' "[48]

Stevenson's behavior mystified Kennedy. He found him more than merely irritating. The Governor lacked a sense of reality. He was holding out even without any evidence of a significant pro-Stevenson movement among the delegates. In June even the vanguard of Stevenson's intellectual supporters—the Schlesingers, Galbraiths, and Commagers—defected and announced themselves for Kennedy. As Galbraith explained to Jack, ". . . intellectuals, like others, are subject to the bandwagon effect or, hopefully, have an eye for a winner."[49] By the time Mayor Daley said Stevenson would only get a piddling vote from his home-state delegation, the outcome had been virtually sealed. The Kennedy camp also had the useful support of the party's national chairman, Paul Butler.[50] As the convention was about to open, estimates of Kennedy's first-ballot strength reported in three weekly magazines ranged from 666 1/2 to 743 possible votes out of the needed 761. Kennedy's own calculation was 740.[51]

Stevenson was hardly as deluded as it seemed. Just before going to Los Angeles, he confided to a friend that he had few doubts that Kennedy would be nominated.[52] Nevertheless, Adlai went to the convention hall with all the aura of an unannounced contender, incited the adulation of his admirers, and, although some later tried to minimize their concern over his tactics, threw a momentary fear into the Kennedy camp. That Stevenson himself could have moved the professionals to deliver those cherished votes to him for a third time was wishful thinking. There is, then, little wonder that all of this led the Kennedys to conclude that Adlai was a fine prima donna but a terrible politician.

One critic rarely noted for sotto voce opinions was Harry Truman, and few were more ardent about stopping Kennedy. For the ex-president, as for Stevenson, that convention was a last hurrah. Truman had seen himself snubbed by Stevenson, his chosen successor, and then unable to advance Harriman four years later. By 1960 a man famous for his visceral reactions had become more enraged than ever. And the rise of young Jack Kennedy was one of the things that made him see red.

Almost nothing about Jack pleased Truman. Not his religion, his father, or his milieu. Geographically the men were separated by half a continent; culturally by a world. What Truman undoubtedly felt like saying about Kennedy—and the whole clan—would have made some of his famous outbursts seem tame. When word got out that the ex-president planned a televised preconvention press conference, the specter of an unleashed Harry stirred visions of a Democratic bloodbath, complete with religious animosity and consequent political suicide. When Clark Clifford told Dean Acheson that "the boss" was about to turn himself loose, the former secretary of state prudently urged restraint. But Harry was Harry. He promised Acheson that the advice would be taken "under consideration."[53]

It turned out that Truman's performance was relatively moderate, but still sharp enough to provoke the Kennedy camp. He said that Kennedy was just too young and "not quite ready" for the presidency. What was really needed was someone with "the greatest maturity and experience."

Despite his dubious qualifications, Jack was prepared to sweep a controlled and prearranged convention, when in reality he should have yielded to any number of other, better qualified men. "May I urge you," asked the former president, "to be patient?"[54] He was even guilty of a slip of the tongue when he called the candidate "Joseph," which may have inadvertently revealed his real target.[55]

Kennedy watched Truman from Hyannis Port, then arranged for a news conference at New York's Roosevelt Hotel. With the convention just one week away, the question of whether he could still be stopped remained interesting. "Mr. Truman," Kennedy began his point-by-point reply, "regards an open convention as one which studies all the candidates, reviews their records and then takes his advice." He kept silent about religion. Truman had not spelled that out, and he was not going to. But it was to the "age issue" that Kennedy directed his most effective thrust. Eloquently he recounted how overlooking fourteen years of experience in elective office merely because of age would have rendered as ineligible "all but three of the ten names put forward by Truman, all but a handful of American Presidents, and every President of the twentieth century—including Wilson, Roosevelt and Truman." Dropping those not yet forty-four would have disqualified Jefferson, Washington, and Madison from their founding roles and "kept Columbus from discovering America."[56]

But Kennedy didn't leave it at that. His reply verged on the audacious. Youth, he said, was not only a virtue; youth had its advantages. "The strength and health and vigor of these young men is equally needed in the White House, for during my lifetime alone four out of our seven Presidents have suffered major heart attacks that impaired at least temporarily their exercise of executive leadership."

Kennedy went on. "Older men may always be appointed to the Cabinet. Their wise counsel of experience will be invaluable, but then if ill health cuts short their work others may replace them." But, where a President is concerned, "the voters deserve to know that his strength and vigor will remain at the helm."[57]

Lyndon Johnson watched the performance from his Washington home. He could hardly have missed the clear reference to his own cardiac problem.

Having provoked the "health" issue, Kennedy had to be prepared for the consequences. In Los Angeles, Mrs. India Edwards, a longtime Democratic Party worker and currently cochairman of Citizens for Johnson, told the press that Kennedy had Addison's disease. Not very well informed for one making such a serious charge, she was unable to go beyond saying that doctors "have told me he would not be alive if it were not for cortisone." All she knew about Addison's was that it had "something to do with lymph glands."[58]

The Kennedy camp was prepared. Several weeks earlier two physicians, Dr. Eugene J. Cohen, a New York endocrinologist, and Dr. Janet Travell, an internist and pharmacologist, had supplied a statement declaring that he was in excellent health, fully capable of handling "an exhausting work load," and of "meeting any obligation of the Presidency without the need for special medical treatment, unusual rest periods or other limitations." Insofar as Addison's was concerned, the statement said that a checkup in late 1958 had shown that "your adrenal glands do function." In response to a hurried call from Sargent Shriver, both doctors consented to publicizing their names along with the document. Ted Sorensen, asked in Washington about reports that Jack was taking cortisone, denied them outright. "I don't know that he is on anything," he said, "any more than you and I are on."[59]

Nor had the medical statement said anything about the steroid. Explicit denials were reserved for such laymen as Sorensen and Robert Kennedy. Cortisone takes over for what the body fails to supply. Patients are not kept on that potentially debilitating drug because they feel so well but for either one of two reasons or a combination of both: the condition needs to be contained, or termination may be more difficult than maintenance. When Dr. Travell was interviewed by Sorensen in 1966, she explained that "Once a person has been put on this regimen, at the present time it is easier and safer just to continue the supplement indefinitely in most people." She also told him that Jack "was one of the early people who received the benefits of the nine alpha fluoro-cortico compounds which could be taken by mouth."[60] Kennedy's friend, Bill Walton, noted his dependence during the 1960 campaign. Wherever Jack went, an aide carried a special little bag because "he had to have medical support all the time." Frequent rests were also necessary.[61] Sargent Shriver, married to Jack's sister, Eunice, another Addisonian, confirmed that his brother-in-law was on cortisone for the rest of his life.[62] Dr. Hans Kraus, the New York surgeon who gave Kennedy extensive physical-therapy treatments in the White House, found that he was taking cortisone "all the time."[63] The medication had relieved the life-threatening condition, and the disease had little to do with his ability to do his job. All the while, however, the definitions offered to the public about both the disease and the treatment were prompted more by political necessity than by a desire to clarify.

While Truman's charges had created the contretemps over health during the preconvention period, some good did come out of the incident. Kennedy's rebuttal from the Roosevelt Hotel helped establish a pattern that became familiar to the public. On the defensive and in response to such challenges, he sparkled and gained more than he lost. Even relatively early in his career his most effective moments came during question-and-answer sessions. Now, during the campaign, he was strongest under pressure. Nobody appreciated his response more than his father. That day, Joe Kennedy listened to his son's performance from a cottage at Lake Tahoe and told a close friend that he thought it had been Jack's best effort.[64]

Inadvertently or not, Truman had slipped the Ambassador's name into the campaign. How much of the former president's hostility toward Jack involved bitterness toward Joe Kennedy cannot be determined precisely, but it must have been considerable. Some years later, Truman told Merle Miller that Joe was a "tight-fisted old son of a bitch," while in the same breath he accused him of having "bought West Virginia" for Jack.[65] Similar references to Joe Kennedy remained a constant undercurrent that never stopped plaguing the candidate. Nixon's strategists, in planning the fall campaign, knew that no reminders were necessary.

Joe Kennedy was clearly anything but "tightfisted."

Expenditures were as lavish as the rumors made them out to be. That was especially true during the preconvention period when less outside funding was available. For that phase the official Kennedy accounting came to $912,500, and estimates were much higher. Whatever the actual figures, one thing is clear: The campaign never faltered for lack of money. There was justification for the Republican pun about "Jack's jack." Of course, there had been vote-buying in West Virginia, which took the form of underwriting slating, the process of compiling recommended names from the complex ballots. Omission from slates meant certain defeat. Offerings were also made for the ostensible purpose of helping to defray the cost of transporting voters from the "hollers" of the hill country to remote polls. Though the Humphrey campaign had far less money (including what they got from the Johnson camp), there is no reason to doubt that they also made such payments. They never could match Kennedy, although the family had to be conscious about avoiding ostentatious uses of wealth.[66] All of the accounting cannot overlook the enormous advantage of having a private airplane, the *Caroline,* which was purchased and maintained by the Ken-Air Corporation, a family enterprise established solely for that purpose.

But the father's role was significant not for spending alone. Joseph P. Kennedy was an impressive and sophisticated man. He drew upon a lifetime of acquaintances, business and personal associates, relationships, and mutual obligations. The bait of potential Kennedy assistance never lost its lure. His circle of media people—the Krocks, Grahams, Luces, Hearsts—did not guarantee any official blessing (witness the heresies in the form of Luce's endorsement of Nixon, or Krock's criticisms) but at least obtained fairer exposure than most Democrats would have gotten. *Life* magazine went out of its way with photoessays showing Jack and Jackie at their glamorous best. Its sister publication, *Time,* which had been rabidly pro-Republican and harsh on Democratic cold-war leadership, became almost mushy toward Jack.[67]

Equally useful was the Ambassador's entree to political leadership. "I think it fair to conclude that the Ambassador was the most effective force behind Jack's election as President," wrote his faithful lieutenant, Frank Morrissey, in an *ex post facto* tribute to a function that had been kept from public view.[68] Another intimate, Charles Spalding, was on target about Joe Kennedy's significance when he recalled that "everybody knew that Mr. Kennedy was there. . . . He worked as hard as anybody, but he had to make it obvious that he had separated himself from his son, that this wasn't a puppet. That probably was something that for somebody with his temperament was a difficult thing to do."[69]

The father pursued anti-Stevenson forces in New York State, especially Bronx boss Charlie Buckley, Peter Crotty of Buffalo, and Dan O'Connell of Albany's durable machine.[70] He was also instrumental elsewhere, working his contacts in New Jersey and doing some effective lobbying with Mayor Daley and Governor David Lawrence of Pennsylvania. Additional politicking was done on the West Coast, where he had old movie-world contacts. But most direct overtures were by telephone. Kenneth O'Donnell and David F. Powers, in their 1972 book, allow themselves the admission that "If Jack had known about some of the telephone calls his father made on his behalf to Tammany-type bosses during the 1960 campaign, Jack's hair would have turned white." When O'Donnell was asked to elaborate, he explained that old Joe was "overanxious" and tended to pound too hard at some contacts.[71]

In contrast to the Ambassador, others in the family were very visible contributors. Bobby took on a major role. Acting as campaign manager, he was the planner, the persuader, wheeler-dealer, delegate-counter. His genius, wrote Schlesinger, "lay in his capacity to address a specific situation, to assemble an able staff, to inspire and flog them into exceptional deeds and to prevail through sheer force of momentum."[72] The reputation for conducting a driving campaign with ruthless pursuit of the objective was also Bobby's. While Jack's approaches seduced, Bobby's often angered. His meeting with a New York reform group that included Eleanor Roosevelt and Herbert Lehman, in which he said "I don't give a damn about anybody in this room," but "only want to elect my brother President of the United States" was more effective than ingratiating.[73] If Jack's mind was more like a computer that absorbed, sifted, and analyzed, Bobby's was less cerebral and more emotional, directed toward immediate results. Ted, their younger brother, was only twenty-eight in 1960 and one year out of law school at the University of Virginia. Campaigning for Jack a second time, he spent the better part of the preconvention period out West, first bucking the region's pro-Johnson sentiments and then its preference for Nixon.[74] All told, Kennedy money and manpower were almost impossible to overcome.

"You just won't believe it," said John Kennedy to his brother, Robert, the morning after he won the nomination.

"What?"

"He wants it."

"Oh, my God!"

"Now," asked the older Kennedy, "what do we do?"

Robert Kennedy, who recalled this little bit of dialogue nearly four and a half years after the event, went on to say that he and his brother soul-searched for "the rest of the day—and we both promised to each other that we'd never tell what happened—but we spent the rest of the day alternating between thinking it was good and thinking that it wasn't good that he'd offered him the vice-presidency, and how could he get out of it."[75]

Pierre Salinger later remembered that Jack Kennedy told him somewhat cryptically, "I don't think anybody will ever really know how this all really came about."[76] The only certainty is that Johnson, through some kind of process, was offered the vice-presidency not many hours after Kennedy had thanked the delegates for his own nomination. That afternoon, Johnson accepted "with all my heart," which set off both hand-wringing and elation. "Don't worry, Jack," advised the temporary occupant of Marion Davies's Beverly Hills villa, Joseph P. Kennedy. "In two weeks everyone will be saying that this is the smartest thing you ever did."[77]

The various renditions of what actually happened closely parallel the Kennedy–Johnson animosities.

The principals have left only fragmentary accounts, Kennedy's in the form of answers to questions at a press conference in Los Angeles on the Saturday immediately after the convention, and Johnson's in an interview given to Philip Potter for *The Reporter* in the spring of 1964. More immediate chronological information comes from Johnson's office diary. Bobby explained his version during three later interviews. As far as is known, Sam Rayburn left no account. Phil Graham, who was close to Johnson, contributed the document that includes a description of how he and Joe Alsop lobbied Kennedy. Beyond that are the secondary impressions of aides who were present at the Biltmore that day.

They were aware of much of what was happening, but lacked entree to the most vital meetings. A back stairway, for example, provided discreet passage between the Kennedy quarters on the eighth and ninth floors and Johnson's seventh-floor suite. Private sessions were often held in bathrooms and locked bedrooms, with many of the telephone messages transmitted over internal lines. A further obstacle to any reconstruction is the considerable confusion that characterized the whole situation. Self-serving fabrications and plain wishful thinking also impede investigators. Nevertheless enough information is now available to explain what really happened.

En route to Los Angeles, Kennedy's mind was preoccupied with the need to accumulate more delegate votes. When he first arrived, he was confident, but doubts became noticeable by Tuesday evening. The Stevenson boom could no longer be dismissed the way some Kennedy partisans have since suggested. John Kennedy himself responded to a news conference question by saying that "I thought on Monday that we were in the clear, but then I began to read the papers and Wednesday I was somewhat not."[78] That meant playing every available card, which included tantalizing the hopefuls with the thought of a wide-open vice-presidential nomination.

Going into Los Angeles, seven men could reasonably have been regarded as potential candidates. However remote Stevenson's chances, and it was never clear that he would have accepted second place on a Kennedy ticket, they vanished during the theatrics at the Sports Arena. Humphrey's had disappeared even earlier, when he had withdrawn his own presidential candidacy without delivering on an earlier understanding about getting behind Kennedy.

That left Symington, Freeman, Henry Jackson of Washington, and Michigan's attractive, wealthy, and liberal bow-tied governor, G. Mennen Williams. Of the entire lot, Symington seemed the most likely. He could offer geographic balance. As a border-state man, his farm support was decent. While liberals were not delirious about Stu, he did have Harry Truman's approval and was not feared. A more important credential in the era of the "missile gap" was defense, and Symington's expertise was reinforced by having been Truman's Air Force secretary. The others were either without an adequate political base, popular appeal, or tended to duplicate Kennedy's own areas of political strength. If not Stu, there could only be Lyndon.

And to many that seemed unthinkable. Even if Kennedy overcame his own prejudices, the Texan would never accept. Exchanging Capitol Hill for the vice-presidency seemed like a bad bargain. Analysts inclined to think he would refuse also cited the strong pressures of his own band of dependents, those primarily interested in how much more he could do for them if he remained as majority leader. Indeed, that was the prevalent view of Johnson's allies. They included not only so powerful a legislator as Robert Kerr of Oklahoma, but—and more significant—Speaker Rayburn himself.[79]

We now have information that, at an early stage, Sorensen and his deputy, Mike Feldman, had Johnson on a list of vice-presidential nominees "as far and away the outstanding candidate."[80] Two weeks before the convention Kennedy consulted Sorensen and was assured of the logic of offering "the number two spot to the man who was his closest competitor . . . in terms of votes, the man who was the leader of the party in the Senate and was already a national figure, to the man who was the leader and had the most strength in the convention of that area which had been opposed to JFK."[81]

On the day the convention opened, Jack was confronted at the Biltmore by Phil Graham and Joe Alsop. Graham counseled that the offer should be made to Johnson and made so persuasively that there would be no doubt about its sincerity. Alsop urged Kennedy to think about the future, not to "risk leaving this country to Stu Symington; you know perfectly well he's too shallow a puddle to dive into." Kennedy grinned and replied, "You know damn well I would never do that," and left both men startled by his quick, almost casual agreement. It was so simple they feared they had gotten a brush-off.[82]

But there were other complications. Bobby was among them. He had assured several delegates that Johnson *would not* be chosen. Ken O'Donnell, working with similar liberal and labor people, had made similar commitments.[83] Then in a chance meeting Kennedy told Symington that he was his "first *available* choice," thereby holding out the enticing prospect that Johnson was not a competitor.[84] All sorts of possibilities were being dangled, all kinds of assurances given, but, with it all, they preserved the tactical advantage of appearing to leave the door open to as many as were eager to rush in.

In his Biltmore suite, Johnson sat at a television set with four close aides. One of them, Mary Margaret Wylie, noted that the majority leader "showed outward calm as he watched the first ballot . . . In the living room were gathered a large group of press, photographers, and television people. He visited with them and then went into a bedroom of the suite to watch most of the balloting. He joked with the press and asked for sandwiches to be sent up and offered everyone a drink."[85]

When Wisconsin put Kennedy over the top, Johnson seemed pleased. Someone said he hated to see Lyndon lose, but Johnson said he didn't mind, and he seemed to mean it. "There was no evidence of sorrow, or sadness or dejection on his part," noted Wylie.[86] "Quite the contrary, he seemed at all times during the evening gay, relaxed and possibly relieved when it was all over with."[87]

Johnson's phone rang. It was Mr. Sam. The speaker was worried, his voice almost grave. Lyndon must not, under any circumstances, accept the vice-presidential nomination. Johnson then got on the phone with "Big John" Connally, then a close aide. Connally, also at the arena, said there were rumors around the place that an offer would be made. Johnson said he didn't believe them, sent Kennedy a congratulatory telegram, and went to bed.[88]

Kennedy, having gone to the hall and briefly expressed his thanks to the delegates, was back in his North Rossmore Avenue apartment with a group of close friends and aides—Torby Macdonald, Evelyn Lincoln, Dave Powers, and his cousin, Ann Gargan. Kennedy drank beer, ate two fried eggs and toast, and then went over the incoming telegrams. Johnson's said, "LBJ now means Let's Back Jack," quite a change from the Kennedy jibe that LBJ stood for "Let's Block Jack."

Kennedy hardly needed that telegram to remind him about Johnson. But he could not have helped suspect that the gesture was more than perfunctory. By then it was the middle of the night, and he tried to reach the majority leader. Johnson had gone to bed and an aide said he could not be disturbed. So Jack tried to get Evelyn Lincoln, who had left minutes earlier to return to the Biltmore. She entered the headquarters suite and found the message from Kennedy for delivery to Johnson. He wanted to see him later that morning. Since Lyndon had gone to bed, the telegram was left with "someone at the door."[89]

At just about the same hour, another call awakened Sargent Shriver. Kennedy's brother-in-law was sharing his room with Harris Wofford. Shriver still cannot recall who phoned that night, but it was somebody close to Johnson and its message was clear: Johnson would accept the vice-presidency if offered. The caller wanted to make sure that Kennedy was clear about that and would make no mistake. Kennedy got the message from Shriver at eight the next morning.[90]

Just about a half hour after his briefing from Shriver, Kennedy, apparently unwilling to await the response to his midnight message, telephoned down to Johnson's seventh-floor suite. When told by Kennedy that he wanted to see him, Johnson offered to go upstairs. Kennedy declined the gesture and said he would go to the seventh floor. At 10:58 A.M., Kennedy entered Johnson's suite.

Before their meeting, each man had taken soundings. Although Kennedy's tone had been suggestive, Johnson told those with him that he couldn't be certain about what the other man had in mind. Still, of course, as Bobby Baker has written, "It was obvious Jack Kennedy wasn't coming over to talk baseball."[91] Baker made a fifty-cent bet with Lady Bird Johnson, who figured that Kennedy's call would only be ceremonial. Mostly, of course, that was wishful thinking. She worried about her husband's physical condition, did not relish his having to campaign that fall, and so "didn't think it was the road for him." She felt "like that moment in the wedding ceremony when it is said if anybody wants to speak out speak out now or forever hold your peace." For Lyndon, Lady Bird thought, it was also a matter of loyalty to go along, loyalty to the party to help swing the election.[92]

Finally, when Kennedy walked down the two flights, he took a back stairway to evade newsmen. When he slipped into Johnson's suite, Lady Bird and several aides were with the majority leader. So was Rayburn. Kennedy and Johnson then disappeared into a bedroom. Less than ten minutes later Kennedy left and Johnson faced his little crew. As Walter Jenkins remembers it, the senator explained that he had been asked to run but had "more or less declined." There was, however, nothing final about the response. At most he had put off Kennedy for a few hours. "I told him I'd have to consult with Speaker Rayburn, with my wife, and with others whose judgment I respect."[93]

In their discussion, Johnson had probed Kennedy about the identity of his consultants. Kennedy reeled off a list of party leaders and included the additional names of Alsop, Graham, and his father.[94] Not good enough for Johnson. Nothing Kennedy said had outweighed Rayburn's caution. What about the liberals? What about organized labor? What about those who would tear the party wide open? Kennedy said he would talk to them.[95]

So Johnson had not really accepted the offer. Nor had he turned thumbs down. He had been shrewd, testing the quality of Kennedy's offer and willingness to unify the party behind a Kennedy–Johnson ticket. Kennedy, then, instead of saying that he could not control disparate forces, instead of shrugging his shoulders and agreeing that the fight would be too messy, bad for the party, bad for the country, bad for the free world in this time of need for great resolve in the face of the coming showdown with the Communists, left the seventh floor determined to satisfy Johnson's considerations.

When Kennedy reached his own suite, a delegation was waiting. Evelyn Lincoln intercepted him to say that his father had left word to be called. Lincoln trailed into the living room while Kennedy was on the phone and heard just one word, *accepted,* which certainly did not explain the whole story.[96]

Meanwhile, on the seventh floor, Hale Boggs entered Johnson's suite and found Sam Rayburn, who told him about what *he* regarded as Johnson's virtual declination and asked what he thought about it. Boggs later reported their conversation:

"Do you want Nixon to be President of the United States?" asked Boggs. "I knew that this was one thing that he didn't want to happen," he later told an interviewer. "That's a gross understatement."

"You know I don't want that to happen," was Rayburn's predictable reply.

"Well," said Boggs, "unless you approve of Lyndon taking the nomination, that's what's going to happen. How can any man turn down being the Vice President?" Boggs thought about Rayburn's 1956 fantasy and added, "You wouldn't turn it down."

As Boggs told it, it was very simple. "Well," said the speaker, "that's right. He's got to do it." Rayburn asked Boggs to get hold of Kennedy.

There they were, the forty-three-year-old nominee and the seventy-eight-year-old veteran, who had been born at virtually the same time as Franklin D. Roosevelt. Kennedy talked about the value of Johnson as insurance against Nixon, by all odds the most likely Republican nominee. He stressed his regard for Johnson's own value, and told him how important he would be in his administration. "Well," said Rayburn, "up until 30 minutes ago I was against it. . . . I'm afraid I was trying to keep him in the legislative end where he could help me. I can see that you need him more. I yield on one condition," he then added, "that you go on the radio or television and tell the people you came to us and asked for this thing." Kennedy agreed.[97] Boggs later recalled that the presidential nominee left that little talk "positively exuberant." From that moment on "Mr. Rayburn was one hundred percent for the Kennedy–Johnson ticket."[98]

Rayburn telephoned his revised views to Johnson.

"I'm a wiser man this morning than I was last night," he explained. "Besides that other fellah [Nixon] called me a traitor and I don't want a man who calls me a traitor to be President."[99]

Having succeeded that far, Kennedy then found, as he would so often in the future, that the most difficult moments were still ahead. Bobby, Ken O'Donnell, Ralph Dungan, all those who had worked to keep important delegates in line with assurances that Johnson would not be on the ticket, were aghast. The three-man group from labor, designated to speak to Kennedy about choosing a vice-president, was totally unprepared for the news.

Facing Arthur Goldberg, Walter Reuther, and Alex Rose of the Hatters Union and a leader of New York's Liberal Party, Kennedy was guarded. Rose and Reuther began by pitching for Humphrey. Symington or Jackson were also acceptable. Tactfully, Kennedy dropped his bomb by saying that "we may have to look toward Texas." The leaders were being asked to support a man who had backed the Landrum–Griffin Labor Bill of 1959. Rose and Reuther were especially heated, and they warned about the possibility of a floor rebellion that even they might not be able to contain. Labor might simply have to put up its own candidate.

As the delegation turned to leave the suite, Kennedy asked Goldberg to remain behind. In the privacy of a bathroom, Jack noted that Goldberg had not said very much. Although the labor lawyer, then general counsel for the United Steelworkers of America, was for Hubert Humphrey, he had not really argued the anti-Johnson case. At that point Kennedy revealed that Johnson had already been chosen and had been approached. He explained that it was his own idea, and that he could not have been certain of his acceptance until he had seen Rayburn. Goldberg was then asked to help bring AFL-CIO President George Meany into line.[100]

Only the Kennedy brothers knew exactly what happened next. "We spent the rest of the day," Bobby later revealed, "alternating between thinking it was good and thinking it wasn't good . . . and how could he get out of it."[101] The only certainty is that Jack Kennedy had begun to waver. Confidence in his decision had been weakened. Four years of trying to woo liberals might only end with a rebellion. Bobby saw the course as suicidal; it had to be undone. Johnson should be told about the opposition, about how embarrassing they would make his candidacy. In all fairness to him he should be given a chance to decline. It should be presented to him that way, as a warning, as a courtesy. Why not? Jack told Bobby that if he wanted to do just that, he should go ahead. Good luck. He was on his own.[102]

What followed showed a candidate with surprisingly little control over events. Having come as far as he had, having precluded a significant convention battle for the nomination, and picking up en route a reputation for leadership over a highly efficient political organization, the plot to abort Johnson was farcical.

Bobby rushed to the seventh-floor suite. Lady Bird, however, intervened. She told her husband to deal with only the candidate himself, so Bobby met with Rayburn. The speaker was told about the predicted floor fight, that dissidents were hopping mad. Such delegations as Michigan's were especially incensed, eager for an open rebellion. So was the little group from the District of Columbia. Kennedy wanted to give Johnson a chance to be spared from the unpleasantness.

There was nothing subtle about the younger Kennedy's approach, and Rayburn, of course, saw through it. Johnson's office diary for that day contains the information that Bobby's mission was to ask Lyndon "not to accept the offer," all in the guise of acting without his brother's knowledge.[103]

Phil Graham, who had entered the seventh-floor suite earlier and was in another room, was delegated to phone Jack Kennedy for some clarification. Just who was in charge? But Kennedy couldn't talk; he was busy contending with people who were trying to persuade him that "no one had anything against Symington." Would Graham call back in three minutes? By this time, Graham's memorandum reported, he and Jim Rowe were "as calm as Chileans on top of an earthquake." Finally, in his third conversation with Kennedy, Graham, additionally exasperated from having to battle the impossibly clogged hotel telephone circuits, told him it was too late to be changing his mind. "You ain't no Adlai," he pointedly reminded Jack. Bobby returned upstairs.

More meetings. Johnson continued to be harangued by outraged pleaders. The Kennedys, meanwhile, resumed hand-wringing. As Bobby later recalled, "We just vacillated back and forth as to whether we wanted him or didn't want him."[104] Graham solicited a Kennedy–Johnson endorsement from Stevenson, whose sense of political practicality had moved him toward Symington. Additional contretemps followed over who would deliver the seconding speeches. Lawrence would place the Johnson name in nomination, but who would talk next? Everybody had ideas. In that confused atmosphere the whole plan seemed about to collapse. Bobby's lobbying had infuriated Rayburn. Johnson was impatient. By midafternoon, with nothing settled, Walter Jenkins remembers that Johnson was ready to start packing and go home.[105] Then Bobby came back.

This time he did face Johnson, whose bedroom was still loaded with jumpy politicians. Their only chance for privacy was in an adjoining room, and there Bobby finally got back to business. He told the majority leader that if he became the Democratic national chairman, he could play an important role in the party. The idea was, as Bobby later explained, "that to run the party he could get a lot of his own people in and then if he wanted to be President . . . he could have the machinery. . . . We didn't really know whether he'd want to go through with it, and, in any case, the President wanted to get rid of him."[106]

Rayburn simply said, "Shit." Johnson countered the overture with stiffened resistance against being dropped. "If I am Jack's choice," he said, "I'll fight for it."[107] That left Bobby with only one thing to say. "Well, it's Jack and Lyndon."

Rayburn asked Graham to call Kennedy again. Graham, informing him about Bobby's latest mission as though the older brother had no idea of what was going on, listened to Jack respond "as calmly as though we were discussing the weather," and heard him explain that Bobby was "out of touch and doesn't know what's been happening." Jack then reassured Johnson about his willingness to fight for him. He had, moreover, just revealed the news to reporters and asked Johnson to do the same.

That brief interlude between Bobby's last mission to Johnson and the Graham call to Jack was when a thoroughly indecisive Kennedy finally made up his mind. Exactly what happened during that interval may never be known, but there is enough reason to suggest that encouragement from Joe Kennedy may have finally clinched the issue. That another father-son exchange took place even while Bobby was downstairs is highly likely. That Joe Kennedy was close to the situation and backed Johnson has already been well established. Even more obvious is that the father's intimate involvement in his son's political fortunes did not suddenly cease at the precise moment of Jack's vital decision. The Ambassador had undoubtedly been as instrumental as anyone at the Biltmore. With the persistent belief among such Johnson friends as Phil Graham that Bobby had acted on his own, however, the episode left an irreparable distrust toward the younger brother from the man who would ultimately become the thirty-sixth President.

Jack had his own mending to do. He made Henry Jackson chairman of the Democratic National Committee, which gave the Washington State senator a key campaign function. Orville Freeman later became Kennedy's secretary of agriculture. Stu Symington was told that he really was the first choice but that, very simply, his area of strength

largely duplicated Kennedy's.[108] Kennedy, conscious of the strong hostility toward Johnson by Wisconsin's two senators, Gaylord Nelson and
William Proxmire, who had opposed the Texan on gas rates and other
interests, told them that Sam Rayburn had come to his Biltmore room
and demanded that he put Johnson on the ticket. He didn't want to go
along, he told Nelson, but Rayburn had threatened the destruction of his
legislative program if Johnson remained as majority leader. And, in the
House, Rayburn could inflict his own damage. That story was concocted
not only for the Wisconsin people, but also spread by Bobby to other
governors and senators.[109]

On the convention floor, the reaction was relatively subdued, with the
Michigan delegation the most rebellious. Governor G. Mennen (Soapy)
Williams later explained that, although "we had given our life's blood
to get Kennedy in and felt a strong tie with him, this was something that,
despite the tradition of supporting the President, we just weren't able to
take lying down."[110] But practical politics and an appetite for winning
behind what was widely acknowledged as the most effective ticket
against Nixon triumphed over ideological purity. The "nays" were no
match for the "ayes."

The convention closed that Friday evening at the vast Los Angeles
Coliseum, a football stadium that also served as the temporary home of
the recently relocated baseball Dodgers. Politics combined with theater as
the final event was preceded by two and a half hours of entertainment
offered by high school bands, jazz musicians, and a drum corps. Mort
Sahl, the comedian who had made his reputation at a San Francisco
nightclub, told the crowd that Jack Kennedy was "on his way back to
school to take care of his affairs and write a term paper called 'What I did
on my summer vacation.' " Sahl added that Vice-President Nixon had just
sent a telegram to Joseph P. Kennedy offering congratulations and consol-
ing him with "You have not lost a son. You have gained a country."[111]

The nominee arrived close to 6:30. The weather was hot and the sun
still high. The band played "Walkin' Down to Washington," the awk-
ward official campaign song. Then, in a display of party unity, Kennedy
was introduced by Adlai Stevenson, who sounded the theme of "revitalization." With the return of Democrats to Washington after eight Republican years, "America will become again what we once were, the guiding
star of the hopes of free men." He described Kennedy as a man devoted
to the "ideals of liberal democracy" and said his nomination had restored
the "best hopes of the American past—the hope of vision, the hope of
vitality, the hope of victory."[112]

With little more than half the 100,000 seats filled, Kennedy began to speak. He faced the sun that was moving toward the horizon, a position better suited for the television cameras than for following the prepared script. He obviously had trouble reading the words, and the delivery was far from exciting. Laboring along, with obvious weariness, Kennedy declared that "we stand today on the edge of a New Frontier—the frontier of the 1960's—a frontier of unknown opportunities and perils—a frontier of unfulfilled hopes and threats." This "New Frontier," he said, was not just "a set of promises," but "a set of challenges" that appealed to the pride of Americans and not to their pocketbooks. It held out "the promise of more sacrifice instead of more security."

Still listless, he began his conclusion. "Now begins another long journey, taking me into your cities and homes all over America. Give me your help, give me your hand, your voice and your vote." He quoted from Isaiah, and added, "As we face the coming great challenge, we too shall wait upon the Lord and ask that He renew our strength. Then we shall be equal to the test. Then we shall not be weary. Then we shall prevail."[113] The crowd applauded; according to one count, for the thirty-sixth time. Now they were on their feet. Democrats had their candidate.

2

"High Hopes"

After the convention Kennedy returned to Hyannis Port for a few weeks of rest before leaving for Washington in August to attend a special session of Congress. That rest period was also a transitional phase in the battle for the White House, an interval between the fight for the nomination itself and the fall campaign. Inevitably most of his attention was devoted to a common postconvention function, for only rarely can a candidate take his prize without having to mollify the wounded, and Jack Kennedy was no exception.

The victory itself had brought disturbing confirmations about the Kennedy machine. In some ways Kennedy power had been too blatant. The exaggerated display of super-efficiency and mechanical invincibility had prompted Agnes Meyer's dyspeptic comment to Stevenson: "Today unless you are as scurrilous as Nixon, you can succeed only by being as shrewd and organization conscious as Kennedy . . . The era of the engineer-statesman has begun."[1]

Most finger-pointing singled out Bobby rather than Jack, and it confirmed that he was by far the more ruthless brother. Clark Clifford has remarked that he "felt that whereas Senator Kennedy had the inclination possibly to use the stiletto or the scalpel, Bobby Kennedy used the meat axe."[2] One observer returned from Los Angeles and wrote privately that "Bobby Kennedy went around wagging his finger at David Lawrence and Sam Rayburn and others when the occasion required," then closed the letter with the advice to "Burn this. My name is already down in Bobby's black book, and I don't want to give any documentary evidence to support the motion for deportation." Stevenson himself had begun to refer to Bobby as the "Black Prince."[3]

Liberals were the most inclined to see Bobby as Kennedy's "storm trooper," but they themselves were a pretty testy lot. They demanded ideals and action, while insisting on kid gloves, purity, and principles. Had Hubert Humphrey, for example, chosen Johnson to run with him, there would have been more falling into line with rhapsodies about the wisdom of it all. When Kennedy made that move, though, it was cynical, nothing more than the expedient stroke of an unprincipled politician. Not even eloquent avowals in support of pet ideals convinced the skeptics on his left.

His other flank was equally vulnerable. At the moment, southern sit-in movements to desegregate public facilities were stirring anger and violence, but the Democratic Party at Los Angeles had endorsed "peaceful demonstrations for first-class citizenship" and fully supported the exertion of all branches of the federal government behind the movement for racial equality. For a variety of reasons the party's southern wing swallowed such heresies in 1960, but that did not make them more palatable. In the aftermath of the convention Senator Richard Russell of Georgia, one of the most respected regional leaders, agreed with a friend that "We are, indeed, in a deplorable condition and I devoutly hope and pray that Divine Providence will give us the strength and wisdom to save our Southland from the evil threat of the Platform adopted at Los Angeles."[4] Earlier Russell had declined Kennedy's invitation to join him on the platform for the acceptance speech.[5] When the Los Angeles convention came to an end, then, Russell, like Harry Truman, was far away.

Eleanor Roosevelt had also decided there was no point in remaining. Her only exchange with Kennedy after the first-ballot victory came when he reached her by phone at the airport. The conversation had been suggested by a mutual friend, but it was cold and brief. She broke it off abruptly by telling Kennedy that he had no reason to worry about her; there were more important things to think about. She could always be reached later if he had anything further to say.[6]

On that last Sunday of July, Stevenson visited Kennedy at Hyannis Port and found most of the family present, including the "Black Prince." Jack seemed pleased to see the "Guv," and at the same time preoccupied with his problems. He told Adlai he was especially worried about New York. He had to attract that state's important black and Jewish vote. And, of course, that was the center of Stevensonian reformers and independents. When Stevenson then suggested that he should have a foreign policy task force to prepare for a possible transition to the presidency, Kennedy surprised him by accepting the idea and, right on the spot, asking Stevenson to take charge. Stevenson, promptly reporting his conversation to Mrs. Roosevelt, wrote, "His interest and concentration seemed to be on organization not ideas at this stage, which I suppose is proper."[7]

Adlai's name came up, as he had assumed it would, the next time Kennedy saw "Mrs. R." They met at her cottage on the Roosevelt estate at Hyde Park, on Sunday, August 14. Jack later called the site their "raft at Tilsit," after the spot where Napoleon and Czar Alexander of Russia had made their peace on the middle of a river in 1807. The Kennedy–Roosevelt rapprochement came about through a Kennedy desire for a meeting, and Ted Sorensen's suggestion that the presence at Hyde Park that day of a group of senior citizens in celebration of the twenty-fifth anniversary of FDR's signing of the Social Security Act would offer an opportunity for such a visit.

Kennedy asked Bill Walton to accompany him. Walton had worked in the primaries and had been given the job of coordinating the New York City campaign. His earlier days as a journalist had given him entree to both the regular Democrats and the rebellious reformers who were working to unseat Carmine DeSapio and Mike Prendergast. Before leaving for Hyde Park, he and Kennedy heard that Mrs. Roosevelt's granddaughter had just been killed in a riding accident. Kennedy assumed that the tragedy would force cancellation of their meeting, but she insisted that they meet at her cottage, named Val-Kill.

While Kennedy talked privately with "Mrs. R.," Walton waited in another room with members of the Roosevelt family and Pierre Salinger. Then, wanting him to tell her about the New York City reformers, Kennedy invited Walton to join them. With both men present, however, she shifted the subject to Stevenson. All the way to Hyde Park, they had anticipated that that would be foremost on her mind, and that she would insist on making him secretary of state as the price of any peace.

What they heard from "Mrs. R." came as a mild shock. She said she well understood what it was like for presidents to contend with pressure for appointments, and therefore she did not intend to attempt to influence a Kennedy cabinet. Jack's relief must have still been visible when she followed that up by saying, "I've come to believe Governor Stevenson may not have some of the characteristics I thought he had." Then, as Walton remembers, she stuck the "knife deeply into Adlai." Kennedy, of course, was unaware of just how recent events had soured her on Stevenson.[8] While she went on, Kennedy rolled his eyes and looked at Walton with disbelief. Walton recalls that the meeting was "a great release to us, opening the reform movement," which thereafter did become more accessible to Kennedy's interests. While she said she would endorse him publicly and accept the cochairmanship of the New York Citizens for Kennedy Committee with Herbert Lehman, Kennedy agreed to work in cooperation with the reform leadership.[9]

Mrs. Roosevelt then telephoned Stevenson about the meeting. She told him that while she had asked for no commitments about the future, Kennedy did have "in mind" the intention to invite him to become secretary of state. But, as Stevenson remembered that conversation with Mrs. Roosevelt, his conclusion was that she did "not know him [Kennedy] well enough to draw any conclusions from his words and manner." Mrs. Roosevelt was also secure about Kennedy's need for Stevenson, appreciating his importance in helping to win New York and California.[10] "I also had the feeling that he was a man who could learn. I liked him better than I ever had before because he seemed so little cock-sure, and I think he has a mind that is open to new ideas," she wrote to another friend. "My final judgment is that here is a man who wants to leave a record (perhaps for ambitious personal reasons, as people say) but I rather think because he really is interested in helping the people of his own country and mankind in general. I will be surer of this as time goes on, but I think I am not mistaken in feeling that he would make a good President if elected."[11] Both letters emphasized her own central role, but the one to Stevenson had stressed her toughness. She informed him that Kennedy had left the meeting feeling "somewhat chastened" and was ready to let her initiate future moves. Kennedy had also seemed "in awe" of her judgment and experience, and was obviously "hungry" for the help she could give him.[12]

However much her ego may have been involved, her importance was genuine. If further evidence was needed, it was provided for Kennedy when the national board of the Americans for Democratic Action met in Washington. Their mood was hardly much brighter than when they had found themselves with little choice but to go along with Truman in 1948. Half the representatives from various chapters throughout the country thought they would solve the problem simply by making no endorsement. Even the favorable delegates were obviously cool. "It isn't what Kennedy believes that worries me," one said. "It's whether he believes anything." But several of the ADA leaders, including Schlesinger, Joe Rauh, Jr., James I. Loeb, Jr., Gus Tyler, Sam Beer, and Senator Joseph Clark of Pennsylvania, urged a strong endorsement, with the group from New York most vigorously behind them. That was, at least, a partial reflection of Mrs. Roosevelt's support. Getting the others to go along required concessions. A statement praising Kennedy for having shown himself to be "an aggressive champion of creative liberalism" in the areas of foreign relations, civil rights, and economic and social policy was dropped. Schlesinger himself, he later wrote to Kennedy, had not been prepared "for the depth of hostility which evidently exists" on the part of grass-roots liberals, some of whom were prepared to vote for Kennedy only because of Nixon. Such apathy hardly promised much of an effort to generate a large vote.[13]

For liberals eager to believe, who preferred to hope that a new leader had arisen after the years in the wilderness, Kennedy supplied some solace. He interpreted the "challenge of the New Frontier" as countering Republican hostility to social programs. In Warm Springs, Georgia, the site of FDR's polio foundation, he proposed a six-point program for the "New Frontiers of health." Before Pittsburgh's Urban Affairs Council, he delivered a fighting speech that asked for a ten-year federal action program "to eradicate slums and blight and help solve the problems of explosive metropolitan growth." He said the emphasis should be on urban renewal, housing, mass transportation, pollution control, and recreational facilities. He told New York's Liberal Party that their faith was "an attitude of mind and heart—a faith in man's ability through the experience of reason and judgment to increase for himself and his fellow man the amount of justice and freedom and brotherhood which all human life deserves."[14]

Among the Democrats hardest for Kennedy to convince were veteran politicians who themselves were Roman Catholics. Collectively, their backing was crucial. Their continued skepticism threatened to undermine the credibility of Kennedy arguments about overcoming the "religious issue." Moreover, such leaders as Billy Green and Jim Finnegan of Philadelphia, Dick Daley of Chicago, Bob Wagner of New York, and Dan O'Connell of Albany were vital for carrying metropolitan areas with key concentrations of Democratic voters. With the possible exception of Daley, even more important were governors Brown of California, Lawrence of Pennsylvania, Mike Di Salle of Ohio, and Steve McNichols of Colorado—all Catholics.

The alarm seemed greatest among Catholic Democrats concerned with local and statewide candidates. Voting for one Catholic candidate on a ticket might be acceptable, even a reaffirmation of tolerance, but more than one could look like a "papal cabal." Even putting that aside, they dreaded the prospect of having Kennedy rekindle a new round of anti-Catholicism. One former governor explained that the Irish had reached a point where the voters tolerated them as governors and senators but that if one ran for the presidency there would be so much anti-Catholic sentiment, especially in the Midwest, that many lesser offices held by Catholics would be swept away.[15]

More exasperating for Kennedy personally was opposition from the clergy itself, which prompted his celebrated comment: "Now I understand why Henry VIII set up his own church."[16] Indeed, it was true that while getting him elected seemed a test of religious toleration, others within the Church felt that a Catholic in the presidency could do less to help their interests than would a Protestant.[17] It was also true that many prelates, among them Francis Cardinal Spellman of New York and James Cardinal McIntyre of Los Angeles, were simply too conservative to accept Kennedy.

The entire experience, and most explicitly with Cardinal Spellman, made Joe Kennedy vow never to give another penny to the Church. The cardinal further angered the Ambassador just a few weeks before the election by publicly meeting President Eisenhower at the airport and escorting him down Fifth Avenue. "So the result was that my father wouldn't speak to him again," Bobby later told an interviewer.[18]

Even Kennedy's victory in the Wisconsin primary did little to reduce anxieties about the religious issue. Throughout the farm areas especially, the circulation of hate pamphlets provoked reminders of 1928. Especially vile was one tract called *Maria Monk, Or Secrets of the Black Nunnery at Montreal, Canada,* which was a direct reminder of the anti-Catholicism of one and a half centuries earlier.[19]

In Wisconsin the major split had clearly gone along Catholic-Protestant, as well as urban-rural, lines. Kennedy's great strength came from the cities and towns with a high percentage of German and Polish Catholics. Humphrey, even while losing statewide, gained sixty-six percent of the Protestant farmers and forty-one percent of the Protestants who lived in cities and towns. Kennedy's candidacy, indeed, did provoke a flare-up of religious controversy in midwestern rural America.[20]

Kennedy's sixty-one percent of the popular vote and triumphant sweep of forty-eight of West Virginia's fifty-five counties became his most decisive preconvention accomplishment, and that was done despite the fact that only 3.9 percent of the population belonged to the Catholic

Church. West Virginia thereby became the best evidence that Catholicism would not necessarily be fatal. "We found at the outset in West Virginia that the problem of Senator Kennedy's religion was acute and that we initially ran considerably behind because of this issue," Robert Kennedy later wrote to Senator A. Willis Robertson of Virginia. "However, after the issue was met forthrightly and Senator Kennedy spoke out and conveyed his convictions on this subject there was a tremendous switch in voter sentiment. We found that by a vigorous but sympathetic effort, people can be convinced."[21] Theodore H. White has agreed. "All other issues were secondary," he wrote.[22] Some reporters, however, had second thoughts. "Looking back," noted Chalmers Roberts, "I think that the press was considerably conned by the Kennedy tactic and that Humphrey had more than a point in his complaint about the emphasis on this single issue."[23]

Religion *was* important in West Virginia. Fundamentalism had strong roots among the hill-folk of a state impoverished by the decline of the coal industry. When Kennedy's pollster, Lou Harris, first went in to canvass in 1958, he found voters favoring Kennedy over Nixon by fifty-two to thirty-eight percent. When Harris returned in December of 1959 to conduct a trial heat of Kennedy against Humphrey, Kennedy showed a decisive seventy to thirty percent lead, a vital factor in enabling Kennedy to decide about entering that primary—even as he let the outside world, including Humphrey, believe that religion would make it an uphill battle. Once Kennedy's faith was publicized, however, the Harris poll taken three weeks before the May 10 election did show a complete reversal. Now Kennedy trailed Humphrey by forty to sixty percent.[24] So Kennedy was at a disadvantage. He did have to counter fear about religion. Ultimately he achieved this, but the salient fact remained that if the West Virginians *were* a single-issue people, *religion was not that issue.*

Of course, that all becomes clearer with hindsight. Kennedy moved in a forthright manner, largely calculated to place opponents on the defensive and make them vulnerable to the appearance of lining up with bigotry by favoring Humphrey. That part of his campaign was highlighted when he went on television two nights before primary day and responded to a planted question asked by Franklin D. Roosevelt, Jr. Very effectively, Kennedy made the point that "when any man stands on the steps of the Capitol and takes the oath of office of President, he is swearing to support the separation of church and state; he puts one hand on the Bible and raises the other hand to God as he takes the oath. And if he breaks his oath, he is not committing a crime against the

Constitution, for which the Congress can impeach him—and should impeach him—but he is committing a sin against God." Theatrically, Kennedy then raised his hand over an imaginary Bible and repeated softly, "A sin against God, for he has sworn on the Bible."[25] The little drama worked, ostensibly demonstrating Jack Kennedy's ability to shame the bigots.

West Virginians simply had concluded that Jack Kennedy was more effective and more likely to defeat the Republicans, which meant that he, unlike Humphrey, would be in a position to do something about their troubles. Kennedy's own eloquent responses to their poverty created for them "the New Deal reincarnated in the smiling personality of Franklin D. Roosevelt."[26] Moreover, Kennedy's Catholicism was something they could live with, for they had been doing that very thing. Catholics had long served in the state legislature, and one had gone on to the United States Senate. In 1960 West Virginia had Catholics at all levels of government, including the state supreme court. Although they had preferred Hoover over Smith in 1928, they had voted for the Catholic in that year's Democratic primary in preference to Senator James Reed of Missouri, a Baptist. Kennedy won on a bread-and-butter New Deal appeal, and he knew it.

At a meeting of the Kennedy staff, one month before the West Virginia vote, Bobby summarized the situation quite succinctly by saying, "It is simply food, family and flag in southern West Virginia."[27] The candidate himself, addressing the American Society of Newspaper Editors that same month, said with characteristic candor that "the great bulk of West Virginians paid very little attention to my religion, until they read repeatedly in the Nation's press that this was the decisive issue in West Virginia. There are many serious problems in that State, problems big enough to dominate any campaign, but religion is not one of them."[28] When Joe Alsop took his own straw poll by going door-to-door in Charleston, he found evidence that, as the Kennedy campaign had calculated, many were planning to vote as a way of countering the talk about bigotry.[29]

It was not, of course, that simple. Had it been, Kennedy's success should have been duplicated more effectively during the fall. Tennessee, after twice having voted for Stevenson over Eisenhower, would hardly have preferred Nixon. Oklahoma, which had given Democratic candidates a shade over fifty percent during the preceding three presidential elections, would not have gone Republican by fifty-nine percent. The Survey Research Center of the University of Michigan later found that Kennedy's faith resulted in a net loss of one and a half million votes.

The possibility of having the religious issue work in his favor naturally never escaped Nixon and the Republican National Committee, and they pursued the simple but effective strategy of deploring such innuendos and bigotry, and repeated that abhorrence as much as possible.[30] The advice Kennedy received that it made "no sense to brush the religious issue under the rug" was patently gratuitous. Only by withdrawing from the field could he have ignored what Billy Graham declared was "a major issue whether we like it or not" that "will go much deeper than in 1928."[31]

That was in August. And Graham, having resisted a Kennedy effort to join other Protestant theologians in a statement criticizing the validity of the religious issue, made his comments from Europe, leaving no doubt that he thought it *was* a valid question. Besides, the evangelist and Nixon had a warm relationship and, in all other ways, he was in greater harmony with the Republican than with Kennedy. Only the resourceful intervention by Brooks Hays, the former Arkansas congressman who was prominent in Baptist affairs, may have kept Graham from openly siding with Nixon.[32]

Meanwhile Kennedy's postconvention spell at Hyannis Port was also devoted to recuperating from a troubling throat infection that had plagued him since leaving Los Angeles. After the traditional Labor Day kickoff in Detroit's Cadillac Square, he moved on to the West Coast. At the Shrine Auditorium in Los Angeles, he was "visibly weary, with deep circles under his eyes and hoarseness creeping into his voice."[33] By then the religious issue, which was clearly not going to disappear, returned with enough force to move him toward Houston.

This time the trouble came from Dr. Norman Vincent Peale. Peale, best known as the author of the immensely popular 1952 volume called, ironically, The Power of Positive Thinking, was also a Republican and a friend of Nixon. He brought together 150 ministers, all conservative and all Protestant, and they called themselves the National Conference of Citizens for Religious Freedom. Their statement, which was issued on September 7, made front-page news and declared that the religious issue was not the fault of any candidate but the creation of "the nature of the Roman Catholic Church which is, in a very real sense, both a church and a temporal state."[34]

The immediate reaction to the group's statement was one of embarrassment, and a number of eminent Protestant and Jewish theologians quickly denounced such premises. The Kennedy people later obtained information linking the meeting with Nixon and the Republican National Committee.[35] This incident preceded Kennedy's appearance before the Houston Ministerial Association on September 12. While his vocal problem remained worrisome, it paled beside the awareness that he would be entering the den of some very agitated Southern Baptists.

Indeed, the general impression of the highly publicized encounter was that Kennedy was stepping onto hostile turf and could not possibly win. He was also conscious of the other danger that criticism had made so obvious: He had to walk a careful tightrope that avoided antagonizing his fellow Roman Catholics while satisfying the immediate audience in Houston.[36] But the inspiration for the event was essentially nonpartisan, with the overture to Kennedy having come at the suggestion of the Reverend Herbert Meza. Meza was a Presbyterian minister in Houston who had been born into a Spanish-speaking Roman Catholic family and converted at the age of eighteen. He was also a supporter of Kennedy, but, to retain the nonpartisan auspices of the event, he tendered the invitation in conjunction with a pro-Nixon colleague.[37] When Kennedy arrived in Houston the night before the event, he found Meza worried that extremists, anti-Catholic Church of God parishioners from Texas, might get on the program and embarrass Lone Star State Protestants on national television.[38] Ground rules that rejected any advance screening of questions seemed to leave that possibility wide open, but the candidate himself welcomed the format. The question really was whether the points raised would be legitimate or whether the lunatic fringe would dominate the affair and, in the process, upset Kennedy. Reverend Meza got some advance indications of the latter possibility when he received a number of long-distance phone calls from people who wanted their questions put before Kennedy. One lady from Washington, D.C., insisted that Kennedy be asked "what those nuns are doing that I see walking up and down the corridors of the Pentagon?"[39]

Kennedy campaigned in Texas on that Monday. At the Alamo, his memorial to the fallen heroes included the observation that "side by side with Bowie and Crockett died McCafferty and Bailey and Carey, but no one knows whether they were Catholics or not, for there was no religious test at the Alamo."[40] After additional speeches in Lubbock and San Antonio, he finally boarded the plane to Houston.

John Cogley, a Catholic scholar, coached him by asking the type of questions that were anticipated. Kennedy's voice was in such bad shape that he replied mostly in writing by handing Cogley long, lined yellow sheets of paper with his answers. Still conscious of the Catholic audience in the rest of the country, he wrote on the pad, "It is hard for a Harvard man to give pointers on theology. What will they think at Fordham and B.C. [Boston College]?"[41]

"The meeting had many of the earmarks of an inquisition," wrote one minister who attended. He also noted that "there had been a strange feeling of tension, uncertainty, perhaps hostility in the air during the session."[42] Yet none of this seemed apparent when Kennedy appeared. The gathering, variously described as from six hundred to one thousand, rose to their feet and applauded as he entered the Crystal Ballroom of the Rice Hotel. He walked to the head table, where he sat down between Reverends Meza and George Reck. They exchanged few words and, as they waited to start, both clerics noted that Kennedy seemed tense.[43] At precisely 9:00 P.M., timed for the start of the telecast, Reverend Reck opened with expressions of hope that the proceedings would be restrained, and then Meza introduced Kennedy.

He spoke deliberately, slowly and with greater clarity than usual. He stuck close to the text prepared by Sorensen, making only the most minor interpolations. One careless phrase could negate whatever gains might be made within the Crystal Ballroom. "There was no doubt in my mind but that it would make or break us," Jim Wine later recalled.[44]

Kennedy reaffirmed his belief in the constitutional presidency and disavowed suggestions of subservience to the Church. "I am not the Catholic candidate for President," he told them. "I am the Democratic Party's candidate for President, who happens also to be a Catholic." He pledged to resign the office if the time ever came when he would be required to "either violate my conscience, or violate the national interest," a vow that Cogley thought was necessary because Kennedy's public position "had suggested to lots of people that if he were a good Catholic, he would bypass the Constitution and do what his 'Catholic' conscience dictated."[45] His tone was earnest and reflective, the idealism of a candidate with faith that separation could be maintained between secular government and individual spiritualism. "If this election is decided on the basis that 40,000,000 Americans lost their chance of being President on the day they were baptized, then it is the whole nation that will be the loser in the eyes of history, and in the eyes of our own people," he declared before making a closing pledge to "preserve, protect and defend the Constitution."[46]

The statement lasted ten and a half minutes. Throughout, his voice showed no sign of throat problems. His audience responded to Kennedy's final words with applause that seemed tentative, as though they were awaiting some cue from others. The lingering suspicions became visible during the subsequent question-and-answer period, when seven ministers kept probing the accuracy of his vows of freedom from the Church hierarchy. Kennedy retained his poise and showed no irritation, but others in the audience were less restrained. A minister of the Church of Christ, the Reverend B. E. Howard, carried several open books to a floor microphone and tried to confront Kennedy with responsibility for quotations that he read from Catholic sources, including the *Catholic Encyclopedia*. The man went on at length, and someone in the audience called out, "I object to this. The time is running out." Kennedy patiently answered his questions and also explained that he could probably do a better job if he knew their complete context.[47]

The final response was much warmer. The ministers rose and applauded, and some rushed up to him to grab his hand or say something encouraging. Going to Houston had been a gamble; he had thought his options were narrow, and now it seemed fairly secure that his cause had not been damaged. The national Citizens for Kennedy organization showed a film of the performance to audiences throughout the country.

Kennedy's real gain was rather subtle. Clearly, preaching about bigotry or the evils of anti-Catholicism did not, by itself, reform many, but more likely hastened the taking of sides. John Harllee, Jack Kennedy's former PT boat associate who led the Citizens for Kennedy in northern California, found that hostility remained so strong among the many Baptists in the area that county chairmen were reluctant to permit the showing of the Houston film.[48] Reformation Sunday, October 30, nearly became the occasion for massive, last-minute anti-Kennedy campaigning by a coalition of conservative Protestant churchmen, but other ministers managed to divert that objective to discussions of bigotry rather than Catholicism as the major problem.[49]

Public attention was finally directed to the so-called "great debates," the four televised Kennedy–Nixon confrontations that created a new precedent for presidential campaigns. As with the Houston appearance, Kennedy profited from just being there. Vice-President Nixon, however, had little choice; he felt he couldn't give the impression of "ducking out," but he also had reasons for not fearing to go before the cameras. His previous television successes, especially during the celebrated "Checkers speech" of 1952, provided some confidence. He had only to hold his own to prove himself worthy of being "Ike's boy."

The face-to-face confrontations highlighted the essentials that separated the two men. Nixon's burdens included the U-2 affair and the failure of the Paris summit conference, together with the dead-end course of the administration's recent efforts at coping with the Soviets, Cuba, and the People's Republic of China. These gave Kennedy the opening to ride hard on widespread impressions that America's international prestige had suffered.

The issue was not whether the cold war could be mitigated, not which man was best equipped to search for peace, but who would face the "Communist threat" with greater resolve. That led Nixon to outdo Eisenhower's enthusiasm for defending the tiny islands of Quemoy and Matsu off the Chinese coast and Kennedy to advocate strengthening the "non-Batista Democratic anti-Castro forces in exile, and in Cuba itself, who offer eventual hope of overthrowing Castro."[50] Kennedy, the Democrat, with an abundant New Deal constituency still out there, linked economic weakness with the inadequacy of federal action and the reduction of America's ability to appeal to the rest of the world. His concluding statement for the first debate tied it all together by asking, "Can freedom in the next generation . . . conquer, or are the Communists going to be successful?" and adding, "If we fail, if we fail to move ahead, if we fail to develop sufficient military and economic and social strength here in this country, then I think that uh—the tide could begin to run against us."[51]

That first debate was relatively bland, which encouraged the electronic audience to respond almost exclusively to cosmetics and style— Kennedy's self-confidence and good looks, his crisp, authoritative, fact-filled delivery made him seem knowledgeable; Nixon's evident discomfort as rivulets of sweat smudged his makeup, and his vagueness and efforts to be agreeable, created a figure uncomfortably incongruous for one who was to be preferred for his "experience."

The initial triumph had been decisive. America suddenly discovered that the vice-president had a credible opponent, a rookie with championship promise. The free promotion made possible by the new age of electronics was a bonanza for Kennedy, and he had made the most of it.

Suddenly, on the day after the first exchange with Nixon, the throngs turning out for Kennedy's appearances became major demonstrations, matching the kind of turnouts Eisenhower had inspired in 1956. Ohioans packed the roadsides during Kennedy's twelve-hour swing through the state, with lunch-hour crowds mobbing his car along Euclid Avenue in downtown Cleveland. Frank Lausche, Ohio's conservative Democratic senator, suddenly decided that Kennedy was his man and joined the entourage with all the conviction of an apostate. From the Southern Governors Conference at Hot Springs, Arkansas, came word that nine formerly tepid Democrats had suddenly become inspired.[52] Bewildered backers of the vice-president wondered whether Nixon had been hurt more by his own weak responses to Kennedy's points or by his appearance. Some even smelled sabotage, and suspected a "treacherous" cosmetician in the studio at Station WBBM in Chicago, which led to crank calls and letters to a beautiful—and truly innocent—young woman, Frances Arnold, for having been the "assassin." The culprit, however, had been Nixon's own makeup expert, who had merely applied some Lazy-Shave to cover his "five o'clock shadow." Kennedy himself was not, as most people thought, entirely without makeup. With much less of a beard problem, he needed only a dusting of powder.[53]

At their next on-camera meeting, Nixon was prepared by someone else at his own home. To counter his own active sweat glands, he ordered the studio chilled to sixty-four degrees, which was then raised to seventy when Kennedy objected to being "frozen" out. Kennedy also made a preliminary test of the floodlighting in the Washington studio and found that his lectern was under a much stronger glare than his opponent's, and so technicians made the proper adjustment. Nixon went on, in that second debate, to give his strongest performance.

While the candidates argued about civil rights, domestic economic conditions, presidential leadership, and the proper role of the federal government, cold-war issues raised the most passion. Kennedy himself had long since accepted the analysis endorsed by a number of defense experts that the Eisenhower administration had contributed to a "missile gap," which would soon enable the Soviets to have at least a temporary and dangerous striking power advantage. Kennedy exploited the post-*Sputnik,* post–U-2 period to argue that Republican policies were making America's military position vulnerable, a position that made some of his liberal friends wince. "J.F.K. has made the point that he isn't soft," John Kenneth Galbraith wrote to Lou Harris. "Henceforth he can only frighten."[54]

That second debate began with Paul Niven of CBS asking Nixon whether Kennedy's charge that the administration must take responsibility for the loss of Cuba could be compared with "your own statements in previous campaigns that the Truman Administration was responsible for the loss of China to the Communists?"[55] Nixon rejected the comparison. China was lost, he pointed out, by 1953, but "Cuba is not lost, and I don't think this kind of defeatist talk by Senator Kennedy helps the situation one bit." Certainly Cuba was an issue that was too good for Kennedy to resist. How could Nixon, he wanted to know, advocate military action to defend Quemoy and Matsu while tolerating a Communist regime only ninety miles off the Florida coast?[56]

Just before the fourth and final debate Kennedy's campaign headquarters at New York's Biltmore Hotel released a statement that said, in part, "We must attempt to strengthen the non-Batista Democratic anti-Castro forces. . . . Thus far these fighters for freedom have had virtually no support from our Government."[57] During that last debate, Nixon termed Kennedy's ideas the most "dangerously irresponsible recommendations that he's made during the course of this campaign." It would not only fail, but would earn our condemnation from the Organization of American States and the United Nations and would, moreover, "be an open invitation for Mr. Khrushchev to come in, to come into Latin America and to engage us in what would be a civil war, and possibly even worse than that."[58]

Nixon has already taken credit for a major role within the administration for working to develop precisely the sort of American initiative advocated by Kennedy. Nevertheless, he later wrote in his memoirs, "I had no choice but to take a completely opposite stand and attack Kennedy's advocacy of open intervention in Cuba."[59] His account, published in Six Crises, went into greater detail about his immediate reaction to Kennedy's predebate statement. He explained that Secretary of the Interior Fred Seaton verified that CIA Director Allen Dulles had included information about the clandestine plans when briefing Kennedy. "I understand and expect hard-hitting attacks in a campaign," Nixon then explained. "But in this instance I thought that Kennedy, with full knowledge of the facts, was jeopardizing the security of a United States foreign policy operation. And my rage was greater because I could do nothing about it." The publication of Six Crises brought a prompt refutation from the Kennedy White House. On March 20, 1962, a statement released by Press Secretary Pierre Salinger denied that Kennedy had received any prior knowledge of secret preparations for a refugee landing on Cuba. Dulles himself confirmed Kennedy's position and stated that the controversy was due to an "honest misunderstanding,"[60] although he acknowledged that the July discussion had indeed included Cuba and the CIA's clandestine radio operations.[61] He also had met with Kennedy again in September. The exact contents of that conversation are similarly unknown, but Kennedy is on record as having told the Scripps-Howard newspapers shortly afterward that "The forces fighting for freedom in exile and in the mountains of Cuba should be sustained and assisted." He was even more explicit in a major speech made in Cincinnati on October 6, when he advocated "encouraging those liberty-loving Cubans who are leading the resistance to Castro."[62] Moreover, by the time he debated with Nixon, the potential fund of information available to Kennedy and his staff was plentiful.

Shortly before the fourth debate, Dick Goodwin, an aggressive top Harvard Law School graduate and Kennedy staff writer, received a long memorandum from Archibald Cox. Cox, on leave from Harvard to supervise the Kennedy data-gathering headquarters in Washington, advised that Nixon was "willing to take action which disregards the charter [of the Organization of American States] and endangers our relations with other Latin American states for the sake of some supposed political advantages." He added that Nixon was "willing to endanger our position in the world and risk war in an effort to get votes. It is time for us," Cox went on, "to take away the claim that the Republicans are the party of peace. No one will suppose that Senator Kennedy is an appeaser."[63]

Goodwin worked along with Sorensen and Salinger to get out a release that would both satisfy Cox's warning and make the papers before the next debate. The statement included much that had been said before, together with the admonition that American collective action against communism in the Caribbean would have to be in concert with both the Organization of American States and the European allies. But it also included the line about supporting the non-Batista, anti-Castro refugees.

Goodwin now contends that that was the one campaign statement not personally cleared by Kennedy. "It was very late at night," he recalls. "I called the Carlyle to read it to Kennedy, but he was asleep and we decided not to wake him. Not knowing about the Bay of Pigs invasion plans, which I didn't know but Kennedy *may very well have known, * the statement didn't have any implication for me that it took on immediately in the press. He had been up and down the coast giving speeches saying we ought to do something to help the anti-Castro forces. So it didn't appear to me to be anything much different from what he had been saying either in released statements or extemporaneously. However, a particular phrase, one or two words used, did in fact suggest the force of military action from the outside, which was not in my mind, to tell you the truth. And I certainly knew nothing about the plans."[64]

But the fact is that the release was issued not during the night, as Goodwin remembers, or even the next morning. The early release on the twentieth, which undoubtedly preoccupied Goodwin and Sorensen the night before, was the three-thousand-word refutation of Nixon's criticism of Kennedy's "misstatements." The Cuban comments were, instead, handed to the press on the evening of the twentieth from the Hotel Biltmore in time to make the morning papers of the twenty-first.[65] If Kennedy was asleep at a crucial point, taking his customary afternoon nap, there was still enough time between then and that evening for him to have cleared the statement. As Goodwin also says, "Nothing went out as a statement of his that he didn't read first, and often [he] edited it as

*Emphasis supplied

time allowed."[66] For that to have been the only release of the entire campaign that Kennedy did not personally clear, and for that to have come just one day before his fourth debate with Nixon, make disclaimers somewhat disingenuous. Moreover, rhetoric about "fighters for freedom" was not routine phrasemaking by Goodwin; since 1956 the Hungarian rebellion had made "freedom-fighters" synonymous with anti-Communist nationalism.

Nixon, of course, always remained outraged. The Eisenhower White House version of the Kennedy briefings was more persuasive than Dulles's, and while admitting that clandestine radio operations had been discussed, the director never attempted to say that Nixon was entirely off base; it was just an "honest misunderstanding."

The immediate stake, it has been argued, was the importance of Florida and its ten electoral votes. That state's population was especially involved with what was going on in the Caribbean. But it was more than merely Cuba, Castro, and alleged threats to the Western Hemisphere. It was the cold war and the need to convince the American public that even Democrats could act forthrightly about communism. Kennedy was tough and meant business, and the debates had made that point. Just before the fourth encounter, Jack's foreign policy adviser, the usually dovish Chester Bowles, had offered encouragement by writing, "You have been brilliantly successful in building up our position in regard to American military strength to a point where no one can call us 'soft on Communism.' "[67] As Reston wrote after the final Kennedy–Nixon round, he "was a much more experienced and competent man than most people thought before the debates began," and, he added, "the general impression here is that he has succeeded in this objective."[68]

The Kennedy tide that had continued to build since his nomination was further spurred by the debates, but it was still far short of assuring victory. The South, especially, remained uncertain. How well could Lyndon Johnson whip "his states" into line, let alone his native Texas? What would be the effect of Harry Byrd's, Virginia's senior senator, "sitting on his hands" in his normally Democratic state as he had done during the Eisenhower campaigns? What about the unpledged electors of Mississippi and Louisiana? Could all potential defections from normal Democratic majorities be balanced by the "safe" states, now presumably secured by the attraction of a Roman Catholic candidate?

The South continued to be a weak spot, not only because of Kennedy's religion. The Democratic Party's platform, written by and for northern liberals, seemed serious about implementing integration and even promised to finally deliver a Fair Employment Practices Commission. Senator Byrd passed the word that Dick Russell had told him that "Kennedy will implement the Democratic platform and advocate Civil Rights legislation beyond what is contained in the platform."[69] Nor could Russell himself give public speeches that, as he held, would endorse a "socialistic platform that I believe to be destructive and which I will largely oppose in the next Senate."[70] Despite some expressed fear of losing committee chairmanships and dissidence by their senators, James O. Eastland and John Stennis, the Mississippi delegation voted unanimously in mid-August to go along with Governor Ross Barnett and place a slate of unpledged electors on the November ballot that would be dedicated to state's rights.[71] "We are having a great deal of difficulty in the Southern states," Robert Kennedy explained to Sargent Shriver in early August, "on the grounds that Jack's views are socialistic, and he wants the state to control both man and business."[72]

Even Lyndon Johnson's presence on the ticket did not help. Lyndon was neither a Deep South segregationist nor a true regional leader like Russell. "I would hate to depend for the defense of the South upon Lyndon Johnson," wrote Augusta, Georgia, attorney Roy V. Harris, an ardent segregationist. "I have often said that in following Lyndon Johnson, we get the little dog's tail cut off an inch at a time and it seems to me that if the tail is going to be amputated it would be more humane to do it all at one time." Johnson, he also recalled, had spoken before a black caucus at Los Angeles and vowed to guarantee them more progress in the field of civil rights in the next four years than had been made in the last 104.[73] For Johnson, then, it was not a simple matter to keep his natural constituents in line, convince the South to vote for the ticket, and, at the same time, satisfy Kennedy's northern followers that he was no racist.[74]

Just how severe those problems were became obvious when the Texas State Democratic Convention met in Dallas on September 20. Governor Price Daniel, who chaired the proceedings, pleaded that "No one should interpret the support of these nominees as support of the platform that was written at Los Angeles." The mention of Johnson's name provoked a barrage of boos because he had "sold out" to the North by becoming Kennedy's running mate. At Daniel's suggestion, the convention finally adopted a state platform that differed in key ways from the party's national policies.[75]

Seeking to supplement Johnson's southern efforts, Kennedy kept close, reassuring contacts with those he had cultivated. Byrd continued to resist personal appeals.

For Jack Kennedy the need to balance regional and ideological forces helped reaffirm his reputation as a politician with plans and tactics that had not much to do with convictions. The consequent suspicions were so strong that Schlesinger saw the need to dash off a little book designed to refute charges that Jack Kennedy was merely a Democratic Nixon.

By 1960, however, a variety of post–World War II developments had made changes inevitable. The Democratic platform, therefore, was not ahead of its time by reflecting the new realities. They had long since been evident not only as a consequence of long-standing efforts to implement the Fourteenth Amendment, but, most recently, because of the student sit-in movement. Begun in Greensboro, North Carolina, just a month after Kennedy had declared for the presidency, the movement had become a massive crusade for the integration of public facilities. All of this meant that the civil rights drive was too far advanced to be ignored by a political leader seeking broad support.

Kennedy's own attitude was unclear. During the constitutional and political debates over the Civil Rights Act of 1957, he had voted both for the provision to give the Justice Department greater enforcement powers, which failed to pass, and, to the distress of liberals, for an amendment requiring criminal contempt cases to be tried by juries. The latter provision, of course, meant that local segregationists would have the final say. There was, then, no end to suspicions that Jack Kennedy's civil rights outlook was limned in political expediency. Doubts were not much encouraged by the early support for his candidacy that came from John Patterson, the Alabama governor who had defeated George Wallace in 1958 by, Wallace maintained, "out-niggering" him. The subsequent choice of Lyndon Johnson at Los Angeles could be rationalized only by liberals with strong faith in Kennedy's ultimate course.

Some skeptics got an early chance to experience Kennedy's attitudes themselves. No state was more ardent for civil rights than Michigan. With a progressive party leader, Neil Staebler, a liberal governor, G. Mennen Williams, and the power of the United Auto Workers under Walter Reuther, racial equality had attained virtually the same importance as traditional bread-and-butter issues. Kennedy had met with Williams and Staebler at the governor's Mackinac Island retreat in March, and although he had come away with the endorsement of Michigan's leadership, representatives of Detroit's black community were far from satisfied. "Conscious of the fact that it was important to get Kennedy on the right track with the Negro and civil rights groups in America," Williams accepted an offer to fly down to Washington on the *Caroline* so the candidate could meet with a black delegation at his Georgetown home. That luncheon meeting several weeks before the convention enabled Kennedy to clarify his position on the sit-ins. "They just couldn't understand why he had to qualify his statement that he was for the Negroes by saying, 'If they act peacefully,' " Williams later said. "They felt that this was a sort of demeaning, condescending position, and the argument went back and forth and back and forth. The Negroes were obviously not getting their point to Jack, and they were unsatisfied with his posture."

At one point during the discussions Jackie appeared and was introduced to the group, which then moved to the tables that had been arranged at the outdoor terrace. Finally, as the conversation continued, the governor won Kennedy's understanding about the objection to his condition that he would support the blacks if they acted peacefully. They feel, Williams told Kennedy, "that it's as if you issued an invitation to them for dinner and said, 'Please come to dinner, but wash your hands before you sit down.' Obviously you would expect your guests to wash their hands before you sat down and you would be insulting them if you said that." That group left Washington as converts to Kennedy's cause and delivered for him at the convention, but, more than any other delegation, felt let down over his choice of Johnson and made the loudest protests.[76]

Johnson campaigned tirelessly for the ticket that fall, concentrating mainly on the South as his whistle-stop train, the so-called "Cornpone Special," carried the earthy senator throughout the region. Neither local politicians nor oil moguls were permitted to forget the consequences implicit in having Johnson return to the next Senate as majority leader because they had failed to deliver. Johnson's contribution also extended to Kennedy's religious problem, a matter that the Texan treated in his usual colorful stump style. Referring to the *PT 109* incident, he would say, "When Jack Kennedy was saving those Americans, they didn't ask him what church he belonged to."[77]

Johnson visited Hyannis Port on the last weekend of July, flying into the airport near Hyannis despite foul weather. Their get-together was their first since Los Angeles, and a time to confirm strategies for both the special rump session of the Congress and how to divide campaign strategies. The next day, with both Lady Bird and Jacqueline present, they held a joint press conference in the "Big House" of the Ambassador. When asked about carrying out the party's civil rights platform, they explained that the question would be taken up with the party's congressional committee chairman. Since the key panels were in the hands of southern segregationists, the response very clearly meant there would be no action on civil rights during the special session.[78]

The record shows continued close Kennedy–Johnson communications before, during, and after that special session, as telephones linked Hyannis Port with the LBJ Ranch near Johnson City. Once in Washington for those few weeks in August, get-togethers were common, and both men met with such party leaders as Henry Jackson, the chairman of the national committee, governors Luther Hodges of North Carolina and Ernest Vandiver of Georgia, George Smathers, and Russell. On August 26 Johnson went to Kennedy's office in Room 362 of the Senate Office Building so the two men could confer with New York City's flamboyant and hard-bargaining Harlem congressman, Adam Clayton Powell, Jr., who had backed Johnson before the convention. Powell's support was obtained at the usual price—a contribution for his church.[79]

One particularly important policymaking session in Johnson's office took place without Kennedy, but in the presence of leaders representing a broad spectrum of civil rights positions. Russell, Orville Freeman, Gene McCarthy, Humphrey, and Joe Clark were all present as Johnson explained his position. Congressional realities virtually guaranteed that boldness in moving for civil rights legislation would merely jeopardize other social programs that were promised by the platform. From what is known about that mission, Johnson convinced at least two of the liberals, Freeman and Clark.[80] And an important message was conveyed to the southern leaders: There was nothing to fear. Russell, in turn, assured both Kennedy and Johnson that only some terrible campaign blunder would cause their electoral vote total to go below 350, which was still a comfortable majority.[81] When the campaign began, Russell's own activity was mostly confined to two days in Texas, and that as a personal favor to Johnson, who needed help "with the so-called conservative vote to off-set the charge that he was a socialist."[82]

During the special congressional session that August, Kennedy was forced to join with other Democrats from the North and the South to table civil rights legislation introduced by the Republicans solely to embarrass and divide the opposition. To compensate he signed a statement in conjunction with the Leadership Conference on Civil Rights, urging President Eisenhower to issue an executive order on housing that could be desegregated "by the stroke of a presidential pen."[83] In his televised debates with Nixon he deplored the inequities retarding black progress and said, "I think we can do better." He called on Nixon to say he would implement the *Brown* decision and back legislation to empower the attorney general to protect constitutional rights. His listeners heard sympathy and understanding, but not a thing was said about what he would do to urge Congress to act. As Harris Wofford has pointed out, "Kennedy grabbed at anything that would bypass the legislative branch."[84]

Nixon, also insecure about his southern standing, refrained from wooing the black vote. One of the fiascos of the Republican campaign was the statement of his running mate, Henry Cabot Lodge, Jr., that suggested both Republican candidates had an obligation to place a black in the cabinet.

Kennedy, on the other hand, made a major effort to spur minority registration, and, under Shriver's general leadership, a special unit was established to attract the black vote. The group included civil rights activists whom Kennedy had used in the past such as Marjorie and Belford Lawson and Harris Wofford, a white attorney on leave from Notre Dame Law School. Wofford, who was close to Dr. King and his wife, Coretta, had also served as a member of the staff of the Civil Rights Commission and had helped to edit Kennedy's *The Strategy of Peace.* [85]

Possibly the most crucial incident came just two days before the final Kennedy–Nixon debate. Dr. King was arrested with fifty-one other "trespassers" for having insisted on being served in the Magnolia Room restaurant of Rich's Department Store in Atlanta. When Wofford heard the news, he managed to intercede with the city's progressive mayor, William Hartsfield, and Morris Abram, the Atlanta lawyer and civil libertarian. Even while that succeeded, a statement from the office of Governor Ernest Vandiver that was issued by Georgia's Kennedy campaign chief, Griffin Bell, denied the possibility of outside interference and declared that King "must stand trial and he will get equal treatment just as any other common law violator."[86]

But Dr. King was the one prisoner not released. Earlier he had been picked up on the technicality that his Alabama's driver's license was no longer valid in Georgia. The fact that he and Coretta were driving with a white woman, novelist Lillian Smith, had not helped matters much. King was fined twenty-five dollars and placed on twelve months' probation. His participation in the sit-in was ruled by De Kalb County Judge Oscar Mitchell as a violation of his probation, and the earlier conviction was reinstated. King was ordered to serve a four-month sentence in a remote rural jail, the Georgia State Prison at Reidsville, two hundred miles south of Atlanta.[87] A statement issued from the Kennedy campaign and released by Salinger expressing hope for a satisfactory outcome had obviously been futile. Any further denunciation, warned both Vandiver and Bell, would cost Kennedy a batch of southern votes, although the governor reportedly promised to get "the son of a bitch" released if Kennedy would make no additional public statements.[88]

Numerous efforts were then made to reassure Coretta King. Wofford arranged for a call to her from Chester Bowles, whom the Kings admired, explaining that every effort would be made to get Dr. King's early release. When Bowles tried to get Stevenson to make a similar call, Adlai shocked him by refusing on the ground that he had never met Mrs. King.[89] Hubert Humphrey sent off a telegram to Richard Russell warning that the incident "can cause [the] Democratic national ticket unbelievable trouble."[90]

It was Wofford, however, who reached Jack Kennedy through Shriver with the suggestion that the candidate himself make a call to Mrs. King. "That's a damn good idea," Kennedy replied without hesitation. "Get her on the phone." And Shriver, who was alone with Kennedy at the time, remembers that he talked to her "maybe a minute and a half. He put down the phone. I walked out of the room, went out in the other room and had coffee with the rest of the guys, and then I went off about my business. I never said anything about it."[91]

The decisive call, however, the one that led to Dr. King's release, came from Bobby Kennedy. According to the younger Kennedy brother, he made it to Judge Mitchell, a good friend of Governor Vandiver, to let him know "that if he was a decent American, he would let King out of jail by sundown. I called him because it made me so damned angry to think of that bastard sentencing a citizen to four months of hard labor for a minor traffic offense and screwing up my brother's campaign and making our country look ridiculous before the world."[92] Bobby's personal attention had obviously flattered the judge. When Dr. King's father announced that he would no longer hold Jack Kennedy's Catholicism against him, the presidential candidate remarked, "Imagine Martin Luther King having a bigot for a father." Then, walking on, he turned to Wofford and added, "Well, we all have fathers, don't we?"[93]

Word of the Kennedy intervention was not allowed to go unnoticed by black voters. Wofford distributed a little blue pamphlet on the King case called *"No Comment" Nixon versus a Candidate with a Heart, Senator Kennedy,* which contained key statements by black leaders attesting to the actions in behalf of Dr. King. Nearly two million copies were distributed during the days before the election, mostly in black churches throughout the country. King himself, according to an early biographer, responded philosophically. "There are moments when the politically expedient is the morally wise," he said, but he continued to withhold any formal endorsement for Kennedy, something that the presidential candidate had been trying to get since the start of the campaign.[94]

Four years later, when interviewed by Anthony Lewis, Robert Kennedy was asked about that key phone call. Either directly or indirectly—Kennedy did not recall which—the suggestion to call judge Mitchell had come from none other than Governor Vandiver of Georgia. Recalling that the judge was a good friend of the governor, Kennedy explained, "And the judge said that if I called and it was a matter of importance, that he'd make the arrangements. So I . . . went into a pay booth and called the judge and said, 'Will he get out on bail?' or something to that effect. I don't know what he did but he got him out. The judge said, 'Bob, it's nice to talk to you. I don't have any objection about doing that.' That's how it happened, and my brother's and my actions were independent of one another." Not that Vandiver had any special sympathy for King; his action was motivated by loyalty to the ticket. Later, shortly before Jack Kennedy assumed the presidency, there was opposition by civil rights groups to the possibility of offering Vandiver a place within the administration.[95]

Jacqueline Kennedy completed the voting ritual as quickly as possible. Then came voter eighty-six, who signed in as John F. Kennedy of 112 Bowdoin Street, Boston, the address of his old, useful apartment across from the State House. The senator's turn lasted almost twice as long as his wife's, which encouraged speculation that he had voted a split ticket. Brusquely, he emerged and led her past the crowd of spectators to the waiting limousine, which sped them to Logan Airport for the short flight to Hyannis.

At the airfield that served Cape Cod, located just above the village of Hyannis, they were confronted with another crew of well-wishers: more photographers, more inane clichés, more infatuation with trivia, more of what his life had become. Mrs. Kennedy smiled obligingly, her advanced pregnancy barely showing under the cloth raincoat. Gently, she edged her husband out of the little entrapment. Then, as though responding to both his wife and his own impatience, the senator abandoned customary campaign behavior. He rejected the offer of a motorcade procession that had been arranged by a local committee and chose to hitch a ride with his cousin, Ann Gargan. Their car, accompanied by a five-motorcycle police escort, sped along the most direct route through Hyannis, to the southwest, in the direction of the sea breezes.

He had hurried only to end up waiting, having to cope with the boredom of the long hours ahead. Not until well after sunset would there be even a trickle of returns, and not until sometime after midnight would matters begin to gel. Until then there would be the usual premature indicators, the isolated reports from "key" precincts, analysis of "trends" based on meaningless fragments. He knew all that. He had been through it before. This, though, was different—the real thing, the national contest. Now he could do nothing but wait. For the first time in years, maybe since he had begun his active drive for the presidency, circumstances were entirely beyond his control. Nothing was more frustrating. He wanted to be alone, to wish away the hours, to know the results, whatever they might be, and to go on from there. If he lost, there would still be the Senate and he had four more years before facing reelection. At least he now had time to think about such things.

For the election story the Hyannis Armory had been converted into a gigantic press headquarters. Desks, typewriters, and communications facilities had been placed everywhere. There were also the inevitable political analysts ready to give significance to returns from insignificant places. Within the compound itself Bobby's house had become an elaborate electronic center, complete with banks of temporary telephones ready to provide instant access to every part of the country.

At about five o'clock that Tuesday afternoon, Jack Kennedy got up from his nap and visited Bobby's house. A phone call to John Bailey in Hartford revealed that some voting machines that had been prematurely opened had shown signs of a big Kennedy landslide developing in Connecticut. That brightened the mood just as the large living room began to fill with Kennedys. The Mayflower Catering Service had already laid out a lavish buffet that included sandwiches of lobster and egg salad, together with an assortment of petit fours, eclairs, and turnovers, as well as plenty of beer and soft drinks. Jack himself said little. He was the calmest person in the room. Cornelius Ryan, the author of popular books about the Second World War, noticed how little he communicated even with Bobby, who was in total command of the situation.[96] Bobby had sent telegrams to key leaders all over giving them eight different phone numbers for calling him with the latest information as "the election takes shape in your area."[97] Meanwhile the Kennedy women scurried about energetically as though warming up for a gala party.

In an upstairs room Lou Harris was much subdued. Early figures were beginning to come in, and he did not like what he saw. There were discouraging returns from some midwestern districts and the city of Louisville. At 7:15, at just about the time that message reached the group gathered downstairs, the large television set in the corner of the room carried the news that CBS's IBM 7090 computer had projected a victory for Richard Nixon. ABC's Univac said the odds were ten to one.[98]

That set off outbursts of shock, disbelief, and expletives. Fortunately the computers soon began to reverse themselves, so completely, in fact, that Kennedy was the new projected winner with an expected fifty-one percent of the popular vote. A Kennedy tide seemed to be developing. The industrial centers of the Northeast, which had been hard hit by unemployment and economic stagnation, were turning in some of the highest pluralities for a Democrat since FDR in 1936. Connecticut, Massachusetts, Rhode Island—the heart of New England—were all falling into line. Without that center of Jack's constituency there would have been no contest. But the vital and less easily predictable states of New York and Pennsylvania were also moving his way. Kennedy then returned to his own house, where he sent Caroline off to bed with a kiss and settled down with Jackie and Bill Walton. At about 10:30 Jacqueline turned to her husband and whispered, "You're President now."

But he knew better. He had yet to transcend his basic strength. The nation's hinterland, with its powerful conservatism, Republicanism, and heavy Nixon support would be much more decisive. Jackie, less anxious now, went to bed, and Kennedy hurried back across the lawn to his brother's place. He found Bobby tracking the national picture with the aid of a large election-night chart put out by the Shell Oil Company. At 11:50 Bob wrote down the information that Los Angeles County had reported ninety percent of its vote. But the pattern was taking on a "peculiar fashion." Despite Kennedy's sixty-five-thousand-vote majority at that point, the overall distribution made for little confidence that California would wind up in Jack's column. Even by 2:00 A.M., those thirty-two electoral votes were uncertain. And, as pluralities became scarcer after the figures from the Northeast had all been recorded, the West Coast was becoming more crucial.

Those postmidnight hours were the most uncertain. Two midwestern states that could have eased matters considerably earlier in the evening —and should have—Ohio and Illinois, were, instead, going all wrong. Despite Governor Mike Di Salle's early endorsement, and despite its urban-industrial base and a thirty percent Catholic electorate, Ohio was leaning strongly toward Nixon. Lyndon Johnson called Kennedy to say, "I heard *you're* losing Ohio, but *we're* doing fine in Pennsylvania."[99] Illinois remained uncertain. The lead there kept changing with Nixon's chances bolstered by strength in the downstate agricultural counties. By the early-morning hours it had become obvious that Kennedy was in desperate need of either Illinois, California, or Minnesota to give him the eleven electoral votes that he needed. At almost 4:00 A.M. Jack returned to his own house.

As he slept, his lead continued to evaporate. California's uncertainty was increased by the suspension of the tabulation for the night, leaving that state's thirty-two votes in doubt. With half the districts uncounted, Kennedy's popular lead there stood at just 100,000 by 5:00 A.M.; the Nixon people could still hope that the whole thing could be thrown for a decision into the House of Representatives by the maneuvering of fourteen unpledged Alabama and Mississippi electors. As the hours went by, that possibility grew. He was still ahead, but his national popular plurality kept shrinking as more votes came in from the West, and he still lacked the vital eleven to go over the top. Guardedly, *The New York Times* ran a headline for its 7:00 A.M. edition that only said that Kennedy was the "Apparent Winner."[100]

Not until shortly after noon did the suspense end. Minnesota's eleven electoral votes were obviously safe. In Los Angeles, Herb Klein, Nixon's press secretary, announced a concession. "All right," Jack Kennedy said in Hyannis Port, "let's go," and Salinger told the press that the President-elect would make a statement in the armory at 1:45.

When he appeared on the stage of the flag-draped armory, he was obviously solemn. On the bleachers behind him were a dozen members of the Kennedy family. For the first time since the start of the primaries, almost a year earlier, the seventy-one-year-old former ambassador, wearing a gray business suit and seated beside his wife in the front row, was seen in public with his son. Bobby stood impassively at the side of the stage, hands in pockets and, like the other Kennedys, gave the impression of having accepted a burden rather than a prize. Facing the three hundred newsmen and massed television cameras, the President-elect acknowledged only that it was "a satisfying moment" and pledged his energy to advancing the "long-range interests of the United States and the cause of freedom around the world." He smiled and looked at Jackie, whose eyes were on him, and said, "So now my wife and I prepare for a new Administration and for a new baby."[101]

Jack was better rested and more poised the next afternoon, when he held his first postelection press conference. When a newsman asked about rumors concerning his health, he answered without hesitation that he "never had Addison's disease. In regard to my health, it was fully explained in a press statement in the middle of July, and my health is excellent. I have been through a long campaign and my health is very good today."

His major news involved appointments. Allen Dulles would stay on as director of the CIA and J. Edgar Hoover would continue to head the FBI. Other than his acknowledgment that the closeness of the election might present problems for his legislative program, the statement about Dulles and Hoover was taken as an obvious concession to the pattern of the ballots, which were still being counted. The two men represented continuity with the past. Their retention was taken for granted as a reassurance to wary conservatives that a liberal *putsch* was not about to overthrow the established order, and that did have its validity. But Dulles could hardly have been replaced while deeply involved with the Cuban scheme, and Hoover's possession of the tapes connecting Jack to Inga Arvad, the Danish woman suspected of spying for the Nazis, made it prudent to keep him happy.[102] So Kennedy was not much inclined to accept the advice of Bill Walton and Ben Bradlee, both of whom had dined with Kennedy the night before and argued that Dulles and Hoover should be the first holdovers to be removed.[103]

While President Eisenhower began cooperating with Kennedy's representatives in starting the process of transition to a new administration, ballot-counting went on. Not until days later did it become clear that Nixon had managed to take California. Only after many weeks did Hawaii finally land in the Democratic column. The final tally showed Kennedy's plurality as just 113,238 out of a two-party total vote of 68,329,540, although the electoral vote was a more decisive 303–219. Less noticeable at the time but equally significant for the future burdens of the Democratic President was his ability to bring in only twenty-seven of his party's thirty-four senatorial candidates. All seven who ran behind him lost, and the overall pattern of congressional returns showed that few had been dependent on his heading the ticket to ensure their own success.[104]

As Kennedy recovered in Hyannis Port and assessed the situation, the close race was more conducive to sobriety than euphoria. There was continued vote-counting, emphasis on Jack's margin representing the equivalent of something like two votes per precinct, and, much more demeaning to one of his temperament, persistent doubts about its legitimacy. Had he really won it on his own? Had Johnson brought home the southern states and allayed the businessmen? Had the Cook County organization of Mayor Daley manipulated the count? An English journalist who visited Kennedy during those postelection days found him considerably uneasy. He thought he was undergoing the first shock of his presidency. "I think it hurt his self-confidence and pride that he won with such a narrow majority. He considered himself so much better than Nixon, and yet there was Nixon, and he didn't do so badly."[105]

3

"Preparing for Power"

It quickly became obvious that Kennedy's handling of the transition was a public-relations triumph. He seemed to be staffing not a government of politicians, or even one of lawyers—Jack was virtually creating a university. He included a real dean of faculty, McGeorge Bundy, recruited from the Charles River academic community to temper the earnest enthusiasts on the Potomac.

While not exactly a haphazard development, the Kennedy version of Roosevelt's "brain trust" was both more academic and more improvised. The request for Stevenson to head a foreign policy task force ultimately involved his two legal assistants George Ball and John Sharon. They headed an astoundingly ambitious prepresidential gathering of expertise. Altogether, seven task forces had been appointed before election day. By January 20 there were seventy-nine, involving around one hundred people, with specialties about evenly distributed between foreign and domestic policy. Their findings supplemented studies made by the Rand Corporation, the Brookings Institution, and Henry Jackson's special Senate Subcommittee on National Machinery.

Kennedy valued the studies as much for the process as the results. He clearly warmed to the notion of rounding up as much information and as many advisers as possible, reserving for himself the political judgments that would ultimately have to be made. Also, with so vast a corps of experts dedicating themselves to his cause, he thereby acquired an endless reservoir of talent. Roswell Gilpatric, who served with Symington's group, observed that they were mainly "useful exercises for the President to find out the sort of the cut of the jib [sic] of the people who were on the task forces, and also bringing into play on his team two very influential senators, namely, Jackson and Symington."[1] When somebody pointed out that advisers were being enrolled without regard to overlapping, Kennedy's logic was simple and understated: "I simply cannot afford to have just one set of advisers."[2]

Preparations to take over power went on while Jack Kennedy commuted between Hyannis Port, Palm Beach, Washington, and New York, gaining, as the days passed, the aura of a conquering hero. Kennedy's people thought Truman had been courageous but ill-prepared for the presidency; they considered Eisenhower as little more than a benign dumbbell. They had few doubts that intelligence, training, energy, and idealism were exactly what the world needed. Brought together by the inspiration of a new leader who combined "a mixture of intelligence and smartness," they seemed cocky, arrogant, and overconfident, giving the impression that the power of the presidency was all that mattered.[3] "I think some of the orderliness of gearing the presidency to the rest of the government were lessons they hadn't learned, and later learned the hard way," was the later recollection of Ed McCabe of Eisenhower's staff.[4]

But nobody could minimize their industry. Before Christmas, with the aid of his "talent scouts," Kennedy had put together a cabinet that Adam Yarmolinsky described as "nine strangers and a brother."[5] Orville Freeman, who became secretary of agriculture, was no stranger, however. Freeman's appointment to the post that ranked high on Kennedy's personal list of the "ten-dullest jobs," was an obvious bid to bolster the President's traditional farm-belt weakness. The Freeman–Kennedy association had already been made public when the Minnesota governor placed Kennedy's name in nomination at Los Angeles. The new secretary of commerce, Luther Hodges, was the governor of North Carolina and had been a Johnson man before Los Angeles. Nearing the age of sixty-three and the oldest Cabinet nominee, Hodges offered southern representation and comfort to worried businessmen.

Several others were brought into the administration by the recruiting efforts of Kennedy's brother-in-law, R. Sargent Shriver. Shriver had no particular qualifications for the job except, as he recalls, that Kennedy "would somehow know that you were able to do that, and then he'd put you in charge of it and he wouldn't be fussing with you all the time."[6] Shriver went to work by instructing his aides to find the best people without regard to availability, a technicality that could always be resolved afterward. He also enlisted Harris Wofford and Adam Yarmolinsky to help with the talent hunt. Meanwhile the sense of activism gave the whole enterprise its magnetism, and potential recruiters were rated according to criteria carefully spelled out on prepared forms. An important item to check was "toughness," which actually led some to phone in saying, "I'm tough."[7]

Their chief find was Robert McNamara, the Ford Motor Company "whiz kid" from Ann Arbor, who beat out such other highly lauded possibilities to head the Defense Department as John McCloy, William Foster, and Paul Nitze.[8] McNamara impressed both Shriver and Kennedy, who liked his precise, efficient mind. Furthermore McNamara was a Republican (Kennedy was relieved that he was not another Catholic) who was as unorthodox politically as he was in business. Kennedy himself did not meet him until he had first been scrutinized by Yarmolinsky and Shriver. At one point, while the matter was supposedly secret, *The Washington Post,* much to Kennedy's annoyance, broke the story. When the "leak" was analyzed, it was traced to Kennedy himself. He had played golf with Phil Graham and had dropped McNamara's name. "So," as Mike Feldman later recalled, "we found it was true that the Ship of State is the only ship that often leaks at the top."[9]

Then there was the attorney general. In a Cabinet with an average age of forty-seven, a full ten years less than Eisenhower's, Robert F. Kennedy was the youngest. His qualifications were also somewhat dubious. Other than serving his brother, Bobby was best known for his anti-Communist credentials through his earlier connection with Joe McCarthy's committee and for his pursuit of organized crime, especially the highly public crusade against Jimmy Hoffa. The Virginia Law School graduate had never practiced and had no apparent claim to the position of the nation's chief law-enforcement officer. He had, in fact, not been the first one mentioned for the post. Abe Ribicoff could have had it, but the governor, circumspect, recoiled against the specter of a Jewish attorney general forcing white Protestant southern schools to accept little black boys and girls.[10] Arthur Goldberg, who was also Jewish, did show some interest, but Kennedy was not nearly as indebted to him as to Ribicoff. When offered the number-two job in the Justice Department, Goldberg rejected having to become an underling.[11] And he had no doubt that his superior would be Bobby Kennedy.

Jack was not surprised when hints of Bobby's coming appointment prompted comments about nepotism, which began to tarnish the transition's lofty tone. One leading Republican senator called the move "a little bit ominous," and Drew Pearson privately advised Bobby that acceptance of the post would inevitably place his brother "in hot water all the time."[12]

More serious was the opposition from Richard Russell, a Capitol Hill power who Jack Kennedy could not afford to ignore. The Georgia senator's concern went beyond propriety and nepotism and centered on the probability that any new attorney general would be making decisions affecting recent civil rights laws. The powers of the office, Russell wrote in a private memorandum, "are too vital to the rights and liberties of all of the American people to be devoted to political purposes."[13] Taking his case directly to the President-elect, Russell found Kennedy in agreement. He understood why his brother should not be appointed. There would be too much litigation involving race relations to keep the Kennedy name from becoming a curse word in the South.

When Russell advised that Bobby should be prudently appointed to some other responsible position within the administration, Kennedy raised the possibility of retaining Eisenhower's secretary of defense, Thomas Gates, and making Bobby the latter's undersecretary for the interim. When Gates finally retired, Bobby could replace him. If not Gates, Robert A. Lovett could hold defense for a while.[14] But the pressure to name Bobby came from a source hard to resist—the Kennedys' father.

Jack sought out Clark Clifford, who had done much previous problem-solving for the Kennedys. Clifford later quoted Jack: "I'm just really not completely comfortable with it. Bobby's bright and he has been doing a marvelous job as campaign chairman. Bobby hasn't practiced law." Jack suggested Clifford meet with Joe Kennedy to try to persuade him that Bobby belonged elsewhere. Clifford did. The older Kennedy listened very politely, and then said, "Thank you very much. I appreciate that. Now we'll turn to some other subject because Bobby is going to be attorney general."[15]

There were advantages to having Bobby with him. Their exact nature became clearer later on, and it is even tempting to suggest that Jack Kennedy, conscious of his own ways, anticipated the unique protective services that could be fulfilled by no one other than his brother. But no such intimation exists, and it would be foolhardly to conjure up some such Machiavellian foresight. For the moment the political consequences were clearly what mattered. His jocularity about announcing Bobby's appointment in the middle of the night when no one was looking, or pointing out that a young lawyer had to get "his experience someplace" was a typical Kennedy way of jesting about his own predicament.[16] Earlier he had protected family interests by deferring to his father and withdrawing a promise to relinquish his vacated Senate seat to his friend, Torby Macdonald. But Jack was able to move with a freer hand elsewhere during the administration-building process.

A good example was the case of Douglas Dillon, whose credentials should have been comforting to Joe Kennedy. As Treasury secretary, the Republican holdover from Eisenhower's administration would serve as a conservative brake against "irresponsible" Democratic fiscal policies. That was the sort of safeguard Kennedy had wanted, and his presence could also immunize Kennedy from partisan criticism. There were even reports that Eisenhower had urged the investment banker to refuse the Treasury post unless he first obtained written guarantees on behalf of "sound" fiscal policies and a lack of "political" interference.[17] Meanwhile his nomination was being boosted by such press stalwarts as Graham and Alsop. The most important dissenters were Bobby and Joe Kennedy.[18] The "founding father's" attitude was simple. He had doubts about Dillon's financial acumen (undoubtedly based on the Eisenhower's administration's tight money policies), which was consistent with Joe Kennedy's nonideological, unorthodox outlook. He also feared the dangers of a committed Republican creating embarrassment someday by walking away from the administration in a huff.[19]

But Jack Kennedy wanted Dillon. Dillon had agreed to a prior condition, but it had nothing to do with finances. In the presence of the two Kennedy brothers, he promised that any break with the administration would be, as Bobby later recalled, "under peaceful circumstances."[20] Moreover, whether or not Dillon satisfied Joe Kennedy, he was the kind of man the administration needed for Treasury. As head of the talent hunt, Shriver had to find somebody who would reassure the financial community. A number of bankers had been considered, including the presidents of the Bank of America, the Continental Bank in Illinois, and the head of the Federal Reserve Bank in New York. Another banker, Lovett, who had served under Truman, was offered the job but declined because of his health.[21]

Kennedy finally decided for Dillon, Shriver recalled, "because Dillon had government experience, both in the State Department and in the Treasury Department. Dillon had impressed Kennedy here in Washington, when Dillon was an official in the Eisenhower administration, with Dillon's judgment, his knowledge, his technical competence, and his nondogmatic politics. In other words, Dillon was not an ideological Republican." The decisive factor, however, was expressed very simply: "I know Dillon and I can trust Dillon."[22]

But that choice gave some others the impression, as Albert Gore has written, that "a new Democratic President would deliver the tax and monetary policies of his Administration to the very crowd that had reversed the policies of Roosevelt and Truman with such hurtful results for our people."[23] Populists like Gore had no reason to expect anything else. Dillon and McNamara were the sort of Republicans who appealed to the Kennedys—effective, independent conservatives who impressed the people who counted. When, on the last day of 1960, forty-one-year-old McGeorge Bundy was announced as Kennedy's special assistant for national security affairs, the New Frontier had still another Republican, one who had twice backed Eisenhower against Stevenson.

Even Abe Ribicoff, the Connecticut governor and early Kennedy backer, for all his reputation as a liberal, was safely moderate. His popularity in Hartford had been based on such things as fiscal caution, and his reputation was further promoted by the highly publicized crusade for highway safety.[24] Kennedy made him secretary of health, education, and welfare.

Then there was Arthur Goldberg. Goldberg was a brilliant, self-made lawyer, most recently special counsel to the Steelworkers union. But, as with many self-made men, Goldberg prided himself on a capacity for cultivating those who might normally have been enemies. His selection as secretary of labor was, in fact, at first opposed by the building-trades unions, and Kennedy had to personally ask Meany to mollify the dissenters.[25] Goldberg would later be accused of "leaning over backwards" to placate managerial viewpoints.

For all that was implied in a slogan like "New Frontier," then, the centers of power were more notable for competence, influence, and energy than for crusading, which is exactly what Kennedy wanted. Easily the most celebrated omission from the inner circle and, in many ways the most poignant, was Stevenson, whose name came up early in connection with the attorney generalship. But Stevenson's behavior at Los Angeles killed whatever chance he had had for anything significant. Nevertheless, when Kennedy handed him the foreign policy task force job, there seemed to still be some chance he might get State after all. But that, too, was illusory. As perhaps Mrs. Roosevelt had begun to perceive, the very strength of Adlai's devoted liberal following had helped make him a totally impossible choice. From the other side, his candidacy was weakened because his two presidential campaigns had left him with too many enemies on Capitol Hill.[26]

Kennedy viewed Stevenson with more than a little awe. His Lake Forest milieu and pedigree were not to be overlooked. Neither was his use of language and appeal to women. More than once Kennedy friends heard envious comments about why females were so attracted to Adlai. None was more revealing than Jack's remark that he stopped fearing his competition after seeing him in a locker room.

But the most denigrating Kennedy views of Stevenson related to what Jack and Bobby both considered his political ineptitude, or just plain innocence. Bobby's contempt showed when Stevenson, as head of the American delegation to the United Nations, fumbled what he thought was a routine request for a personal favor. The attorney general had had a female classmate who "was attractive then and has remained so," and he wanted to know whether Adlai could help her get a job at the UN. When Stevenson responded with an explanation that there were certain budgetary limitations and that, anyhow, she should first be interviewed by the proper channels, the President's brother made the following handwritten comment: "This letter shows one of the main reasons why Adlai never became President! He will never learn, I expect."[27] None of this was apart from fear of Stevensonian "softness" in the management of America's global affairs.

A much livelier possibility for secretary of state was J. William Fulbright. As Robert Kennedy later wrote, Jack "had worked with Fulbright, knew him better, was very impressed with the way he ran his committee. Before Fulbright became chairman of the Senate Foreign Relations Committee, Kennedy regarded him as somewhat pompous and opinionated, but he later came to respect the man from Arkansas.[28]

Former Secretary of State Dean Acheson told Kennedy he considered the senator somewhat of a dilettante and felt he was less solid and serious than the kind of man needed for the job. When Acheson suggested John McCloy as an alternative, Kennedy said it would not behoove a Democratic President to imply that his own party had nobody capable of being secretary of state. Acheson then boosted Dean Rusk, remembering how during the Truman years Rusk had voluntarily accepted a demotion to take on the politically sensitive job of assistant secretary in charge of the Far East.[29] More than a week later, however, when Kennedy went to see Walter Lippmann, who favored Bundy, he gave the columnist "the distinct impression that he was inclined to appoint Senator Fulbright . . ." Both agreed that Stevenson would not do.[30] Kennedy then had Clifford and Richard Russell sound out the senator.

Fulbright responded by telling both Clifford and Russell that he thought himself temperamentally unsuited and felt he would be better off remaining in the Senate. Fully consistent with such private discussions were his comments to the press that he was "not a candidate."[31] Fulbright was obviously conscious of how his signing the Southern Manifesto in defiance of the Supreme Court's desegregation decision had antagonized civil rights groups. That would cripple his dealings with the sensitive third world. But that was not all. By taking positions that appeared to subordinate the interests of Israel to the needs of American foreign policy, Fulbright had also antagonized another important constituency that Jack Kennedy had worked to attract. The additional opposition from organized labor raised the price still higher.[32]

He also had important support: Lyndon Johnson wanted him. So did Russell. A substantial portion of the party's southern wing would clearly be pleased.

But the dissent was strong, and Bobby especially argued against going with Fulbright.[33] Fulbright went to Palm Beach, where Joe Kennedy outlined the political liabilities that must ultimately govern his son's preferences. Fulbright, then, had had enough. He asked Dick Russell to request Jack Kennedy not make the offer.[34]

With the nomination in obvious trouble, Kennedy called on Russell and mentioned the man touted by Acheson: Dean Rusk. He wanted to know whether Rusk was sufficiently "tough-fibered."[35] Along with David Bruce, the senior ambassador, Rusk emerged as the top choice. When Robert Lovett preferred Rusk, the decision was made.[36]

The Rusk appointment was announced from Palm Beach on December 12. Four days earlier Stevenson had seen Kennedy in Georgetown. The Governor's handwritten notes prepared for that encounter leave no doubt that, even at that late date, he still hoped to head State, or, if he had to settle for something less, a Cabinet-level post with a direct role in policymaking.[37] The offer of the ambassadorship to the UN, even with Cabinet-level rank, nevertheless came as a shock. He told Kennedy he needed some more time to decide, which irritated the President-elect almost to the point of withdrawing the offer.[38] Stevenson told his close associates he wanted no part of the UN. "That's an errand boy's job," he said to Newton Minow. But finally, on December 10, after reassurances about his policymaking and personnel responsibilities, Stevenson accepted. Two days later Kennedy revealed that decision together with the announcement about Rusk.

There was little criticism anyone could make of the Rusk appointment. All anybody knew about him was his Rockefeller Foundation connection and his recent *Foreign Affairs* article, which came out just before the Eisenhower–Khrushchev fiasco in Paris and now seemed prophetic for its warning about summit conferences. Other than that he had served in the State Department under Acheson and had recently headed the Stevenson-for-President Committee in Scarsdale, New York.

The almost constant sense of movement toward forming a new administration stimulated confidence in Kennedy's assumption of power. Even Bobby's appointment gave off few sparks. While Americans once again demonstrated how optimistically they greet new presidents, conservatives remained wary, harboring nightmares about socialists, civil rights agitators, and bureaucrats eager to give money to the wrong people. Since the election, for example, Richard Russell kept in contact not only with Kennedy himself but with Johnson. Information he obtained gave him enough confidence to assure a friend that, while he was "not enamored of Kennedy," he could not see any reason to prefer Nixon to Kennedy. "On matters of vital concern to us," Russell added, "their thinking is almost identical."[39]

From the Left, financier James Warburg, who had helped bankroll the Institute for Policy Studies, privately admitted that he did not know where Kennedy stood, but was pleased that "we shall have a man in the White House who has intelligence, courage and energy, instead of a man who to my mind would have been little more than a weather-vane."[40] Ken Galbraith, the only academic who had established a social relationship with the Kennedys, was given encouraging words. Sheer activity is often its own virtue; and after the Eisenhower era it was more attractive than ever. If the Russells were placated, the Warburgs hopeful, and the Galbraiths seduced, who can fault their human dreams? Or give Kennedy low grades for keeping them happy?

Kennedy enjoyed Palm Beach that fall. He got there from Hyannis after a big crowd gave him an enthusiastic send-off at the Barnstable County Airport. For the first time six of the *Caroline*'s eighteen seats were occupied by Secret Service men. With his pilot, Howard Baird, at the controls, the plane first stopped at Washington, where Kennedy's daughter and Jackie were to remain until after the expected birth. When the plane reached Palm Beach's International Airport shortly after 10:00 P.M. that Friday night, several thousand well-wishers were on hand to greet the President-elect.

Conservative influences were plentiful in Florida. Taken by his father to a reception honoring former president Hoover, Kennedy found that one thing led to another. At Joe Kennedy's request Hoover telephoned Richard Nixon to set up a conciliatory meeting.[41] So Kennedy boarded a helicopter for Key Biscayne that Monday morning, and they met in a resort hotel situated on a palm tree–covered island about ten miles southeast of Miami. Their conversation was friendly and animated, a replay of election strategies. Afterward there was speculation that Republican participation and advice would be welcomed, although Nixon himself would not be offered any role. When the press asked Kennedy what they had talked about, he smiled and said, "I asked him how he took Ohio, but he did not tell me. He must be keeping it secret for 1964."[42]

A more significant Florida meeting was with Allen Dulles. That was the session that supposedly gave the President-elect his first information about the anti-Castro plan. Whatever he heard from the CIA director on November 18 merely supplemented the daily intelligence reports already being received through the Eisenhower administration's cooperation with Clark Clifford. Altogether, Kennedy had by that date a fairly comprehensive view of how the plans had matured from infiltration and guerrilla war to an outright invasion. Kennedy himself was not yet clear about whether he was about to take over a plan so advanced that it could not be revised.

Other problems were more immediate. Some of them were gone over with a group of aides at his father's Palm Beach place on the Monday before Thanksgiving. With Jackie back in Georgetown, where he planned to join her for the holiday—and the expected birth of their second child still weeks away—Kennedy devoted himself to some of the more prosaic matters confronting his preparation for power, detailing how the new administration would operate the Executive Office.

That afternoon Clifford set the tone by boldly announcing to reporters that the new, more activist presidency would not insulate itself behind a barricade of subordinates. The military-style staff system favored by Eisenhower would be abandoned. There would be no designated assistant to the President, the title originally held by Sherman Adams and passed on to Wilton B. (Jerry) Persons after revelations of corruption forced the change in 1958. The nearest individual to that kind of responsibility would be Sorensen, whatever his title—and that matter would be left to the President. Elsewhere, there would be a sharp reduction in the size of the White House staff. Policymaking, it was explained, would be accomplished directly between the President and his top officials.[43]

Nothing extraordinary marked the Kennedy Thanksgiving dinner in Georgetown. Outside the brick town house the curious kept watching for signs of prominent faces while newsmen did their duty and waited for something to happen. But there was little to see. The Kennedys remained indoors, their holiday meal intimate.

With them was Bill Walton. Jackie enjoyed his warm, bright, sophisticated conversations that were considerably more fascinating than the purely political talk she heard from most of Jack's friends. She and Walton had traveled in the same circles in the old days, along with some of the others who had tagged along with Kathleen and Jack Kennedy. They could talk about art and books and enjoy the best that Washington then had to offer.

Walton and the Kennedys broke up early that evening. Jack, still preoccupied with filling State, Defense, and Treasury, had to return to Palm Beach. His Corvair left Washington shortly after eight. Three hours later, while Walton was in bed at his Georgetown home, a *New York Herald Tribune* reporter called with word that Jackie was in labor at Georgetown University Hospital. There had been no sign of anything about to happen when Kennedy left Washington, but at about ten o'clock she had to call Dr. John A. Walsh. Jackie had suffered two miscarriages before Caroline was born, and now nobody was taking any chances. The ambulance driver found her in the upstairs bedroom lying in a nightgown and overshirt. "She was smiling and looked like a baby doll," he told reporters.[44] She was carried down on a stretcher and taken to the nearby hospital. Walton, meanwhile, called the Palm Beach airport and told the ticket seller who answered the phone to notify him as soon as the Kennedy plane arrived. Forty-five minutes before midnight the Corvair was some thirteen thousand feet over the east coast of Florida and heading south toward Palm Beach. On his radio pilot Howard Baird heard that Jackie had been rushed to the hospital, and he immediately made the announcement on the plane's loudspeaker. A burst of applause erupted within the twin-engine plane. Kennedy himself then appeared at the door of his compartment, smiling and waving in appreciation of the congratulations.

Jacqueline gave birth, by cesarean section, at 12:22 A.M., to a six-pound two-ounce boy. When that moment came, Jack was on the ground at the Palm Beach airport ready to board a faster, four-engine plane back to Washington. A half hour later he was back in the air and able to follow the progress of both John Fitzgerald Kennedy, Jr., and his wife by radio from a newspaper reporter in the airport's control tower. At 4:18 A.M. he entered the hospital, took a quick glimpse of the baby through the nursery window, and headed for room 3020, where he found his wife awake and fine. He then learned that it had not been all that simple. The emergency operation for the premature birth was a critical procedure, and, as Jacqueline's biographer has written, "For long hours the baby's life hung in the balance but, in the end, he survived," after spending his first five days in an incubator.[45] In Georgetown, Kennedy made repeated hospital visits, seven within the first forty-eight hours, and kept a close rein on Caroline. At the Holy Trinity Church that Sunday she was dressed for her birthday in a pink hat and a blue dress with white knit leggings. The child then showed her boredom by wandering through the pews, while Kennedy remained seated and showed no annoyance. "Caroline demonstrated that no matter who her father might be," reported the papers the following day, "she was a normal three-year-old."[46] When Jack returned to Holy Trinity the next Sunday, the child was not with him.

The major news during those December days centered on the succession of announcements from Georgetown about the latest appointments. Many designees stood on the front steps of the Kennedy home, hatless and coatless like the President-elect, as television cameras made them familiar images on home screens. Someone observed that the 3300 block of N Street was enjoying its most impressive spectacle since 1824, when an earlier resident, Major John Cox, entertained the Marquis de Lafayette.[47] The entire transition, especially in this the most public of all its phases, was perfectly orchestrated to inspire a romantic sense of drama and high expectations.

The very imagery of a "New Frontier" acquired its aura from the shortcomings of the Eisenhower administration. The first Kennedyite contacts with the Republican White House confirmed that the old crew was not only hopelessly conservative and myopic about the world but more concerned with procedures than with substance. Culturally Eisenhower himself was closer to the world of Lyndon Johnson than to a New England Irish Catholic milieu, glossed by a Harvard patina. His contempt was not only toward Jack but extended to all the Kennedys. Privately he talked about the oldest brother as "Little Boy Blue," and dismissed Bobby as "that little shit." Teddy was simply the "Bonus Baby." The President thought that Kennedy had been quite mediocre in the Senate and regarded him as someone who would have been nothing without his father's money. Johnson and Rayburn were even reported to have advised the Republican President that Kennedy must not be permitted to reach the White House because he was "a dangerous man," and Eisenhower never did forget how they persisted in calling Kennedy "dangerous." That was especially recalled when he watched the Democratic convention. "The next thing I knew," he said, "I turned on television and there was that son of a bitch becoming a vice-presidential candidate with this 'dangerous man.' Haven't talked to him since."[48]

Eisenhower felt that an illegitimacy existed about the whole Kennedy enterprise. He damned whatever forces had made it possible. The transfer of power, then, as when Eisenhower took over from Truman, took place between two of the least compatible men. That the oldest President was about to make way for the youngest, twenty-seven years younger, did nothing to help matters. During Kennedy's own turn in office he took care to cultivate Eisenhower's patriotic obligations and, wherever possible, publicize the former president's support. The two consulted often by telephone. If Ike himself went astray, thereby threatening to legitimatize Republican attacks on Kennedy politics, the administration could work to keep "Ike restrained and moderate," as Harris Wofford reminded the President, by cultivating Milton Eisenhower.[49] However much Kennedy managed to squeeze bipartisan support from the aging General, he had no illusions about the older man's attitude. "He probably glories in my failures," Kennedy told a *Washington Post* correspondent during the dark days of the 1961 Berlin crisis.[50]

Before Kennedy's swearing in, the two men had met only twice. The first session came on December 6. Before the scheduled 9:00 A.M. meeting at the White House, Kennedy read the accumulated paper work: from John Sharon and George Ball, who had been advised by Clark Clifford about what Eisenhower would want to talk about, he received eight reports on policy fields. On the evening of the visit Kennedy conferred with Paul Nitze on disarmament. He also read a Rand Corporation paper on "Political Implications of Posture Choices," which was very direct in warning that the perception of possessing powerful military capacity would, for both the consumption of the Soviet Union and American voters, be the most likely stance for great political gains.

Arms limitation, it advised, was also vital. The public would hesitate to support a military buildup unless there was confidence that "their governments are actively and aggressively seeking to arrive at arms control agreements." The paper viewed nuclear blackmail as the most serious Soviet threat, and warned that it could best be neutralized by military strength and not merely by the capacity for retaliation. What Kennedy and his advisers took to heart, and underlined as they read, was the following sentence:

Political history does not support that it is more dangerous to be strong than to be weak, more dangerous to threaten than to betray fear, more dangerous to be as "provocative" as an Adenauer or a De Gaulle than to be as conciliatory as a Macmillan.[51]

Here was an area where Kennedy and Eisenhower did not differ. The assumptions were similar. Only the style contrasted.

So eager was Kennedy to be punctual for his White House meeting that he drove away from his Georgetown home with far too much time to spare, and the Lincoln took a circuitous route to avoid arriving too early. But at one minute to nine, when the car reached the northwest gate, a smiling President, wearing a brown felt hat and brown suit (not, some White House aides had long since learned, a good omen about what mood Ike would display that day), stood at the north portico. Kennedy stepped from the Lincoln with something uncharacteristic, a concession to the dignity of the occasion, a hat—although, true to his character, he held it in his hand. He smiled, saluted, and said, "Good morning, Mr. President." A small flurry of excitement arose among knowledgeable insiders when Eisenhower paid his own respects by calling Kennedy "Senator."[52]

They conferred far longer than anybody had anticipated. Mostly Kennedy listened as Eisenhower went on and on about the workings of the National Security Council and the intricacies of the White House bureaucracy. He heard the President on other favorite topics: the importance of NATO to America's system of alliances; the balance-of-payments problem, he pointed out, made it essential to prod the European partners to help stem the gold drain. Together they talked about Berlin, the Far East, and Cuba. "He had previously been briefed by Allen Dulles a number of times," Eisenhower noted in a memo, "and had some familiarity with the details of these three subjects."[53]

Eisenhower's response was far more positive than Kennedy's. Nothing about the session dispelled Kennedy's view of Eisenhower as a "non-president" who had only limited awareness of his powers. He was fully as ponderous and shallow as Kennedy had anticipated.[54] Robert Kennedy later told Arthur Schlesinger, Jr., that while his brother found that Eisenhower had not done his homework and was thin about areas that he should have known, the strength of his personality enabled him to understand why he had become President of the United States.[55] Eisenhower, however, had Jerry Persons call Clifford to say that he had been misinformed about Kennedy. The youthful successor was an impressive man.[56] The President also recorded the observation that Kennedy's attitude was "that of a serious, earnest seeker for information and the implication was that he will give full consideration to the facts and suggestions we presented."[57] "Little Boy Blue" was not so bad after all.

During the second week in December Jacqueline accompanied her husband to the family's winter home in Palm Beach, for continued recuperation. "Jack read Robert Walpole in one night," she wrote to Ken Galbraith; "it has taken me two weeks to finish [Archibald] MacLeish and

[John] Betjeman—isn't that awful," and then she added, "I can't tell you the peace they have brought me, reading them at night, in these days when I have to fuss with things like mail and evening dresses all day."⁵⁸

Kennedy, meanwhile, presided over more conferences, meeting with political figures who were far removed from the world of Jackie's interests. One session involved the party's congressional hierarchy, which should have included House Majority Leader John McCormack. But although Lyndon Johnson, Sam Rayburn, and Mike Mansfield made it to Palm Beach, Kennedy's old rival for the control of Massachusetts Democrats was notably absent. Explaining that his failure to attend had absolutely no significance, McCormack said he had had a previous commitment to preside at the opening of a new bank in Waltham. "Congressional leaders often meet with the President or President-elect, but a new bank doesn't open every day," McCormack pointed out.⁵⁹

Kennedy–McCormack interests were colliding once again. McCormack had wanted his nephew appointed to the Senate seat Kennedy was about to vacate, and Edward McCormack, Jr., the state's attorney general, was eager. He said he would run for the seat in 1962 regardless of who became the interim candidate. The Kennedys, eager for a seat-warmer willing to yield to Teddy—or Bobby, as they told the press— would no more go along than give the McCormacks a prized family heirloom. At the moment John McCormack should have been meeting with the President-elect at Palm Beach, word came that several weeks of negotiations between Governor Foster Furcolo and Ken O'Donnell would result in the naming of Ben Smith II of Gloucester, Joe Kennedy, Jr.'s, old Harvard football teammate.⁶⁰

The Palm Beach session left Lyndon Johnson with two functions delegated by Kennedy. As vice-president, he would have two chairmanships. One involved the Committee on Contract Compliance to supervise the enforcement of nondiscriminatory provisions under which private industry was obligated to perform work paid for by the federal budget. The other was the Space Council, an area of deep interest to Johnson and his state of Texas. Left unresolved, however, was how to handle the House Rules Committee situation. Under the chairmanship of Howard W. Smith of Virginia, whose hold over the committee was as authoritarian as it was conservative, that body was an obvious obstacle that faced the expansive economic or social programs Kennedy and the Democrats had urged during the campaign. Already there was talk of a move within the new Congress to weaken Smith's grip by expanding the committee itself, much as Roosevelt had wanted to do with the Supreme Court, but

Rayburn came away from the Florida meeting unwilling to specify a preferred tactic. He only said that he believed that Kennedy's program would get through the new Congress.[61] Finally, with the holiday season over, Kennedy returned to the Carlyle Hotel in New York. In January the hotel became the major preinaugural headquarters.

From that New York base, Kennedy sought to contend with the loose ends. He appointed Walter W. Heller to head the three-member Council of Economic Advisers (CEA). Heller, a tall, slender economist from the University of Minnesota, had been introduced to Kennedy during the campaign by Hubert Humphrey. "You'll find that I'm a good deal more interested in economics than my predecessor," Kennedy told him when he called him to Georgetown in December, "and maybe a little bit better informed on it!" Heller, a Keynesian with faith in government's ability to stimulate demand and guide economic ebbs and flows, was told by Kennedy that he was needed as a counterweight to Secretary of the Treasury–designate Douglas Dillon. "He will have conservative leanings," said Kennedy, "and I know that you are a liberal."[62] On the day his chairmanship was announced, Heller told Kennedy, according to a 1980 reconstruction of their conversation, that "I'm going to be in there pitching for a tax cut to handle the recession, as an anti-recession measure." Kennedy, almost as fearful as his predecessor about saying the economy was in a recession, replied, "Do you think for a minute that I, coming in on a platform of sacrifice, can, as the very first thing, hand the voters a tax cut?"[63]

With Heller's guidance, the council was completed with the addition of James Tobin of Yale and Kermit Gordon of Williams College, both brilliant young economists; both were as Keynesian as most of their colleagues, who had come to believe that balanced budgets were neither moral goals nor necessarily the essence of economic wisdom. Together with Dillon, and with the addition of the newly appointed director of the budget, David E. Bell, a Harvard economist and former Truman aide, the council rounded out Kennedy's fiscal team.

Two of them, Heller and Tobin, served on Paul Samuelson's task force and had already learned that as much as Kennedy's campaign had stressed Eisenhower inaction and the need to "get the country moving again," neither he nor his staff had given much thought to exactly what that goal would require. Tobin found a lack of understanding and sympathy from Kennedy with the idea of fiscal stimuli to get out of the recession. Sorensen warned them that getting the reputation of being a reckless spender was the very last thing Kennedy wanted. He did want to balance the budget, and would not ask for a deficit. "They just hoped they could get away with an anti-recession program which did not involve deficits," said one of Samuelson's colleagues. An additional restraint was the budget that Eisenhower had already proposed for the coming fiscal year.[64]

Nevertheless, at a New Year's Day press conference before he returned to the Carlyle, Kennedy pledged to take prompt action to relieve and rehabilitate economically distressed areas. That cause had already been taken up during the West Virginia primary, where, as Brooks Hays recalled, "The confrontation of stark poverty in the midst of an area that had scenic beauty and vast human resources . . . stirred his imagination."[65] During the campaign Kennedy had returned to that theme over and over again, making it an integral part of his New Frontier approach to domestic needs. "We all tended to oversell it as a cure for everything," remembered William L. Batt, Jr., who later headed Kennedy's Area Redevelopment Administration.[66] The problems of depressed areas had been studied during the transition by a twenty-three-member task force headed by Paul H. Douglas, who had twice sponsored bills in the Senate during the 1950's to bring relief to such regions, only to have both vetoed by President Eisenhower. With the new administration assistance for such human needs would be an intrinsic part of the approach to the entire economy. Within sixty days after taking office, Kennedy told his news conference, he would propose a program to combat unemployment.[67]

During the coming months economic policy would be molded to suit a variety of circumstances. Statements spelled out in January, however thoughtful and prudent, could only serve as general objectives. But the economic situation, as urgent as it was during a recessionary period, and in view of Kennedy's campaign commitments, was a relatively academic matter compared with the percolating racial developments. In later years Kennedy would be criticized for omitting civil rights from the array of significant areas covered by task force studies.[68]

A preinaugural foreshadowing of future civil rights problems came then not from any task force study or specific plan of action but from the nomination of a fifty-three-year-old black economist, Robert C. Weaver, as administrator of the Housing and Home Finance Agency. Kennedy felt committed to offer a significant post to a black appointee, and made his first attempt by tapping Congressman William Dawson of Chicago. Dawson had the qualification of being black but not militant on civil rights. When Dawson declined, Weaver was brought in. "My name came up through people who knew me both in civil rights and in housing," Weaver recalls. Although he was also chairman of the board of directors of the NAACP and was a lot more involved in the area of racial equality than Dawson, he has been described as a "moderate," an appraisal that he doubts the President-elect would have shared "because my position was a little more than moderate from his point of view."[69]

When Weaver met Kennedy at Palm Beach, he attached two conditions to his acceptance. About the first Kennedy was forthright, assuring him that he fully intended to issue the housing order. Kennedy hedged somewhat about the second, whether Weaver would later be elevated to head the department upon the possible creation of a Cabinet-level Department of Urban Affairs. His agreement that Weaver would be a "logical contender" was about all that could be expected at that point, and the New Yorker accepted.[70]

That provoked Kennedy's first serious snag. Mississippi's James Eastland, one of the Senate's most outspoken unreconstructed members, charged that Weaver had a "pro-Communist background" because of connections with "front" groups during the 1930's. The chairman of the Senate Banking and Currency Committee, A. Willis Robertson of Virginia, said he would work to block the nomination within his panel because Kennedy had failed to give him advance notification, and Alabama's John Sparkman, who led the group's housing subcommittee, chimed in with a *pro forma* complaint that Weaver had helped keep Fulbright from becoming secretary of state. Vested interests behind the southern senators included builders fearful of a discrimination ban.[71] Not until February did Kennedy get Weaver confirmed, and then only after the President granted Robertson's request for written assurances about the nominee's loyalty.[72]

On January 9, after a triumphant speech at Boston, Kennedy visited the Cambridge home of Arthur Schlesinger, Jr. Schlesinger was not easy to place. The Pulitzer prize–winning historian was already somewhat of a controversial figure. During most of the fifties he had been close to Stevenson. As an Americans for Democratic Action stalwart he had a reputation for strong New Deal liberalism. Like his good friend and colleague, Galbraith, Schlesinger was more interested in the use of power to attain social and economic objectives. He would be predictably outspoken about ideas that could raise hell among certain elements on Capitol Hill and within the Democratic Party. Kennedy enjoyed Schlesinger, admired his intelligence and accomplishments, and respected his idealism, just as he did the strong views of a Galbraith or a Rostow; but too often such academics tended to toss around ideas that slighted the political considerations of the real world. Still, Kennedy felt he owed

Schlesinger some role within the administration. He wanted him nearby. He resolved the matter by designating him as special assistant to the President. The title, as many of his appointees were to learn, was largely inconsequential and mostly useful to shelter talent. By the time Kennedy left Cambridge that Monday, he had also enrolled Abram Chayes, an aide to Chester Bowles, as legal adviser to the State Department, and invited Jerome B. Wiesner, the MIT professor who had advised the campaign on scientific matters, to take the White House advisory position that Dr. James Killian held under Eisenhower.[73]

The *Caroline* returned Jack to New York that evening. He dined at the 21 Club, and went to see *Do Re Mi*, a musical at the St. James Theater, where the opening curtain had to be delayed for five minutes following an ovation from the audience. The Secret Service escorted the next president up the aisle and out of the theater before the final curtain, and he was driven back to the Carlyle.[74]

Shortly after noon on the tenth of January, Kennedy shut down his preinaugural headquarters and headed south. He flew to Washington in the company of George Kennan, who gave him an analysis of Khrushchev's position and, in particular, the overtures made to Kennedy by Mikhail Menshikov. After listening to Kennan, Kennedy said that he was giving thought to the problem of his staff with relation to foreign policy. He was coming around to the idea of having a small group within the White House that would be responsible directly to him without representing other departments. He told Kennan that he did not want to be put in a position where he had only one or two people to whom he could turn for certain types of advice. Dean Rusk, for example, had already approached him about possible American intervention in Laos, and Kennedy considered that too narrow a base for the making of decisions of such importance. He did not want to lean as heavily for foreign policy advice on a single man, as Truman had with Dean Acheson.[75] In Washington, after Kennedy parted from Kennan, he went with Lyndon Johnson and the chairman of the Senate Public Works Appropriations subcommittee, Robert Kerr of Oklahoma, to see Eisenhower's secretary of the treasury, Robert B. Anderson. Anderson had recently been to Bonn because of his concern over the West German contribution to the balance-of-payments problem. From Anderson's office Kennedy went into a conference with Douglas Dillon, his own designee to head Treasury. Not until 12:43 A.M. that night, after a four-hour flight from Washington, did the President-elect reach Palm Beach.[76]

Such physical endurance had long since become routine, most effectively minimizing whatever suspicions remained about his having Addison's. An article in a magazine published by the American Medical Association, *Today's Health,* reported that he was in "superb physical condition," fully ready and "capable of shouldering the burdens of the presidency." Prepared from information supplied by people around Kennedy, especially Bobby, the pre–Inauguration Day item reviewed his early illnesses and minimized the problems of Addison's. That term, it explained, was a loose one that "has come to include all grades of adrenal insufficiency." Going beyond the admissions made in July, it acknowledged that he was taking medication "by mouth" to guard against any consequence of the problem, but said he needed no special diet and kept his weight at about 165. His personal habits involved only mild use of tobacco and alcohol, which largely consisted of some cold beer with dinner and an occasional daiquiri.[77]

One could hardly miss the point: This was no hard-drinking, improvident Irishman. This child of Rose and Joseph Kennedy was like all children of that "lace-curtain" family: sober, responsible, and dedicated to both family and society. Spiritually they were with the Roman Catholic Church. But as Americans worthy of the nation's highest trust, their behavior was as pure as the Founding Fathers'. Jack Kennedy's wholesomeness was made amply clear. Colleagues familiar with the playboy personality thus observed some tailoring for public consumption.

He was healthy, clean-cut, pleasant, and moderate; he knew when to work and when to play. The papers showed him relaxing during those last prepresidential days at Palm Beach. That final weekend Lyndon Johnson was his houseguest. On Saturday and Sunday the two men golfed and swam. When Kennedy returned to Washington, Jackie's domestic requirements during that hectic period forced him to do much of his work in Bill Walton's house. That was his temporary quarters on the day he had his final preinaugural meeting with President Eisenhower at the White House.

The conference, on Thursday, January 19, was, according to Clark Clifford (who kept the only known set of notes), "one of the best meetings that will ever be held, where each president had his three top Cabinet men and the discussion was completely candid and open and forthright."[78] Clifford had worked with Jerry Persons, his counterpart on Eisenhower's staff, to prepare the agenda.

The morning began with Eisenhower demonstrating to Kennedy, with some relish, how pressing a button could bring a helicopter and provide instant escape from the White House. He actually fingered the device, and Kennedy looked through the window of the Oval Office and saw a whirlybird setting down on the back lawn. Eisenhower then took him into the Cabinet Room. There, in the presence of their staffs, he assured Kennedy that presidential authority would not always be a magic wand.

His preoccupation was almost entirely on Laos. Vietnam was mentioned only peripherally. It was in Laos, Eisenhower told Kennedy, where communism would threaten all of Southeast Asia. Hostile forces securing the strategic Plain of Jars and controlling the main north–south road along the Mekong Valley would pose an immediate threat to Thailand, Cambodia, and South Vietnam. He would even be willing, *"as a last desperate hope, to intervene unilaterally."* He firmly ruled out any political solution, because that would involve a coalition government with Communist participation. Within recent days, moreover, the position of Prince Boun Oum's Royal Laotian government was becoming more desperate. An antigovernment coalition had staged a counteroffensive that threatened the regime. Key objectives in the vital Plain of Jars were being retaken.[79]

Even before the session with Eisenhower, Allen Dulles had warned Kennedy about the deterioration in Laos. "Whatever's going to happen in Laos," Kennedy then said to Sorensen, "an American invasion, a Communist victory or whatever, I wish it would happen before we take over and get blamed for it."[80] Eisenhower, of course, was challenging his successor, in effect daring Kennedy to prove himself capable of handling the situation. He himself was about to leave the White House unscathed by further developments in Southeast Asia and Cuba. Kennedy would have to take over the task of keeping the world from becoming half "slave." The first Democratic President since the "soft-on-communism" preoccupation left the meeting puzzled. How could Eisenhower be so casual in the face of such potential disaster?[81]

That very day James Reston wrote that the problems facing the new administration were bound to be much more difficult than the nation had believed. The solutions, he thought, would inevitably be a lot more radical than anything in American politics since the first administration of Franklin D. Roosevelt.[82]

With the coming of a new administration, something akin to religious fervor distracts most Americans, an extension of the endless quest for a future that has something more to offer. With Kennedy this spirit was compounded, exaggerated, made more irrational. Few asked why, if Eisenhower remained so popular and could doubtless have been re-elected, did the change bring such elation? The national capital itself, which always has a holiday atmosphere for presidential inaugurations, was even more than usually jubilant.

Every attention was directed toward witnessing the most glamorous and festive of such occasions, the American version of royal pageantry. The National Park Service had simulated a touch of spring by spraying green dye on the grass around the Washington Monument. Other chemicals were used on the trees along the parade route to discourage roosting starlings. But weather forecasts reflected the season rather than the illusion, and snow began to fall by Thursday evening. Within the next few hours nearly eight inches buried the make-believe spring. Cars were abandoned in the drifts. Streets were blocked. Crews of men went to work, shoveling, plowing, salting. The city had to be reopened for the next day.

That night it was still bogged down. At Constitution Hall, where Frank Sinatra had prepared an inaugural gala, they were two hours late in getting started. When the program finally began, it did so with a noteworthy event—to many, another hint that there *was* a new spirit in the land. Marian Anderson, the black contralto who had been prevented from singing in that hall by the Daughters of the American Revolution back in 1939, rendered the National Anthem. The show finally ended at 2:00 A.M., after Kennedy rose to praise Sinatra's efforts. The Democrats, he added, would still have a deficit in 1965, so Sinatra would be needed again.[83]

As the Kennedy limousine left Constitution Hall and drove down the mall in the falling snow, the President-elect asked the driver to turn on the lights so the crowd could admire his beautiful wife. Kennedy then glanced at a copy of Jefferson's Inaugural Address and said to her, "It was better than mine."[84] She was then dropped off at their Georgetown home, and he went on to a reception given by his father and mother at Paul Young's Restaurant on Connecticut Avenue. He did not get home until 3:48 A.M. It had been a long day.

4

"Idealism and Cynicism"

Together with Kennedy's personality, the challenge to "get America moving again" had penetrated the nation's conscience, and that meant confronting enemies wherever they existed and transforming them into allies. If there was no longer such a reality as monolithic international communism, if nationalistic versions had gone beyond Kremlin control, the potential danger was even greater. The split was not something America ought to "look forward to with comfort."[1] "It could bring us harm," Kennedy told an off-the-record briefing of journalists at the State Department, "if Khrushchev has to prove his revolutionary intensity." For too long American policy had reacted, not initiated. Like prewar England the "free world" was too lethargic. An active America, demonstrating the blessings of liberty, could sell values that fostered confidence and respect. There was enough potential for the excitement and satisfaction of natural desires without Communist authoritarianism. All this Kennedy believed, but he also knew it was easy to rhapsodize.

He had gone from plateau to plateau. He had overcome the hurdles and was not about to stop. He was a hard man to know. His exterior revealed very little of what churned inside. One European visitor, an especially perceptive student of character and minds who had the opportunity to engage him in long talks, perceived an inner struggle that was constantly working to retain self-control. Drift and boredom were perhaps the greatest, unaffordable indulgences. He knew exactly what he wanted. From his parents he had unceasingly absorbed the inevitability of success.

Still, he never got very far from the realization that disaster was waiting, that all his margins of survival—from the *Amigari* that sliced open *PT 109* to the victory over Nixon—had been exceedingly narrow. More than any other President since Abe Lincoln, thought Walt Rostow, Kennedy combined that sense of tragedy and the possibility of tragedy, "but the idealism in his stance was another counterpoint in him." He was, after all, the man who was going to bring sense to the chaos.[2] Queries directed to the White House about Kennedy's favorite quotations received the standard response that the one he liked best of all came from Edmund Burke, the great English Whig: "The only thing necessary for the triumph of evil is for good men to do nothing."[3] "The White House intrigued him," remembered Kennedy's journalist friend, Charles Bartlett. "He was just burning with the things he could do. He really was challenged by the opportunity to do something for the country."[4]

After the Eisenhower fifties Americans were ready to "honeymoon" with the Kennedys. The First Family becomes the republic's Royal Family. In a world of electronic images constantly communicating lifestyles and values, the White House sets the pace. Kennedy was the first telegenic President of a people who knew that "seeing is believing." So, for all the reverence for Ike and Mamie, there was a seamless transition to the semi-aristocratic chic of Jack and Jackie. When presidential Press Secretary Pierre Salinger and Mrs. Kennedy's personal secretary, Pamela Turnure, announced that the new First Lady was having the White House sponsor a program for the creative arts, the change seemed authentic. Eleanor, Bess, Mamie—they belonged to the past.

In a very few words Fred Dutton spelled out what ultimately became the most characteristic mark of the Kennedy presidency, the one element that defied all the *Congressional Quarterly* boxscores of legislation proposed and accepted. At Bobby's urging Dutton, a thirty-seven-year-old Californian, had joined Kennedy's staff after two years as executive secretary to Governor Pat Brown. "The nature of the overriding task for this Office," he wrote in a memorandum, "remains not so much just more legislation, nor more executive orders, but to evoke more of a willingness by people to give of themselves to accomplish all the hard things which need to be done."[5]

The innovative Hundred Days of Roosevelt, a time when the entire nation had to be rescued from despair, had created new criteria for judging early success. With Eisenhower there were different ground rules. He came into office surrounded by every kind of contention *except* economic, and so becoming the great conciliator earned him a place in history. These two men, the one offering new departures to save the system and the other pacifiers, were the most successful of recent Presidents.

For Kennedy the Inaugural Address had done its job. He needed only to build on that tone.

A solemn journey, a mission of revitalization and reform, had begun. The glow lent the "honeymoon" an almost magical aura; if not the dynamic, somber rolling up of sleeves and restructuring of Roosevelt's time, there at least was another kind of appeal: the spark of confidence. America really seemed to be "moving again." Both within and outside the White House there was a new kind of bravado or even audacity. While news and analysis columns did not hesitate to delineate just how cautious the new administration really was, the *Times* nevertheless declared, after he had been in office sixty days, that the "Kennedy personality has turned the White House into a beehive of action and ideas."[6] "Our faith in him and in what he was trying to do was absolute," Pierre Salinger later wrote, "and he could impart to our work together a sense of challenge and adventure—a feeling that he was moving, and the world with him, toward a better time."[7]

There were areas where Kennedy could get immediate and substantive results. He had only to place his name on a document to boost the quantity and quality of food for the needy. His first executive order directed Orville Freeman to use funds already available to expand food distribution to the needy, thereby fulfilling a pledge made during the West Virginia primary.[8] On Inauguration Day he had noted few black faces among the Coast Guard contingent that marched along Pennsylvania Avenue, so one of his first acts was to pick up the telephone and personally ask the Coast Guard commander whether that reflected an exclusionary policy. Assured that none existed, he replied, "Well, I didn't see any yesterday in the parade."[9] Before the week was out, he sent a memo to Chester Bowles directing the undersecretary to investigate the small number of minorities in the Foreign Service and throughout the State Department.[10] He also dispatched Arthur Goldberg to New York to settle a costly tugboat strike that had stymied much of the nation's commerce, and within fourteen hours of his arrival the secretary of labor was able to announce a settlement.[11] But the most dramatic breakthrough came on the last day of January, and that seemed to demonstrate that the Kennedyites were as good as their word. On Capitol Hill, after a fight led by Sam Rayburn, with close monitoring by Kennedy since he and the speaker had discussed the strategy at Palm Beach, the administration won its vote to enlarge the Rules Committee. Their margin was only five votes, as slim as most Kennedy crucial battles seemed to be, but it meant that the addition of two Democrats and one Republican might weaken the grip of Chairman Howard W. Smith and expedite the flow of vital legislation. With the administration only eleven days old, whether this would have any substantial future effect was secondary to the symbolic impact.[12]

One gain seemed certain. Doubts about Kennedy's youth and inexperience had been neutralized. Headiness had bolstered his staff and assured the nation, and the staging of his first press conference on January 25 further stimulated the popular acceptance. From the Indian Treaty Room of the Old State Department Building where Eisenhower's conferences had been held, the quasi-theatrical event was moved to the amphitheater of the New State Department Building. On hand were all the paraphernalia of modern electronics. Kennedy, in a pin-striped suit and white shirt, strode to the lectern at 6:00 P.M., dinner hour on the East Coast. He stood apart from the more than four hundred people in the auditorium, separated by a spacious hollow, beyond which his live audience sat in elevated tiers ready to record and interrogate. The scene, wrote Russell Baker, was about as warm as "an execution chamber"; but with that performance Kennedy brought presidential press conferences into the realm of effective public relations.[13] He sold himself even more than his views.

His spontaneous and televised news conferences became an integral part of a public relations "blitz," and he held ten during those first three months. From the start he became an instant champion of the art. He stood there, confident, cameras focused on his tanned face, triumphant and in command. His opening statement told of early decisions—to delay the Geneva atomic test ban negotiations until the American position could be more adequately prepared; to substantially increase food assistance for civil war–torn Congo. Then, with no real change in demeanor, came his coup: The Soviet government had ordered the release of both survivors from an RB-47, which had been shot down over the USSR while on an "electro-magnetic survey." This removed "a serious obstacle to improvement of Soviet-American relations." Offering no additional interpretation, he merely said the matter had been under discussion with Llewellyn Thompson, the American ambassador in Moscow, and that the men were en route home. He neither thanked Khrushchev nor offered any apologies for possible intrusion into Soviet air space, which the

Eisenhower administration had denied, but volunteered that, like his predecessor, he had banned additional flights. Offering no hint of new departures, he left an impression of prudent continuity.

Nor did he extend an olive branch. Less than three weeks before Kennedy came to power the Eisenhower administration increased the Havana–Washington tensions by breaking diplomatic relations. Acting in the immediate afterglow of the inauguration, Castro warned that Cubans were ready to meet the "threat of imminent aggression," a matter that had become plain to all with open eyes in the entire region from Miami to Guatemala, and challenged the new American President to "make the first move" in restoring friendly relations.[14] That, replied Kennedy, was "a matter that should be negotiated," and then proceeded to declare that the Cubans were repugnant to American interests because they were less concerned about the welfare of their own people than in "imposing an ideology which is alien to this hemisphere." Castro was not a legitimate force but an intruder who threatened the "security" and "peace" of the Americas.[15]

There was no softening when Kennedy faced his first joint session of Congress on January 30 and spoke on the State of the Union. The language was portentous, the style of a man with a mission—Lincoln at Gettysburg, Churchill during the Battle of Britain. "It is one of the ironies of our time," he declared, "that the techniques of a harsh and repressive system should be able to instill discipline and ardor in its servants—while the blessings of liberty have too often stood for privilege, materialism and a life of ease."[16]

Self-consciously, then, he girded himself for the test and loaded his message with the cataclysmic tones of a man about to preside either over a new creation or Armageddon:

> *I speak today in an hour of national peril and national opportunity. . . . We shall have to test anew whether a nation organized and governed such as ours can endure. . . . our national household is cluttered with unfinished and neglected tasks. . . . Each day we draw nearer the hour of maximum danger, as weapons spread and hostile forces grow stronger. . . . the tide of events has been running out and time has not been our friend. . . . We cannot escape our dangers—neither must we let them drive us into panic or narrow isolation. . . . There will be further setbacks before the tide is turned. But turn it must. The hopes of mankind rest upon us.*[17]

Walt Rostow likes to recall that they belonged to an extended family, each with his own official title but each prepared to pitch in with whatever had to be done. Assignments sometimes landed on the fellow who happened to be in the Oval Office at the particular moment of need. "The informality was amazing," recalled Dutton. "Kennedy really didn't get himself involved in what might be called housekeeping functions; he didn't care about them."[18] He had little patience for the niceties of administration, for the pipelines that structured bureaucracies. Especially at the start, he would use his own telephone to make those calls to surprised subordinates. He wanted action above all.

Delegations of authority were minimal. The Cabinet, the National Security Council, and the whole chain of command were all transformed from the carefully structured Eisenhower format to Kennedy's personal style.[19] He shunned long-winded discussions, preferring to question and get right to the point. He was the best interrogator they had ever met. He learned much by listening, but more by reading, digesting every possible document. "As soon as it got around to the town that Kennedy was reading our memos," Roger Hilsman has recalled, "everybody in town began to read our memos."[20] Aides quickly caught on that the best route to "the boss" was through the written word. Even so he was not isolated behind a wall of paper. "We were few enough so that the President had some idea of who we were and what we were doing," Carl Kaysen says when contemplating how White House staffs have grown since Kennedy's time. "There wasn't anybody there who had not some personal contact with Kennedy from time to time."[21]

"The Kennedy Administration is an odd mixture of idealism and cynicism," wrote James Reston, "of liberals and conservatives, of professors and politicians, of Harvard grafted on to the Boston Irish."[22] He had, Rostow recalls, "a marvelous gift for orchestrating people. The people he wove together represented almost geological layers in Kennedy's experiences—old friends from pre-war days, college friends, the PT boat friends, and these people all respected one another." His administrative techniques in handling was indeed the skill of a man who had grown up in a big family, and it "appeared almost an extension of that style and experience."[23] They had their jealousies, their territorial prerogatives, that occasionally marred the superficial appearance of perfect harmony, but, almost to a man, their loyalty to Jack Kennedy was the great unifier.

Afterward the veterans of the New Frontier read the retrospective views of "Camelot." Increasingly they found themselves on the defensive, criticizing detractors as writers of "pseudohistory" who failed to understand what the New Frontier was really like. They did not doubt that, in that early post-Eisenhower era, they had something to offer a world headed toward either nuclear annihilation or totalitarianism.

America was also about to decide whether the Second Reconstruction would collapse like the first, with similar consequences, or whether, in their hands, the pattern would be broken, rational solutions achieved; and unlike the backlashes against abolitionism and "black Republicanism," this time there could be racial civility. They liked the challenges (*challenge* was one of the boss's favorite words) of maneuvering in a complex and dangerous world. Literary critic Alfred Kazin, skeptical that all the intellectuality was but power wrapped in tinsel, approached them warily. But even Kazin came away convinced that they gave "the glow of those who have not merely conceived a great work but are in a position to finish it."[24]

It was only February, and Jack Kennedy had not been sworn in for very long when John Kenneth Galbraith suggested to him that "the problem of the new Administration is going to be neither liberalism nor conservatism but caution. I am a little appalled," he wrote, "at the eloquence of the explanations as to why things, neither radical nor reactionary but only wise, cannot be done."[25]

To insiders around Kennedy, Galbraith would never become a legitimate builder. He was a visionary, an idealist, equipped with a master plan for salvation. He was witty and articulate, and had contributed important books about countervailing powers protecting capitalism from capitalists and the dearth of spending for the public sector. With the First Family, Galbraith was a favorite; his social relationship with the Kennedys made fellow New Frontiersmen jealous. With Jacqueline he exchanged views about books and art. Both Kennedys found him insightful and stimulating; his letters were pithy and entertaining. "The Republic may be in decline," Galbraith wrote in his diary as the administration was getting under way, "but more likely it is only becoming less stuffy."[26] He was good to have around.

So was Walt Rostow. He bubbled. He excited Kennedy, fascinated him with a broad vision of how the world could be made safe for democratic American capitalism. Like Galbraith he did not sin by boring. But their ideas were another matter. Kennedy could enjoy Rostow's intellect, marvel at his calculations on how matters could be taken in hand, and yet consider his designs dangerous. The combination of Walt's OSS work during World War II and his faith in bombing as the end-all in Southeast Asia made him the "Air Marshal" in Jack Kennedy's mind.[27] Rostow, with his comprehensive view of the world order, a Descartes in gray flannel, was pawned off by Rusk and made Mac Bundy's deputy. Galbraith, convinced about the need to create demand through public spending and unimpressed by budget-balancers, was far too audacious for the President. It was one thing to have an aroused intellect, but quite another to misperceive the world. Galbraith became ambassador to India, where he and Nehru could enjoy each other.

Kennedy also had the support of his staff in their belief that men like Galbraith were too far ahead of the possible. It was one thing for the Executive Branch to be daring, to move ahead with executive orders and requests for legislation that would suit important segments of the constituency, but there was a real world out there. The powers on Capitol Hill must be mollified, and almost all had been elected by bigger margins than Jack. They owed him little. It all added up to little leverage, especially with key congressional seats still in the hands of older, experienced, and largely hard-nosed politicians more eager to service their sponsors and voters than presidential desires. Sam Rayburn helped him enlarge the Rules Committee, but who could say what that would really mean? The symbolic value was there all right. But Judge Smith remained at its head, and he was not about to fly the white flag. Were that the full extent of congressional obstacles, the fight might have been more equitable. But who could ignore such heavies as Richard Russell, Wilbur Mills, Harry Byrd, A. Willis Robertson, Jim Eastland, and, in some ways the most obstructive and most powerful, Robert Kerr. Disproportionately southern and conservative, they often controlled key committee chairmanships and had other means that made the young, untested President not much of a match.

Kennedy privately told Chalmers Roberts of *The Washington Post* that the idea of Americans as anything other than complacent and contented was a myth, a myth furthered by the dominance of the Democratic Party. In this century, the era when the party had become most conspicuous for reforms, only FDR had won with votes that transcended the "complacent-contented attitude." When Americans are ready to sacrifice, they will do so when they feel that the burdens are national consecrations. So if the Democrats remained strong on the Hill, it was for no better reason than the continuing margins made possible by Dixie power. And, nobody doubted (Kennedy did not need to remind Roberts) that the South had made the difference in the election, and securing its support took the craft of a Lyndon Johnson.[28]

Kennedy's appraisal was hard to dispute. He had honed a capacity for digesting the intricacies of precinct politics during his climb to the White House. Now he had the additional advantage of the staff and intelligence-gathering machinery. His voracious daily reading included virtually every newspaper of consequence, neglecting only those from the West Coast.[29] He also kept up with books to a degree uncommon among

American politicians, and digested an eclectic array of periodicals, from *The New Republic* to the *Economist* of London. Nor did significant public-opinion surveys escape his attention. So he, more than anybody else, appreciated the fact that, despite the 8.1 percent unemployment level reached in February, much of the country was relatively unaffected. Not only the congressional lineup stood in the way, but it was hard to find much of a constituency for combating unemployment on a grand scale. Asked whether they or their families had in any way been touched by the current business situation, seventy-three percent of the respondents—replying during the depth of the downturn—said they had felt nothing. When, in January and then half a year later, the Gallup poll showed how well Kennedy's policies were meshing with popular desires, they found that fully two thirds wanted them to remain in the middle or even more toward the right. A more liberal direction was preferred by just twenty-three percent in January and by only fifteen percent in July.[30]

Kennedy naturally slid into a pattern of convincing the public that dogmatic liberals had not captured the White House. And they had not. He really was not one of them. Life had made him a Democrat, but that did not mean he was the liberal some of the more hopeful thought they had corralled.[31]

If he was a skinflint with his own money, he was not much looser with public funds. He intrigued David Bell, his director of the budget, by responding to information about how many gardeners were needed to maintain the White House grounds with the comment that "the man we have handling our grounds at Hyannis Port could do this whole thing with the assistance of maybe a boy." And, just as his father would have done, he brought down his own man from the Cape.[32] Nor was there much his own advisers could say to convince him of the wisdom of attacking the recession through public-works spending or stimulative tax cuts. Five months before Ronald Reagan's election in 1980 Walter Heller recalled Kennedy's fear that "he could not break the grip of the balanced budget psychology, that it would hurt him a lot politically if he seemed to go far out. A public that had just been asked to sacrifice could not overnight be placed on the dole."[33] So the President asked Heller to "use the White House as a pulpit for public education in economics, especially on the desirable effects of a Federal deficit in a recession," but he quickly added, "always make clear that the recession started *last year.*"[34] The rationale given to Heller was an accurate reflection of Kennedy's political fear. It also illustrated how a fiscal conservative handled advisers who wanted their President to be a social democrat.

It was Kennedy, too, much more than his Keynesian colleagues, who was most receptive to Douglas Dillon's warnings about the balance-of-payments situation. As an Eisenhower holdover Dillon was familiar with how the last administration had worried over the problem. Walt Rostow also shared that concern, and he worked long hours reinforcing Kennedy's consciousness.[35] Kennedy had given it more than passing reference in a Palm Beach speech late in 1959, and Robert B. Anderson, Eisenhower's last treasury secretary, discovered that the President-elect "was one of the few people who really understood what the balance-of-payments problem was."[36]

When Douglas Dillon pressed the balance-of-payments issue at the very first Cabinet meeting, Kennedy was with him. The predicament threatened to limit the domestic promotion of economic expansion while inhibiting military operations abroad, and the President ordered a Defense Department study.[37] "He had to live constantly in fear of this two-edged blade," recalled Walt Rostow.[38] That, among other things, helped seal Kennedy's closeness to Dillon, the Republican holdover who had lacked Joe Kennedy's confidence. Few outside the little circle of New Frontiersmen realized how influential Dillon became, most others often underestimating his relative standing. After the economic advisers, "Dillon was the most important influence," Heller says.[39] Moreover, the secretary was both shrewd and able. Some thought no Cabinet member, even Bob McNamara, was more effective, and a journalist who assessed the administration's early months observed that "Dillon has marched exactly in step with Kennedy."[40] But Kennedy didn't march. He tip-toed.

In mid-February he moved to deal with the situation on the wage and price front. A twenty-one-member labor-management advisory committee was established to recommend policies that would promote "free and responsible collective bargaining, industrial peace, sound wage and price policies, higher standards of living and increased productivity."[41] Privately, when he was asked what Americans could do to comply with his request to "do for your country," he replied that they could demonstrate their patriotism by restraining wage demands.[42]

During those early weeks he outlined his domestic program as though he were setting off on another Roosevelt Hundred Days. But Dillon, who was in a particularly good position to evaluate Kennedy alongside his immediate predecessor, acknowledged that the differences between the new administration and Eisenhower's approaches were nil. Each President, through his own partisan needs, exaggerated the actual differences.[43]

Eager to gloss over the record, liberals hailed as evidence of a return to liberal government Kennedy's action in following up on his first executive order, the one that boosted food distribution for the needy, by his second. That placed the Food for Peace Program within his own Executive Office.[44] But those were the easy programs, the ones that were implemented "by the stroke of a pen."

Despite the hopes of an increasing number of supporters, he, with considerable support within his administration and the established black leadership, stayed clear of even hinting at the need for new civil rights legislation. Here was one area where the odds for success were overwhelmingly negative. Asking for new laws to strengthen the voting rights regulations already enacted, desegregating public accommodations, and outlawing discrimination in hiring and firing would not only be futile, but would be lost in Howard Smith's Rules Committee or Jim Eastland's Judiciary Committee, while being sufficiently divisive to kill whatever other proposals had a chance of surviving.

Then, of course, he had to contend with the Federal Reserve System. Created in Wilson's time to govern the nation's monetary policies, it was also designed to be independent of any particular administration. That never ruled out a little arm-twisting, but William McChesney Martin, Jr., a traditionalist, was determined to preserve his prerogatives. Stories had appeared during the 1960 campaign that, with monetary policy an issue and Democrats criticizing tight money, the chairman would be encouraged to retire. Martin, a symbol of fiscal integrity to many, upheld his principles and was not about to be budged. Right after the inauguration Kennedy told Walter Heller, "Frankly, I need Martin and Dillon. I need these Republicans to maintain a strong front as far as the financial community is concerned."[45] But some requests for "cooperation," a little lobbying, could be done legitimately. The good-natured "Fed" chairman was easy to talk to, but the resultant impression was deceptive. Martin was one of seven men charged with guiding the economy who came in to see the President on the morning of February 17, and he seemed open-minded about the argument that long-term interest rates could be brought down only if the Treasury and the Fed cooperated in reducing the supplies of long-term government bonds available for private holders.[46] "True," Heller wrote to Fred Dutton, "Martin's first steps toward Administration policy have been cooperative and significant. And he *does* need to save face—but we need to be watchful that the face-saving doesn't become a half-hearted effort in behalf of lower interest rates."[47]

With the President still resistant to stimulation by cutting taxes, Heller turned to his colleagues in late February and suggested they argue the matter by posing the following question: "Is good economics bad politics?"[48] A few days later he advised the President to "recommend a truly adequate program in April," adding that defeat in Congress would plainly place the political blame for persistent unemployment "clearly and justifiably on the opposition. If it is passed, there will be a healthy recovery, for which the administration can claim credit."[49] O'Brien also informed the White House that more "education" was needed to "allay liberal and conservative fears about tax credits."[50]

On April 20 Kennedy did send Congress a special message on taxation. It included broad reform objectives, pointing out the existing inequities that "have developed into an increasing source of preferential treatment to various groups." It also emphasized the importance of private capital formation through "a series of investment tax credits."[51] Presented at the height of the Bay of Pigs crisis and caught between conflicting views, the proposals died. One of the administration's more liberal critics later called the reforms section the closest the New Frontier had come to the image that it had projected during the campaign.[52]

Heller and his council had moved Kennedy about as far as they could.[53] Frustrated at their inability to bolster the economy through fiscal policies and blocked by those who blamed high unemployment on structural factors and by those worried more about sparking inflation, the trio of economic advisers was forced to settle. As a broad objective the concept of economic growth was much more palatable; it offered something for everybody. Accordingly growth became the sine qua non of everybody's economic utopia. From the outset, in fact, all desks in Commerce sported placards that asked, "What have you done for growth today?"[54] Kennedy himself told a business group that "Economic growth has come to resemble the Washington weather—everyone talks about it, no one says precisely what to do about it, and our only satisfaction is that it can't get any worse."[55]

Then economic indicators began to turn upward, recovering from February's low point. Arthur Goldberg had predicted that natural forces would reassert themselves, and that seemed to be happening. In early April the National Bureau of Economic Research reported that a study of cyclical phenomena indicated that the economy may have entered a phase that was always followed by recovery and expansion, and cash registers were providing additional evidence. March auto sales were thirty-four percent over February's. Home building and retail sales were similarly up.[56] On May 10 Heller gave the President the good news that "It *is* fairly widespread. It is *not* yet vigorous. It *will* set 'new records'

. . . starting sometime in the summer."[57] Those around Kennedy nevertheless were not eager to abandon the "second-stage" proposals suggested as a possibility by the economic message of February 2. They wanted direct public-works expenditures at all levels of government, together with legislation to counter long-range unemployment.[58] Goldberg especially pressed for large-scale public expenditures for a wide range of domestic programs, including training and relocation, housing, a youth corps, and public facilities.[59] But Kennedy held firm: The immediate commitment should be limited to standby programs, with temporary action directed only toward areas with exceptionally high unemployment.[60] Thus the economy bumped along, not substantially better and certainly not worse. What Galbraith, the Council of Economic Advisers, and other liberal economists had failed to get Kennedy to do, Khrushchev managed artfully.

Soviet conduct became the spur for higher military spending, an incremental process that ultimately set new peacetime records. The start, however, was modest. In three separate requests between late March and July, Kennedy asked the Congress for some six billion dollars in new outlays, but the overall increase above Eisenhower's original projections for fiscal 1962 came to two billion dollars. While Kennedy's primary interest always was, and remained, in the area of international relations, such considerations impinged on the domestic economy even more than he had anticipated. In later years portraits of the President as a "cold warrior" included accusations that he boosted defense spending as the most politic route toward economic recovery and growth.

Such notions assume a far less complex economy, a system somehow immune from the hazards of inflationary stimuli, a commonwealth in which conservatives were all too eager to ignore balanced budgets and ledger books over the joy of additional military hardware. The fact is that neither Kennedy nor his economic consultants and advisers prescribed stimulation through that kind of buildup. When Kennedy issued his calls for increased military appropriations, the economy was already showing signs of recovery. Moreover, in March, economic planning by the CEA concerned itself less with the potential boost from more spending for arms but with adjusting the economy to any possible moves toward disarmament. Neither the Soviets nor the Americans had been testing nuclear weapons since 1958. Within the administration's first week word was out that disarmament was one of the most promising areas for negotiations with Moscow.[61]

With global strategy planning concentrating on Laos, Cuba, and Berlin, arms limitation was not viewed as a contradictory goal but as a feasible simultaneous pursuit, an area of possible value to the economies of both countries. As far as the United States was concerned, Heller advised the President on March 24 that "preliminary thinking strongly suggests that the problem of economic adjustment need not be a road-block—real or psychological—to disarmament efforts. We believe plans can be devised for cutting taxes, adjusting non-defense programs, and tempering the wind to the shorn lambs of the defense industry in such a way as to make economic adjustments tolerable, indeed, to turn disarmament to major economic advantage."[62] Kennedy's requests for more defense spending were made while the CEA was finding virtues in arms reductions and coincided with the international situation rather than domestic requirements.

But the Laotian situation was getting messier, and that was the initial focal point of concentration. Then, too, the Kremlin's responses to Dag Hammarskjöld after the murder of Patrice Lumumba in the Congo jolted Kennedy and set back his hopes that the Russians were prepared to reach some kind of mutual solution. That April also brought Moscow's announcement of Yuri Gagarin's orbital space flight and, within the next week, the disaster at the Bay of Pigs.

It was then that Kennedy responded with a buildup. "Earlier setbacks in Southeast Asia had already convinced Kennedy and the National Security Council that spending for conventional armed forces and on guerrilla tactical operations would have to be raised," wrote Hobart Rowen shortly afterward. "The civilian spending program, which had already been whittled down, went out the window altogether, when Kennedy decided that our national prestige required a massive effort to land a man on the moon and return him safely to earth."[63] When asked about the Soviet space exploits, Kennedy agreed that "If we can get to the moon before the Russians, we should."[64] Considerations of space, military spending, and arms limitations were all part of dealing with the Russians. Shortly afterward Khrushchev's fulminations over Berlin and the prospect of nuclear blackmail seemed to give Kennedy and his planners little choice. Given the realities of Soviet behavior, they logically concluded that the risks of not having a usable force were greater than having one.

All told, Kennedy's legislative objectives were closely tuned to what was possible. In March, during a conversation with Dean Acheson, Kennedy cited the following comment from Lord Acton's "An Essay on Nationality": "The pursuit of a remote and ideal object, which captivates the imagination by its splendor and the reason by its simplicity, evokes an energy which would not be inspired by a rational, possible end, limited by many antagonistic claims, and confined to what is reasonable, practical and just."[65] By that standard Kennedy succeeded magnificently. On May 1 he signed into law the Area Redevelopment Act to pump federal funds toward the rejuvenation of depressed areas. Only four days later minimum wages were raised to $1.25 an hour. Social Security benefits were also widened. A $4.88 billion ominibus housing bill was the most comprehensive measure in that field since the Taft–Ellender Act of 1949, and was aimed largely for the benefit of low- and moderate-income families. There was also more aid for localities to battle water pollution, and more money toward public works.

But, as with any presidency, the inevitable prices had to be paid. Minimum-wage legislation was almost decimated by the traditional Republican–Southern Democratic conservative coalition, and the administration's victory had to come at the price of sacrificing tens of thousands of the most miserably paid, including 150,000 laundry workers. Few were more in need of such protection, but a well-organized laundry association lobby made their desperation quite irrelevant.[66] When at last Area Redevelopment grants started, the first were targeted not toward the most vital areas, but, as has already been pointed out, "to serve a shirt factory deep in the Ozark Mountains of Senator Fulbright's Arkansas. . . . a nonunion, low-wage enterprise of the very type whose competition has been so keenly felt in the depressed manufacturing centers of the North."[67] Other major parts of the program requested in February—health care, aid to education—were either in jeopardy or without any chance of success.

Kennedy's critics would later focus on such things and lament the absence of "real" accomplishments. But mostly they were voicing their own frustrations, speaking out about a people, a Congress, and a President not out to achieve New Deal–style reforms for American society but a modification of the past decade's mild conservatism. Among those expressing other preferences, the tilt was toward the right.[68]

But promises were being fulfilled. The nation was going forward. At the start of March, Kennedy sent a special message, creating a Peace Corps and signed an executive order establishing the agency on a temporary basis. His brother-in-law, R. Sargent Shriver, began serving as its director. The suite that opened to serve as its headquarters, at 806 Connecticut Avenue, was immediately inundated by mail and phone calls from eager young people.[69] Then on March 13 the President addressed Latin American diplomats at the White House and called "on

all the people of the hemisphere to join in a new Alliance for Progress
—*Alianza para Progreso*—a vast cooperative effort, unparalleled in mag-
nitude and nobility of purpose, to satisfy the basic needs of the American
people for homes, work and land, health and schools."[70] "It was quite
an occasion," career diplomat Thomas Mann remarked years later when
recalling that scene. The Alliance held out the hope of a middle way in
Latin America, the promotion of popular democracies capable of countering Castroite revolutionary sentiments seeking to overturn the hemisphere's rightist dictatorships. That and the Peace Corps were imbued
with missionary nobility, tapping latent desires to assert the universality
of the American dream.[71]

All that combined with a very visible presidency boosted Kennedy's
standing far above November's figures. A *Newsweek* survey reported that
the "new, young, and untried President—one who had been elected by
only 49.7 per cent of the electorate—now had the great part of the
American people behind him."[72] In a confidential analysis, Kennedy's
own pollster wrote that the ability to "get things done" was winning the
highest rating of popular approval. While critics duly pointed out that
Kennedy had not set his sights very high, both the Gallup pollsters and
Lou Harris, who made confidential studies for the White House, concluded that the expectations of most Americans had been "exceeded."
Harris's calculations had Kennedy's favorable ratings at an incredibly
high ninety-two to eight, and the Gallup organization's somewhat more
modest figures still showed a substantially impressive seventy-two to six
margin among those with an opinion.[73]

On Capitol Hill, Kennedy had managed to achieve a fairly reliable
working majority through a coalition of northern and western Democrats and liberal Republicans. Still, the steps were tempered, the requests
moderate, the compromises forthcoming. Why, then, was he so cautious?
Why did he fail to exert his personal leadership to achieve a more
impressive legislative record? "It is true," Walter Heller explained in
1980, "that, for all his national popularity, for all the effective troops that
he had in the White House in terms of relations with Congress, he was
not confident of his ability to get things through Congress." In sharp
contrast to Kennedy's responses to global events, in the realm of domestic politics, Heller explained, "I think he had a deep-seated belief that
he had to condition and educate the country in his first term and he'd
get his payoff in the second term."[74] The need to postpone action until
reelection became a common explanation, almost giving the impression
that the man who had run for the presidency on the theme of getting the
country "moving again" was guilty of the same kind of procrastination
as his predecessor.

If Kennedy was cautious, hesitant, calculating the probable cost of each move, he managed to approach foreign policy with a freer hand. Certainly, it was in the nature of the presidency, and the Founding Fathers had made clear the Chief Executive's responsibility. There in the very arena where the stakes risked nuclear disaster rather than the alienation of some domestic interest group, Kennedy was less hesitant about using those powers. Foreign crises were, of course, also more urgent and far less likely to permit delay. Moreover, the international order was of much greater personal interest and, from the start of his presidency, not a day passed without reminders of its primacy. In late March, Adolf Berle wrote in his diary that Kennedy "has had more rough crises thrown at him in the first sixty days of his Administration than any President since Lincoln." Before the anti-Castro brigade even attempted to land on Cuban soil, a writer for *The Nation* praised Kennedy for his "ability to live with chaos."[75] Springtime had come, bringing out the cherry blossoms in Washington, and the President was finding his challenges.

5

"Home Life in the White House"

John Kennedy's game was football, not baseball, but he was President of the United States, and so he helped open the season at Griffith Stadium by throwing out the first ball for the home team Washington Senators. One press aide, Barbara Gamarekian, had momentarily embarrassed Kennedy in the Rose Garden a few days earlier when she found him doing his "homework" for the event. He and his administrative assistant, Ted Reardon, were equipped with baseball gloves, and the President was tuning up his "pitching" arm. At the ballpark, such preparations paid off when he impressed everybody by throwing two ceremonial tosses about ninety feet. Kennedy then sat back and rooted for the Senators. An inept expansion club making their debut after the old Senators had become the Twins of Minnesota, whatever inspiration they may have drawn from his presence failed to keep them from suffering the first of that season's one hundred losses.[1]

Along with the crowd of 26,725 and the President was a gaggle of politicos, congressional leaders from both parties, aides, and such old friends as George Smathers. One who was both an aide and a friend was Dave Powers. The resident baseball expert, Powers was able to keep the game's vital statistics in the same memory bank that stored accurate mental printouts of election results. Dave also excelled at telling funny stories, with his rich Boston Irish accent flavoring the folksy ethnic touch. Not surprisingly he was nicknamed the "Court Jester," but he was also present for whatever task was required. That included caring for the President's personal needs, providing companionship in the White House swimming pool, or even greeting official visitors—all managed with the right touch of levity. A famous Powers one-liner came during the visit of Iran's monarch in 1962. "You're my kind of Shah," was the Powers compliment.[2]

The common notion that the boss created the tone was reaffirmed within the Kennedy White House. It was set quickly, and observers were not always amused. During the early evening of the second Sunday in office, there was a White House ceremony that swore in fifteen additional appointees, mostly assistant secretaries but also including the entire Council of Economic Advisers. After each man had raised his right hand and taken his oath before Chief Justice Earl Warren, they, their wives, and their children joined President and Mrs. Kennedy and Vice-President and Mrs. Johnson in the Blue Room for the first gala reception. "There was a tremendous difference in the atmosphere of the White House from the military receptions of the Truman time," recalled Air Force Secretary Eugene Zuckert, "and this gathering of people thoroughly enjoyed themselves," feeling as though they were in the President's home and not in the White House.[3] But much more memorable than the presence of Washington's power elite was the real live liquor on the table, brought down by the new President from its previous confinement in the upstairs living quarters. It was the first time guests had ever seen spirits served at a White House reception. "Everybody just lit up even before they got to the liquor," said Zuckert.

The word got around quickly. The Baptist General Convention of Texas rounded up a unanimous resolution of condemnation from their five hundred delegates.[4] A church official associated with the temperance department of the Columbia Union Conference of Adventists in Ohio told a youth conference of Seventh-Day Adventists that the President had misstepped by setting up a bar in the White House for social functions.[5] Completely overlooked in all this, and in marked contrast to their complaints, was the President's own alcoholic moderation.

Still, the most significant Kennedy imprimatur upon the White House was Jackie's restoration work. Much of it consisted of perpetually shifting things around, especially paintings. The portraits of ex-presidents were sometimes switched so frequently that they wound up precisely where they had begun. But it went far beyond that. She worked toward restoring the mansion's original decor by acquiring, with the assistance of private donations, authentic early-nineteenth-century pieces.[6] Sometimes the responses were too quickly forthcoming, even embarrassingly so, as when she had to explain her diligence to Adlai Stevenson. "I am just heartbroken to be writing you this," she wrote that first July, "because you were so fantastic to respond so quickly and generously to Mary Lasker's plea—and because it would have been so fitting to have you give the Lincoln settee and chairs—but the sad thing is I got someone to give them—probably the very day Mary wrote to you—as I was so scared we could lose them. I really jumped the gun on myself. . . . I hope Lincoln will forgive me . . . and that you will too."[7] Under Mrs. Kennedy's impetus a White House Fine Arts Committee was organized, the mansion was declared a national monument by Congress, and a White House Historical Association incorporated.[8] Her efforts also brought, in 1962, the publication of a *White House Guide Book*. Inevitably it became impossible to distinguish between public dedication and the demands of the First Lady's own personality. Before that first Christmas in the White House, for example, Letitia (Tish) Baldrige, the social secretary, notified Evelyn Lincoln how to respond to inquiries about what kind of gifts Jacqueline would prefer to get. "She wants art books," wrote Tish, "and she wants a little sterling coffee pot with a wooden handle—George I— holding only two cups. (Tiffany, of course!)"[9] If the President thought his wife was indulging herself, he showed no signs of displeasure. That was a valuable function, and he encouraged her work. Together, they would change both the symbols and the country.

The short-range effect was something else. The icons lent credibility to the aura of change; the New Frontier, and the very concept of the term, became synonymous with a touch of class, ultimately romanticized through identification with the Camelot legend. In his concern for appearances John Kennedy resembled all the Kennedys. And all seemed to be paying off. His wife's stature, which had hitherto been most useful ornamentally, began to assume political connotations. That first spring the flow of visitors to the mansion set new records. From a daily high of 8,074 in early April, the number went to 13,575 by the end of the month.[10]

But not everything carried Jackie's imprint. The President's father arranged to have the White House pool, which had been built during FDR's time, enhanced by a mural on all four walls. The design, personally supervised by the Ambassador, depicted the harbor at Saint Croix in the Virgin Islands, and was complete with a lighting system that adjusted the swimmer's ambience to reflect the time of day.[11] The President himself took a personal interest in the beautification of the Rose Garden. During his first year in office he often commented that he thought it looked too barren, and so he directed its rehabilitation. Before the actual planting began, he designed the steps that led from the top of the walk down to the garden, and provided for a platform from which he could address gatherings.[12]

As in her other homes his wife guarded her privacy. She was especially involved with keeping the children away from prying tourists with their cameras. She maintained a protectiveness toward everything that comprised her world. One day in January of 1963, she was especially incensed, and quickly dictated a note for Evelyn Lincoln to pass along to Larry O'Brien. "I was passing by Mrs. Lincoln's office today," complained the First Lady, "and I saw a man (Congressman [Wayne N.] Aspinall) being photographed in the Rose Garden with an enormous bunch of celery. I think it is most undignified for any picture of this nature to be taken on the steps leading to the President's office or on the South grounds. If they want their picture taken, they can pose by the West Lobby. This also includes pictures of bathing beauties, etc."[13]

The Kennedy desire for culinary distinction led to some publicity, although the implications of that incident were not pleasing. First there was the revelation that, before the inauguration, an attempt had been made to lure away from the French embassy in London a Vietnamese chef named Bui Van Han. Bui had supervised the ambassador's personal kitchen for twenty-two years and had a reputation for having a way with sauces and duck. Janet Auchincloss, Jacqueline's mother, had heard about him and suggested the idea. The entire procedure was somewhat indelicate, for chef-snatching was the upper-class equivalent of horse-stealing. Nevertheless the thought of a gourmet French chef in the White House intrigued Jackie, and she had Tish call London. The chef, however, vowed his loyalty to the ambassador; worse than that he talked to the press. Somewhat embarrassed when it all came out in mid-February, the White House issued a statement acknowledging the incident. As he did so often, the President promptly made himself the butt of his own joke when he told a Gridiron Dinner gathering that "we were anxious to get an expert in French cooking who wasn't named Pierre."[14] Then in early April, Pierre Salinger revealed that a White House luncheon given for Prime Minister Harold Macmillan of Great Britain had been prepared by one René Verdon, a thirty-six year old Frenchman who had worked for one of Joseph P. Kennedy's favorite restaurants, Caravelle. "The verdict," reported The New York Times, "was that there was nothing like French cooking to promote good Anglo-American relations." There was, however, one hitch: Verdon was not an American citizen. Not until that could be rectified could he be on the government payroll. Little wonder, then, that the executive powers rushed to correct the situation with the urgency of getting Henry IV baptized.[15]

When the Kennedys sold their Georgetown home shortly after the inauguration, they concentrated on their official residence in the mansion and, of special importance to Jacqueline, on locating a place where she could also escape the constant frenzy that characterized the environment of her husband's family. She therefore spent as much time as possible at Glen Ora, especially during her convalesence after John's birth.[16]

Glen Ora, a nineteenth-century French provincial estate, was two miles from Middleburg, in the heart of Virginia's "hunt" country. The hilly countryside was in the past best known as the Civil War base of John F. Mosby and his Rangers, guerrilla raiders of the Confederacy. By Kennedy's time it had become a favorite of Washington's well-heeled brass, whose money enabled them to join the indigenous old Virginia families in their fox-hunting. (Later, when political success brought him to the East, Ronald Reagan also rented an estate in the area.) For the Kennedys it was ideal. Jacqueline was an accomplished rider and an honorary member of the Orange County Hunt. The main building, with its six bedrooms, was augmented by a large guesthouse that contained an ample two-story party room. The four-hundred-acre property, which Kennedy rented, also had a swimming pool and a tennis court. About all that it lacked, and that was a significant omission for anyone who is President of the United States, was an appropriate house of worship. In the absence of a Roman Catholic church anywhere in the vicinity, the Kennedys attended mass at the Middleburg Community Center.[17] After Jacqueline came north from Palm Beach with her two children in early February, she got her first taste of Glen Ora over the Lincoln's Birthday weekend. When warmer weather came, Jackie practiced her riding and jumping, and the President kept up with golf at the Fauquier Springs Country Club.[18]

Until later in the spring, however, Kennedy spent most weekends at Palm Beach, where he never lacked a constant flow of guests. His old Choate pal, Lem Billings, was on hand almost all the time, virtually a perpetual weekend houseguest. But there were other friends from school-days who came and went, including Rip Horton and especially Torbert Macdonald, who had long since become a member of the House from Massachusetts. Jack's golfing companions that spring at the Palm Beach Country Club included not only his father, but brothers-in-law Steve Smith and Peter Lawford. They also joined with such celebrities as Bing

Crosby and businessmen Christopher Dunphy and Carroll Rosenbloom, owner of the Baltimore Colts. There, too, the President socialized with Earl E. T. Smith and his wife, Flo, and made use of his father's screening room to see the latest movies.

But Glen Ora—and later their home at Atoka—was much more Jackie's place than Palm Beach or Hyannis Port. Regardless of where her husband chose to spend his out-of-town weekends, and he was always gone for at least one or two of the days, she preferred a place of her own. Such desire for a refuge of her own characterized her life as First Lady, from that very first evening in the White House when, despite a family reunion, she chose to remain in seclusion in the upstairs Queen's Room.[19]

One of Jack Kennedy's friends has said that marriage never kept him from having fun. That point has been made by many others, and in many different ways. Jack's reputation was an important reason why many senatorial colleagues were not convinced that he would have a serious shot at higher office. During the years after Kennedy's death it became clear that his relationships with women after he reached the White House followed his old pattern. The one female in his life who brought unmitigated joy was little Caroline; the others, obligations and anxieties along with a pleasurable sense of danger.

His mother Rose has become legendary. Ask a Kennedy confidant or admirer, and she is immediately portrayed as Mother Courage, the woman who withstood her husband's wanderings. She was the "cement that kept the family together," the steady, devout figure who kept the candles burning and illusions alive. One fashion columnist said of the lady who thought it sinful to neglect either the texture of her skin, the perfection of her figure, or the quality of her wardrobe that "there's something, somehow, *regal* about Rose Kennedy."[20] All the while, either with her husband absent or present, she tended to the needs of nine children, guided their educational and spiritual growth, and tracked their health on index cards. Her own book, *Times to Remember,* concocts the best portrait of such maternal perfection, of a world with neither nasty thoughts nor deeds, where tragedies amply demonstrate that God's will touches the hallowed. Truman Capote put it best when he remarked that Rose Kennedy "really is a public perfect person."[21]

When the veil is brushed aside, a more lifelike portrait emerges. She was much less important, much less central to her children's lives than the mythical Rose Kennedy. Domestics were forever at hand; and when her children were away at school, masters served as surrogate parents. While she often traveled all over the world, including annual visits to Paris to examine the latest fashions, not once did she bother to venture a few miles north of New Haven at a time when young Jack was at Choate and constantly confined to infirmaries. When Jack was asked by a good friend what she had been doing when he really needed Mother, he explained that "she was on her knees in churches all over the world."[22] When her daughter, Kathleen, strayed from the faith to marry Billy Hartington, Rose, unlike Joe Kennedy, literally took to her bed in Boston and Hot Springs, and sent no message of maternal blessing to her daughter.[23] After Kathleen died in an airplane crash in the company of a second Protestant, the truth about her daughter's last days was carefully confined to the same closet with the other skeletons. The beneficiary of her husband's standing order to those who ran his office that she was not to be disturbed or upset about household matters and to be given whatever she needed without any questions or hesitation, her existence indeed approximated the regal. The Ambassador's nurse has reported that "Mrs. Kennedy never allowed a 'paid' person to share her table. This dictum went so far as to include some of the most highly respected doctors and specialists in this country."[24] After her husband's stroke in late 1961, he, too, was cared for by surrogates, especially his devoted niece, Ann Gargan. Rose broke few strides. Always the lady, she kept her rituals in order, the rounds of golf, visits to Paris, travels whenever possible. "She appeared regularly, and often unexpectedly, at most of the important artistic and social events of the season," writes her biographer.[25]

She had assisted with Jack's political career. In Massachusetts her presence at teas and gatherings of supporters made her an almost legendary figure. She was the "mother of the year" every year. Rose Kennedy —elegant, sophisticated, the embodiment of the best Irish society in America, a marked progression from the generation of her father, the vulgar pol known as "Honey Fitz"—captured popular awe. Her devotion to family and church, bearing with stoicism repeated tragedies, was somehow more admirable from one with her wealth and position. Perhaps tales of her husband's philanderings made her seem more brave. Her son's presidency further embellished that image, and Jacqueline's frequent absences from the White House enabled Rose to stand in as the hostess. Never tiring of her function, her satisfaction at her son's rise was so complete that she delighted at having her chauffeur stop for hitchhikers so she could have the thrill of informing the innocents that they were "riding with the President's mother."[26]

Neither privately nor publicly did Jack accord her the respect that he did his father. While the Ambassador was often overbearing and oppressive, and all too often outrageous, he was at least of this world. Rose was not. She bore the cross, and Jack winced, in his youth siding with Kathleen in her little rebellions. In his maturity, unlike Rose, Jack's religious faith was expressed more in the privacy of his room than in church. He was, paradoxically, a Catholic deist. Having been raised as the second son of Joe and Rose Kennedy, and having had to virtually remake his temperament to suit what has been called the "Kennedy neurosis," he had his own not unnatural ambivalences toward the very background to which popular lore ascribed much of his strength. In a moment of pique perhaps, or possibly of reflection, he confided to his close friend Bill Walton that it might not be a bad idea for the state rather than parents to bring up children.[27]

Nor was Jacqueline comfortable with Rose. Much more private, much more withdrawn, she remained far from enamored with the hectic world that forever surrounded the Kennedys. Once she broke her ankle playing touch football, she virtually despaired of adjusting herself to their desires. Whatever chances for overcoming inherent temperamental differences had been they were further reduced by the political distance that separated the Kennedys from the Bouviers and Auchinclosses. But the tensions that confronted Jackie came mainly from Rose, not her father-in-law, toward whom, by all accounts, she developed considerable affection. No appraisal of the two most important women in Jack Kennedy's life makes much of an effort to glorify their relationship. The recollection of one of Jackie's secretaries, Mary Barelli Gallagher, is especially revealing.

"Do you know if Jackie is getting out of bed today?" she quotes Rose as having asked. Told that Gallagher could not be certain, she made the following snippy comment: "Well, you might remind her that we're having some important guests for lunch. It would be nice if she would join us." Jacqueline, when told about her mother-in-law's suggestion, mocked Rose in a singsong voice and went right on with her own plan, which was to remain absent.[28] In his memoirs J. B. West, the White House usher, reports that "Rose Kennedy came to the White House more often when her daughter-in-law was away, than when she was in residence." She also kept her son and his family supplied with a constant flow of "prayers, rosary beads, and religious artifacts."[29]

Her daughter-in-law's own strong-minded independence could not have made matters simple for Rose Kennedy. Much more than Bobby's wife, Jackie resisted surrendering her own identity so she could become a full-fledged member of the extended family. Rose was also conscious of her son's less than idyllic marriage.

But after Jack's election to the presidency they were "trapped there together," a mutual friend has pointed out, and their marriage "blossomed." Life together in the mansion may have brought greater intimacy, but their basic differences remained.[30] Nor did much about Jackie's character change enough to satisfy what had troubled the President's mother.

Jacqueline never did share Rose's devotion to Jack's political friends and career. She felt uncomfortable with the old hangers-on, lamenting in terms that were hardly complimentary the almost perpetual weekend presence of someone like Lem Billings. Unlike Rose's zest for participation in her son's career, Jackie had to be cajoled to play a political role. Newsmen who observed her close up doubted that she ever became emotionally involved in the process.[31] During the Wisconsin primary, Edwin Bayley, then Governor Gaylord Nelson's executive secretary, noticed that fear of Jackie's political naiveté (which Bayley thought unjustified) made Kennedy's staff want to keep her "bottled up."[32] At Hyannis Port shortly after her husband had won the Democratic presidential nomination, she complained to one of Lyndon Johnson's secretaries that she felt "so totally inadequate, so totally at a loss, and I'm pregnant; and I don't know how to do anything."[33] While preparations were being made for her trip to India in 1962, Chester Bowles advised the President to have her spend less time with the country's elite inspecting monuments, and more in the villages where community-development programs were being carried out. She could also, Bowles suggested, get around to some universities and a representative selection of the public schools.[34]

Jackie's obsessive spending was one of the greater threats to her marriage. That also upset the tranquil world of Rose, for the specter of marital separation had very ominous implications for Jack's political career. Jackie was a spender of legendary proportions, and her habits caused severe strains with her husband. During that Wisconsin primary she went off alone one day to campaign by visiting some black churches. Later, when Jack Kennedy's car picked her up and she squeezed into the rear seat between some aides, her husband glanced back at her and asked, "Jackie, how did you do?"

She replied, "Oh, I did very well. I met the loveliest minister of the loveliest black church, and he has all kinds of financial troubles. So I thought it would be awfully nice to help him out, so I gave him two hundred dollars."

"Well," said Kennedy, "that was nice." Then, with a quick second thought, he added, "Goddamn it, it wasn't my money, was it?"[35]

Burdened with all his other distractions, the President demanded from his wife's financial manager closer scrutiny over Jackie's spending, which, in 1961 and 1962, exceeded his own $100,000 salary. Almost half was for clothes.[36] One chairman of a powerful congressional committee recalled the only time he ever saw Jack show anger. The congressman happened to be in the Oval Office when an agitated President suddenly displayed his bills for forty thousand dollars' worth of clothes that Jackie had bought. "What would you do if your wife did that?" he asked. The visitor from the Hill, a longtime fixture in the House, assured the President that his own bank balance would spare him that danger.[37]

Such spending habits were especially irritating for a President so concerned about the mansion's household budget, and he insisted that Jackie and Chef Verdon order groceries from more reasonably priced stores. He was constantly irritated over costs, mulling over entertainment bills that required personal checks to compensate for the limitations imposed by the official White House budget. He often complained bitterly about the liquor consumption, and ordered the mansion's butlers not to open bottles of champagne until the last one was finished. He admonished them about having several open simultaneously, and advised that they were not to rush about trying to refill half-empty glasses.[38] Exasperated, the President finally called upon Carmine Bellino, the accountant who had helped Bobby's investigation of organized crime, to make a cost study of the White House.[39]

But the greatest threat to the marriage, and to Kennedy plans for their son's presidency, came from another source—Jack's continued wanderings. Jacqueline's most credible recent biographer has repeated how close her husband's affairs brought her to a separation, with, of course, all the problems divorce would have created in a Catholic family, not to mention the political implications when Jack was aiming for the White House. She consulted both the Kennedys and the Auchinclosses, and, of course, there was no relief. But as Stephen Birmingham recalls, the situation produced rumors that Joe Kennedy offered Jacqueline a cash payment of one million dollars to keep the peace, and that has never been denied.[40] It is understandable that Rose, who bore her cross with her own husband's philanderings, was less tolerant of her daughter-in-law's attitude. Joe Kennedy's nurse, who cared for him after he became an invalid, observed that Jackie "loved and respected her father-in-law and was grateful for any help he received."[41]

Jacqueline finally learned, as her mother-in-law had long since done, how to live with infidelity. Such patterns were, after all, similar to those of her own father, John (Black Jack) Bouvier III. She asked few questions. As much as possible she left the White House for other diversions, including several extensive overseas trips. They seemed entirely appropriate, even helpful, for a First Lady. The last one taken during her husband's lifetime included a journey to Greece and a visit aboard Aristotle Onassis's yacht. That was after the death of Patrick, her infant son, and nobody was eager to criticize her at that time. As far as the President's extramarital activities were concerned, Bill Walton, who was on close terms with both, recalls that they remained "vague and shadowy."[42]

Not until the mid-seventies did outsiders learn much about their President's private life, but those better acquainted with the center of power knew about the "vague and shadowy" affairs. Kennedy had not reformed his playboy ways, and close observers knew that much of the gossip was substantive. When Joe Alsop gave parties for the President at his Georgetown place, he was always careful to include as many attractive women as possible. They were imported from as far away as New York because, as Alsop has explained, "there aren't that many beautiful women in Washington," and Kennedy liked having them around for his enjoyment.[43] Other journalists, less close to Kennedy than Alsop, suspected that he was especially fond of a young correspondent from the Midwest who worked for one of the major organizations. "There were always rumors around about the President and girls, and especially one member of the press," recalled a newsman who went to work with the Peace Corps.[44]

They also talked about Fiddle, who was the partner of Faddle, more formally known as Priscilla Wear and Jill Cowan. They had only recently graduated from Goucher, had both served in his presidential campaign, and were Washington roommates. Fiddle, Priscilla, worked for Evelyn Lincoln; Faddle, Jill, for Pierre Salinger. Winsome, innocent, and "cute," they were office amusements. Like the two Filipino stewards who were called "Quemoy" and "Matsu" by Dave Powers, their nicknames reflected inseparability. Fiddle, however, was considered the presidential favorite, her meager secretarial talents and frequent proximity to him feeding that suspicion. Another young woman, whose acquaintanceship with Kennedy went back to his Senate days, was on the staff of the National Security Council. *Time* later referred to her as one who had fallen "in love" with the President and "was always available."[45]

An alleged special relationship between the President and Pamela Turnure, Jacqueline's personal secretary, aroused crusading efforts by a woman singlehandedly determined to expose the "debaucher of a girl young enough to be his daughter." She displayed a snapshot of a Kennedy look-alike figure shielding his face from the camera and turning away furtively in the dark. The photographic "evidence" could have been a view of any man, at any place, and at any time, but the accuser was not discouraged. She "alerted" all the major media—plus the B'nai B'rith, the Catholic Daughters of America, and the Daughters of the American Revolution—with the information that Turnure was having an "illicit sexual relationship with President John F. Kennedy." In a letter to the attorney general she complained that his brother's "cynical knowledge that the Press will cover up for him is such that he has brought her into the White House itself as his wife's press secretary."[46]

But public exposure was a very tangible problem with what Ben Bradlee has called the "John's other wife story." Alleged evidence of a previous marriage hit the Oval Office hard, creating considerable agitation, precisely when international attention was focused on the newly constructed Berlin Wall and the testing of Khrushchev by a convoy of American troops along the *Autobahn*. It seemed to correspond somewhat too neatly with everything else known about Jack Kennedy, and, furthermore, was flavored with the aura of legitimacy by appearing in print and in a source that was impeccably innocent, as but one of the twenty-five thousand capsule biographical entries that comprised the *Blauvelt Family Genealogy*. Nor could anyone easily relegate its compiler to the crackpot category, as, perhaps, Miss Turnure's accuser. Louis L. Blauvelt was a skilled toolmaker who had worked for General Electric in New Jersey. He was also meticulous about his avocation, a genealogy which was published in 1957, just two years before he died at the age of seventy-nine. The most that has been said to impugn his reliability is that he may have been senile. But even that fails to suggest a motive, and nobody has ever come forward to say that Blauvelt was incapable of recognizing that such an allegation would ultimately create somewhat of a stir. Sometime during the summer of 1961 an unknown person found the entry and photoduplication promptly multiplied its readership. On page 884 of the genealogy was the following information:

(12,427) DURIE, (Kerr), MALCOM, (Isabel O. Cooper. 11.304.) We have no birth date. She was born Kerr, but took the name of her stepfather. She first married Firmin Desloge, IV. They were divorced. Durie then married F. John Bersbach. They were divorced, and she

married, third, John F. Kennedy, son of Joseph P. Kennedy, one time Ambassador to England. There were no children of the second or third marriages.

The Blauvelt affair jolted the White House. Both the President and the attorney general warned reporters that they would find themselves in the courts if they tried to use the story. "I'll wind up owning your magazine," the President told Laura Bergquist.[47] When J. Edgar Hoover began getting reports from "concerned citizens," Robert Kennedy told the director that he "hoped" the press would print it because then "we" could all retire for life on what "we" collect.[48] Four months after that telephone conversation between the attorney general and the FBI director an internal memorandum was forwarded to Hoover at his home with the unconfirmed report that Kennedy had married Durie in 1939, when he was only twenty-two. A Reno divorce was supposedly granted in 1948, but then invalidated. Then, after an earlier attempt to get one in New Jersey, a sealed divorce was finally secured there in 1953. The report also asserted that the then Archbishop Cushing applied to the Papal Court in 1951 for an annulment, and, in 1953, that was also granted.[49] With such allegations in the air it was not surprising that Kennedy turned to his old troubleshooter, Clark Clifford.

Clifford had the item copied at the Library of Congress, where, as Bradlee found out, a waiting list for the volume included ten members of Congress.[50] Clifford called the woman, who was living in Palm Beach with her third husband, Thomas L. Shevlin,* in a colonial mansion opposite the North Ocean Boulevard home of Joseph P. Kennedy. She assured the attorney that there was nothing to the story, but found the whole fuss flattering.[51] A butler who worked in the Shevlin home later remembered how they "just had an enormous laugh around that house all that time: newspaper people calling up. They laughed so much I just figured there was nothing to it."[52]

Both Durie, who was nicknamed Dede, and Kennedy admitted to having known each other. The woman, who had been described at her coming-out party in 1934 as "radiant, with golden-brown hair, blue-green eyes and a sunny smile," was seen with Kennedy in a Miami nightclub in 1947. He was just taking his congressional seat and she, one year older, was fresh from her second marriage. Kennedy told Clark Clifford that he certainly remembered Dede. He had dated her "once or twice" and she was very attractive.[53] Both Kennedy brothers also explained that Joe Junior had dated her more often.[54]

*She has since remarried for a fourth time.

The explanations were finally put together by Clifford, including the presence of other obvious inaccuracies in Blauvelt's entry. Durie Malcolm's surname was misspelled. The order of her first two marriages was reversed, and no mention was made of Shevlin, who married her a full decade before the publication. Bradlee reports that one member of the family, "who insisted on being unidentified," speculated that old Louis Blauvelt "may well have concluded that the family hadn't done much and likely just formed the idea in his mind. That's all."[55] When an interviewer got Clifford to discuss the case in 1974, the prominent Washington attorney and presidential adviser said, quite logically, "How this mistake was made by somebody writing that genealogy, no one could possibly fathom. Unless it could have been some other person named Kennedy and the author was old and one thing and another and got the names confused."[56]

But the most obvious point remained unsaid. At the time Jack Kennedy had allegedly taken that step, he had just been elected to office from the largely Roman Catholic Eleventh District of Massachusetts. Marriage to a woman just getting her second divorce would have required a much more light-headed response to crucial decisions than characterized him at even that age. While he was not above the common masculine ploy of promising marriage, neither was he then persuaded that the time had come to actually take a wife. Finally, after the "secret marriage" story had circulated underground for a year, it could no longer be ignored, and the President wanted to "clear the air" through Phil Graham's publications. Whether that satisfied doubters is another matter. Seventeen years after he had personally investigated the alleged affair for the press, Fletcher Knebel could still say, "I don't know yet whether it was true or not."[57]

As the first Roman Catholic President, Kennedy was especially vulnerable to vicious gossip. Dating back to Colonial American pamphleteers and penny-presses, more conventional Presidents have not been spared that by-product of democracy. And, moreover, the Kennedy administration coincided with one of the more turbulent periods of social change, with questions of race once again transcending and blurring class tensions. The Blauvelt matter, any possible moral indiscretion, any departure from acceptable standards, had its monitors and exploiters. Before the "official" explanations of the "secret marriage," the underground market was swamped with exposés. Time noted that "racist organizations in the South and crackpot groups everywhere photostated these pieces and sent them out as junk mail by the scores of thousands; it is estimated that at least 100,000 were received by mailbox holders in Massachusetts alone."[58]

Nor did antiadministration papers, even the most "respectable" ones, ignore other opportunities to tar the Kennedy image. The *New York Journal American,* the flagship Hearst paper in New York City—now bitterly opposed to Jack's politics despite his family's old friendship with the publisher and his own brief service as a Hearst correspondent—tried to link him with the Profumo affair then agitating Great Britain and threatening the Macmillan government's survival.

The year's great sex scandal broke when John D. Profumo, the secretary of state for war and a Conservative member of Parliament, resigned both his office and his seat. He admitted to having lied to the Commons by saying that there had been "no impropriety whatsoever" about his relationship with "a party girl," Christine Keeler. The affair suddenly became a national-security sensation as well. Through a Dr. Stephen Ward, who served as a procurer for high-class prostitutes, Profumo entered the milieu of Captain Yevgeny M. Ivanov, a Soviet deputy naval attaché in London. In June, the Prime Minister told Commons that Miss Keeler had told police that Ward had asked her to discover from Profumo when the Americans would supply atomic weapons to Germany. But her denial stood up, and the matter turned out to be more an example of Profumo's human weakness than international intrigue, such as the Philby spy case, which also generated headlines that summer in Britain and America.[59]

Kennedy himself had a noblesse oblige view of such matters. When one prominent student of Russian thought tried to tell him about an affair Lenin had had with a lady, he took exception to that information. "I had the feeling that one mustn't talk about the private affairs of great heads of state in quite that tone of voice," said the scholar, who prefers anonymity. Unquestionably the British upper class, to which Kennedy always felt so close, was in that category. Furthermore he especially sympathized with the Macmillan government. Despite earlier difficulties, he and the Prime Minister had by then managed a harmonious and even close relationship. Privately he was also charitable about Profumo himself. He understood that Profumo's circumstances exposed him to that kind of scrutiny and disdained offering any strong criticism. "He was very tolerant that way," explained Charles Spalding.[60] Kennedy had, by then, already been at the near-disaster stage himself and was undoubtedly self-conscious about his own vulnerability. When in late June, after he had spoken to the nation most eloquently about the need for long overdue civil rights legislation, he met Dr. Martin Luther King, Jr., he advised the black leader to avoid two associates being monitored by the FBI for potential Communist connections. He specifically cited Profumo's threat to Macmillan's government.[61] The Hearst article appeared just one week later: its implication was that the President was linked to the Profumo affair.

It did not name John F. Kennedy. The front-page story headlined "HIGH U.S. AIDE IMPLICATED IN V-GIRL SCANDAL," told that it involved one of the "biggest names in American politics," a man who holds "a very high" elective office. Under the joint byline of James D. Horan and Dom Frasca, the story was based on a revelation made via transatlantic telephone of the knowledge of the "American affair" as given by another London "party girl," Marie Novotny. The U.S. official had had his indiscretion with a beautiful Chinese-American woman identified by the paper as Susy Chang. She had been involved in a celebrated vice case in New York in 1961, was implicated as having been in the city with Christine Keeler and Mandy Rice-Davies, and was apparently then operating from Dr. Ward's fashionable Chelsea apartment.[62]

To insiders it must have long since become understandable why Jack Kennedy had made his brother attorney general. Once again Bobby handled a presidential lapse, or if not an actual lapse, vulnerability that came directly from both his behavior and reputation. Late on the afternoon of the first of July, two days after the article appeared, the attorney general met in his office with the two reporters, presumably at his request. When challenged to identify the "high" U.S. official, they conceded that they meant the President. Their concern, however, only extended to the "security implications." Then they played back the twenty-minute tape of the accusatory call from London with the voice of British newspaperman Peter Earle, whose News of the World was doing handsomely with the Profumo affair. Marie Novotny could be heard offering corroboration. "Like our Mr. Profumo," she said, "your man also has access to government secrets," but Earle attributed the situation to "human frailties." Robert Kennedy also heard that the information had been solicited by the Journal American.

Bobby then asked whether the story had been corroborated by any other source. Had there been further checking? They replied that additional information existed but was confidential. The attorney general then told the men not to say that he ever asked a journalist to violate a confidence. If the reporter had any other corroboration, he was clearly not forthcoming; nor did he supply the nature of additional allegations. The whole procedure was monitored by the FBI, with Courtney Evans of the bureau then reporting back to Director Hoover that the office conference "ended most coolly and, in fact, that there was almost an air of hostility between the Attorney General and the reporters."[63] Coincidentally the President himself was in London seeing Macmillan that same day.

By that time Kennedy had presumably weathered the most serious risk posed by his taste for women. That liaison dated back to shortly after his press conference of January 2, 1960, when he announced his candidacy. Within the next few days he made a number of additional political appearances. Then the newly declared presidential aspirant moved on to campaign in New Hampshire, Indiana, and Utah; then on to the Southwest. On Sunday, February 7, he left Albuquerque and reached Las Vegas.

The visit was a stopover en route to further campaigning in Oregon and Washington. At that night spot and gambling capital, he joined brother Teddy and sister Patricia, who was then married to Peter Lawford. The Hollywood actor belonged to the so-called "Rat Pack," which included such other entertainment personalities as Frank Sinatra, Sammy Davis, Jr., and Dean Martin. At the moment, they were involved in the filming of *Ocean's Eleven,* which featured the robbery of a gambling casino. Later that evening, in the lounge of the Sands Hotel, Sinatra introduced Jack Kennedy to a woman named Judith Campbell.[64]

A twenty-five-year-old divorcee from an upper-middle-class family who had introduced her to Hollywood from childhood, Campbell was one of the women whose charms were shared by the Rat Pack and various underworld figures who flitted among several adult playlands. Her first meeting with Kennedy was only casual. That Sunday, Ted was more attentive, but Jack took her out to lunch the next day before he left for Oregon. By Campbell's own account their intimacy did not begin until they met in New York City's Plaza Hotel on March 7. FBI records show that Kennedy's proximity to the Rat Pack, and to that particular feminine associate, was already being tracked.

The bureau's Los Angeles office gathered information about intense efforts by hoodlums associated with gambling operations in Las Vegas, Miami, and Havana to insinuate themselves into the graces of the potential President. Through a criminal informant the FBI heard that a visit to the Miami area had revealed that "members of the underworld element . . . and other unidentifiable hoodlums are financially supporting and actively endeavoring to secure the nomination for the presidency as Democratic candidate, Senator John F. Kennedy. He said that Frank Sinatra is going to campaign for Kennedy in several of the primaries . . ." The singer's songwriter, the bureau learned, was also writing Kennedy campaign lyrics. Sinatra himself had made a recording of "High Hopes" for the candidate and was also cultivating Lawford. The bureau's Los Angeles station area chief, who also confirmed that Kennedy spent time at the Sands with Sinatra, added that "it is a known fact that the Sands is owned by hoodlums and that while the Senator,

Sinatra and Lawford were there, show girls from all over the town were running in and out of the Senator's suite."[65] A long sketch of Kennedy's background also reported that he had been "compromised" with a woman in Los Angeles and that in the recent past he and Sinatra had been involved in parties in Palm Springs, Las Vegas, and New York City. While the bureau was accumulating raw data about Kennedy activities, one informant expressed dismay at what was being heard "as he would hate to see a pawn of the hoodlum element such as Sinatra have access to the White House."[66] Kennedy's "fondness for Frank Sinatra," Dave Powers and Ken O'Donnell later explained, "was simply based on the fact that Sinatra told him a lot of inside gossip about celebrities and their romances in Hollywood."[67]

Judith Campbell (who later became Judith Campbell Exner) was a beautiful woman, twenty-five years old, dark-haired, with slim hips and legs, and a full bosom. She was often compared with Elizabeth Taylor. Of medium height, she was not typical of Kennedy's general preference for tall blondes. Her account of their relations, which was published in 1977, is often simple-minded and tedious. Specific items lack authority. Most of all, however, other than its intended exploitative value, the tone is defensive. Such close members of the Kennedy circle as Evelyn Lincoln and Dave Powers had loyally denied ever having known of her existence.[68] Powers, in his inimitable way, said that the only Campbell he knew was "chunky vegetable soup."[69] When the question of her visibility around the Kennedy White House was raised with Ken O'Donnell, he denigrated the importance of the log showing over seventy calls from the woman. He said they were received by Mrs. Lincoln. Anybody could have spoken to her. That was not unusual. The entries were no evidence that she had actually spoken to the President. Such calls would have had to go via O'Donnell, and he never got "a single one." But when Judith's memoirs appeared several months after the O'Donnell interview, they contained enough specific information (including the private telephone numbers to the White House) to validate her essential claims.[70]

By her own account her visits were concentrated during the summer of 1961, when she saw him five times.[71] Kennedy's physical condition was then at its worst point in years. Not for a long time had he been in such agony. Moreover, that period was particularly difficult, because it coincided with the Berlin crisis and his realization that a nuclear exchange was entirely possible.

That spring's international crisis was sparked in Vienna, but Kennedy's physical distress began in Ottawa, Canada. At a tree-planting ceremony on May 16, the President himself wielded a shovel, and his fragile back was left with painful muscle spasms. Nevertheless he fulfilled crucial diplomatic visits to London, Paris, and Vienna, where the famous meeting with Khrushchev lasted over a two-day period in June. That first weekend back in the States was spent at the home of the Ambassador's Palm Beach neighbors, Mr. and Mrs. Charles Wrightsman. In seclusion, Kennedy rested and, according to the White House appointment books, participated in no activity except "swimming to help correct his back trouble."[72] Shortly afterward, Ken Galbraith visited him in the White House and found him in bed. "I think he is suffering a good deal from his back," the new ambassador to India noted in his journal. "Certainly it is more serious than he admits or wants to admit."[73]

Possibly also related to his stress of the moment was a severe viral infection, which came soon after the Galbraith visit and forced the cancellation of all presidential appointments on June 22. Much more serious than publicly acknowledged, the brief illness involved an acute sore throat, coughing, chills, and a fever that reached 105 degrees. He was treated with large doses of penicillin, and was given an intravenous injection as well as cold sponge baths. By the following morning the fever was reduced to 101. That day the President conducted his meetings in the mansion, including an early-morning farewell call by Prime Minister Ikeda of Japan.[74] But his condition continued to be dominated by excruciating back pain.

Once again he walked with crutches. He used the elevator rather than the curving staircase to get from the second to the first floor of the mansion. The White House pool became an important therapeutic aid. His leather canvas supporter covered his lower abdominal region. When receiving guests he sat in the rocking chair that had been supplied by Dr. Janet Travell many years earlier. He seemed to like it, and used it often, although one of his attending physicians pooh-poohed it as "nonsense," more of a public-relations gimmick than of any medical value.[75]

Kennedy's always sensitive physical state further taxed the resources of the experts. In view of his history they had done everything possible to protect him from his various vulnerabilities. His Addison's was contained, for example, by continued use of steroids, with the dosages varied periodically. Special attention had also been given to potential allergens. Collections were made of all dust from the mansion's second floor, including bits of camel hair from throw rugs and Caroline's Welsh terrier, Charlie, and a vaccine was then produced to immunize him from his environment. Since Kennedy was also allergic to horsehair, his mattresses, which were made more rigid by heavy supporting boards, consisted of cattle-tail hair. An additional mattress was made for carrying on *Air Force One* so he could have it wherever he went. When he woke up in the morning with puffy eyes because the slope of his bed permitted fluids to accumulate during the night, special blocks were built to elevate his position.[76] But it was his back that remained most painful.

It was in the middle of all this concern that Judith Campbell came to the White House to practice her specialty.

She excelled at her profession and satisfied his desires, engaging with the President in assignations that were, for him, more functional than anything else. "Because of his back problem there were times when there was nothing else he could do," she writes. "I understood about the position he had to assume in lovemaking when his back was troubling him, but slowly he began excluding all other positions, until finally our lovemaking was reduced to this one position." Lest anyone doubt that she, too, had her standards, her public confession explains that "the feeling that I was there to service him began to really trouble me."[77]

Also hidden from the public eye was the effort to remedy his back condition. Just as the White House appointment books make no mention of Campbell, they omit the physicians and therapists brought in to cope with the problem.

Dealing with the Kennedy medical history is in some ways like trying to uncover aspects of vital national-security operations. From the very start of his political rise, of course, there was the potential for exposés of his actual condition. Bad as it was, it could easily have been exaggerated by competitors; just before the 1960 convention the attempt made by John Connally and India Edwards had been beaten back and, except for rumors about Addison's, not much remained that seemed to pose an immediate threat. There is, however, ample reason to believe that safeguards were necessary and precautions had to be taken against efforts to magnify what was actually going on. Even after the inauguration, of course, there was always the problem of reelection and his ability to govern. Blowing the cover of the President's physical fitness facade had the potential for devastating political advantage.

Initially, Kennedy's primary care was in the hands of Dr. Travell. Originally trained as an internist, she developed a reputation as a pharmacologist. Her special expertise became the treatment of muscular disorders through the use of injections at the trigger points of the body that refer pain to other areas.[78] Other than the allergist, Dr. Paul F. de Gara, Kennedy's medical problems also involved Dr. Preston A. Wade, Dr. Eugene J. Cohen, Dr. Hans Kraus, and Dr. George C. Burkley. Dr. Burkley, an admiral from the Naval Dispensary in Washington, was brought in at the start of the administration to become part of the White House medical staff.

During the 1960 campaign Dr. Cohen's New York office was ransacked. The doctor had wisely taken the precaution of filing Kennedy's records under a different name, and the intruders succeeded only in leaving scattered records of other patients on the office floor. But at about the same time, as though to remove any doubts about the motivation behind that break-in, Dr. Travell found that someone had tried to break the lock on her door. She then rounded up all existing Kennedy medical records and deposited them for safekeeping.[79] When Dr. Kraus became a White House consultant, his office was also entered, but the Kennedy material had been placed in a separate file and without his name. "I reported that to the White House right away, of course," the doctor recalls, and they sent experts to equip the office telephone with devices to counter wiretaps. "And I had a secret button so that I could talk without being heard outside. I accepted it as an expected procedure when treating someone in an important office."[80]

Not until 1972 did some investigative reporting by *The New York Times* reveal that the President was among the celebrities treated by "Dr. Feelgood." That was Dr. Max Jacobson, who dispensed amphetamine "pep pills," better known as "speed," to patients in high-powered, competitive positions who needed to combat depression and fatigue. Dr. Jacobson was one of the unofficial White House visitors. He also traveled with the Kennedys, and treated Jacqueline along with the Radziwills and Mark Shaw, the Kennedy photographer. A published collection of Shaw's pictures shows the doctor with Kennedy, Charles Spalding, and Prince Radziwill near Palm Beach in February of 1963. But the Kennedy reliance on the hyperactivity-inducing drug had actually begun early in his administration. Only later was there concern within medical circles about potential side effects, which included addiction and psychiatric complications.[81] For Kennedy at the time, it seemed to be just the kind of stimulant he needed.

Only now, however, can the problem of Dr. Travell and the President's more persistent problem, the state of his back, be reconstructed. Dr. Travell's reliance on continued procaine injections began to raise increasing concern, not only among the specialists at the Bethesda Naval Hospital, but with Dr. Burkley as well. As the body became tolerant to the drug, there was fear that narcotics would be the next necessity. Burkley, when interviewed for the Kennedy Library in 1967, was cautious about respecting medical ethics and reluctant to criticize his colleague, but nevertheless he did explain that "it was felt that my management of the President's health was more general and not as limited to the use of the procaine injections which Dr. Travell advocated at all times."[82] Interviewed fourteen years later, the doctor explained that "it was simply that if you had a strained back playing golf or something like that and you went to the doctor and you had a muscle that was in spasm and procaine was injected, it would relieve the spasm. But following the relief of the spasm you should get the muscle back in shape by physical means rather than by use of medication of that nature."[83] Dr. Travell's published account virtually ignores Dr. Burkley's existence, and she denies that there ever was any controversy over procaine. After some trouble with her "memory" she agreed that additional help was sought. "If there were a consultation and we had a doctor in," she says, "you know, this was not generally known. We could have anybody in we wanted to."[84] There is also reason to believe that the President himself had begun to despair over the lack of progress and wanted a consultant.

Dr. Cohen suggested Hans Kraus, a New York orthopedic surgeon who had been practicing physical therapy. For several weeks Travell opposed the move. Finally, Dr. Burkley warned that he would make the call himself if she refused, and only after that threat did she agree. Dr. Kraus began an almost daily commutation to the White House after his regular office hours in New York City.

He learned that the President was getting "more and more injections and needed two or three injections a day and then finally they got concerned and asked me." First he examined the President in Dr. Travell's White House office, and then he suggested starting with three physical-therapy treatments a week. He found Kennedy worried about undertaking the process without the outside world learning about it. Dr. Kraus suggested that they respond to any questions by saying that the President's physical condition was so good that he simply needed exercises to get into top shape and the doctor was there merely to assist. For the sake of appearances he gave him treatments in the exercise area. That would help confirm explanations that he was just there for the President's workouts. His importance, however, was underscored by the telephone placed in his automobile, so that he could be summoned immediately, whether the President was at the Cape or in Washington.[85] When Dr. Kraus began his treatments in October, he found the President "completely unrehabilitated." His back was stiff and his abdominal muscles were weak.[86]

The therapy proceeded in the gymnasium adjacent to the pool. In an atmosphere further enhanced by the President's favorite relaxation music (mostly country and western, with a mixture of some contemporary tunes), he underwent daily workouts under the guidance of Chief Petty Officer Ellis Hendrix, a pleasant, proper, and highly skilled man who had served under Admiral Burkley at the Naval Dispensary. By December the improvement was significant. When four doctors examined him that month, they found that the therapeutic work that had largely been substituted for the continued procaine dosages had advanced his muscular development by at least fifty percent.[87]

Dr. Travell retained her title, but in fact Dr. Burkley had been informed that he was to have complete charge of the President's future medical care.[88] Carrying out a mission for the President, Ken O'Donnell had asked for her resignation. On Christmas Day the story that she was on her way out appeared in the press. According to her own account, that came as a complete surprise. Nor does it contain any conjecture as to how and why it originated. All she explains is that she confronted the President with the front-page item from *The Washington Post* and said, "I will do anything I can for you as long as you wish. But I am ready to leave at a moment's notice, if that is your pleasure," which drew his response that "I don't want you to leave. If I do, *I* will let you know." Then he had Salinger issue a denial.[89] Questioned in 1980 about the origin of that report, she firmly responded with "I have no idea."[90]

In reality Dr. Travell's position had long since undergone a transformation. At a "summit conference" of doctors who attended the President at Palm Beach just before Christmas, it was reaffirmed before all those present. The physicians included Dr. Wade, the surgeon who had operated on Kennedy's back; Dr. Burkley; Dr. Travell; and Dr. Kraus, who had been angered to learn about the consultation only inadvertently while en route to Palm Beach on *Air Force Two*. Neither Burkley nor Kraus, then, was well disposed toward her, and the President was still in pain and despairing of overcoming his problem. Wade first examined Kennedy privately. They then all gathered around his bed. In the presence of her colleagues, Dr. Travell was told that she would have nothing further to do with Kennedy's care, not in any way. Any recommended use of procaine would be at the direction of either Dr. Burkley or Dr. Kraus. The physiotherapist from New York, a short, decisive, athletic man who spoke with a heavy German accent, was very direct: he would either have complete control of his patient or would quit. And the patient, the President of the United States, agreed. The White House appointment calendar for that day stated that the Chief Executive was "recovering from a cold." "We always tried to hide the business of his back," explains Dr. Kraus. Dr. Travell denies that such a conference ever took place.[91]

Why did the President cling to her? Dr. Burkley was asked. "He didn't cling to her," he replied. "She sat. She wasn't stubborn; she had been appointed and she was going to stay."[92] But there was more to it than that. It was easier to let her stay on and retain her dignity, than to turn loose a discontented physician eager for revenge through her pen. She had served her function, and no harm would be done by permitting her to remain with the First Family in a rather innocuous position. She had always been helpful in the past, and it was also the humane thing to do. To the outside world Travell remained *the* White House physician, and the press accorded her that treatment. But most of her work was thereafter confined to a variety of related matters, including taking care of inquiries, such as the one from a Philadelphia physician who was concerned when he saw a newspaper photograph showing Kennedy at La Guardia Airport walking through a snowstorm without an overcoat. On June 14, 1963, long after the de facto change had been made, Rear Admiral George C. Burkley received formal orders assigning him to his duty as "physician to the President of the United States."[93] The papers then hastened to explain that Travell had not resigned. Her duties were to care for the pregnant First Lady.[94] "The President came up every weekend," she recalls; "spent three or four days at Hyannis Port, and I was with him half of every week, and our relationship never changed in any way as far as our personal involvement and personal relationships. . . . I was there practically straight through the whole summer until she lost the baby in August. I was there all summer and through August."[95]

Meanwhile the President's physical condition had improved dramatically. A better golfer than most people realized (and, during a period that followed Eisenhower's presidency, a greater enthusiast than he cared to have publicized), he began to take more liberties with his game. His physicians had, all along, worried that swinging the clubs might "precipitate something that we didn't want to have precipitated."[96] Insisting that he could play, at one point he took photographers out to see him hit golf balls. By analyzing his own motions and muscular contortions, John Kennedy was able to show off his condition by swinging a club without involving his back.[97]

The President's father was also playing golf when he felt the first signs of his own illness. On the Tuesday before Christmas of 1961, Joe Kennedy sat down on the fairway leading to the sixteenth hole of the Palm Beach Golf Club. He should not have been surprised. Repeatedly, he had been warned that he was a candidate for a stroke. Stubbornly, he had refused to take the anticoagulants that had been prescribed. Now, too, he resisted, preferring to blame his cold. But his appearance betrayed such assurances. An ambulance was called, and he was removed to St. Mary's Hospital, where the chaplain immediately administered the last rites of the Church to the patient. He was seventy-three, and his condition remained critical for many weeks.

The President had flown back from Palm Beach only that morning. He was still in the air when his father was stricken. Until Bobby finally called him with the news, he managed to meet with General Maxwell Taylor, receive his daily briefing from his military aide, confer with the Council of Economic Advisers, and spend an hour presiding over the National Security Council. Then, upon hearing Bobby's message, he looked stunned. "Dad's gotten sick," he told Pierre Salinger. By 5:45 P.M., together with his brother and sister Jean, he was on *Air Force One* headed for Florida. When he arrived, he didn't get to see the Ambassador, but met with a team of physicians. Told about the seriousness of the condition, he telephoned Dr. Travell to call in a vascular specialist from New York. Dr. William T. Foley then arrived on the same Air Force plane that brought Ted Kennedy.

Their father was conscious, but unable to speak. Dr. Foley examined him and told the President that his illness was grave. Not until John Kennedy's third visit to the bedside, which took place on the second day at St. Mary's, was the father able to recognize his son.[98] The Ambassador lived on, but barely: his right side was paralyzed, and the stroke had also left him speechless. The remainder of his life, in and out of rehabilitative institutions, and at Palm Beach and Hyannis Port, was dominated by a pathetic struggle to talk (he often thought he was communicating when only gibberish came from his mouth) and to walk. He also suffered from an attack of pneumonia, which required a tracheotomy to enable him to breathe, and from two cardiac arrests. When at last he finally managed his first steps, his son, the President, was dead.[99]

But his mind was sound. He constantly fought the imprisonment of his condition, and was largely assisted by Ann Gargan. Being on the sidelines had never suited him. On Friday afternoons he would sit watching the sky and wait for the helicopter that would bring his son from the White House for the weekend visit. "It really made a big difference in his life," said Bobby, who, like his older brother, would not outlive the father. "And then on Sunday afternoon, he'd take off and my father'd come out and see him leave in the helicopter."[100]

Long before the illness the Ambassador's previous backstage presence had been minimized. He had become less prominent in the daily lives of his two oldest surviving sons. Acquaintances noted that he was less part of their daily conversations. They loved, admired, and respected him. Jack was especially good at making him laugh by saying outrageous things, and he always liked to go on exchanging ideas with his father. Nevertheless the reality was that their relationship had changed. The shy, bookish, introspective second son had grown up, had overcome the force of his own nature and met the paternal demands. He had become the leader. "We're prehistoric," one of the Ambassador's friends, a newspaper executive, recalled him saying many times. "We're antediluvian in our points of view. They're leaving us behind. They're thinking in forward terms, and this is going to be the kind of philosophy that is going to prevail in this country."[101]

Joseph Kennedy's close involvement with his sons' careers had naturally brought him into contact with J. Edgar Hoover. Over the years the two men had enjoyed a mutual cordiality similar to the Ambassador's many other business relationships. Deep in the bureau's files were the titillating records, complete with the sound of Jack's voice, detailing the young man's liaisons with Inga Arvad. During those early wartime days the director had been amused by the adventures of the Ambassador's son. But this was something else. In the months after the older Kennedy's stroke, Hoover was receiving strong evidence that Judith Campbell, then in such frequent contact with the White House, was also a friend of two underworld figures, Sam Giancana of Chicago and John Rosselli of Los Angeles. In the early 1940s Inga had only been a suspected enemy agent, and Jack Kennedy an ensign in the Office of Naval Intelligence. Now Hoover was confronting something much more formidable. He could hardly ignore the possibility that the woman was a conduit between mobsters and the President. Over a year before the Profumo case startled the British; now, the President of the United States himself was in the middle of a potentially incendiary situation. The American counterpart of Dr. Stephen Ward was Frank Sinatra. Whatever may have been true of Kennedy's innocence of what was going on around him, associations with Sinatra and Campbell had to stop.

On March 22, 1962, Director Hoover went to the White House for a luncheon appointment with the President. Before that date, the presumed purpose of the meeting had been clarified in a memorandum Hoover had sent to both the attorney general and Ken O'Donnell. They were informed that a concentrated FBI investigation had shown that the President's friend, Judith Campbell, was in touch with John Rosselli. Rosselli was a middle-level Mafia figure who had been in and out of jail since his association with Al Capone in Chicago. Fifty-seven years old in 1962, he was a fashionably dressed, gray-haired, slight figure easily recognizable in Las Vegas gambling casinos. His connections included Frank Sinatra, who would later sponsor Rosselli for membership in the Friar's Club in Beverly Hills (only to be ultimately charged with conspiracy to cheat its members by using electronic devices during gin-rummy games).[102] Rosselli also had powerful colleagues. One of them was Sam Giancana, the "boss" of organized crime in Chicago. Before the age of twenty he had been arrested and rearrested in three murder investigations, and had served time for various other offenses. All told, he had been placed behind bars some sixty-three times.[103] He had been cited before the McClellan Rackets Committee, and Bobby Kennedy, who had been that group's chief counsel, had referred to Giancana in his 1960 book as "the gunman for the remnants of the Capone mob."[104] Even before the Kennedy administration took office, both hoodlums were involved in another enterprise. Having himself been recruited by former FBI agent Robert Maheu, Rosselli turned to Giancana. Senior CIA officials in the Eisenhower administration had approved the payment of $150,000 to mobsters to assassinate Cuban Premier Fidel Castro. Such was the universe of the President's friend, Judith Campbell. No wonder he could later commiserate with Profumo![105]

Nobody can be certain about the exact conversation that took place between the President and the director. Only one other person has claimed to have been with them, and that was Ken O'Donnell. O'Donnell has maintained that his boss and the director had no private conversation that day, or that the name of Judith Campbell ever came up. Afterward he remembered Kennedy telling him, "Get rid of that bastard. He's the biggest bore." Hoover was seeing "commies" under every bed.[106]

White House logs show that the last Kennedy–Campbell telephone conversation took place only a few hours later, strongly suggesting that the President quickly severed that relationship. Later he spurned the further company of Sinatra by staying clear of the singer's Palm Springs, California, home.[107] Hoover followed up his conversation with the President by asking the CIA's director of the office of security whether the agency would object to wiretap prosecutions because the "introduction of evidence concerning the CIA operation would be embarrassing to the Government." As the director probably anticipated, they did, thereby acting to safeguard against possible exposure of Giancana's and Rosselli's connection with the anti-Castro operation.[108]

Whether Hoover knew the precise details of the CIA–Mafia association when he met with the President is unknown. Nor did Kennedy himself betray any knowledge of the plans when he saw John McCone and Richard Helms on April 2.[109] But Hoover found out soon enough. A memorandum he sent on April 10 referred to "exposure of most sensitive information relating to the abortive Cuban invasion in April 1961," a reference to plans for doing away with Castro simultaneously. On May 7 the attorney general was briefed about the Maheu–Rosselli–Giancana plotting. As CIA General Counsel Lawrence Houston later recalled, the younger Kennedy's response was, "If you have seen Mr. Kennedy's eyes get steely and his jaw set and his voice get low and precise, you get a definite feeling of unhappiness."[110] Robert Kennedy was then given the misleading information that the operation had been disbanded. When he met with Hoover two days later, the attorney general explained that the CIA had been explicitly warned against such operations without prior Justice Department clearance. Hoover, according to his notes, was in full agreement. He also thought using someone like Giancana represented "horrible judgment." But for the record he included the additional confidential explanation that Bobby "well knew the 'gutter gossip' was that the reason nothing had been done against Giancana was because of Giancana's close relationship with Frank Sinatra who, in turn, claimed to be a close friend of the Kennedy family. The Attorney General stated he realized this and it was for that reason that he was quite concerned when he received the information from CIA about Giancana and Maheu."[111]

All this, however, touched only Jack Kennedy's private life-style and the administration's confidential dealings. The public knew nothing, and at that moment his political stock was extraordinarily high. Still, he could hardly have escaped self-consciousness when a reporter opened a presidential news conference, only two months after the Hoover visit, by starting a discussion about the proper handling of a current scandal involving a Washington manipulator, Billy Sol Estes. "Improprieties," said the President after some thought, "occur in a good many different kinds of life, whether it's labor, management, Government. Not all people are able to withstand these pressures. But we intend that the personnel of the United States Government will meet the highest ethical standards possible, and when they do not, action will be taken."[112]

No suggestions of wrongdoing ever brushed the President himself, and the massive popular support included representatives of the most skeptical community in American life, intellectuals. Implicit in creating such an alliance was an identification with a common humanistic reform view of the world, and no administration had ever worked as self-consciously to court their support. The President's symbolic role was strengthened by having a gala White House evening devoted to a performance by the cellist Pablo Casals, whose presence at the mansion was made more notable because it marked the end of his self-imposed silence in protest over the demise of Spanish democracy. In extending the invitation to Casals, Kennedy ignored an FBI check of the artist that branded him a supporter of every sort of identification he feared: admiration for the Castro revolution in Cuba and condemnation of American support of Franco and prevailing cold-war policies.[113] Such were the hazards of buying "culture." Five months after the Casals appearance Nobel prize winners of the Western Hemisphere—authors, artists, composers, scientists—were invited to dine in the Executive Mansion. It was one of the brightest of White House evenings. Kennedy's own greetings to the assemblage made the occasion even more notable. "I think," he told them, "this is the most extraordinary collection of talent, of human knowledge, that has ever been gathered together at the White House, with the possible exception of when Thomas Jefferson dined alone."[114] Less than two weeks later he offered another toast at a White House cultural affair, this time at a dinner honoring French Minister of Culture André Malraux. "I am very glad to welcome here some of our most distinguished artists," Kennedy said on that occasion. "This is becoming a sort of eating place for artists. But they never ask us out!"[115]

Nothing could have been more appealing. An American President was showing himself to cherish more than just politics and statesmanship. Intellectuals had finally found a kindred soul at 1600 Pennsylvania Avenue, perhaps the first since the days of Teddy Roosevelt and Woodrow Wilson. And Kennedy's popularity was building, bolstered by an image that transcended educational and economic lines. A recent Gallup poll had shown his performance winning a seventy-nine percent approval level. His political "capital" was abundant, and as long as that remained strong, the presidency could contemplate long-range objectives on its own timetable. Ultimately popular support would sway the Congress and cushion hard times.

Yet nobody was more conscious than Kennedy of the remaining hurdles. Only days after the Gallup survey had confirmed the persistence of overwhelming support, the organization released some other interesting findings. George Romney of Michigan, the Mormon Republican exemplar of moral rectitude, was ahead of the GOP's possible 1964 contenders in the level of "favorable" responses, with a powerful eighty-five percent. Nor did Kennedy miss the fact that Governor Rockefeller, who ranked second to Romney, was not only behind by a considerable distance but was thought of negatively by well over twice as many people.[116]

If the ways of the world were simple, the Republicans would pick Goldwater, but things had never come that easily to Jack Kennedy. As Charles Bartlett has recalled, "I don't think he ever thought he'd be lucky enough to get Barry Goldwater as his opponent."[117] Rockefeller was clearly a greater threat. He was strongly opposed by vital segments within his own party, but once past the Republican nominating convention he would make a powerful appeal to the great center of American politics, drawing far more Democrats than Goldwater ever could.

But so could Romney. "I always had the impression that he viewed George Romney as his stiffest [opponent]," Bartlett said. "I think he had a sort of sinister feeling that Romney would be there."[118] Bobby Kennedy later agreed that his brother was most concerned about Romney because the former automobile executive from Michigan had appeal to "God and Country and all of these matters," while Rockefeller had been weakened by his divorce and quick remarriage.[119] Even without knowing what was going on "backstairs" at the White House, the public might well fall for Romney's appeal to traditional American virtues. Also Kennedy began to see that, unlike Rockefeller, the Romney strength in the North could well be augmented by support from the South.[120] Forever conscious of his thin margins, Kennedy was a long way from feeling secure.

6

"Making the World Safe: Laos"

"I used to ask my brother each week about whether he liked the job," Bob Kennedy told an interviewer after it was all over. "And he always answered he did. During that period of time he'd say . . . what a fantastic job it would be if you didn't have the Russians."[1] It was also possible to note, as did John Fischer, that "While he was still trying to move in the furniture, in effect, he found the roof falling in and the doors blowing off."[2] But Kennedy never complained; he had asked for the challenges, and his appetite was satisfied. It was probably also true that, as President, he faced each situation with the fatalism implicit in his comment that "there is always inequity in life. . . . It's very hard in military or in personal life to assure complete equality. Life is unfair."[3]

His on-the-job training was very brief. Very quickly he learned that the world was even more complex than he had imagined. When he spoke at the University of California more than a year after his inauguration, the trumpets were gone from his rhetoric. He rejected the notion that "American power is unlimited, or that the American mission is to re-make the world in the American image." He spoke of a "free and diverse world," where it might be possible to "shape our policies to speed progress toward a more flexible world order."[4] That world view was consistent with the Jack Kennedy who had complained that too many school-children were still being taught an exaggerated concept of nationalism.[5] If the United States had a mission, and Kennedy thought it did, it was not necessarily to alter different societies so they would adhere to American concepts of democracy but to promote a more rational world order. Whereas Woodrow Wilson had wanted America to make the "world safe for democracy," John Kennedy, who was born the year of that pledge, decided that it ought to be made safe for diversity.

That meant harnessing the instruments of war. The continued suspension of atomic tests, a carry-over from Eisenhower's last years, could provide a wedge to force an opening toward arms limitations and the peaceful resolution of basic East–West differences. Those, after all, were the prerequisites for a satisfactory economic existence. Without the Kremlin's recognition of similar realities the mission was hopeless. Ironically "TRB" wrote in *The New Republic* that "No really great President gets 78 percent public support till he's dead. We trust Kennedy's burning desire to be 'great' will take care of this."[6] The comment, drawn from Kennedy's own *Profiles in Courage,* suited his own view of presidential leadership. He would have been profoundly disturbed to know that so many historians would later stress that his contribution to human existence was the extension of the cold war and the escalation of the arms race.

Kennedy had long-standing convictions about the hazards of unilateral action under circumstances unfavorable for military solutions. As a senator, in 1953 and 1954, he was forceful about French persistence in combating Indochinese anticolonialism; in 1957 he made an especially celebrated speech about the Algerian war, where, he charged, the French were also guilty of misplaced faith in military reconquest and pacification. In 1959 his direct reference was to American policy, the support then being given to the Chinese Nationalists in their determination to hold on to the offshore islands of Quemoy and Matsu. "To become bogged down in such a conflict, without allies, without the support of world opinion," he warned, "might well be a disaster far worse than any we have heretofore known."[7] His life would end, nevertheless, with an unresolved debate about how inevitable he had made the commitment of American forces to Indochina.

And it was Laos that became his test case. Not Cuba, not Berlin, not the new African states, or even the Middle East, but Laos, a landlocked hinterland in what had once been Indochina.[8] Its location in Southeast Asia resembled a jigsaw-puzzle piece that filled the void between China,

Cambodia, divided Vietnam, Thailand, and even a bit of Burma. When Kennedy met Eisenhower at Camp David in the immediate wake of the Bay of Pigs, he told the former president that losing Laos would imperil Thailand.[9] Of course, Kennedy was telling Eisenhower that he also shared his notion of the domino reaction in Southeast Asia. That remote, impoverished little kingdom, with its factional, ideological, tribal, and nationalistic loyalties, had become the playing field of Southeast Asia, a land less important to occupy than to deny to others.

Together with the question of arms limitations, Laos was one area where it seemed possible for common interests to provide a basis for a Soviet–American arrangement, and that could become a pattern for accommodations elsewhere. At the very least Laos might expose Russian intentions in an era when they were continually giving off alternating hot and cold signals. The CIA also reported that the "governments of the area tended to regard the Laotian crisis as a symbolic test of strength between the two major powers of the West and the Communist bloc."[10] Kennedy voiced that sentiment later when he toasted Souvanna Phouma at a White House luncheon with the statement that "the future not only of Laos but of a good deal of the rest of the world" depended on the resolution of that conflict.[11]

The situation gave Kennedy somewhat more maneuverability than did other hot spots. Unlike both Berlin and Cuba, not many American votes hinged on the outcome of rivalries in such an obscure place. "This is the end of nowhere," said an American official in Vientiane, the Laotian administrative capital. "We can do anything we want here because Washington doesn't seem to know it exists."[12]

That didn't mean it could be ignored. If Laos fell and took the other "dominoes" with it, and, like Eastern Europe, Cuba, or China, they came under some sort of Communist regime, the domestic political hazards would nevertheless be great. For still another Democrat to yield in Asia, especially in the wake of Eisenhower's creation of the Southeast Asia Treaty Organization (SEATO) with its protective clauses for Indochina, could easily encourage another "Who lost China?" debate.

Kennedy could hardly have forgotten those days, especially since he had been among the accusers. His education had since broadened. He knew that the ambitions of local potentates, landed interests, political naiveté, and the legacy of colonialism had made appropriate responses elusive. Both Moscow and Peking viewed such "emerging nations" as ideal recruits for future communization. Kennedy agreed with his British friend, David Ormsby-Gore, that the United States had been inept in staking its interests on corrupt right-wing dictators. Only a truly neutral coalition government made much sense in a place like Laos, and that also brought him close to the view that diplomacy to reduce local frictions was far preferable in an area where military commitments were already too great. But recognizing the circumstances does not necessarily make the choice simple. In this case Kennedy felt trapped by a political and military climate that had as its only clear consensus the blocking of communism and thwarting expansion of the "international conspiracy."

Trying to protect Laos from such evils had indeed been an objective of the Eisenhower administration. "Despite its remoteness," the former president later wrote, "we are determined to preserve the independence of Laos against a takeover backed by its neighbors to the north—Communist China and North Vietnam."[13] What he did not say was that the determination had long since taken the form of covert military operations. Laos became one of the earlier testing grounds for CIA covert actions. Under the Military Assistance Program some $300 million was spent to resist left-wing insurgency by the Pathet Lao. During subsequent hearings held in Washington it was reported that Laos had become the "only country in the world where the United States supports the military budget 100%." Nowhere else was the per capita outlay greater, a process that was in itself destructive because it intensified corruption and sharpened the contrasts between the abundance of goods available in Vientiane and the impoverishment of the provinces.[14]

The immediate objective was to keep from power Prince Souvanna Phouma and his plans for a neutral coalition government under his concept of national unity. That meant representation for the Pathet Lao rebels. American intelligence operations, money, and rigged elections had "saved" Laos from the prince twice before. A coalition regime that Souvanna Phouma had established with the aid of battlefield victories achieved by an obscure paratrooper, Kong-Le, served as a provisional government until the Eisenhower administration decided that the prince was too intransigent. "My political position has not changed since 1956," said Souvanna Phouma. "The United States is free to make its choice and if U.S. aid is not continued, the Lao Government will get it someplace else."[15] For the third time, in the fall of 1960, the United States used its leverage with the assistance of a blockade of Laotian imports imposed by nearby Thailand, which was under the dictatorship of Marshal Sarit Thanarit, a cousin of Souvanna Phouma's chief rival. That enabled General Phoumi Nosavan's forces to sweep through the Mekong Valley and capture the cities located at either end, Vientiane and Luang Prabang. On December 13 Prince Boun Oum was named as the head of a new government, and the United States quickly gave its recognition.[16]

Souvanna Phouma fled to Cambodia and Kong-Le rushed to the Pathet Lao. The Soviet Union, accordingly, stepped up its airlift of supplies to the antigovernment forces. Washington's achievement had been, as Bernard Fall wrote, to throw "into Communism's arms a great many people who essentially were *not* Communists . . . but who, by deliberate action on our side, were left with no alternative."[17]

All this helped make Souvanna's uneasy alliance with the Communists a self-fulfilling prophecy. With Kong-Le and the Pathet Lao now heavily aided by the Russians, the antigovernment coalition took the counteroffensive and captured key objectives in the vital Plain of Jars and threatened the Vientiane regime.[18] In turn that escalated the counterinsurgency activities by the U.S. Army's Special Forces.[19] This had been fully described to Kennedy before he appeared for his January 19 meeting with the outgoing President. "Whatever's going to happen in Laos, an American invasion, a Communist victory or whatever," Kennedy told Ted Sorensen, "I wish it would happen before we take over and get blamed for it."[20]

Even before Kennedy became President the State Department had agreed with the British suggestion for reviving the three-nation International Control and Supervisory Commission (ICC) for Laos that had come out of the cease-fire negotiated at Geneva in 1954.[21] But that was hardly more than a gesture; by itself it did nothing to change American policy. The main unresolved question was whether Washington would continue backing the Boun Oum/Phoumi regime as *the* legitimate government. Moreover the ICC was composed of India, Canada, and Poland. The Indians were "neutralists" and the Poles would obviously accommodate Moscow.

Once he had charge over the situation, Kennedy's inheritance left him with few choices. Going along with the Eisenhower policy seemed unfeasible, especially since the Phoumists were doing nothing to gain confidence that they were winning over the various Laotian groups, let alone the tribesmen from some of the more remote regions. The self-defeating aspects of past policy had become obvious. The only choice was how, then, to keep the country from falling under the control of the North Vietnamese without direct American intervention. Just letting it happen was unthinkable. Without any evidence of firm American resistance, he had few doubts that the Soviets would complete their penetration, and little would dissuade them from similar expectations elsewhere.

Despite the reasoning of the American ambassador in Vientiane, Winthrop Brown, that having Lao T-6s bomb the enemy would only invite military retaliation, CINCPAC (Commander in Chief, Pacific Admiral

Henry Felt) had advised that force should be built up starting "with ground-strafing sorties against Kong-Le/Pathet Lao/Viet Minh supply trains and dumps. Bombs should not be ruled out." Any subsequent retaliation by Communist bloc nations would then "fully expose them as the aggressor and is unlikely for that reason."[22] They continued to argue Phoumi's cause, advancing the proposition that, with proper support, he had the capacity to capture the Plain of Jars and, from there, protect the Mekong River.

"If it hadn't been for Cuba, we might be about to intervene in Laos," Kennedy told Arthur Schlesinger, Jr., in early May.[23] Sorensen also recalls Kennedy thanking God that the Bay of Pigs prevented an even more disastrous commitment in Asia.[24] Bobby Kennedy has also agreed that Cuba was the decisive factor.[25]

However, Schlesinger recalls that the post–Bay of Pigs deliberations did not "altogether exclude" from Kennedy's mind some kind of limited intervention.[26] But he also includes a comment by the President made at a luncheon with Walter Lippmann as early as March 20, nearly a month before the attempted landing in Cuba. "I don't see why we have to be more royalist than the king," Kennedy said that day. "India is more directly threatened than we are; and, if they are not wildly excited, why should we be?"[27] Too much may have been made, then, of how the presidential decision was shaped by events in the Caribbean.

Kennedy well understood how difficult it would have been to dispatch American troops across the Pacific without *first* doing something about Cuba.[28] The island nation had also become the most contentious topic of foreign policy debates.

Kennedy's only real recourse on Laos was to maneuver between what he was actually doing and what he appeared to be doing. All the while, diplomatic and military means had to be pursued to the limit. That also included convincing the Joint Chiefs that their military solutions were less applicable than they believed, and the congressional leaders had to confront similar truths. But while getting these points across to the military and the politicians, Kennedy had to convince the Russians that he *could* take the bolder step.

Back in 1958 Kennedy had talked about "Sputnik diplomacy, limited brush-fire war, indirect, non-overt aggression, intimidation and subversion, internal revolution," and his concern was strengthened by Khrushchev's "wars of national liberation" comments.[29] One of Kennedy's responses to the Soviet leader was to ask Major General Chester V. Clifton, his military aide, to compile whatever information he could gather about guerrilla warfare. Clifton soon found that the military manuals, however, were useless in the area of the type of warfare that had become increasingly characteristic.[30] Only gradually did the American military command begin to realize that subversive insurgency was a form of politico-military conflict rivaling the importance of conventional warfare. Essential for countering that threat were the kinds of social reforms that could gain the allegiance of the peasantry. The Eisenhower administration had been developing a plan for that purpose, and this was the one approved by Kennedy on January 28, 1961.[31]

While the situation in South Vietnam was not directly related to Laos, the relationship between the two was obvious. The Eisenhower administration, having installed Ngo Dinh Diem as president, had made a formal commitment to South Vietnam in 1954 after the partition at Geneva. Colonel Edward Lansdale, fresh from his heroics against Huk insurgents in the Philippines, had gone to Saigon as head of the American Military Assistance Advisory Group (MAAG) and had helped to consolidate the Diem regime.

Now Lansdale, a brigadier general, returned from a secret trip to South Vietnam to report on new findings. The general pointed out that the failure of a November coup had probably given the Americans a reprieve. Had it been successful, he wrote, "I believe that a number of highly selfish and mediocre people would be squabbling among themselves for power while the Communists took over. The Communists," he added, "will be more alert to exploit the next coup attempt." Most emphatically General Lansdale also stressed that the U.S. could demonstrate its support for Diem as well as help the Saigon regime command the peasantry by adopting an immediate program to implement social, economic, and political reforms along with military programs. Failure to take such remedial action would leave the regime extremely vulnerable before a major springtime Vietcong offensive.[32]

The President digested the lengthy report, then looked up at Walt Rostow and said, "This is the worst one we've got, isn't it?" Lansdale's account, both pessimistic and sobering, strengthened the realization that the Laotian efforts could not be divorced from the work of stabilizing the South Vietnamese situation. Kennedy was sufficiently impressed by its reasoning to suggest that it would make "an excellent article for something like *The Saturday Evening Post*" under, of course, somebody else's signature.[33] In February an item for the NSC agenda explained that "We need to develop a doctrine and a policy for the deterrence of guerrilla warfare and begin to apply it soon in concrete cases."[34] Rostow then took the lead in getting the Pentagon and the bureaucracy to pursue

Kennedy's interest in antiguerrilla warfare.[35] A firm believer in military strength, Rostow nevertheless advised Sorensen that the President's foreign aid message "should underline the fact that the struggle of these hard pressed areas against Communist pressure can never be wholly a military struggle. Efforts at reform and development are a legitimate part of the struggle to maintain their independence against Communist pressure," and that by itself should be no "excuse for deferring thought and effort on development problems."[36]

In mid-February the administration began negotiations with Diem. There was an offer of troops, which the South Vietnamese president rejected. But under the counterinsurgency program there was also pressure for him to accommodate some of the political leaders in his cabinet and to strengthen the authority of the National Assembly. Other reforms were also advised, all aimed at enabling him to appeal to the peasants. Once digesting the counterinsurgency concept fully, Kennedy created a unit known as "Jungle Jim," which became the predecessor for the Air Force's antiguerrilla warfare strategy.[37] But nothing better illustrates the President's own infatuation with the concept than his overruling the Pentagon's objections to establish a separate, elite command for the Special Forces, the Green Berets. Here, before the Bay of Pigs, was the genesis of Kennedy's later creation of a new National Security Council committee that would be designated as Special Group (Counterinsurgency) to operate in such specific areas as Laos.[38]

Starting in mid-February negotiations opened with Diem to implement the Kennedy plan. That resulted in some $42 million in additional assistance to an aid program already getting $220 million. The American suggestions for reforms inspired constructive-sounding decrees from the presidential palace, but nothing changed.

Michael Forrestal, who worked on Bundy's NSC staff, later went to Saigon with Roger Hilsman and met with Diem. He found the Vietnamese president to be an intellectual "one-way street." Diem could talk for hours and hours and displayed remarkable knowledge of the countryside. He was proud of having walked across the entire land, both from north to south and east to west. If he thought something was in his own interest, he was immovable. Basically an aristocrat, a mandarin, he deigned to consult only notables. He was obviously under the strong influence of his brother, Ngo Dinh Nhu and his sister-in-law, Madame Nhu (soon to be known to Americans as the "dragon lady" of South Vietnam). He remained optimistic about power ultimately attracting the loyalty of the villagers. There was, he held, no real need for reforms; full power and force to protect the peasants would suffice. To Diem the war was strictly an effort directed by Hanoi. Forrestal considered him the strongest figure he had ever met.[39]

Kennedy had yet to appreciate how serious an obstacle Diem was, but, in those early days of his administration, his first priority was securing Laotian stability. He was not ready to yield on the Boun Oum/Phoumi government, but neither was he going to betray indifference. He was far from convinced about the wisdom of sending American troops, but he would not let Moscow miscalculate his determination.

At his first news conference the President expressed his desire for "an independent country not dominated by either side but concerned with the life of the people within the country."[40] He called Brown home from the Vientiane embassy and quizzed the ambassador in a manner that clearly indicated a preference for some kind of neutralization. Ambassador Llewellyn Thompson returned from his post in Moscow and began a round of conferences with principal administration officials, the President, and two of his predecessors, George F. Kennan and Charles Bohlen. On March 8 the President remarked at his news conference that he hoped to "achieve a result which will bring stability to Laos, permit it to maintain its independence, and bring peace to the area, and self-determination."[41]

Kennedy followed the lead of his military planners by going along with a proposal to create a neutral commission consisting of Cambodia, Burma, and Malaya. In effect that would have solicited recognition of the Phoumist's legitimacy while rallying world opinion against Soviet intervention. King Savang Vatthana of Laos was told to announce the proposal as his own, and Washington promptly went to work trying to round up support. Success came from two likely quarters, New Zealand and Australia, but resistance came from a more vital sector, Prince Sihanouk of Cambodia, who was much more interested in having the international community pursue agreement on a conference he had previously suggested. He announced that the plan was unacceptable because it meant recognizing Boun Oum.[42]

Could the American President have it both ways? That seemed less and less likely as Kennedy resisted either a vulnerable coalition or intervention. Without Moscow's agreement on the lesser of two evils he would have no choice. If need be, committing American forces would have been inevitable—at that moment easier than acquiescence. At an important strategy meeting in early March he agreed that military preparations had to be advanced, but he would not go beyond that.[43] His roving ambassador, Averell Harriman, meanwhile, delivered a presidential note to Prime Minister Nehru of India, and another was sent to the representative of the People's Republic of China through their envoy in Warsaw. The message was simple: Laos would not be abandoned even if American forces had to intervene. The United States was prepared to accept a truly neutral Laos, but the Russians would first have to stop their airlift.[44]

But the military advisers themselves were almost as confused as conditions on the Plain of Jars. Roswell Gilpatric remembered how the President, who had yet to appreciate their own uncertainty, convened "all five of the military chiefs . . . and each one had a different point of view, and he just literally and figuratively threw up his hands and walked out of the room, it was so discouraging."[45] Secretary of War Eugene Zuckert found that "when we went to the White House and met with the President, he got about seven different recommendations." The whole business hardly seemed worth the fight. There was little apparent zest for full-scale war in Laos. Walt Rostow, who had fewer reservations about intervention as a possible option, recalled that "they were wrong about the situation on the ground; they were wrong in the structure of their planning; they were wrong about Communist logistical capabilities, which they grossly overrated."[46] There was advice to hold the Mekong River Valley from the Thailand side of the border. Others, including Zuckert, proposed air strikes. "If you were to convince the Thais and Sarit that you really were still on his side, you had to do something, and you had to do something affirmative," he explained.[47] To General Lyman Lemnitzer, the chairman of the Joint Chiefs of Staff, and also General George H. Decker, the Army chief of staff, doing "something affirmative" was foolhardy without being prepared to use nuclear weapons to "guarantee victory," together with the realization that such open American warfare could only force counteraction by the Russians and the Chinese. We could, additionally, then find ourselves bogged down up north, in a reopened Korean War.[48]

That was not how Kennedy was about to handle matters. By questioning the military about logistics, by pointing out the flimsiness of certain assumptions, including how little they were able to take into account the potential effect of indigenous diseases, the President emphasized the weaknesses of their arguments without confronting them with blanket White House rejection. He was also preserving his options because retreating from the enemy was no way to inaugurate the New Frontier. His difficulty with the military, however, also presaged a situation that, as a contemporary journalist observed, was creating "a breakdown of communication between the political and the military sides of the government, and this would contribute largely to the failure of Kennedy's next venture."[49]

But he had less and less reason for confidence in General Phoumi's ability to keep the Boun Oum government afloat. Their entire military outlook seemed dubious. Laos was a nation of elephants, parasols, and not much zest for the more civilized notions of killing to win. As a military ally, Ken Galbraith wrote to the President from New Delhi, "the entire Laos nation is clearly inferior to a battalion of conscientious objectors from World War I."[50] Kennedy and the Joint Chiefs had banked on Phoumi to hold the Plain of Jars and the major connecting highway. But leftist forces managed to hold firm on the strategic plain and, without much apparent difficulty, bisected the main north-south road, threatening the royal capital at Luang Prabang. Government troops were near panic, and the increased number of American advisers seemed to be having little effect.[51] Clearly it was getting harder for Kennedy to continue backing the Phoumists. Even their will to fight was in doubt; Washington's gamble was obviously misplaced.

If the American clients in Laos had little appetite for fighting, it seemed to Kennedy that Moscow would have less. His senior Kremlinologists, Thompson in Russia and Charles Bohlen in the State Department, doubted that Khrushchev wanted to flirt with American power. They thought that he was also worried about keeping out the Chinese, but that premise had to be secured by convincing the Soviets that he would not hesitate to move in with force to protect the Phoumist government. For all three reasons, then—political, diplomatic, and military— Kennedy embraced a hard line that he was convinced would not lead to military action.

He said nothing about military moves, but newsmen heard about rumblings in the Pacific. He was asked about "reports that some portion of our Navy, some portions of our Marines, have been alerted and are moving toward that area," but, rather than a flat denial of the point, he emphasized his hope for "a peaceful solution."[52]

Military options had been thoroughly discussed some forty-eight hours earlier, and some of the arguments were unnerving. Walt Rostow wanted troops moved to the Thailand side of the Mekong, poised to cross into Laos at a moment's notice. Admiral Arleigh Burke objected; that would only provoke massive North Vietnamese intervention. Instead the Joint Chiefs suggested something much more overwhelming. At least sixty thousand American troops should be sent in with the warning that they would be supported even if it meant getting into a nuclear war.

When congressional leaders were consulted, both by the vice-president and Dean Rusk, it became obvious that even those who had displayed the greatest bravado in public had no real taste for military action. At a coffee hour with the legislators Kennedy listened but made no commitments. He didn't have to. The sense of nonintervention was clear. Foreign Relations Committee Chairman J. William Fulbright later added the thought to the President that "the extent to which you might be willing to go in defending Laos could possibly be influenced by the stability in Viet-Nam. It would be embarrassing, to say the least, to have Viet-Nam collapse just as we are extended in Laos."[53]

Meanwhile the strategy of warning Khrushchev that we *could* and *were willing* to respond militarily governed the deployment of American combat forces toward the area. Just as Rostow had suggested, five hundred Marines were flown to the west bank of the Mekong, on the Thailand side. The U.S.S. *Midway* sailed for the Gulf of Siam while the Seventh Fleet moved into the China Sea. Bases adjacent to Laos were provisioned and further fortified. The two regiments of the 3rd Marine Division on Okinawa, together with Marine Air Group 16, the 2nd Airborne Battle Group of the 503rd Infantry Combat Team, and the 1st Special Forces Group, were alerted for action and prepared for an emergency airlift into Laos on C-130 turboprop transports. Khrushchev was given a full accounting.[54] Having revealed his military hand, Kennedy turned to diplomacy.

The following Monday he received a visitor from Moscow, Andrei Gromyko. They sat together on a bench in the Rose Garden, and the President warned against miscalculating American determination to act. Gromyko seemed more receptive than Rusk had found him a week earlier, leaving Kennedy with some hope for movement toward negotiations.[55] That same day, however, on the other side of the world, with Rusk in attendance, the SEATO partners offered less encouragement. Only Thailand, Pakistan, and the Philippines were ready to support Kennedy's threat of intervention by contributing troops. Especially strong opposition to the idea came from the French. The SEATO communiqué hoped that negotiations could achieve "a united, independent and sovereign Laos" rather than "neutrality." Disappointed but not surprised, Kennedy tried to compensate by sending Moscow a much stronger note.[56] Khrushchev, of course, was convinced that Laos would "fall into our laps like a ripe apple" without the need for war. He also then indicated that he accepted at least the principle of a British proposal, but that was still short of agreeing to a cease-fire as a prerequisite to an international conference.[57]

During that period the American President had his first face-to-face meeting with the British Prime Minister, Harold Macmillan. The differences between them were largely superficial. The most obvious was

Macmillan's twenty-four-year advantage. He was also leader of Britain's Conservative Party. American Democrats, however, differed mainly in their accents and less in their ideology from those who, in England, were at the center or even a bit to the right. Kennedy, in fact, was temperamentally closer to most British Conservatives than to the Labourites; he was more a part of their world. Macmillan's Edwardian manner did, however, make him somewhat intimidating to the younger man, and Kennedy wanted to know about the correct protocol for greeting his English visitor. He was encouraged to begin with formality. Then when the relationship had been established, Macmillan could simply be called "Mr. Prime."[58]

Of course the process was helped by Kennedy's Anglophilia. While Joe Kennedy had concluded his ambassadorship so disastrously that he was virtually anathema to the British, Jack's infatuation with Churchill and English history and literature had strengthened his identification. Especially through Kathleen, but even before her marriage to a British nobleman, he had become enticed by London society. No foreign country had become less foreign to Jack Kennedy. There was the additional, and obvious, point that Macmillan had also gotten his own fill of the seamier side of politics. Not much ice remained to be broken.

The first session came right after Kennedy's dramatic news conference on Laos and while American troops were being deployed in Southeast Asia. Kennedy had taken his usual weekend away from Washington. That Sunday he also flew from Palm Beach to the Boca Chica Naval Air Station at Key West for an impromptu meeting with Macmillan. Since the Prime Minister was touring the Caribbean before a scheduled visit to Washington and the SEATO meeting was due for Bangkok the next day, it was the right time for a brief talk.

The Prime Minister hesitated about endorsing Laotian intervention. He feared "being sucked into these inhospitable areas without a base, without any clear political or strategic aims and without any effective system of deploying armed forces or controlling local administration."[59] English apprehension was compounded by the specter of American intervention inevitably following along the lines of massive military schemes they had heard from the mouths of John Foster Dulles and Admiral Radford; they could hardly have forgotten Operation Vulture and the proposed, but never materialized, Dien Bien Phu strike. Only three years before, Marines had waded onto the beaches of Lebanon in another dubious enterprise. If going along with such adventurism was the price of alliance, with its potential provocation of big-power differences, the British intended to review matters more carefully.[60]

On this point Kennedy mollified the Prime Minister, but not entirely, because the Briton remained to be convinced that sending in troops was a sensible option. Macmillan did agree to grant diplomatic support and contribute one contingent that was stationed in Malaya. When the inevitable communiqué was issued after their three-hour meeting, that point was omitted. The stress was laid on their vital exchange of views before the SEATO discussions, and on their agreement that Moscow's explicit backing of the British proposals was the most likely route to peace and neutrality.[61]

Their Washington meetings came on April 6 and 8. The two men and their staffs talked during three separate sessions for a total of nearly eleven hours. Meanwhile the SEATO rejection of unified action became known. Events of the following weeks substantiated the denials of American military-aid officials that the Laotian problem was primarily caused by a North Vietnamese invasion. Soviet supplies were being flown in and trucked to help the Pathet Lao, but Kennedy himself denied that the process was accelerating. Obviously matters were far more complex than the propaganda portrait of sovereign people being overwhelmed by aggressors.[62] Such Laotian realities brought the President closer to the Prime Minister's position.

He also knew that countering the Pathet Lao with overt American force would only provoke a greater flow from North Vietnam. But, having advertised the war as an example of Soviet aggression, having gone before the American people with visualizations of expanding red terrain, how could he reverse his stand? How could the powerful United States decide that Laos had suddenly become unimportant? There was also the very real problem that Premier Boun Oum and Phoumi Nosavan had, like Syngman Rhee before them, become American clients and would use every device to exploit the notion that effective resistance of "invasion" required help from Washington.

The President was with Macmillan on Thursday and Saturday. That Friday he granted an off-the-record interview to Chalmers Roberts of *The Washington Post*. He told the correspondent of his certainty that the country would support a decision to go into Laos. He betrayed some sensitivity that it would be viewed by opponents as a "Democratic war," but, according to Roberts's notes, he "said that if he had to go in and if it meant he would be around only one term, nonetheless he would do it. All that was said in a highly convincing manner."*[63] Off-the-record

---

*The President also told Roberts that Eisenhower's plan to strike at Cuba had been vetoed. While a CIA operation had been percolating for some time, he said, the government wants to "keep out of this."

or not, Kennedy was taking no chances. He could not risk any hint that the administration was not fully prepared for a tough stand. When he saw Macmillan the next day, the emphasis was very different.

Kennedy told Macmillan that political pressures for military intervention were great. Doing nothing while Communists were gaining would renew the old charges of "sellout" and "appeasement" that had plagued Truman and Acheson. Macmillan could be helpful. He could send a personal and confidential letter to General Eisenhower, explaining why the military option was not really feasible. Placating the former president might not get his actual support; nor would it eliminate damaging accusations, but it might at least temper the debate and mollify public statements likely to come from more moderate Republicans.

Kennedy's request for help with Ike reflected his own anxiety. Laos, of all places, was immediately the most sensitive. That had been Eisenhower's targeted crisis area, and there can be no question that Kennedy had interpreted his January 19 meeting with the outgoing President as a challenge. From that moment he never lost sight of Eisenhower's influence, playing on the General's sense of duty to be a good bipartisan on diplomatic matters but, at the same time, sensitive about his continuing presence. Bob Kennedy later explained that Ike never did come through with helpful advice. "I think he always felt that Eisenhower was unhappy with him," said the attorney general, "that he was so young and that he was elected President and . . . feeling that Eisenhower was important and his election was so close that he went out of his way to make sure that Eisenhower was brought in on more matters and that Eisenhower couldn't hurt the administration by going off on a tangent and that's why he made such an effort over Eisenhower."[64] Kennedy often sent someone like John McCone shuttling to Gettysburg to keep the General informed. An early accommodation of Ike's desires was the decision of the Kennedy brothers not to bring charges against Eisenhower's former assistant, Sherman Adams (who had been forced to resign in 1958 for "indiscretions" involving acceptance of gifts and favors) for, as Bobby privately noted, having received "more than $150,000 in cash over the period of about five years" from industrialist Bernard Goldfine.[65] Eisenhower, of course, was also motivated by his own concept of bipartisanship in foreign matters, so that it was true—at least publicly —that every time Kennedy got into hot water, Ike gave his support, which is what Kennedy wanted.[66]

Having Eisenhower on his side on Laos was a major Kennedy consideration. On the day after his meeting with the President, Macmillan tried to advance that need by sending the following confidential letter to the General:

It was very good to hear your voice over the telephone on Friday. I was very sorry that we could not meet.

As you will have seen from the Communiqué, we have had good talks and covered a lot of ground.

We discussed a lot of problems, but we naturally spent a good deal of time on Laos. I know you feel very strongly that we must keep Laos out of Communist hands. So do I. So, I know, does the new President. But I need not tell you what a bad country this is for military operations. Indeed, I doubt whether we could save the situation by military action; and I am sure that, even if we could, the cost in men and money would be absurdly high, to say nothing of the difficulties of Asian opinion. I am sure, therefore, that we ought to go all out for a political settlement, if we can get one; and I believe that by political action we have a chance to make the country a neutral pad between Thailand and the Communists.

As I understand it, President Kennedy is under considerable pressure about "appeasement" in Laos. I quite see why this should be so: we have not forgotten the lessons of history. I should however be very sorry if our two countries became involved in an open-ended commitment on this dangerous and unprofitable terrain. So I would hope that in anything which you felt it necessary to say about Laos you would not encourage those who think that a military solution in Laos is the only way of stopping the Communists in that area. . . .[67]

The situation in Southeast Asia temporarily receded into the background when the Bay of Pigs crisis broke. Ken Galbraith thought that viewing the Cuban affair from the embassy in New Delhi was seeing the situation from the "worst station." The United States had just shattered the principle of nonintervention, and that was a "most important force in the unpowerful part of the world, where it is naturally regarded as a vital protection." The Indian press was doing everything possible to make the situation appear even worse than it was, and Prime Minister Nehru was under considerable pressure to further discomfort Washington.[68] When Galbraith later reconsidered Southeast Asia, he faulted Kennedy for overreacting to how "many votes were affected by what happened in Laos."[69]

But, as Galbraith candidly acknowledged, that was hindsight. That was not how the world, and all the domestic implications, appeared to Jack Kennedy at the time. The Congo seemed to be creating another cavity for Soviet infiltration; the Berlin front remained vulnerable to a momentary move from the east; Moscow had won some glory in the days before the Bay of Pigs, when Cosmonaut Yuri Gagarin completed an orbital flight in less than two hours; and now the guardian of the "free world," the colossus of the West, was reduced to salvaging its pawns from Cuban beaches. Kennedy never doubted that Laotian neutrality was only slightly less obnoxious than a Pathet Lao victory. Arthur Krock, after meeting with the President in early May, noted his acknowledgment that "a lot of people will complain about the Communist representation that will probably occur in a 'neutralist' government in Laos, if that should become attainable. But we have no better alternative there."[70] Only a few days earlier Krock received a letter from Eisenhower's chairman of the Atomic Energy Commission, John McCone, which expressed the view of more than just a parochial minority. "This is quite a departure from the efforts of the prior administration and most particularly Mr. Dulles," wrote McCone. "Neutralism seems to spell ultimate Communist domination by one means or another."[71] Weighing these developments, and the realities of his own impotence in dealing with the situation, Kennedy privately wished the world would permit the kind of jingoistic coup that was called for by the conservative *National Review*. "What is crucial," wrote James Burnham, "is that we should *somewhere*, in *some* theater on *some* vital issue, make a stand of unconditional firmness: that we should strike a blow against the enemy. That blow will reverberate around the world, and will mark, or could mark, the decisive turn."[72]

The McCones and the Burnhams were ready to assume that a "neutralist" Laos was but a wedge for an eventual Communist take-over, and Kennedy was not sure they were wrong. For as long as possible he had tried to arrange a coalition government without Souvanna Phouma, but the desirable was no longer possible. The Phoumist government was using unfounded allegations about a Communist invasion from North Vietnam as bait for continued American help. Soviet supplies were being airlifted in from Hanoi, but U.S. military-aid officials in Vientiane were finding themselves unable to convince Boun Oum's people that the material assistance had no broader implications.[73]

Although Kennedy told his press conference on April 20 that he hoped Moscow would soon agree to a cease-fire, it would have been wrong to infer that that would be sufficient to control the battlefield situation. As in Germany the Russians were still pressing the line that the issues had to be resolved by the Laotians themselves. But the risk of that sort of outcome was hardly more congenial to Washington than to Moscow. "The fall of Laos will have a profound effect throughout the area and will inevitably incline these countries toward either neutralism or accommodations to the Communists," advised Lyndon Johnson's military aide.[74] On the battlefield itself, the Pathet Lao were launching powerful attacks at all vital points controlled by the Royal Laotians. The Phoumists were melting rapidly, and the situation was serious enough for people like Burnham and McCone to urge a strong American military stand.

At dawn on the twenty-sixth, Military Assistance Advisory Group headquarters in Vientiane sent a cable to CINCPAC warning that the government forces were "on the ropes" because the enemy had taken positions enabling them to grab "any of the major population centers now held by the FAL [Laotian Armed Forces]." If they took advantage of their capability, nothing could stop them short of open U.S. or SEATO intervention backed by B-26s.[75] Before that day was over, Ambassador Winthrop Brown cabled the State Department for formal authority to authorize air strikes to deprive the enemy of key objectives. The request was being made, said Brown, although "I realize that such action would blow whole cease-fire negotiations wide open: torpedo conference and most likely involve immediate intervention US/SEATO forces, but see no alternative if enemy presses beyond limits indicated above."[76] Before that night was over, the Joint Chiefs alerted CINCPAC to be prepared to move against North Vietnam, and possibly even southern China.[77]

That potential crisis point became the basis for Kennedy's decisive commitment to Southeast Asia. Distaste for open military action, as in the Bay of Pigs, did not imply backing away from force and acceptance of a purely political arrangement. He was ready to move toward negotiations aiming at a coalition government. But, at the same time, the objective remained to salvage Laos from Communist domination, or even from a regime that would have a "neutralist" influence. That meant covert measures, and therein was the continuation of the fine line between Kennedy's political objectives and the solutions of those who favored military action. Such differences between the President and the military, especially after he had heard their own somewhat incoherent solutions, were perhaps as significant as the Cuban situation in promoting his own skepticism of their expertise.[78]

At a stormy NSC meeting on the twenty-seventh of April, Kennedy got an earful of how force could save Southeast Asia. Bobby Kennedy later recalled how, at that session, "everybody was in favor of . . . sending troops in Laos."[79] Admiral Harry Felt wanted his Pacific command empowered to protect the Mekong Valley on a limited basis. Admiral Burke, who, along with Air Force Chief of Staff General Thomas White, remained confident of a military solution, suggested trying SEATO Plan

#5. That involved unlimited intervention in the main cities along the supply route running through the valley.[80]

The younger Kennedy, interviewed three years later, recalled his brother's impatience at that military prescription. "Well, now, first," he remembered that the President asked, "how will they get in there?"

"They're going to land at these two airports," Burke replied.

"How many will be able to land?" the President wanted to know.

"Well," came the reply, "if you have perfect conditions you can land a thousand a day."

"How many troops of the Communists are in the surrounding area?" Kennedy asked. About three thousand, the President was told, which prompted him to wonder aloud about how long it would take the enemy to bring in from five to eight thousand. When told that four more days would be needed, he asked the chief of naval operations, "Now, what's going to happen if on the third day you've landed three thousand men and then they bomb the airport? And then they bring up five or six thousand more, what's going to happen? Or if they land two thousand and they bomb the airport?" The admiral left no doubt that, in that case, an atomic bomb would have to be dropped on Hanoi.[81]

Some solution!

Other than his own probing the only significant dissent came from Chester Bowles. The undersecretary's doubts about military responses had long since given the military men a sense of *déjà vu*. But with Rusk absent while trying to arrange a diplomatic agreement to move toward a conference at Geneva, Bowles was in a position to speak for State. He had no more reticence than before about making his feelings known, and that upset the department's deputy undersecretary, U. Alexis Johnson, a career Foreign Service officer and strong advocate of America's need to assume international policing responsibilities.

Johnson was too much of a career man to be casual about protocol. When the President called on him, he responded strongly about willingness to use military power as the best way to avoid actually having to go to war. He argued that holding the Mekong Valley part of Laos would be the most effective way to protect Thailand and the rest of Southeast Asia. The President listened to Johnson, as to Bowles, without commenting. But it was obvious, Johnson reminisced, "that he was deeply disturbed that he was exposing a body of Americans to a situation in which he might have to take very extreme measures to protect them."[82]

At that meeting, however, the essentials came down to the oral presentation by Roswell Gilpatric of his Laotian Task Force report, which the President had ordered only one week earlier. The examination, coming at a time when the Laotian situation was at its most critical point, was undertaken by an interdepartmental group. "As far as current problems," Gilpatric has explained, "the emphasis was all on Laos. They were almost overpreoccupied with Laos to the exclusion of everything else."[83] And little wonder: the most underscored point of the Task Force draft was that "U.S. objectives in Vietnam will depend largely on effectively blocking the land corridors in Laos through which much of the Communist support to the Viet Cong passes." The Viet Cong had been making significant gains through a "program of infiltration, subversion, sabotage and assassination designed to achieve the destruction of Diem's government. It was all part of a Communist "master plan" for conquering Southeast Asia. Hard-core Vietcong Communists had increased from forty-four hundred in early 1960 to an estimated twelve thousand, and the average number of violent incidents per month was averaging 650. Even more alarming, "58% of the country is under some degree of Communist control, ranging from harassment and night raids to almost complete administrative jurisdiction in the Communist 'secure areas.' " The American objective of creating "a viable and increasingly democratic society in South Vietnam and to prevent Communist domination of the country" required a counterinsurgency plan that safeguarded pro-Western "neutrality" through continuing CIA operations within Laos.[84] When interviewed later, Gilpatric implied that the Defense study had not much choice about the acceptance of the counterinsurgency feature, explaining that not until then did his department have "very much of a handle" about the CIA use of Meo tribesmen in Laos and the Montagnards in South Vietnam.[85] A future director of the agency who was a CIA agent in South Vietnam has written that "Thus the task of meeting Hanoi's pressure in the area would have to be undertaken by CIA's tribal friends, if at all—and the Kennedys had no doubt that it had to be undertaken."[86]

The President acted despite the qualms of key aides. Not only did Bowles dissent, but Mac Bundy, Sorensen, and Dave Bell, whose Budget Department had to be concerned about funding covert operations through the cover of foreign aid funds, all urged the President to approve only the "internal security effort to save Vietnam." Sorensen argued that the surreptitious plan was not terribly realistic because to "the extent that this plan depends on the communists being tied down in Laos or lacking further forces, on our blocking land corridors through which communist support flows, or on our obtaining effective anti-infiltration action from Laos, Cambodia and the Laotian negotiations, the outcome is highly doubtful."[87] Moreover, even before that session was over, the

President summoned congressional leaders. To a man they opposed sending American troops into Laos.[88]

Between that Thursday and the following Tuesday there were three more full-dress NSC meetings, and it was during that period that diplomacy appears to have won out over military action. The British and Russians had already appealed for a cease-fire, but little had changed on the battlefield itself. It was also unclear that a truce could be implemented and policed. Both Galbraith and Averell Harriman sought Prime Minister Nehru's help in winning over the Chinese and the Russians to acceptance of a reconstituted ICC at Geneva.[89] At the UN efforts were also made to convince the British and French, among others, to back cease-fire initiatives by India, which headed the ICC. That matter almost certainly came up on Friday, when Kennedy's visit to Herbert Hoover and Douglas MacArthur at the Waldorf-Astoria included a luncheon with Stevenson and Hammarskjöld.[90] When he returned to Washington at midnight, after his speech to Chicago Democrats earlier that evening, he caught a few hours of sleep before Saturday morning's meeting. Dean Rusk, dominating that discussion, supported limited military actions to demonstrate America's commitment but opposed large-scale operations. Even he conceded, however, the spill-over effect on other nations if Laos were not defended, and Secretary of Defense McNamara warned that giving up there would inevitably mean we would have to attack North Vietnam.[91] Going in with full force had clearly not been foreclosed.

But the breakthrough came just as the military was getting harder to contain. In Vientiane, Ambassador Winthrop Brown advised General Phoumi to accept a cease-fire arranged by Prince Sihanouk of Cambodia. At the same time, Souvanna Phouma called for a meeting between the three concerned parties—Boun Oum's Royal Laotian government, the Pathet Lao, and Souvanna's neutralists—to prepare for a cease-fire and the formation of a provisional government, together with a Laotian delegation to the fourteen-nation conference at Geneva.[92] In New Delhi, Galbraith noted in his journal that that Sunday had been spent "from morning to night trying to arrange a cease-fire in Laos. This morning, to my delight, there is indication that we may have one."[93] At Glen Ora, the President heard that the Communists had agreed to meet with the military representatives of the government in Vientiane. He cut short his weekend and returned to Washington, where he had a ninety-minute meeting with Rusk and the military advisers.[94] While presiding over an NSC meeting late that Monday afternoon, Kennedy agreed that no final decisions would be taken on further actions pending the outcome of the cease-fire situation.[95] That same day the cease-fire was apparently a reality, and the ICC soon afterward confirmed "a general and obvious discontinuance of hostilities." On May 12 the Geneva Conference began, the start of a frustrating, erratic process that did not end until July 23 of the following year, when Souvanna Phouma's coalition government was formally accepted.[96]

Nevertheless the Kennedy administration, relieved at not having to go into Laos, worked to prevent the creation of a "neutralist" government. Rusk had advised the President that the best hope was for "Laos to become a loose confederation of somewhat autonomous strong men. Given the military capability of the Pathet Lao, a centralized government led by a coalition would tend to become a communist satellite. Even partition would be a better outcome than unity under leadership responsible to the communists."[97]

Four days after the cease-fire was announced, Senator Fulbright followed an early-evening meeting with the President by giving reporters the impression that Laotian pressures were forcing the consideration of stationing American troops in South Vietnam.[98] National Security Action Memorandum 2425, which came out of that morning's NSC meeting, recorded that "efforts should be made to reassure [Marshal] Sarit and Diem that we are not abandoning Southeast Asia." Also noted was the President's view that Sarit could be told that consideration was being given to the inclusion of American troops with SEATO forces to be stationed in Thailand, their training to be dependent on developments during or after the forthcoming fourteen-nation Geneva Conference.[99] A few hours later, at his press conference, Kennedy announced that he was sending Vice-President Johnson on a "special fact-finding mission to Asia." When a reporter asked about Fulbright's indication that troops might follow, the President would only say that it was "still under consideration" until he could study the vice-president's findings.[100] Not revealed, however, were decisions that laid the basis for a much more emphatic role behind the Diem government, and for actively countering either Pathet Lao or North Vietnamese efforts to control Laos.

In essence they constituted an American commitment that preceded Johnson's symbolic trip to Saigon. Kennedy's own concerns were indicated in an April 28 memorandum that explained the "considerable doubt" among Southeast Asians whether Communist advances in the area could any longer be stemmed. Therefore, said the paper from Johnson's military aide, "even with a new and bold effort there remain possibilities and even temptations for the nations of the area to seek at least neutral positions in a new hope for survival."[101]

That was also how it was tailored to appear for history: The transition from Eisenhower to Kennedy had given Laos a legitimate opportunity for autonomy. But in reality little had changed. Hubert Humphrey, whose position as the Democratic Senate whip had given him access to congressional briefings of what was actually happening, dictated his private misgivings on May 13. "The Eisenhower-Dulles period was identified with two forces that made a great appeal, jingoism and morality," he said, and then asked, "What are we doing now that is different? . . . We never should have been in Laos militarily. . . . I think we underestimated Dulles and his affect [sic] on the thinking of the people, on the thinking of men in government. This is why President Kennedy or Secretary of Defense McNamara or Secretary of State Rusk get very much the same advice that Eisenhower got. The reason is quite simple. The same people are handing up the advice. They are the same Joint Chiefs of Staff. There are the same people at the second or third echelon in State and Defense."[102]

Humphrey fully appreciated, then, that Kennedy had not resigned himself to permitting the deterioration of pro-Western positions. The President's moves following that Saturday's NSC meeting were counterinitiatives to combat North Vietnamese-supplied and equipped guerrillas. At the heart of the American response was an enhanced MAAG role. One hundred additional men sent to train an enlarged South Vietnamese army would be bolstered by about four hundred new Special Forces troops. There would also be the expansion of "present operations in the field of intelligence, unconventional warfare, and political-psychological activities to support the U.S. objective as stated," which would promote covert actions as "operations against Communist forces in South Vietnam and against North Vietnam." In the north itself counterinsurgency teams would be infiltrated to "form networks of resistance, covert bases and teams for sabotage and light harassment." The operations would aim to "counteract tendencies toward a 'political solution' while the Communists are attacking" the South Vietnamese government, and creating a "psychological program in Vietnam and elsewhere exploiting Communist brutality and aggression in North Vietnam."[103] One year later National Security Action Memorandum 162, which underwrote the expansion of counterinsurgency activities, noted the "success which has resulted from CIA/U.S. Army Special Forces efforts with tribal groups in Southeast Asia."[104]

It is, however, doubtful that even Humphrey fully appreciated the role of the CIA and the counterinsurgency program. That summer, after the drawn-out, on-and-off-again Geneva talks had begun, General Lansdale reported that "about 9,000 Meo tribesmen have been equipped for guerrilla operations, which they are now conducting with considerable effectiveness in Communist-dominated territory in Laos."[105] Harriman, the American negotiator at Geneva, backed the CIA's organization of the Meo tribesmen into a fighting force, "and to fight in the way they fought best: as guerrillas behind the North Vietnamese lines."[106] As the Church Committee's report later declared, the Laotian operation "eventually became the largest paramilitary effort in post-war history." Although not intended by its creators to "become a pervasive foreign policy tool, it stepped up its paramilitary strength in Vietnam, beginning gradually in 1962 and later assisting the military's covert activities against North Vietnam."[107]

Indeed, the conflict had been removed from the central U.S.–Soviet cold-war confrontation. But that was the best that could be said because the substitute was a secret war, one that could not be fully controlled by any of the major powers most involved in Southeast Asia: the U.S., the Soviet Union, or the People's Republic of China. As the new CIA director, John McCone, advised the President in 1962, "we believe that none of the Communist powers involved would respond with major military moves designed to change the nature of the conflict." Rather than risk escalation they "would be more likely to rely on a continuing war of attrition and on intensive propaganda and political maneuvering aimed at isolating the U.S. and building up pressure for an international conference to 'neutralize' South Vietnam."[108] Under their CIA sponsors the Meo warriors grew from guerrilla-size units to a thirty-thousand-man army with battalion-size units to disrupt North Vietnamese supplies along the patchwork of routes that became known as the Ho Chi Minh Trail. The North Vietnamese themselves, of course, were just as determined to maintain their access to the South through the Mekong Valley. Meanwhile, with the security of Diem's government linked to operations in Laos, General Phoumi became dependent on the CIA, and the enterprise began to mount to some three million dollars a month. The corresponding escalation from Hanoi similarly helped make the whole involvement even more inextricable. In the process, a quarter of a million Meos were virtually destroyed.[109]

Documentation now available substantiates the recognition by the Kennedy administration that Moscow's influence over the situation was nil. Their major hope was to thwart their Communist competitors in Peking, and the historic relationship between the Vietnamese and the Chinese gave Ho Chi Minh the greatest stake in "containing" their corevolutionaries from the north. Nationalism and ideology were thus in sharp conflict, with Hanoi seeking to become the prime agents of promoting civil war against the clients of the former colonialists. Kennedy himself well understood, as his British friend David Ormsby-Gore had reminded him in February, that it was ridiculous to conceive of Laos as a bastion of Western democracy.[110]

At home the political opposition was mounting. Beginning with a partisan attack on the administration's spending policies, it had already broadened to include foreign policy. When it came to basic cold-war issues, not a single Republican voice questioned the need for a more militant approach. Barry Goldwater, regarded by some as a possible running mate for Rockefeller in 1964, accused Kennedy of having "blundered" into disaster over Cuba. Both Senator Hugh Scott of Pennsylvania, a moderate, and the party's new national chairman, New York Representative William Miller, claimed that the President had crippled the invasion by aborting Eisenhower's air-cover plan. Eisenhower continued his public bipartisanship and denied that there had ever been such a specific plan, but joined with Nixon in a "loyal opposition" telecast. In what was viewed as a Republican kickoff for the 1962 congressional campaign, Nixon castigated the administration for having been "brilliant as far as what it has been saying," but "very sadly lacking in what it has been doing."[111] When Kennedy's own vice-president, Lyndon Johnson, returned from Saigon, the President learned that the decision to begin negotiations at Geneva had shaken Diem's confidence in the United States. There would be a further decline in morale unless the words were soon followed by deeds, and that meant additional aid so he could expand his army by 100,000 troops.[112]

All of this—the Cuban debacle at the Bay of Pigs and the decision not to make a military stand in Laos—left Kennedy exposed to both Khrushchev and the American public. With the Russians the question of continuing the voluntary ban on nuclear testing and the closely related matter of arms limitations were still unresolved. Moreover, on May 12 Kennedy received a message from Khrushchev accepting a summit conference for Vienna in early June. The President had no doubt that, after what he had been through, the Russians were ready to probe his toughness, especially over the long-simmering Berlin question. At home voters were also convinced that the best way to prevent a nuclear war against international communism was to take the kind of stand that did not blink at the prospect of a holocaust.

7

"The Bay of Pigs"

Suddenly the promising world of the New Frontier lost its credibility. The question arose whether the Kennedy administration was competent to cope with its global objectives. A surge of protest, both at home and abroad, condemned a genuine disaster, a perfect failure: the Bay of Pigs. Instead of overthrowing Castro, 1,214 prisoners had been left behind. Instead of a delicate covert operation in harmony with the President's very recent disavowal of American military contribution to an invasion, the United States could no longer deny, as an uninformed Adlai Stevenson had tried to do at the United Nations, that it had been guilty of violating the sovereignty of a neighbor.

Kennedy did not try to dismiss the intrusion or shift the responsibility. He told the press that "There's an old saying that victory has 100 fathers and defeat is an orphan," and then continued his response to Sander Vanocur's question about foreign policy with the statement that "I'm the responsible officer of the Government—and that is quite obvious." A later White House statement reaffirmed his strong opposition to blaming anyone else.[1]

No Cuba Study Group was needed to tell him about the collective responsibility. The CIA had been wrong. The military had been wrong.

His most important civilian advisers had been wrong. He later responded by shifting personnel, launching an investigation into the mishap, and reinstituting an advisory board for better control over intelligence operations. The disaster, however, was Kennedy's. The operation was launched and failed because John Kennedy not only believed those around him but *wanted to* believe they were right.

Cuba was very different from Laos. As with Berlin for Khrushchev, Castro had become a "bone" in the American throat. During the presidential campaign Kennedy had defensively stolen Nixon's point about how to cope with a Marxist island in an American sea. The opportunity had become a personal challenge to one eager to demonstrate that youth and inexperience were not handicaps. The extravagant emphasis on vigor, toughness, on "getting this country moving again" had begun to substitute for rational analyses. The Kennedy campaign themes had actually offered the Cubans less hope for conciliatory policies than they had received from Eisenhower. Sorensen, in what has rightly been called the nearest thing to the memoirs that Kennedy himself would have liked to have left behind, has written that backing down would have been "a show of weakness inconsistent with his general stance." Kennedy later told his close aide that he "really thought they had a good chance" to topple Castro."[2]

Castro himself was hardly keeping quiet about American anti-Cuban activities. He warned that United States sponsorship of a movement by Cuban exiles would justify his actions in promoting revolutionary activity throughout Latin America, including among Puerto Rican nationalists. "That is the reason President Kennedy can't sleep at night," said the Cuban premier. "Our success is the reason for the nervousness and the hysteria in the United States."[3] Having rung the alarm, Castro then held out his olive branch to the Americans. He said that Cuba would do its part to reduce tensions if Kennedy would act to halt the Pentagon and CIA airdrops of weapons to guerrilla forces in the Escambray Mountains.[4] At about the same time, Kennedy received a report from the Argentine government that their envoy in Havana had had conversations with the Cuban leader which could possibly settle U.S.–Cuban differences.[5]

Even if the legitimacy of such overtures were unquestioned, the cold-war climate precluded any serious negotiation. Moreover, both Kennedy brothers had Fidel in their sights as though they were conducting a long-standing vendetta, another version of Bobby versus Jimmy Hoffa. Sorensen has written that Jack "should never have permitted his own deep feeling against Castro (unusual for him) and considerations of public opinion . . . to overcome his innate suspicions."[6] Allen Dulles found him in a "feisty mood" about getting Castro.[7] At no point did Kennedy ask Dulles or his deputy for planning, Richard Bissell, to prepare a detailed plan for dismantling the Brigade and calling off the project. Contemplating those events from the vantage point of two decades later, Bissell wondered at the fact that one had not been drawn up.[8] Just before the invasion Kennedy told Sorensen, "I know everybody is grabbing their nuts on this." At least he was not going to be "chicken" about getting Castro.[9] McGeorge Bundy now says, "I never realized until after he made the decision what I now believe, that he really was looking for ways to make it work, that he wanted it to work, and allowed himself to be persuaded it would work and the risks were acceptable."[10] Although Bobby was not in on the decision, the two brothers' thinking had long since meshed. Dulles's biographer quotes a CIA source as having said that "Where Castro and Cuba were concerned, Bobby Kennedy went further than Henry the Second, and everybody covered up for him."[11]

After virtually having ignored the bloody final years of the deposed dictatorship, the American press had by then also become passionate about Castro's anti-Yankee fulminations and crimes. Readers who had been earlier persuaded that Cuba had been liberated by social democrats were now outraged by accounts of the nearby regime that depicted an oppressive dictatorship and the vanguard of Communist bloc intrusion into the Western Hemisphere. Castro's personal power was so great that, as the last American ambassador to Cuba has observed, "The same masses who in 1959 roared their approval of his democratic and then of his humanistic pronouncements shouted themselves hoarse approving his Marxism in 1961."[12] The actions of the bearded leader were decisive, dramatic, and much more expeditious than reforms by those who valued bourgeois notions of liberty and property. Just before Kennedy's inauguration, the Eisenhower administration broke diplomatic ties with the man who has been called "the greatest demagogue ever to have appeared anywhere in Latin America."[13]

But that was not the entire reason for Washington's grievances. Castro created havoc with American commercial arrangements—a fact far more ominous than his geographic proximity. "The initial efforts of the Soviet Union to tie other countries to the tail of the Communist kite has usually been through trade," declared a State Department white paper in August of 1960. There was "a pattern of political and economic intervention by the Soviet Union and Communist China inimical to the peace and security of the Hemisphere." There was also concern about

Castro-supported armed incursions against the Dominican Republic, Panama, Haiti, and Nicaragua as well as Castro's desire "to make contact with and actively assist a handful of Puerto Rican radicals whose avowed policy is the overthrow of the Government of Puerto Rico by violent means and to bring about revolutionary changes contrary to the will of the people of Puerto Rico." Moreover, the Soviet Union was threatening to intervene in the hemisphere "to the extent of suggesting missile warfare," because of the "alleged intention of the United States to intervene in Cuba with military force." If wars of national liberation were exportable across the Atlantic, Castro would surely become their prime agent.[14]

In the sense that he was looking for a way out of what he had inherited, Kennedy was far from trapped. His search was for guarantees that it could be done without *visible* American involvement. Neither the Cuban exiles who comprised the Brigade nor the planners really thought that would be possible. But they were correct about Kennedy's appetite. As Sorensen tells it, the anti-Castro coalition was "so intent on action that they were either blind or willing to assume that the President could be pressured into reversing his insistence on avoiding visible American participation once the necessity arose."[15] Moreover, it can be argued that what happened was made possible less by what was inherited than because of the rejection of safeguards that had been recommended during the final month of the previous administration.

Desire and inexperience helped to gull him even more insidiously. He was not so much swept along as a victim of "shared illusions."[16] Bissell did most of the selling, taking over much of the initiative from Dulles.

The deputy for planning, which really meant covert operations, was a man of high character, a type Kennedy could admire, considered even by critics as among the four or five brightest men in the government.[17] Kennedy was fascinated by the articulate intelligence of the Ivy Leaguer from Connecticut who had also attended the London School of Economics and held a doctorate in economics from Yale. He had taught both there and at MIT, and his students had included Walt Rostow and the Bundy brothers, McGeorge and William. Mac Bundy had, in fact, worked under Bissell to help administer the Marshall Plan. After he joined the CIA in 1954, Bissell was a central figure in helping to overthrow Arbenz in Guatemala and masterminding the U-2 spy plane operation. Kennedy had gotten to know him through their mutual friend, Joe Alsop. Bissell was a Stevenson Democrat and also close to Chester Bowles, who had wanted him as deputy undersecretary for political affairs. But Kennedy stood in the way, hoping to make Bissell Dulles's successor.[18]

It was Bissell who, even before Kennedy's inauguration, had backed a scheme to assassinate Castro. American underworld figures had been badly hurt by the Cuban revolution, losing their prized hold over Havana's gambling casinos, the dope trade, and prostitution. They had, indeed, helped make Cuba "the whorehouse of the Western Hemisphere."[19] All such sources of fortunes were wiped away by the revolution. The effort to kill Castro ended temporarily just before the Bay of Pigs invasion. That project, which led to Robert Maheu's recruitment of mobsters, was frustrated by some Keystone comedy circumstances, including poison pills that failed to dissolve in water. The enterprise began without the knowledge of Kennedy or anybody in his administration, but Dulles had at least acquiesced by nodding his head.[20]

Dulles, sixty-eight that April, had intelligence experience going back to the wartime Office of Strategic Services and the plot to kill Hitler. To Jack Kennedy he was somewhat of a legendary figure, but more congenial than his secretary of state brother, Foster, who had died in 1959. As with Bissell, Allen Dulles and Kennedy traveled in the same circles. Dulles often went to the Charles Wrightsman estate near Joe Kennedy's Palm Beach house. As far back as Jack's early days they socialized down in Florida, much of the time while swimming and playing golf. Finding himself working in a Democratic administration, Dulles tended to back off from his usual certitude. The restraint probably came more from uncertainty about the crowd around Kennedy than from reservations about the President himself. Dulles and Kennedy were "comfortable with one another and there was a lot of mutual respect," Bissell said in an interview.[21]

If during those March and April weeks of deliberations and planning Dulles had had any doubts about the plan, as his biographer contends, he never let on. Rather, Carl Kaysen and Theodore Sorensen have both agreed, the director effectively relieved Kennedy's fears when he told him, "Mr. President, I know you're doubtful about this, but I stood at this very desk and said to President Eisenhower about a similar operation in Guatemala, 'I believe it will work.' And I say to you now, Mr. President, that the prospects for this plan are even better than our prospects were in Guatemala."[22]

Some did voice their dissent; others suggested ways of avoiding disaster. At the UN, Stevenson was opposed, wondering whether Kennedy had given the enterprise much thought.[23] Bundy seemed ambivalent, with some associates forever remaining uncertain of exactly where he had stood, and Rusk was cautious; as usual the secretary of state kept mum when facing the President on policy matters when others were around. Above all, however, Rusk was adamantly against overt American assistance and air strikes that could easily be traced to U.S. planes. Bowles, as Rusk's undersecretary, sent long memoranda and at least once confronted the President personally with his misgivings, but too easily he was dismissed as windy and soft—even worse, a "knee-jerk liberal"—and it was easy to suspect him of talking freely to the press about internal differences.[24]

As a special adviser who had also become closely involved in Latin American affairs, Schlesinger complied with the President's request for a white paper detailing Castro's "betrayal" of the Cuban Revolution. He later "reproached" himself for "having kept so silent during those crucial decisions in the Cabinet Room," but his memoranda were examples of determined and articulate pieces of dissent.[25]

He sent warning after warning to the President about singling out for destruction dictatorships guilty of expropriating U.S. businesses, letting foreign policy be determined by fear of a dispersed brigade. He reported that Castro still commanded strong internal support while the U.S. remained identified with Batista, and spoke of the exiles' extravagant expectations of forthcoming American help.[26] He was indignant when the CIA produced a "Free Cuban Manifesto," thereupon complaining to the agency's Tracy Barnes about his "fear that this will sound to a lot of Cubans like an attempt to turn back the clock and restore the old order," when the "emphasis should not be on what the post-Castro regime will do for businessmen, owners of dispossessed property, foreign investors, etc., but on what it will do for the oppressed, the poor, the humble and the downtrodden."[27] When the green light seemed certain, Schlesinger sent one final, long memorandum. He warned that the United States would inevitably be held accountable by the world. Many "simply do not at this moment see that Cuba presents so grave and compelling a threat to our national security as to justify a course of action which much of the world will interpret as calculated aggression against a small nation in defiance both of treaty obligations and of the international standards we have repeatedly asserted against the Communist world." He reminded the President that "we profess to be acting according to higher motives and higher principles than the Russians," and of the dangers of reverting to pre–World War I gunboat-diplomacy and economic imperialism. Counterreactions, supported by international revulsions, might even include "José Martí" and "Abraham Lincoln" brigades, directed at the United States and bolstering Soviet attempts to portray themselves "as the patron and protector of nationalists" in contrast to the capitalistic "gangs." If the invasion must take place, Schlesinger agreed with Rusk's point that the final decision should be made by a subordinate in the President's absence, "someone whose head can later be placed in the block if things go terribly wrong." And if "lies must be told, they should be told by subordinate officials."[28]

If that emanated from Kennedy's "gutless" Left, there were other voices of dissent. Fulbright, the man who had been Kennedy's personal favorite to head the State Department, and who sat as the chairman of the Senate Foreign Relations Committee, was outspoken both in the "brilliant" memo of March 29 and at a meeting in the White House on April 4. There was also a former secretary of state, Dean Acheson. A dove only to the lunatic Right, Acheson had warned Kennedy in person that, as Acheson later recalled, "it was not necessary to call in Price, Waterhouse [the prominent accounting firm] to discover that fifteen hundred Cubans weren't as good as twenty-five thousand Cubans."[29] But Kennedy was fortified by those "realists" who assured him that the invasion would be Cuban-sponsored and Cuban-fought. To establish that deception the CIA had combined the anti-Castro groups and set up an exile "government" known as the Cuban Revolutionary Council under the leadership of former Castro premier, José Miró Cardona.[30]

Actually several articles had already appeared in various publications with informed descriptions of the activities taking place in the region. A Tad Szulc dispatch about to come out on the front page of the April 7 *New York Times,* under a four-column headline, became a central concern in the newsroom. Managing Editor Turner Catledge had misgivings about the journalistic propriety of predicting the "imminence" of an invasion, which the Szulc piece highlighted. But it also revealed—and Catledge worried about that, too—that the CIA was involved. Publisher Orvil Dreyfoos expressed a more general concern about the "national interest." When Catledge called James Reston, he found the paper's Washington correspondent also fearful about subverting the country and wanting to do the "patriotic thing." Over the objection of some other editors the controversial references were deleted, the headline was reduced to a single column, and the news impact was minimized.

Kennedy, who had wanted both an invasion and invisibility, also preferred to have it both ways with the press. He later reprimanded the *Times* for printing too much, but also, as Catledge later wrote, "condemned us for printing too little." The President told Catledge, "Maybe if you had printed more about the operation you would have saved us from a colossal mistake." And, Catledge concludes in his account of the affair, "we might have caused the cancellation of the invasion."[31]

But Kennedy's personal commitment was already too thorough. When D day came, the President told his brother Bob, "I'd rather be an aggressor in victory than a bum in defeat."[32] Bissell has argued that "the one point never to be forgotten about the Bay of Pigs was that the plans for that activity and its progress were meticulously reviewed for weeks before it came off by the President and the whole circle of his advisers, and in even more detail daily by a committee of the Joint Staff of the Pentagon, and by a group in the Western Hemisphere bureau of the State Department who were working actively on the political aspects . . . So I think the answer has to be that if there's anything clear on the record of the Bay of Pigs, it is that lack of supervision and coordination was not the reason for failure."[33]

When logic succumbed to desire, all hands shared in the blunder. As the subsequent Taylor Report explained, the "impossibility of running Zapata [the peninsula at the Bay of Pigs] as a covert operation under CIA should have been recognized and the situation reviewed" as early as November 1960.[34] The anti-Castro Brigade had been encouraged to believe that their mission would provoke open American military intervention, and that seemed essential to the plan. Dulles later denigrated the supposed reliance on a "spontaneous" uprising, and Bissell has agreed that too much has been made of such expectations. A special national intelligence estimate put out by the agency just before the invasion showed abundant disaffection but nevertheless cautioned against optimism about a spontaneous uprising. The operative assumption was that such popular support would only be possible after substantial military control had been achieved, not before. Insufficient thought was given to anything beyond consolidating the beachhead. Hope rested on stabilizing the foothold as a base from which the B-26s could attack communications, sow confusion, and, in Bissell's words, "create a fluid situation." Privately, and never part of the official plan, it was Bissell's hope to then get the Organization of American States to call for a cease-fire and elections.[35] Kennedy's doubts were somewhat allayed by the understanding that, as a last resort, the invaders would be able to "melt" into the mountains and conduct protracted guerrilla warfare. That had been the reason for targeting the original landing site near the town of Trinidad on the southern shore adjacent to the Escambray Mountains rather than at the Bahia de Cochinos (Bay of Pigs), which was considerably to the west and virtually surrounded by swamps. Bissell, who pointed out that the revised landing site had served to shelter outlaws and escaped slaves, acknowledged that the President was "encouraged" to continue to believe in the guerrilla fallback option.[36]

When the revised plan was presented before the Joint Chiefs on March 15, as a subsequent inquiry put it, they "did not oppose the plan and by their acquiescing in it gave others the impression of approval."[37] Intelligence reports also guessed that the time was ripe because of the large numbers supposedly engaged in resistance to the government. A quarter of the total population might actually support a well-organized invasion force, it was suggested.[38] Informers reported that the regime's popularity was continuing to shrink. Havana was crowded with aliens, Communists from Russia, China, and other nations from the bloc. "The people have begun to lose their fear of the government, and public sabotage is common," with rebelliousness spreading throughout the provinces. Nor did the Cuban army appear ready to offer resistance in the event of a showdown, and the police would also cooperate.[39] A last-minute report to the President from Colonel Jack Hawkins, a veteran Marine assigned to inspect the Brigade, could have been written by a cheering squad. "They say it is a Cuban tradition to join a winner and they have supreme confidence they will win against whatever Castro has to offer," he assured Washington.[40]

On the twelfth, Kennedy separated himself from any hint of American participation, and he may have thereby killed whatever chance may have existed of unarmed Cubans rising against Castro. At a news conference he pledged that "there will not be, under any conditions, an intervention in Cuba by the United States Armed Forces." He added that the hands-off policy had been adopted because the basic issue was not between the two nations but "between the Cubans and themselves."[41] Such thoughts were still being emphasized as American policy two days later when he went to the Pan American Building. His talk had been drafted by Schlesinger, but the President added his own words about the Organization of American States as the viable instrument for hemispheric unity that should continue to receive trust and support. He had not wanted to mix up the Alliance for Progress with Cuba, and so had asked Schlesinger to delete two explicit anti-Castro passages.[42] But in retrospect one cannot overlook such remarks that the Pan-American mission was "to demonstrate to a world struggling for a better life that free men working through free institutions can best achieve an economic progress to which all of us aspire," and that the commitment to freedom "must confirm our resolution to enlarge the area of freedom every year in our hemisphere."[43] Meanwhile he had yet to grant his final approval for the invasion plan.

That Friday, Chester Bowles made one last attempt to head off disaster. He sat down and hand wrote a plea to heed the warnings. By the time he brought it to his State Department office the next morning for typing and delivery, it was too late.[44] The wire services were reporting simultaneous attacks on three Cuban air bases by World War II vintage, propeller driven, twin-engine B-26 bombers. They were of a type that had been purchased from the United States by the Batista regime, and their use was part of the effort to make more credible the cover story that they had been commandeered from Castro's own air force. Castro's response was to order a general mobilization of the armed forces and civilian militia. He vowed that the country would resist "and destroy with an iron hand any force which attempts to disembark on our soil." Castro, of course, never doubted their origin. He gave the Cuban UN delegation instructions to condemn the United States.[45]

The President had an unusually crowded Saturday schedule. After an early briefing by McGeorge Bundy, he attended a business-as-usual ceremonial session in the Conference Room, where an international group of physicians was meeting with Dr. Travell. Then there were further consultations with his military aide, General Clifton, Secretary Rusk, and a noon-hour session that had the additional participation of Bissell, Schlesinger, and Adolf Berle. He had Salinger issue a statement denying any White House knowledge of the bombings and explaining that efforts were being made to get as much information as possible.[46] By 12:40 the President was in the helicopter taking off from the White House lawn to spend the rest of the weekend at Glen Ora. He attended Sunday morning mass and played golf with his sister Jean and brother-in-law Steve Smith.

Kennedy's Middleburg stay was part of the plan to camouflage American participation. Allen Dulles, also following a business-as-usual schedule, kept a speaking engagement in Puerto Rico. But not many hours passed before the subterfuges had clearly become transparent. At the United Nations an exchange of charges and countercharges had already commanded central attention. Dr. Raúl Roa, the Cuban foreign minister, had immediately attributed the raids to Washington. That brought Adlai Stevenson's indignant denials. The UN representative thought he had been assured that nothing would occur in the Caribbean while the forum debated existing Cuban complaints about American behavior. Only three days earlier the text of a speech that had been approved by the President and then forwarded to him by Rusk for delivery at the UN condemned the "oft-repeated and unproved charges that the United States is planning armed attack against Cuba."[47] Aware of neither the truth about the bombings nor the imminence of the raids, the American representative displayed his usual eloquence, but he was sadly out of touch with reality.

If Stevenson was misled, so was Rusk; so were the leaders of the Cuban

Revolutionary Council, the members of the Brigade, the chairman of the Joint Chiefs of Staff, congressional leaders (who were not informed until the mission was well under way), and even the President of the United States. The CIA had not even attempted to use the talents of Robert Amory, their own deputy director for intelligence. Such was the concern with secrecy as perhaps *the* top priority, but ironically that very precaution became the weakest link of the whole project. Bissell emphasized the difficulty of getting the Cubans to understand and maintain that requirement of security,[48] using this to rationalize deceptions and misinformation involving virtually all who were concerned. In the process Dulles and Bissell had, of course, deceived themselves. Deception as a root cause was never singled out as such by General Taylor's inquiry; but of course, as Schlesinger has already pointed out, with Bob Kennedy, Dulles, and Admiral Arleigh Burke comprising the balance of that board, their "real function was to preserve the CIA and JCS from feelings of persecution," while the attorney general worked to preserve the "presidential interest."[49] Even the postmortem was a charade in that they were really investigating themselves, and succeeded in perpetuating their illusions by concentrating on operational failures.

The initial deception had blown up even while Kennedy was still at Glen Ora. In New York, Dr. José Miró Cardona, the Cuban Revolutionary Council leader, "confirmed" that the raids had originated from within Cuba. But in Miami, Washington, and New York, a vital CIA cover story that was to have veiled the situation for at least forty-eight hours had begun to break down. On Saturday morning a B-26, apparently battle-scarred and with Cuban markings, flew into Miami's International Airport. The pilot, Mario Zuniga, explained that he was a renegade captain from Castro's air force. He had defected with his plane from San Antonio de los Banos after having witnessed the raids on the airfields that had been carried out by his comrades. Zuniga was promptly taken away by immigration authorities. They were "protecting" him from reprisals, and his name was withheld, but his partially hidden face showed up in news photos. Did his identity have to remain secret because Castro would not know that he had lost an air force captain with a B-26? Reports in Miami also noted that his aircraft's machine guns had not been fired and that its nose was of solid metal. Castro's B-26s had plastic. Moreover, the visible damage could easily have been fabricated, as indeed it was.

On Manhattan's East Side a debate took place within the General Assembly's Political Committee. Dr. Roa charged that the raids were merely the "prologue to the large-scale invasion" his country had been predicting was about to be launched by the United States. Stevenson, after getting "confirmation" from a State Department equally in the dark about the CIA's cover story (in 1981 Bissell still couldn't explain why Rusk didn't know), replied that there would be no United States intervention under any conditions. His government would also do everything possible to "make sure no American participates in any actions against Cuba." He then read a statement from the still unidentified Zuniga that said he and two other fliers had decided to defect. Another B-26 had landed at Key West. Stevenson then held up a photograph of one of the planes that had Castro's air force markings. Dr. Roa, with the confidence of one secure in his logic, replied that it could have been painted by anyone. Kennedy, appreciative of Stevenson's assets as a respected spokesman for the country but unimpressed by what he considered his lack of strength, dispatched Bundy to New York to "calm him down and hold his hand."[50]

On Sunday the President was obviously in no hurry to reach Bissell with the go-ahead signal for the landings. Not much imagination is needed to contemplate what he was thinking about as he attended mass and played golf with the Smiths. Correspondents were still asking questions about the alleged defector, and each passing hour was compounding the difficulty of concealment. Could that fiasco and the raids be separated from the operation itself? Had he already gone too far in encouraging preparations for the invasion due to start shortly after midnight? Could the Brigade, and those ready to fly the B-26s from the air base at Puerto Cabezas (which carried the CIA code name of Happy Valley) having already been inspired by pep talks from their Yankee advisers, be simply told that it was no dice? What about the disposal problem? Trying to jettison it all at the last minute might be enough for open mutiny. A secondary contingency plan of having them sail to Puerto Rico in the event of a cancellation had begun to seem like a moot point. Nearly two hours had lapsed since the deadline when Kennedy finally gave the word to Bissell.

After more golf at the Fauquier Springs Country Club, he returned with Jackie and Lem Billings, and the phone rang. It was Rusk. The secretary of state, whose misgivings had come through during the meetings, was also upset about Stevenson, who had borne his predicament with dignity and courage. Stevenson had been let down, and Rusk now feared exacerbating the mess. Should they go ahead with a second strike at Castro's air bases before a sufficient beachhead could be established and the airstrip captured to make it look as though it was all coming from defectors inside Cuba? In the absence of "overriding considerations," Rusk requested presidential approval for canceling the strike, and Kennedy agreed. Both the President and the secretary then resisted a direct appeal from General Charles P. Cabell of the CIA. Bissell was surprised about the decision and equally agitated, but felt that a protest would have been useless.[51]

That decision would later cause nearly as much anger as the controversial plan itself. Less well known is that the original plan had called for three air strikes. Saturday's, or D day minus two, would have been the first in any case; but the D day strike now aborted was to have been the third. Another, a follow-up scheduled for Sunday, D day minus one, was the original second strike. On Friday, Kennedy's concern that the papers were already making too much of the situation had led to his order that the first be reduced from sixteen B-26s to a "minimal" amount, which dropped the number to six.[52] But about a week earlier, probably with Rusk's advice, Kennedy ruled out what was to have been the second strike.[53]

But it was Castro's ability to move much more rapidly than anyone had anticipated that was probably the most decisive factor. The Cuban dictator had taken the precaution of dispersing his planes on the ground, and right after the invasion began he quickly moved fifty antiaircraft guns to the area. Schlesinger has pointed out that even if there had been a "successful" air strike, the Cubans who presumably would have secured their beachhead would have merely found themselves surrounded by an overwhelming enemy force some two hundred times their size.[54]

Kennedy was awakened at Glen Ora that morning with news of the invasion. One landing was at Playa Larga (Red Beach) at the head of the Bay of Pigs. The other, to the east, was at Giron (Blue Beach), where the prize was an airstrip. Kennedy's predawn caller was Dean Rusk, who told him that General Cabell had returned with a second request. He wanted jets from the aircraft carrier *Essex,* stationed just off the coast, to provide cover for the vessels that were unloading. But Kennedy held fast. He ordered the carrier moved away, out of sight of Cuban territory, to at least thirty miles out at sea.[55] That decision having been made, he boarded the helicopter at nine o'clock with his wife and daughter for the brief return flight to the White House.

With the exception of Monday's periodic briefings he followed his normally heavy White House appointment schedule. Only by early evening, when he was able to give full attention to the Cuban situation, did the profile of impending disaster become sufficiently clear.

Everything, it seemed, had gone wrong. Popular support for the liberators, a fundamental assumption of the planners, was simply not materializing. The 3:00 A.M. appeal of Radio Swan, the CIA transmitter off Honduras that called for Cubans to join the "general" uprising, had absolutely no effect. Castro issued a call for his 200,000-man militia. The invaders unexpectedly encountered offshore coral reefs, which damaged some of the landing craft and forced men to wade ashore through deep water, thereby knocking out much of the portable radio equipment. Too many of the eager anti-Castro Cubans also succumbed to the common trap of inexperienced fighters, the premature firing of excessive rounds of ammunition. With Castro's T-33 rocket-equipped jet trainers already in action, along with MIG fighters and Soviet-built tanks, it quickly became obvious that the planners had totally miscalculated by positing that the Havana regime had not yet been bolstered by Russian technology and supplies. By far the most damaging stroke, however, was delivered not by Soviet hardware but by a British-made Sea Fury bomber. Although the aircraft was sluggish, propeller-driven, and easily outmaneuverable, the antiquated little freighters in the water below (which had been secured from the United Fruit Company) were ridiculously easy targets. Two were hit right away, including the *Rio Escondido* with its ten-day supply of communications equipment and ammunition. Two other freighters scattered for the safety of the high seas.

In New York, meanwhile, Dr. Roa told the UN that his country's invasion had been undertaken by "mercenaries, organized, financed and armed by the Government of the United States," while Stevenson continued to deny American aggression against Cuba, adding that "no offensive has been launched from Florida or from any other part of the United States."[56] "He was disgusted," one of his colleagues has said. "Upset. He was a man who was very jealous of his image—and rightly. And he felt that this had tarnished his image."[57] Circumstances had hardly helped to improve his attitude toward Kennedy, who was then still determined not to look "chicken." Bobby thought he was prepared to go "as far as necessary to insure success."[58]

Tuesday was a day of having to face the ultimate reality. B-26s dispatched against Castro's planes from Nicaragua had been foiled by a heavy haze over the airport. On the beachhead the exiles were mired in the swamp, desperately low on ammo, completely vulnerable to the enemy tank assault. Castro himself was directing Cuban operations, and his communiqué over Havana radio announced that "our armed forces are continuing to fight the enemy heroically."[59] Any possibility of internal uprisings was further made unlikely by mass arrests that put some 200,000 suspected dissidents out of commission. Elsewhere in Latin

America the fallout was becoming widespread, with protest demonstrations already vilifying the U.S. in six cities, including the stoning of the U.S. Information Agency office in Brazil.[60] Soon, disorders spread to the United States, with Fair Play for Cuba rallies in New York and San Francisco.

At the UN, Soviet Ambassador Zorin read the text of a message from Khrushchev to Kennedy that alluded to the warning of July 1960 that America was within the range of Russian rockets. The new message said that the USSR would give the Cuban government assistance in repelling the attack, a statement that may have been made with the confidence that it would not really be necessary.[61] Kennedy held back from issuing an immediate response, clinging to the hope that the situation was not irreversible.

But the beachhead was lost. The invaders were about to be encircled, and American responsibility was more obvious than ever. In desperation Bissell contracted U.S. civilians to fly combat missions.[62] The President, meanwhile, starting with a 7:00 A.M. Cabinet Room session, met with his advisers almost continuously. As usual Vice-President Johnson was invited to attend, and, also as usual, let the others do the talking. Dulles and Bissell could only describe the continuing deterioration. The sometimes agitated discussion, which involved Admiral Burke's attempts to bolster the military contribution to minimize the losses, revolved mainly around salvaging the besieged exiles. Harlan Cleveland was chagrined that Kennedy was making it obvious that his only "executive experience had been as commander of a PT boat," but Rostow saw that in a more positive light. He thought the President had "a small unit commander's attitude toward these people."[63] Most of the men around the table, including the President, Dean Rusk, and General Lyman Lemnitzer, the chairman of the Joint Chiefs, were surprised when Bissell told them that the exiles were not where they could find safety in the hills and become guerrillas as they would have under the original Trinidad landing plans. Rostow noted that Kennedy "really didn't have a very good visual picture of the whole thing."[64] Admiral Burke kept pressing for doing something to cut the losses, but the President, even while agreeing that we were in the thing up to our necks, kept trying to stick to his point about American invisibility. Finally, realizing that his position conflicted with realities and motivated by his desire to rescue the men, he permitted a one-hour flight of six unmarked Skylark jets from the *Essex* to cover for a B-26 attack from Nicaragua, a purely salvage operation. But even then they were given explicit instructions not to fire unless forced to defend the bombers.

Through it all, however, Kennedy kept his composure, remarkably well. His luncheon companions found him "free, calm and candid," as well as effectively in control.[65] In contrast, his younger brother, Bobby, distraught over the accumulating bad news, was cautioning those in the Cabinet Room against making any statements not fully supportive of the President's judgments. His evident agitation upset some of the other advisers.[66]

The President's afternoon concluded with the draft of a reply to Khrushchev. The message, handed to the Russian ambassador by Dean Rusk early that evening, advised the Soviet premier that he was "under a serious misapprehension in regard to events in Cuba," and cautioned that outside interference would have to be met by treaty obligations to "protect the hemisphere from external aggression."[67]

After the Khrushchev message had been completed, Kennedy met with Republican congressional leaders. Again Lyndon Johnson was present. Earlier Kennedy and his vice-president had relieved the grim confinements of the day by walking together for fifteen minutes on the White House grounds. By 9:45, however, just before the annual congressional reception, Johnson and Lady Bird, accompanied by Sam Rayburn, visited the Kennedys in the upstairs living quarters of the mansion.

The East Room reception was a white-tie affair. Afterward, from 11:58 P.M. until nearly three in the morning, the Oval Office was the scene of a hastily arranged meeting that once more took up the problem of trying to mitigate the situation and also considered the plight of the leaders of the Cuban Revolutionary Council, who constituted another kind of disposal problem. They had been victims of one of the CIA's cruelest deceptions, another thing Kennedy had known nothing about.

Led out of New York's Lexington Hotel on Sunday by the agency, they were taken away to where they supposed they would join the invasion force. Instead they were removed to Florida and held incommunicado by the CIA on a deserted air force base at Opa-locka near Miami. It was from there that they heard the radio announcement, prepared by the CIA and put out under the name of the Revolutionary Council, that the invasion had begun. Their numbers included Dr. Cardona, the council's president, and also Manuel Ray, a former minister of public works under Castro who had rebelled and then headed the underground *Movimiento Revolucionario del Pueblo* (MRP). Ray, who had directed sabotage activities, was possibly the most articulate as well as popular resistance leader. He was also considered by such CIA people as E. Howard Hunt as a "communist."[68] Consequently the agency all but ignored him, funded the more conservative leaders, and installed the twenty-nine-year-old Manuel Artime as leader of the exile invasion forces.[69] The Cubans at Opa-locka realized that the CIA had completely undercut their role. "One member is threatening suicide," Kennedy explained. "Others want to be put on the beachhead. All are furious with the CIA."[70]

The President then asked Berle and Schlesinger to meet with the Cuban leaders at Opa-locka, listen to their stories, and free them from detention. After hearing their grievances, Schlesinger reached Dean Rusk by telephone and got an agreement that they should be brought to Washington where, it was hoped, they might be forestalled from their threat of denouncing both the U.S. and the CIA by a personal session with the President.

By the time they returned to Washington with the Cubans, the operation in the Caribbean was just about over. The remnants of the Brigade were being wiped out or captured; some fled into the swamps. The evacuation, using Brigade ships, came that night, and was mainly performed by Navy landing craft manned by Americans wearing T-shirts. One hundred and fourteen had been lost and 1,189 captured, with about 150 finally making their way back.[71]

Schlesinger, Berle, and their group of agitated anti-Castro Cubans finally did see the President late the next afternoon. They found Kennedy in his rocking chair looking "exceptionally drawn and tired." Nevertheless, Schlesinger thought, he remained, "as usual, self-possessed." As they sat on the two couches facing each other before the fireplace, Kennedy expressed his sorrow and explained why he had not been able to intervene more fully. Action by the United States could have had serious consequences elsewhere in the world. Two of the men had sons with the Brigade on the Cuban beach, and they and their colleagues were most concerned with the rescue problem. Kennedy told them he understood; he had lost a brother in war and had experienced action in the South Pacific. "We were not charging Mr. Kennedy with anything," one of the men later told interviewers. "We knew that he didn't have any direct knowledge of the problem, and we knew that he was not in charge of the military efforts directly. Nevertheless, President Kennedy, to finish the talks, told us he was the one—the only one responsible." He also stressed that they would leave the White House as free men, "free to go wherever you want, free to say anything you want, free to talk to anyone you want." Schlesinger had never seen the President more impressive. He had touched the men despite themselves. A Harvard professor who served as the interpreter wondered at the President's composure and said afterward, "You suddenly know why these guys are born to command."[72]

Kennedy then went on to a conference with the vice-president, his military chiefs, and the congressional leaders. There, he looked glum and very upset.[73] The next day the Castro government claimed to have "completely defeated" the invasion force. The last strongholds had been overrun at 5:30 P.M. the day before. Many among the remaining force, which had been on Cuban soil for less than seventy-two hours, had been trapped in a swampy area near their landing group in Las Villas Province.[74] The news wires were carrying analyses claiming that the magnification of the project to the world had made it appear to be a major American undertaking, and its effect would strengthen Castro's regime, make Khrushchev more credible as the protector of small nations, and check the revived confidence in the United States and its new leadership.[75]

Kennedy entered that late-morning Cabinet meeting obviously wrung out. He was disturbed and introspective. He began to talk, the first session at which he had talked at great length, and it turned into a fifteen-minute monologue. He told them the responsibility for what had happened was his. "But he was really talking more to himself than anybody else," said Fred Dutton. When others spoke up, the reaction to the Cuban fiasco was one of resentment, and indignation that Castro "had done this to us." They seemed eager to retaliate, to teach him a lesson. Chester Bowles later recollected that if "the President had at that point decided on that course, to send troops or drop bombs, I think it would have had the affirmative vote of at least ninety percent of the people at that meeting."[76] At the end of the session the President got up and walked into Evelyn Lincoln's office, then he continued through the door and out to the lawn. Bobby saw him and followed. The two brothers walked along together. ""It was quite a moving thing," Dutton remembers. "Even with the Cabinet there at a moment like that, he didn't ask them to rally round; he didn't say that they were to avoid criticism; he didn't give them a public line they were to take. It was very much the inner dignity and the strength of the man coming out."[77]

Chester Bowles talked to the President on the morning of that Cabinet meeting, then he returned to his office and wrote a letter. The "immediate objective should be quickly to get the Cuban situation in perspective . . . to minimize its implications at home and abroad, and to switch our focus and the nation's interest to new areas where we can more readily secure the initiative."[78] Nevertheless, the conventional wisdom at that moment, as Bowles wrote in his memoirs many years later, was that "the humiliating failure of the invasion shattered the myth of a New Frontier run by a new breed of incisive, fault-free supermen. However costly, it may have been a necessary lesson." It was, Cardinal Cushing remem-

bered later about the President, "the first time in my life that I ever saw
tears come into his eyes."[79]

That Saturday the President went to Camp David to await his guest,
Dwight D. Eisenhower.

The two men alighted from their respective helicopters. Eisenhower
had just flown from his retirement home at Gettysburg, not far from the
Maryland border. Kennedy had left the White House lawn with Pierre
Salinger and his naval aide, Taz Shepard, at three minutes past noon.
Thirty-five minutes later he was atop Maryland's Cactoctin Mountains
at Camp David. Eisenhower had gotten to know the preserve well, had
in fact dropped FDR's name for the place (Shangri-la), and called it after
his grandson, David. Since his own presidency had begun ninety-two
days earlier, Kennedy had not been there. Saturdays were normally spent
at one of his favorite weekend spots. But he had personally telephoned
Gettysburg to suggest lunch together at the camp. As he had expected,
Eisenhower was ready to do what he could.

Within the 125-acre preserve security was tight. The electrified steel
fence was backed up by a platoon of armed Marines. Reporters and
photographers were carefully restricted. The two men wanted privacy.

They went to the Aspen Cottage on the terrace. Over fried chicken the
forty-three-year-old President and the seventy-year-old General picked
apart the disastrous operation as carefully as their food. Eisenhower's
advice was not solicited. He understood that Kennedy wanted him to
listen and to understand. The President talked about logistics, objectives,
and the anticipated results. When Eisenhower asked about the timing of
the support the Naval Air Force had supposedly given to the landing,
he was told that there was so much anxiety about concealing American
involvement that no such help was given. When it was obvious that it
was needed, Kennedy explained, it was too late. Moreover, the situation
was further complicated by the failure of communications. Too much
specialized equipment had been placed on a single ship, and when that
was destroyed, the troops on the beach were defenseless. The operation
had been botched, all right, but listening to his successor's explanation,
it seemed even more amateurish.

They left Aspen Cottage and walked together through a clearing,
Kennedy still talking. He explained that General Maxwell Taylor was
going to conduct a postmortem into all phases of the operation because
there might be lessons for similar situations in the coming years. His
words assured Eisenhower that the objective was not to find scapegoats
and that he was taking full responsibility for his own decision, which
suggested that the national interest would not be served by a partisan

splurge of retribution. Eisenhower accepted that spirit and added his own assurance that "I would support anything that had as its objective the *prevention of a Communist entry and solidification of bases in the Western hemisphere.*"[80] He also urged on Kennedy unified action by the Organization of American States to keep out communism through any "necessary action" that would prevent penetration. That was "something that had to be worked on all the time."[81]

Kennedy then brought up Laos. Eisenhower's account makes no mention of the Macmillan letter, but it does relate that the President outlined the situation there and said that "the British were very reluctant to participate in any military intervention and of course the French positively refused to do so." He was also "quite sure that there was no possibility of saving Laos by unilateral military action," and looked forward to the cease-fire that was promised for Monday. The General replied that his current status kept him from giving any advice, but, as he then wrote, "I could just say that as a generality in order to keep your position strong at the conference table you had constantly to let the enemy see that our country was not afraid. We believe in what is right and attempt to insist upon it."[82]

When Eisenhower and Kennedy then strolled back to the front of Aspen Cottage, they were ready for the press. The President heard what he wanted to hear when the General told them that he was "all in favor of the United States supporting the man who has to carry the responsibility for our foreign affairs." Kennedy added that the invitation to meet at Camp David had been given to "bring him up to date on recent events, and get the benefits of his thoughts and experience."[83]

The next day, after mass at the Middleburg Community Center, the President returned to his golf, spending virtually all afternoon "whacking some of these balls into the corn field just to take his mind off what was going on." Spalding had never seen him so despondent; it was "the only time in all the time that I knew him that he was really beside himself over a mistake." He kept blaming himself and wondered how he could have done it. How could it have happened? "The presidency was never easy from there on in," recalled Spalding. "It was just a series of difficult situations which he responded to in that manner, in a very sober mood."[84]

But at least that Sunday's papers carried front-page stories showing Kennedy with Eisenhower. Additional dividends came the next week when Eisenhower resisted pressure from the costars of what had come to be known as the "Ev and Charlie Show," Everett Dirksen and Charlie Halleck, the Republican congressional leaders who did televised reports of politics according to the viewpoint of the Grand Old Party. They went to Gettysburg pleading for the General to hit hard at the administration. Instead he cautioned against turning the investigation into a "witch-hunt." He told reporters, "Don't go back and rake over the ashes, but see what we can do better in the future." His entire approach was bipartisan, and when asked to evaluate Kennedy's first hundred days he generously sidestepped criticism by saying that "this Administration is preoccupied with the most important question there is in the world" at the moment. He also declined to say whether he thought American troops should be sent to Laos.[85]

Privately, however, Eisenhower showed his contempt. As he did so often, he confined his impressions to paper. Speculating that there would be a public outcry "if the whole story ever becomes known to the American people," he concluded that it "could be called a 'Profile in Timidity and Indecision.' "[86]

On April 20 Kennedy went to the Statler Hilton in Washington and told the annual conference of the American Society of Newspaper Editors that United States restraint toward Cuba was "not inexhaustible" and that he had no intention of "abandoning the country to communism."[87] It was a sabre-rattling, jingoistic speech that blamed the victim for the failure of the aggressor, but the American press applauded.[88]

Nor did Richard Nixon think the Cuban effort should be abandoned. The "father" of the scheme as Eisenhower's vice-president, Nixon arrived at the White House at Kennedy's request. He recalled that Kennedy complained that he had been "assured by every son of a bitch I checked with—all the military experts and the CIA—that the plan would succeed." When Nixon then advised finding a "proper legal cover" for getting the job done, the President cited the risk of a possible Soviet countermove on Berlin. Nor did he think we should get involved in Laos, citing the prospect of "fighting millions of Chinese troops in the jungles."[89] Even after that meeting with Kennedy, Nixon maintained that the Cuban situation deserved bipartisan support. Some Republicans grumbled, but with Eisenhower and Nixon having spoken, their complaints were muted.[90] Reaching out to another wing of the Republican Party, Kennedy then brought in Nelson Rockefeller, the New York governor who had won big in 1958 despite the national Democratic sweep of governorships and congressional seats. They met for an hour in the Oval Office and emerged with a plea for Americans to support whatever action was needed to meet the Cuban problem.[91]

At least for the moment, then, Kennedy had neutralized the three men who were then considered the most significant among his opposition:

Eisenhower for his presumed influence with both the country and his party; Nixon, before his losing effort to become California's governor, a possibility for 1964 after having lost so narrowly to Kennedy; and Rockefeller, a potentially natural, powerful, and attractive alternate who could appeal to the broad center of American politics.

On Friday, April 28, six days after his meeting with Eisenhower, came even more energetic efforts. He had flown to New York the day before, delivered a speech, and spent the night at the Carlyle. The following morning he was driven to the Waldorf-Astoria Towers. First, he went to suite 31A for a brief visit with another Republican ex-president, Herbert Hoover, then eighty-seven years old. After their sixteen-minute conversation Kennedy went up to suite 37A for a visit with eighty-one-year-old General Douglas MacArthur. Kennedy assumed that MacArthur was a "stuffy and pompous egocentric." Instead the President said afterward that he "turned out to be one of the most interesting men he had ever met, politically shrewd, intellectually sharp and a gifted conversationalist."[92]

Both Schlesinger and Sorensen have attached great importance to the advice Kennedy heard from MacArthur that day, right after the Bay of Pigs and with Laos still unresolved. They both agree that MacArthur gave him the "unforgettable" advice not to commit American troops on the Asian mainland. Anyone doing so without being prepared to use nuclear weapons against the Chinese "should have his head examined." Undoubtedly that version came from Kennedy himself, who gave William Manchester a similar account later that year.[93]

However this version does not agree with the notes John Kennedy made shortly after he left suite 37A. They reveal that MacArthur did say that "it would be a mistake to fight in Laos. It would suit the Chinese Communists whom he feels we should have destroyed at the time of the Korean War." But, as Kennedy then wrote, "He thinks we should fight a rear-guard action in the southeast of Asia." When Kennedy related his conversation to Arthur Krock on May 4, the journalist wrote that the sense of the discussion with the general was that "our policy must be to avoid a positive, formal withdrawal and help protect the areas as long as governments and peoples want this."[94] The MacArthur view was clearly one of agreement with those who believed that Laos was no place to make a stand, but he accepted the idea that its loss could spill the other dominoes.

Kennedy also failed to report the general's comment about Cuba. "He does not feel we should intervene at this time in Cuba," Kennedy wrote in his notes, "because it does not represent a military danger to us

although the time may come when we may have to do so." Also un-
reported was MacArthur's urging that it was important for the United
States to "take the initiative with regard to peace with the Russians as
they always make us appear to be the aggressor." Furthermore, he added
that "the 'chickens are coming home to roost' from Eisenhower's years,"
and that Kennedy was living in the chicken coop. Eisenhower "should
have done something about Cuba sooner," which, of course, reflected the
general's view that his former colleague was not much more estimable
than Truman.[95]

After the thirty-five-minute MacArthur visit Kennedy went to Stevenson's suite, where the UN representative gave a luncheon for both the
President and Secretary-General Dag Hammarskjöld. Other than his
itinerary nothing was disclosed to the press. Shortly after three that
afternoon Kennedy was aboard *Air Force One* at Idlewild Airport, ready
to continue his whirlwind day by flying to Chicago's O'Hare.

That was the final lap of his schedule before returning to Washington
after midnight, but it was the easiest. He was stimulated by the enthusiasm of those Democrats at Chicago's new lakeside Exposition Hall who
had paid one hundred dollars for Mayor Daley's Cook County fund-
raising dinner. In the aftermath of the Bay of Pigs the Gallup poll was
showing Kennedy's popularity zooming to a high point of eighty-three
percent (with just five percent registering negative reactions) and the
loyal Democrats of the nation's most efficient urban party organization
were no exception.[96] They whooped and cheered. They shouted and
applauded. Kennedy could do no wrong. He had restored vigorous
leadership. American power and American idealism were both on the
offensive.

8

"Discovering the World"

Kennedy's doubts about the utility of summit conferences had helped attract him to Dean Rusk, whose own doubts had been expressed in the pages of *Foreign Affairs*. Right after that article appeared, Rusk's words seemed even more credible when the Eisenhower–Khrushchev brouhaha over the Francis Gary Powers U-2 plane destroyed their planned Paris meeting. Rusk's reasoning was logical. The presidency, he explained, was peculiarly unsuitable for negotiations at the head-of-state level. Such diplomacy should be "approached with the wariness with which a prudent physician prescribes a habit-forming drug—a technique to be employed rarely and under the most exceptional circumstances, with rigorous safeguards against its becoming a debilitating or dangerous habit."[1]

Kennedy was determined to avoid similar traps. "Summitry," Sorensen has explained, "raised undue hopes and public attention, thus producing unjustifiable relaxations, disappointments or tensions. It injected considerations of personal prestige, face-saving and politics into grave international conflicts."[2] Considering the multiple crises all over the globe—in Cuba, Laos, the Congo, and Berlin—Kennedy hoped, at least, to limit his initial sessions with Khrushchev to personal probes, avoiding diplomatic negotiations.

Khrushchev had his own reasons, of course. But whatever they were —desire to gauge the young President for himself, pressures from within the Soviet Presidium, or difficulties with the Chinese Communists—it was the Russian who took the initiative. Even before he had made the grand gesture of releasing the RB-47 fliers, Khrushchev's desire to meet Kennedy was plain. Llewellyn Thompson, Kennedy's most experienced Kremlinologist, agreed that the risk had to be taken: America must not permit Russia to dominate peace initiatives. Moreover little would be lost by the President taking stock of the erratic Russian, as long as serious diplomacy was ruled out. Kennedy then offered to meet in either Stockholm or Vienna. Khrushchev responded affirmatively (despite the Bay of Pigs) to meeting in Vienna. The White House diplomatically delayed a public announcement until after the President had completed a previously scheduled Canadian trip, which was advertised as his first foreign journey.

Kennedy's address before the Canadian Parliament emphasized the strengthening of both conventional and nuclear forces, and emphasis was given to the importance of reforms within the underdeveloped nations. As Kennedy told the Canadians, "For our historic task in this embattled age is not merely to defend freedom. It is to extend its writ and strengthen its covenant—to peoples of different cultures and creeds and colors, whose policy or economic system may differ from ours, but whose desire to be free is no less fervent than our own."

Later the President joined Prime Minister John Diefenbaker in a tree-planting ceremony on the grounds of Government House. He turned the soil without properly flexing his body and felt an immediate twinge in his back. From that moment on the pain was constant, "something like a steady toothache," said Dr. Travell. The muscular spasms emanated from the area between his lumbar vertebrae and the sacrum, and he began to be treated with injections of novocaine.[3]

Remarkably, all during this period and until *The New York Times* published a fairly explicit account on June 9, the President's condition was known only to his doctors. With a round of delicate European visits coming up, to De Gaulle in Paris, Khrushchev in Vienna, and Macmillan in London, not a hint of his indisposition went beyond the Oval Office. An examination of his activities before the trip similarly reveals that the official schedule made no observable concessions to the problem. There were the usual ceremonial exchanges, meetings with the National Security Council, an appearance at the White House news photographers' dinner, a session with a large group of Soviet editors, a major address before a joint session of Congress on urgent national needs, a conference with the Joint Chiefs of Staff, and the usual get-togethers—both formal and informal—with legislative leaders. He later acknowledged to his military aide that he simply was not going to meet the imperious De Gaulle or Khrushchev while on crutches.[4] But having Dr. Jacobson along in Vienna so that "Dr. Feelgood" could treat him for the stressful situation was a much less conspicuous matter.[5]

Kennedy was as eager as Khrushchev to "take the measure" of his rival. The Soviet hand was seen exacerbating local conflicts that covered a staggering number of global flash points: the continuing differences between Israelis and Arabs over land and Palestinian refugees; threats to the Shah's rule in Iran; the Congo; the southern tier of Asia, from India's neutralism to insurrections in Laos and South Vietnam; Castro and the extension of Cuba's revolution to rightist, oligarchic regimes throughout Latin America. More than any other area, however, Berlin had become the symbol of where a stand had to be taken against Communist expansion. That was the one point that brought general American agreement about firmness, though not necessarily consensus about risking nuclear war. In Kennedy's mind Khrushchev had to be convinced that the United States had both the power and the will to restrict further deterioration of Western strategic interests, and it might be possible to make that point in a face-to-face meeting. He might then force a wedge toward a breakthrough to the single agreement most likely to result in a kind of détente, the formal continuation of what had been the voluntary suspension of atmospheric nuclear tests. Still, as Kennedy declared in his televised message to Congress on May 25, "No formal agenda is planned and no negotiations will be undertaken."[6]

"Berlin was no Laos," Sorensen has written. "It was a matter of the highest concern to the United States."[7] Khrushchev had been dangling the threat of a separate peace treaty that would ultimately jeopardize the West Berlin legacy of World War II diplomacy. A "free city" status proposed by the Russians in a diplomatic note in late 1958 demanded mutual guarantees from all sides that would, in effect, have given the satellite German Democratic Republic control of all access routes, making Berlin dependent on the Communist powers for its means of survival. Also implicit in the arrangement, and therefore also unacceptable, was diplomatic recognition for East Germany. That would have wiped out any further claim by the Bonn government as the only legitimate representative of the German people. Khrushchev's continuing rejection of the concept of free elections would, when added to all the other stipulations, have also removed any possibility of reunification as a viable (however implausible) goal. Lacking any agreement along such lines, the Soviets were threatening a unilateral accommodation with the German Democratic Republic.[8] Had Eisenhower and Khrushchev been able to get together in the spring of 1960, or had détente made sufficient progress to have permitted Eisenhower's projected visit to Moscow, resolving that point of East-West contention would have inevitably received the highest priority. But the U-2 fiasco ended all that, and Berlin joined Cuba, Southeast Asia, and the Congo among Kennedy's inherited crises. During that year's presidential campaign, Kennedy was forthright about the importance of defending the city. In a major foreign policy speech delivered before the Senate, he explained that the ideal was "a free Berlin, in a united Germany in a Europe where tensions and armaments have been reduced."[9] In a published interview with John Fischer, Kennedy had also said that Berlin was "really a great area for a power struggle."[10]

Khrushchev seemed to be creating, in effect, a straw man for his own strategy. Forcing summit diplomacy, which he relished, may have been among his objectives. He has also been suspected of having been under pressure for a harder line from the Chinese as well as from his own military people, who hoped to manufacture the proper climate for the resumption of nuclear testing.[11] Finally on February 17 he reopened the crisis. He sent an *aide-mémoire* to the West Germans saying that there was no longer any justification for delaying taking the path leading to a peace treaty that would "solve the problem of the occupied status of West Berlin, making it a free city." He later let Ambassador Thompson know just how important he viewed achieving a Berlin settlement.[12]

Kennedy's examination of the probable American responses never contemplated acquiescence under any sort of pretext. There was some sentiment for having the President take advantage of the friendly overtures made by the Russians by moving toward something like the Rapacki Plan for a demilitarized nuclear-free zone in Central Europe. George Kennan had proposed a variation of the scheme, and shortly after Kennedy became President, Senator Fulbright suggested consideration of an agreement that would guarantee free access to Berlin while establishing an international zone patterned after Vatican City. Kennedy merely listened to that as he did to many other proposals, and then indicated that it could be discussed whenever the Russians were willing to go through regular diplomatic channels, but he took no action.[13] When Khrushchev in effect challenged the status quo, Kennedy concluded that his administration had no other choice but to demonstrate its ability to take a firm stand.[14]

But that didn't mean he was ready to buy Acheson's more provocative suggestions. After having been asked to study the problems of NATO and Germany, the former secretary of state was invited by Kennedy to a White House meeting on the afternoon of April 5. In the presence of the visiting British Prime Minister and his foreign secretary, Lord Home, Acheson calmly proposed that when Khrushchev finally carried out the inevitable stroke of cutting off West Berlin, Kennedy should make the most of the opportunity to respond with unmistakable firmness. An allied division should test the issue of access rights by moving a convoy with supplies from the checkpoint at Helmstedt in West Germany eastward along the *Autobahn* toward Berlin. If the Russians tried to interfere, their real intentions would be made clear, and the military would be able to respond with all the justification that it had had at the start of the Korean War. In Acheson's view there was little to be negotiated but a great deal at stake in convincing the Communists of our readiness to draw the line firmly whatever the dangers.[15]

Understandably the British guests were disturbed, even shaken. This was no longer a mere theoretical discussion of options. Americans like Acheson really seemed to be accepting World War III as a fact of life. But not all Americans, even in that room, in particular Harriman and Stevenson. Acheson was not alone among our "elder statesmen in the field of foreign affairs," Schlesinger promptly reminded the President. Harriman and Stevenson combined some formidable experience. "All have served the republic brilliantly, and all are honorable and towering figures. As a rule of thumb," he wrote, "I would vote with any of them against the third."[16]

Acheson's position had important support from State. Paul Nitze, Foy Kohler, and George McGhee all agreed that the Russians would weigh carefully any intransigence that could lead to general nuclear war. The President had to give the Communists the kind of stiff confrontation their challenge deserved and not betray any sign of weakness.[17] Almost alone among Kennedy's principal foreign policy advisers, Harriman counseled against trying to settle anything directly with Khrushchev while at Vienna. The President should humor the Chairman, talk gently, discuss their mutual view of the world. At the same time, the dilemma of the West Germans can be stated by saying they had three things to fear: 1) that the U.S. would make a tough response; 2) that the U.S. would make a soft response; 3) that the U.S. would have no response.

As he prepared to leave for Europe, Kennedy's mood wavered between optimism and pessimism. He showed some evidence of strain.[18] He called Harris Wofford, and, without his usual light approach, urged getting his "friends off those buses," a reference to the Freedom Riders, who were then making headlines and filling southern jails by civil-disobedience challenges of segregation laws.[19] Didn't they realize how they were embarrassing him and the country at that vital moment? He also wondered why, given the generally troubled situation, the Russians were not moving more decisively to resolve the Berlin situation.

On his forty-fourth birthday Kennedy went to the Boston Armory for a giant birthday dinner sponsored by five thousand Massachusetts Democrats. "I am only 44," he told them, "but I have lived in my 44 years through three wars . . . No one can study the origins of any of those three struggles without realizing the serious miscalculations, the serious misapprehensions, about the possible actions of the other side which existed in the minds of the adversaries which helped to bring about all those wars."[20] Afterward he left from Logan on the short flight to Hyannis, finally settling in late that night at his father's Cape Cod house.

Tuesday was Memorial Day, and the President went sailing on the *Marlin* off Hyannis Port with the Ambassador, Ann Gargan, and Lem Billings. Jacqueline had remained behind, probably at Glen Ora. By the middle of that afternoon, however, the brief respite had ended. Kennedy returned to Barnstable Airport at Hyannis and flew to New York, where he addressed the American Cancer Foundation at the Waldorf-Astoria. From there the presidential party went directly to Idlewild, where they were joined by Jackie. By 10:00 P.M. they were airborne and headed toward Europe.

During the days immediately preceding the European trip, according to Dr. Travell, his pain had become more severe. She had even flown hurriedly up to the Cape for a special treatment. While in Europe he undoubtedly required additional injections. One of the first things he did when he reached Paris was to get his painful back into a hot tub.[21] Soon after his return, he secluded himself for several days at the Wrightsman estate in Palm Beach (his father's home having closed for the summer), and, with the diplomatic journey over, he accepted the need for crutches.

Jackie remained with her husband for only the six days spent in Paris, Vienna, and London. When the state visits ended and he returned home, she flew to Athens with her sister, Princess Radziwill, for an eight-day holiday that included an Aegean cruise.[22] Somewhat disingenuously, Pierre Salinger later told inquiring newsmen that she had probably left without knowing about the President's back problem.[23]

But the press was enchanted by the public elegance of the presidential couple. Charles Bohlen remembered their evening together at the Palace of Versailles: "The President handsome, slim, filled with the vitality of youth and good humor; his wife regal with an elaborate coiffure and a white gown sweeping to the ground. We were proud of them."[24] "I was there at the airport when they left for Vienna," recalled Abe Chayes, "and they looked great. My God, they looked beautiful."[25] De Gaulle himself, austere, forebodingly pompous, had been charmed and infatuated by Jackie's beauty and knowledge of French. A Parisian paper, *Libération,* lampooned his attention to her.[26] When the Kennedys got to Vienna and met with Khrushchev, the Russian's response to Jacqueline was almost one of childish exuberance. "I'd like to shake her hand first," he said as soon as he saw her. Then after dinner in the Schönbrunn Palace she was treated to the Chairman's fondest anecdotes. There she was also joined by Madame Khrushchev. The Russian "first lady" was plain indeed in comparison with Jackie, whose sleeveless, low-waisted, floor-length dress of pale pink paillettes had been designed for the occasion by Oleg Cassini. When the First Lady was driven through downtown Vienna, the crowds created a near stampede. When she arrived in Paris, she rode in a Citroen from Orly Field to the Quai d'Orsay. As she sat in the back of the car next to Madame de Gaulle, at least half a million people strained for a glimpse. She wore a pillbox hat and looked more like a movie queen than did many Hollywood heroines. While the President stood up in his bubble-top car waving to the crowds that lined the Champs-Elysées, wiping his face as a cold rain began to fall, Jackie nevertheless drew more curiosity. Whether en route to a dinner with her husband at the Elysée Palace, visiting a museum while being escorted by Minister of Culture André Malraux, or dropping in at a child day-care center with Madame de Gaulle, her Gallic heritage, beauty, and linguistic fluency made her the constant center of attention. Not inappropriately the President introduced himself at a press luncheon as "the man who accompanied Jacqueline Kennedy to Paris, and I have enjoyed it."[27]

When they reached London, on the final stop of the trip, they found the British less excited about Jackie and more attentive to the youthful President, whose arrival at the gates of Buckingham Palace provoked cries of "We want Jack! We want Jack!" His wife's presence provoked some controversy in England when the official censor banned a sketch that was scheduled for inclusion in a revue with the following lyrics spoken by an actress portraying the First Lady:

> *Since I have married Jack, how*
> *Dame Fortune has smiled,*
> *For his temper is sunny, his*
> *outlook is mild.*

Though we don't discuss Cuba
in front of the child.
We shall tell her the facts at
sixteen. . . .
While Jack fumbles with Russia,
I use all my guile.
So the press and the public won't
guess for a while.
He is just like Ike dressed up
Madison Avenue style.[28]

Most of all, however, the trip constituted the President's memorable introduction to Charles de Gaulle and Nikita Khrushchev. That first visit with De Gaulle, while less tense than the hours at Vienna, was nevertheless stressful. De Gaulle had invited him, and despite last-minute complications that almost made the trip unthinkable, Kennedy was eager to do what he could to reconcile outstanding differences. French fears of a rearmed Germany were not unlike the Russians' and De Gaulle was after American assistance for the development of their own nuclear program. At the same time, the Gaullist vision of a "third force" minimized NATO participation and, in the American view, was inimical to the strengthening of a European structure that Kennedy considered so vital. As far as De Gaulle was concerned, there was no room to negotiate over Berlin; even at the risk of war, the West had to continue the firm stand taken in 1958. Nevertheless he thought Kennedy ought to move toward peace. So, as firm as De Gaulle was over Berlin, he dissented from Acheson's scenario of a probe along the *Autobahn.* He was also blunt about saying that Kennedy would be a damned fool to get further involved in Southeast Asia. He warned that intervention there would mean "entanglement without end," and predicted that "the more you commit yourself there against communism, the more communists will appear to be champions of national independence." America would be "sucked into a bottomless military and political quagmire despite the losses and expenditures that you may squander."[29] But the real purpose of the Kennedy–De Gaulle meeting was the visible show of unity and reaffirmation of American willingness to deploy an army in Europe to confront any threat from the east, a point that needed bolstering after Washington's recent experiences with Cuba and Laos.[30]

As host, De Gaulle staged a show honoring the President and the First Lady that was reminiscent of the France of Louis XIV. Paris was brilliantly festive for the occasion, with lavish displays of the Tricolor and Stars and Stripes along the Champs-Elysées. "After dinner at the Galerie de Glace and a ballet at the Louis Seize Theater, which had just been renovated," Bohlen has written, "we went out on a balcony of the Palace of Versailles and watched the fireworks."[31] There were magnificent state dinners: Wednesday at the Elysée Palace, Thursday in the Hall of Mirrors, and a Friday luncheon at the Palais de Chaillot. The ornamentation was enhanced by the presence of the American President, who made what one observer called "an extraordinarily pleasant and attractive and interesting appearance."[32]

De Gaulle's subsequent, postmortem recollections of Kennedy were tactful. He had been "dealing with a man whose ability" and "whose justifiable ambition inspired immense hopes," words that are more restrained than effusive. At that occasion, just before meeting Khrushchev, the American seemed both anxious and cautious. "I am going to Vienna to show willingness to make contact and exchange views," was the way De Gaulle quoted him.[33] The irony remains that in some ways the adversary he went on to meet in Vienna—earthy, dogmatic, and tempestuous, a peasant even at his most powerful—was a more sympathetic figure.[34]

Kennedy, in turn, told Sir Alec Douglas-Home that the French president had a touch of megalomania and cared for nothing except what he himself decided were the "selfish" interests of his country.[35] No doubt Kennedy appreciated the jibe of still another Englishman, his good friend David Ormsby-Gore, who wrote to Bobby Kennedy that perhaps De Gaulle "should be declared an Ancient Monument and become the subject of a magnificent 'Son et Lumière' we could all go to see on our holiday in France."[36] Khrushchev was at least human, which Kennedy learned to appreciate, and that made him more tractable than a monument.

The Vienna talks did not so much provoke as confirm the existence of a crisis, and the subsequent publication by the Soviets of their *aide-mémoire* that had been given to Kennedy at the start of the talks at once emphasized the challenge to the West and limited the President's options. Inevitably Kennedy returned home determined to show strength through willingness to stand firm even at the risk of sparking the nuclear clash that had been dreaded ever since the end of World War II. In retrospect Kennedy could hardly have been surprised at Khrushchev's determination to support "wars of national liberation" and advance toward the "sovereign rights of the German Democratic Republic." Only Khrushchev's demeanor was difficult to anticipate, simply because he was so erratic. Their concluding joint statement explained that they had "reaffirmed their support of a neutral and independent Laos under a government chosen by the Laotians themselves," and merely confirmed that the other outstanding issues had been "discussed." Ominously, the communiqué offered no additional hope save for the obligatory comment about their agreement "to maintain contact on all questions of interest to the two countries and for the whole world."[37]

Khrushchev had approached the summit without his customary fanfare. Although subdued at the end, he nevertheless left Vienna in a relatively expansive mood. He told the Austrian president that he and the American had made "a very good beginning" toward improving relations with the new United States administration. The talks had accomplished their objective, which was merely to exchange views. His official statement to the Austrian government explained that the talks "will be conducive to the achievement of these talks as well as to the establishment of permanent peace." When he reached Moscow, he omitted the customary triumphal homecoming speech but in every other way displayed good spirits.[38] Khrushchev was clearly conscious of having taken the initiative.

Those who saw Kennedy in the American embassy immediately after the sessions found a decidedly less confident leader. James Reston later wrote that he was "shaken and angry," and that Khrushchev had bullied him and threatened him with war over Berlin.[39] In a *Times* dispatch obviously based on his conversation with the President, Reston reported that the two-day meeting had ended with "a limited agreement on Laos and a sharp three-hour disagreement on all questions concerning Germany and Berlin." Their encounter, Reston reported, ended in "hard controversy," and Kennedy left for London "in a solemn, although confident, mood," with "absolutely no new grounds for encouragement."[40] Another newsman, Peter Lisagor of the *Chicago Daily News*, left Vienna on Kennedy's plane and found that the President refused to comment beyond generalities. Referring to their next stop, London, he said, it was "going to be like child's play." He told Lisagor that he could describe the presidential mood as "somber." Ken O'Donnell, meanwhile, helped make the flight somewhat more colorful by making Khrushchev the object of some of his more pungent expletives. All of them, Lisagor remembered, were "a pretty innocent and green bunch." But they were also "a chastened group. . . . they had come face-to-face with the enemy, a cunning, shrewd, clever, earthy, incisive, wild in many ways face of the enemy, which was Khrushchev, who was unlike anything anybody's ever seen. . . . Kennedy looked kind of tired and a bit used up when we went into London."[41]

In an oral-history interview given in 1964, Bobby Kennedy conceded that George Kennan's assertion that Kennedy was "a tongue-tied young man" was essentially correct. But, Bobby added, Jack returned the next day and was more forceful, spelling out the American position with great clarity and warning that the "wars of national liberation" could get out of hand and lead to miscalculation. He also reminded Khrushchev rather pointedly that the United States had defended Europe in two wars and gave the clear message that his country would assume a similar responsibility for West Germany. It was at the end of their two-day discussion when Khrushchev clung to the argument of his *aide-mémoire* about the importance of signing a separate peace treaty with East Germany in six months that Kennedy commented that it would "be a cold winter."[42]

Yet Khrushchev himself, in his memoirs, was charitable toward Kennedy, praising his preparation and grasp of international issues. He experienced "quite a difference from Eisenhower's behavior in Geneva and Washington, when first Dulles and then Herter were always prompting him."[43] Bohlen suggested that Kennedy's error was to permit himself to engage in debate on grounds where he was no match for the Russian: Marxist theory and colonialism. "He didn't really understand it," Bohlen has pointed out. "I don't believe I ever had the impression that President Kennedy had seriously read . . . Lenin or any of the Soviet theoretical writers." He had only a general notion of what it was all about.[44] As Khrushchev later wrote, "Kennedy wanted to maintain the status quo in the world," and had in mind "the inviolability of borders *plus the enforced preservation of a country's internal social and political system.* In other words, he wanted countries with capitalist systems to remain capitalist, and he wanted us to agree to a guarantee to that effect."[45] The exchange gave Khrushchev the aura of the libertarian championing the aspirations of freedom in the third world with Kennedy placed on the defensive in the role of the colonialist. "In order that there should not be any conflict between us," said Khrushchev, according to an excerpt from the transcript, "you wish that these ideas not be propagated beyond the already existing socialist countries. But I repeat, Mr. President, that ideas cannot be stopped."[46]

While no account of their exchange specifically accuses Khrushchev of having used that particular occasion for nuclear blackmail (as he had done at other times), it was Kennedy's firmness against accepting a separate East German treaty that actually raised the holocaust option. Much to Khrushchev's annoyance, he kept warning about "miscalculation." He warned that if the Soviets pressed their point, they would force a showdown because the West could not retreat from what were considered its vital interests. "Time and again," Sorensen has pointed out, the President "returned to that point during the two days of talks."[47]

Perhaps most devastating was the subsequent Soviet publication of Khrushchev's *aide-mémoire*. That document had all the paranoia that characterized Soviet diplomacy. The West was charged with rebuilding German military power, with stockpiling weapons and establishing a strong military base "on German soil," all aimed at dividing "the former Allies in the anti-Nazi coalition." The city of West Berlin, "deprived of a firm international status, is now a place where Bonn's revenge-seeking elements constantly maintain extreme tension and stage all kinds of provocations very dangerous to the cause of peace." The solution was its conversion to a free, demilitarized city. Occupation rights would end with a peace treaty, and West Berlin would become "strictly neutral" with respect for the "sovereign rights of the German Democratic Republic." Nor did the document mince any words about the implications of access rights to the enclave 110 miles behind the East German frontier. That question would be settled "through appropriate agreements with the German Democratic Republic." And if the West had any remaining doubts about what that implied, the Soviet document reiterated that it would have to be consistent with the "inalienable right of any sovereign state." The changeover should be possible after six months.[48]

Immediately after Vienna, Dean Rusk returned to Paris, where his briefing of De Gaulle and the NATO Council left little hope for a peaceful settlement. That ominous outlook, however, was not fully shared by the British. When Kennedy got to London on the last stop of his European journey, he found that Macmillan shared his views on a Laotian accord. Both men continued to view Soviet support for the Geneva negotiations as a test of Moscow's intentions. But Macmillan had preferred to confine reactions to the Berlin crisis to a statement of principles that would avoid a precipitous movement toward a showdown, although it was true that the Kennedy–Macmillan communiqué dutifully declared the "necessity of maintaining the right and obligations of the Allied governments in Berlin."[49]

The only choice, Kennedy knew, was a blend of overwhelming strength to remind the Russians that, as he had warned in his Inaugural Address, we were "ready to pay any price," with a sufficient opening to permit room for a peaceful resolution. Kennedy's rejection of Acheson's call for the declaration of a state of emergency in the Berlin affair foreshadowed his similar reluctance to heed the call by the former secretary of state (whom the Republicans had pilloried for "selling out" to international communism) for a military strike against Cuba during the missile crisis. Essential for an understanding of Kennedy during the Berlin threat is the rejection of the simplistic concept of the President as a "cold warrior" and an understanding of the style of his leadership. The grim firmness, the soaring rhetoric so consciously patterned to counterpoint the Eisenhower monotony, were inseparable from the qualities that helped shape the national mood and attract international attention. It was, moreover, the same style that brought approval from the political Left when used so effectively to appeal to the national conscience when civil rights outrages became unendurable.

As Kennedy himself came to realize, his position may well have been too articulate, the alarm too strident. But it was a fine line, one that had to maneuver between avoiding hysteria while convincing the Russians and Western Europe that the United States would not back away from that position even if faced with the ultimate consequences. Not much was heard at the time about secondary options, and it is most unlikely that Kennedy's political opposition, recharged in the months after the Bay of Pigs, would have permitted a more conciliatory choice. Even before the President's plane landed at Andrews Air Force Base and he had had a chance to make his report to the American people, *The New York Times* (hardly the most hawkish of papers) editorialized that while compromises were inevitable on such matters as the nuclear test ban and Laos, "there are some points on which no compromise can be made, and all the compromise cannot come from our side alone."[50]

Later much would be written about how Kennedy's "on-the-job training" tempered some of his enthusiasms and gave him a more realistic view of the world. But such commentaries often forget that his basic outlook never did change. Where it did, it was largely a matter of events overwhelming him at home. But Jack Kennedy's determination to eject Castro was just as great, if not greater, after the failure of the Cuban invasion. Thus once Khrushchev had made clear his own determination, once Kennedy had been faced with the dramatic truth of how the Russians viewed the world, Kennedy went into action much as he later did when U-2 planes detected the presence of missile sites in Cuba.

Within less than twelve hours after his plane had touched down at Andrews Air Force Base, Kennedy went before the public with a televised report. His tone was moderate and showed less anxiety than he had displayed at that afternoon's meeting with congressional leaders.[51] He was firm but not apocalyptic. He conveyed Khrushchev's position in remarkably judicious terms, with considerably less cold-war sloganeering than had been customary.

He made little effort to moralize, to delineate the issues as choices between good and evil. The Russians were not the devilish aggressors. Americans had not been hearing the type of candor that told them, as did Kennedy that evening, "that the Soviets and ourselves give wholly different meanings to the same words—war, peace, democracy, and popular will." Facing Khrushchev directly had been much more sobering than reading his speeches. It had offered confirmation of "how differently we view the present and the future. Our views contrasted sharply but at least we knew better at the end where we both stood." He explained that the mood of the talks "was not cause for elation or relaxation, nor was it cause for undue pessimism or fear." He found that Khrushchev "believes the world will move his way without resort to force" and said he had "predicted the triumph of communism in the new and less developed countries." The Russian was certain "that the tide was moving his way, that the revolution of rising peoples would eventually be a Communist revolution, and that the so-called wars of liberation, supported by the Kremlin, would replace the old methods of direct aggression and invasion." Even more candid was Kennedy's subsequent statement that "It is easy to dismiss as Communist-inspired every anti-government or anti-American riot, every overthrow of a corrupt regime, or every mass protest against misery and despair. These are not all Communist inspired." Nor, he added, had the Communists created "the conditions which caused them."[52]

Afterward, and not immediately following his return from Vienna, Soviet–American relations began to deteriorate. The Russians' inexplicable publication of the full text of the *aide-mémoire* they had given Kennedy at Vienna alone confirmed the more portentous implications of the Soviet position. Reprinted in the American press, it portrayed Soviet–American differences more ominously than the President's public explanation of June 6. By graphically delineating the challenge, Moscow had undercut any possibility of minimizing the threat. Khrushchev then followed through with an alarming radio and television report to the Russian people. He mixed praise for the American President with the warning that "a peace treaty with Germany cannot be put off any longer." He referred to the impending East German sovereignty by terming as "aggression" any possible effort to cross the borders by land, air, or water, and promised that such an act would be "duly repulsed." He also alluded to "wars of national liberation" by saying that the Soviet Union did not intend to interfere with the Laotian guerrillas who were jeopardizing the cease-fire. In the Kremlin one week later Khrushchev wore the uniform of a Soviet lieutenant general and spoke in terms that were reassuring to his own hard-liners.[53]

Nobody thought Khrushchev would intentionally push matters to the edge of war, but as Kennedy himself had warned the Chairman, miscalculation was a constant danger. And there was little disagreement that the safest course lay with emphasizing American willingness to respond to Russian provocations. At a White House luncheon with congressional leaders an alternative course was not even debated: military forces had to be built up and Russian toughness matched.[54] Bob Kennedy later explained that Khrushchev thought his brother was "not going to be a strong figure based, in my judgment, on the fact that we didn't use American forces to crush Cuba . . . and thought he was a young, inexperienced figure."[55] At his June 28 news conference the President himself observed that the comments since Vienna were "apparently designed to heighten tension."[56] Dean Acheson told a National Security Council meeting the next day that testing the American will to resist was their basic objective.[57]

So there was little choice but to react, and react with authority. As things stood, the Russians were dealing the cards, fine-tuning the Berlin tensions, and maintaining, at the same time, luxurious detachment over developments in the Congo and Southeast Asia. Only the German question contained ingredients for a direct showdown, and, as Kennedy evaluated his options, he feared that the real danger lay in preferring to talk rather than to fight.

Apprehension began to intensify. The situation had no acceptable fallback position. No clients could be counted on to substitute for the major powers. When Acheson gave the NSC the plan for his *Autobahn* probe and pressed for the declaration of a national emergency, all with the assumption that Khrushchev was merely testing our general will to resist and so undermine America's world influence, the President held back. He listened to the objections at the table and solicited the views of such people as Robert Lovett and others.[58] He seemed obsessed about being maneuvered by Khrushchev into a formal summit conference. Undoubtedly he had the nightmare of allowing Germany to become to Khrushchev what Poland became to Stalin in his dealings with FDR.

There is ample reason for believing that Kennedy was well aware that the whole Soviet campaign on Berlin was contrived, and that Khrushchev's dilemma was in satisfying the Kremlin and his own military while his real interests were elsewhere, more in tune with those specialists eager to stimulate agricultural production.[59] At the same time, the State Department's long delay in getting out a response to the *aidemémoire* was most irritating. "I think the moral of it is that no one was really riding herd all the way through," Bundy noted to the President a few days after it finally came out, but Rusk later claimed that he had stalled intentionally because he feared that Kennedy was too eager to negotiate.[60] The President's annoyance with Rusk and State showed when he told Adolf Berle that, as Berle noted in his journal, "he was entirely disillusioned about the 'old pros' in the State Department; their capacity to deal with situations."[61]

Kennedy considered the State Department's reply on Berlin as insufficiently spirited, too full of worn clichés, to convince the Russians. Nor would it "lessen the crisis by developing any new areas of negotiation."[62] Kennedy's preoccupation was with the possible consequences of Berlin and the need to maneuver between the twin evils of "holocaust or humiliation"—as he saw the choices—and convincing Moscow that he was ready for war if that became inevitable.[63] Even Chester Bowles, one of Kennedy's leading doves, agreed that the United States had to make clear the willingness to fight.[64]

Gradually that summer, as he contemplated his public stand, Kennedy had faced that possibility. He felt that the chance of war was close. Robert Kennedy has said that the odds were about one in five.[65] "I think it's fair to say," Martin Hillenbrand has explained, "that the President's employment of our nuclear capacity as a diplomatic weapon in the Berlin situation was a very measured and tempered one, one which reflected his responsibilities as President."[66] Kennedy had concluded that the U.S. could no longer afford to be bound by the traditional policy of excluding a preemptive first strike.[67] He had concluded that Khrushchev "won't pay attention to words. He has to see you move."[68]

The working assumption, as remembered by Paul Nitze, was that the Russians would first seek alternatives to nuclear war. The President agreed with McNamara that such Soviet hesitations could be overcome if American retaliatory capacity were limited to knocking out Soviet population centers. Nitze recalled that the argument emphasized developing sufficient power and survivability for second-strike response more effective than the initial Soviet blow. Kennedy accepted this general principle. He discussed it with McNamara several times during the Berlin crisis. Throughout Kennedy's determination to save Berlin, he remained all too conscious of the need to make decisions that would bring closer the ultimate one of finally "having to press that button."[69] In the interest of safeguarding against miscalculation the Russians had to be convinced that Kennedy was capable of going that far. In September the attorney general said during a televised interview that the importance of defending Berlin was so great to the President that "he will use nuclear weapons."[70] Stewart Alsop later interviewed the President, and quoted him in a popular magazine article as saying that "Khrushchev must *not* be certain that, where its vital interests are threatened, the United States will never strike first." Kennedy had also told him that "in some circumstances we might have to take the initiative."[71] But he accepted the notion of giving Khrushchev an "escape hatch" so he could back down without political humiliation.[72]

Later generations have replayed Kennedy's actions and found them unjustifiably provocative. He did just about everything short of ordering full mobilization. His televised counter-challenge of July 25 has been called "one of the most alarming speeches by an American President in the whole, nerve-wracking course of the Cold War."[73] He sat at his desk before the presidential seal and was flanked by flags. The delivery itself matched the grimness of its message. It evoked the horrors of the nuclear nightmare, and, especially when he went on about the advisability of building shelters, it was enough to jolt those who had been loath to think the unthinkable. The impact was powerful, and the most effective parts —as Sorensen has fairly acknowledged—conveyed that intent, but it was far from an ultimatum. The "escape hatches" were there, although weakly perceived in comparison with the stress on a tough stance. He noted that the Russians had raised the ante. They had prescribed the date for a separate peace; they had jeopardized the security of the Berlin accesses; and they had increased the military budget. While Kennedy emphasized that the West had no intention of yielding to the pressures and enumerated the ingredients of the partial mobilization, he also stressed that the United States intended "to have a wider choice than humiliation or all-out nuclear action." The American reactions would not be all military or all negative, but they would be strong. "If we do not meet our commitments in Berlin, where will we later stand?" he asked. His call included doubling the number of draftees, reactivating reserve units, and increasing the armed forces by over 200,000 men. The economic burden was spelled out through the call for an additional $3.25 billion for the armed forces, nearly two billion more for nonnuclear weapons, ammunition, and equipment, plus a $207 million civil defense increase. Military outlays sent to Congress the next day involved an increase of $3,454,600,000.[74]

The civil defense call, unlike previous tentative suggestions on the subject, now carried the urgency of an immediate crisis. Recommendations for the construction of public and private shelters encouraged somewhat hysterical debates that prompted many Americans to rationalize why lifeboats should be used on a first-come, first-served basis with unfortunates left to scramble for their own survival. Would it be moral to protect loved ones even at the cost of shooting those desperately trying to share their restricted space, air, and food? Clare Boothe Luce, quick to find an incentive for those most capable of providing for themselves, suggested that private construction might be stimulated by making such shelters deductible as medical expenses.[75] Others argued the academic question of whether such civilian defense measures would induce a psychological acceptance of war or would become part of the nuclear age deterrent. Eleanor Roosevelt, who was much more sympathetic with the former point of view, expressed that fear in a newspaper column. Kennedy responded with a warm note and added the thought that the "prospect of a nuclear exchange is so terrible that I conceive that it would be preferable to be among the dead than among the quick."[76] Nevertheless a military-diplomatic point had to be made, and requests for a shelter program went on to Congress.

In passing it along to Senate Armed Forces Committee Chairman Richard Russell, the President reasoned that expanded appropriations would "greatly increase the capacity of this country to survive and recover after a nuclear blow" and that "large numbers of lives could be saved by adequate fallout shelter space." He also informed Russell that the cost would come to just three or four dollars for every American. "We may well take satisfaction in this achievement."[77] By early 1962, in a special issue devoted entirely to civilian defense, The New Republic considered that a total of $692.3 million had been requested for the shelter program. To make the whole thing credible would require "a massive, nationwide, deep shelter program, one that would provide 'hardened' holes for a very substantial number of civilians. But there is no indication," said the magazine, "that the authorities, federal, state or local, intend to undertake anything so radical or so expensive."[78] Kennedy himself later realized that the stress on shelters (inspired in part by deterrence, the need for toughness, and to undercut Rockefeller politically) had been overdrawn.

"I don't know when I've been happier," wrote Harry Truman to the President, "than when I listened to your great speech on the situation with which we are faced. . . . Keep it up."[79] Senator Fulbright, who had received an advance copy, heard the speech after dinner at Clark Clifford's home. "The response," he informed the President the next day, "was very favorable."[80] And the public was also with their President. The next Gallup poll showed that, if necessary, seventy-one percent agreed that Americans should fight their way into Berlin.[81]

Khrushchev's solution came swiftly, unexpectedly. The response took the form of the Berlin Wall, first a barbed-wire barrier, and, within the next few days, a mortar and cinder-block divide that separated the city into two sectors, sealing off the escape routes that had been draining manpower from the Communists. "There had been zero warning of any such activity," recalled Kennedy's military aide, General Clifton, although the CIA had warned the President that the Communists were worried about the exodus. The news came on a Sunday when the President was at Hyannis Port. Clifton, whose code name was "Watchman," called in Kennedy from his outing on the *Marlin* and gave him the news as he got into his golf cart. The President was furious.[82] More extreme responses from agitated Americans were expressed through moral outrage and numerous demands for tearing down the barrier.

It was not surprising in retrospect; inevitably it was a face-saving solution that both backed off from confrontation and coped with the refugee drain. "It had become clear to many of us who were dealing with the Berlin problem," Martin J. Hillenbrand told an interviewer, "that the East German regime and the Soviet Union would have to do something, somehow about the ever-increasing flow of refugees, which was reaching almost runaway proportions by mid-summer of 1961."[83] The President, of course, retained his composure during that provocation far more than those who would have liked to have seen America take action across the border. General Lucius Clay, soon to become Kennedy's personal representative in Berlin, volunteered to offer any assistance in a possible congressional investigation of the lack of a reaction. "To have stopped this," he explained, "we would have had to be prepared to move in force across the border unilaterally and indeed with probably complete Allied disapproval. Such a movement might indeed have had far reaching consequences."[84] From the administration's point of view the act was merely another in a long series of violations. It did not, however, fall within the scope of the basic rights we had been threatening to take military action to defend.[85]

Kennedy responded by sending to West Germany both Vice-President Johnson and General Clay, who had been American high commissioner for Germany at the time of the 1948 blockade. More dramatically, however, the President made a token gesture that reinforced the credibility of the tough stand he had been taking over access rights to West Berlin. Although the wall was essentially a defensive and not an offensive act, Kennedy sent a convoy of fifteen hundred American troops along the *Autobahn*. "It was," Sorensen later wrote, "his most anxious moment during the prolonged Berlin crisis, his first order of American military units into a potential confrontation with Soviet forces."[86] While the vehicles were on the highway, General Clifton retained communications with the convoy's commander. The gesture was not really the same as Acheson's plan, since the Communists had said nothing about barring entry through East Germany territory. But it was sufficiently nerve-wracking for General Maxwell Taylor to fear a Soviet reaction.[87] Kennedy himself canceled his usual weekend absence from Washington until he heard that they had gotten through. But in an off-the-record background briefing he held at the State Department earlier that week, the day after news came about the barbed wire, his fear of an outbreak of nuclear war was genuine.[88]

For a few hours during the final weekend in August the confrontation seemed to be imminent. General Clay, eager to relieve the mounting pressures placed against Western positions by East German police, drew American tanks into a line facing Soviet-controlled territory only yards away across the East-West boundary in Berlin. Soviet tanks responded and, for that chilling period, an "eyeball-to-eyeball" meeting placed world peace at the risk of a single individual's hotheaded response. Quietly the Russian tanks withdrew that Sunday, thereby backing off from what may have been the most dangerous moment of the entire crisis. Just before that showdown Khrushchev had announced the withdrawal of the six-month deadline for signing a separate peace with East Germany. For a while, at least, the crisis had subsided, but there still was no solution.

At Vienna, Khrushchev had said that he would not act unilaterally to break the moratorium against atmospheric nuclear bomb testing. Suddenly, however, at the end of August he announced that the informal cessation had come to an end. Russian testing would resume, which was what his military chiefs had hoped for all along.

Congressional responses came rapidly, some of them denunciations of the Russians for having broken an "agreement" not to test. Of course that was not true; there had been no such accord. But Kennedy had hoped that the pause could nevertheless aid the Geneva process of finding some way out of continuing to poison the atmosphere with radioactive fallout. Restricting testing had, in fact, become very much part of his long-term desire for effective arms control. Unfortunately Soviet resumption made the American choice of pursuing the moratorium single-handedly a virtually nonexistent option. Within hours of the Soviet announcement Vice-President Johnson, hitherto portrayed as opposed to American resumption, sent the President a memorandum urging a new round of tests because "our nation's security is threatened. Testing," Johnson reminded Kennedy, "is an essential to relative modernity in weapons development."[89] When Carl Kaysen suggested exploiting the situation in a different way, by a presidential speech piously stating America's refusal to play the same dirty game, Kennedy responded by saying, "They'd kick me in the nuts. I couldn't get away with it."[90] Within the administration a great debate broke out. In effect it was a postscript to the Berlin crisis of 1961. The Russians went ahead with a two-month series of tests of forty nuclear weapons.

Skeptics will continue to doubt Kennedy's disappointment. Schlesinger quotes from a Robert Kennedy memorandum, written just after the Khrushchev announcement, that the decision to resume testing produced "the most gloomy meeting at the White House . . . since early in the Berlin crisis." In much the same vein, Sorensen reveals that Kennedy's first reaction "is unprintable. It was one of personal anger at the Soviets for deceiving him and at himself for believing them."[91] Still, from Bundy, by way of Chalmers Roberts, we learn that Kennedy told Schlesinger, Sorensen, and the correspondent what they wanted to hear: He was, in fact, happy to let the Russians "take the heat for awhile. . . . Sorensen was 100% wrong about JFK agonizing over resumption of nuclear testing, that he was convinced K [Kennedy] had made the decision and called the meeting only to ratify it."[92]

The March announcements to resume atmospheric testing won the support of two thirds of the American public.[93] Those who argue that Kennedy should have provided the leadership in the opposite direction, by "sailing against the wind," were essentially asking him to gamble with his political base. Robert Kennedy later told John Bartlow Martin that his brother "was never very enthusiastic about the testing."[94] Still, his anxiety for progress in the entire field of arms control and nuclear proliferation was understandably tempered by the realities of American politics. During those months between the Soviet resumption and the start of the American atmospheric series in the Pacific in April, he vacillated between his own desires and his limited options. All the while he pursued a centrist position. He joined with Macmillan in a statement urging Soviet acceptance of a three-power agreement to end atmospheric tests productive of radioactive fallout.[95] Two days later, on September 5, he announced that underground testing would begin in the Nevada desert.[96]

When Kennedy finally announced his decision to resume, it came by way of a radio and television address to the American people. And he did so on March 2, a full half year after the Khrushchev move. On August 31, when he was trying to delay having to resume, the White House had issued a statement of confidence that the U.S. nuclear stockpile assured ample freedom to ignore Khrushchev's "blackmail." Now, however, Kennedy underlined the American need to "maintain an effective quantity and quality of nuclear weapons." He explained that safeguards on radioactive fallout would be "far less than the contamination created by last fall's Soviet series." But his most candid admission was the following: "In the absence of any major shift in Soviet policies, no American President—responsible for the freedom and the safety of so many people—could in good faith make any other decision."[97]

9

"Playing the Game"

Two important changes came about at the end of 1961, one in the State Department and the other in Congress. Chester Bowles had been pushed out as undersecretary of state, becoming what was, in effect, a special presidential representative to the third world. His leaving had been brewing for at least half a year and became the centerpiece of a State Department reorganization, a shakeup quickly known as the "Thanksgiving Day massacre."

Bowles was the New Dealer sacrificed to gladden New Frontier tacticians. Ted Sorensen assured Bowles that he was getting the "Harry Hopkins spot" in the Kennedy administration, which Bowles later recalled to the President as a description he "could not take too seriously."[1] It would be a bad mistake, Harris Wofford had warned Kennedy back in July, for "his to be the first head to fall in the aftermath of Cuba."[2] But Kennedy's animus toward Bowles was nothing new. Bowles had been sluggish about standing up for Kennedy before Los Angeles. He had insisted he would never campaign against Humphrey and had conditioned his original commitment to Kennedy on that vow. One close Bowles associate thought he "never knew how fully he accepted Kennedy as a real exemplar of the liberal tradition in American politics or how fully he was accepted by Kennedy."[3]

He was obviously there as a sop to the liberals. Also Bowles was too verbose for Jack Kennedy, both orally and on paper, and he wanted to remake the world by taking giant leaps. He retained too much of his family's reformist, mugwump tradition. He was unrealistic, soft, a tinkerer rather than a doer, a visionary.

And Bowles, rather than Rusk, bore much of the responsibility for the inefficiency of the State Department. He "preferred exploring long-range ideas to expediting short-gap expedients," Sorensen has explained.[4] Almost two years before it was acceptable, Bowles urged Kennedy to develop "possible alternate leadership to Diem in South Vietnam."[5] An important reason for moving him out, however, was that he was too free with the press, telling newspapermen about differences within the administration, and especially about his dissent before the Bay of Pigs.[6] The end seemed imminent during the summer of 1961, when the President's friend, Charles Bartlett, wrote that Bowles's scalp was in jeopardy because he "has created a sense of disorder and insecurity" in the State Department.[7] On July 17 *The New York Times* reported that the President was about to call for his resignation. Bowles's supporters (the "Chet Set"), especially Harris Wofford and Sorensen, came to his aid. They guessed that it was the President who was playing the leaking game. Schlesinger describes Kennedy reading the *Times* article on a return flight from Hyannis and commenting: "You can tell how that story was written. You can tell where every paragraph came from. One paragraph is from Bowles or his people. The next paragraph is from someone at State trying to make a case against Bowles."[8] When Bobby was interviewed in 1964, however, he said very plainly that "the President was going to move him out and he leaked to the press that he was going to be moved out." And that he agreed that the publicity had been embarrassing, had raised too much of a fuss, and the controversy was allowed to cool.[9] Indeed the effort to clarify the lines of authority within the State Department was the cover under which Bowles was deftly yanked out during that Thanksgiving Day massacre and replaced by George Ball. "The President snuck up on him one day and got him fired before he knew it," explained Bobby with evident satisfaction.[10]

Bowles later told a Kennedy Library interviewer that he was the victim of two groups out to get him. Both were close to the President and antagonistic to his liberal influences. Earlier they had worked to block Stevenson; then they wanted to undercut his UN position, but Adlai was too prominent at the UN, and Bowles was "an easier target." His memoirs later repeated essentially the same thing, but the interview that was conducted in 1965 stressed that while one cabal consisted of such conservative newspaper buddies as Joe Alsop, the other was the "rather fashionable, well-to-do group" that socialized with the President. In that interview Bowles also said that "I don't think Rusk had much to do with the matter, although I may be wrong."[11]

Another loss was of an entirely different order. The death of Sam Rayburn on November 16, 1961, had deprived Kennedy of an effective speaker. John McCormack was no match. Rayburn had served there longer than any other man. "Mr. Sam" was a fixture; if anyone could work wonders with Kennedy's slim margin of congressional support, it was Rayburn—and, during the Rules Committee fight, he did exactly that, although the results hardly justified the battle. Still, as one student of Kennedy and the Congress has written, "No member of the leadership, House or Senate, was more challenging (or important) to [Larry] O'Brien at the outset than Mr. Sam."[12] O'Brien's congressional liaison staff had worked hard and intimately with the speaker, and the President himself had succeeded remarkably well in bridging the chronological and cultural gaps that separated him from Rayburn. McCormack, however, although from Kennedy's own city, was more troublesome. Their very proximity in home-state politics had created rivalry rather than cooperation. The 1962 Democratic senatorial primary contest between Ted Kennedy and Edward McCormack, the speaker's nephew, hardly healed matters even if they "were determined not to let it interfere with their collaboration."[13] The reality was quite another matter. On the education bill McCormack actively opposed Kennedy's attempt to keep public funds from going to parochial schools; indeed, when James J. Delaney of New York City teamed up with the Republicans, the bill never came out of the Rules Committee.

One historian who interviewed McCormack shortly before his death in 1981 came away from that meeting and immediately recorded his observation that "when I turned to his relationship with John Kennedy . . . the change in atmosphere was quite dramatic. The speaker stiffened in his chair, his voice changed, and he became formal and quite strained. I knew at once that it would not be possible to probe realistically into the Kennedy–McCormack relationship. The speaker refused to discuss or even admit that any differences existed and repeatedly insisted that his ties to Kennedy were very positive. . . . It is my considered view as an historian that Speaker McCormack's response demonstrated that his relationship with John Kennedy was charged with tension, which, for personal and other reasons, the speaker does not intend to discuss or document."[14]

If McCormack was unreliable, the situation in the Senate was hardly better. Mike Mansfield lacked Johnson's power. O'Brien's staff, with specialists assigned to work each chamber, conducted an efficient operation, counting heads with accuracy, cajoling individual legislators, keeping careful tabs on potentially useful members with detailed lists of favors rendered by the White House to be cashed in for some helpful vote or influence with colleagues. And the upper chamber was more cooperative, granting the administration's wishes in a number of key areas not possible from the House, such as aid to education. Even so, the power of entrenched southern conservatism that lingered on can be seen by the letter Dick Russell wrote to a friend in which he described that body as the "most radical one that has ever met together in the history of this nation."[15] Even allowing for hyperbole, it must be assumed that Russell was referring to the Senate's actions in the Eighty-seventh Congress in going along with administration requests in the fields of aiding depressed areas, hiking minimum wages, housing and farm legislation, and, unlike the House, aid to education.

The Kennedy congressional record would afterward be gone over endlessly, mostly caught up in a debate about whether it was as weak as its critics charged and whether such bills as the ones providing for Medicare, civil rights, tax reductions, immigration reform, and the establishment of a Department of Urban Affairs would have been possible without Lyndon Johnson's later leadership. Johnson's partisans preferred to cite the somewhat deceptive figures compiled by *Congressional Quarterly* that showed that the President got just 44.3 percent of his legislative requests in 1962. With the election of the Eighty-eighth Congress that figure plummeted to a disastrous 27.2 percent, a level that the service pointed out was the "lowest score for a President in ten years."[16]

Others have pointed to a respectable body of social welfare legislation, in addition to the Trade Expansion Act, the Peace Corps, the manpower retraining program, and the creation of the Arms Control and Disarmament Agency. Much of the analysis, however, gives surprisingly little attention to Kennedy's own role. For a man who was to many "just a wise-ass Catholic kid" who had never been part of the Senate's inner circle and had far less seasoning than the congressional leaders, he was well liked.[17] At the weekly Tuesday morning breakfasts his ability to relax and banter was appreciated. There were, though, rumblings of discontent (mostly from southern members) that he should have given Vice-President Johnson more to do on Capitol Hill to move legislation.[18] But Johnson at least was always at those leadership meetings and breakfasts, and doubt remains about whether that kind of involvement by the vice-president would have made him more unpopular or whether it was resisted because, as Wilbur Mills believes, Kennedy feared that it could become a way of enhancing his political power.[19]

A consensus does emerge from the Capitol Hill view of the Kennedy presidency. He was cooperative, worked well with the members, and was always polite. When at one point the powerful chairman of the Ways and Means Committee objected to a ten percent write-off in the tax bill, Kennedy responded in a typical manner. He assumed not that Wilbur Mills was mistaken but that the bill was defective. But while Mills could recall such incidents as examples of harmony, he did not hesitate to label Kennedy's approach as "timid."[20] Allen Ellender of Louisiana went beyond that, saying he could not recall a President who was "less aggressive."[21] Hale Boggs suggested that while Kennedy took positions and held to them, "he felt that the House hierarchy, so to speak, was pretty well lined up in other hands."[22] Kennedy preferred to submit a bill, according to his longtime colleague Leverett Saltonstall, "and then hope or expect Congress to do something about it because of the public interest in it."[23] Other comments flow into the same vein: the staff was hardworking, but the President was detached.[24] One member of O'Brien's staff remembered his personal frustration at the President's remoteness. While specifically excluding Torby Macdonald, he lamented Kennedy's friendships that had little to do with congressional effectiveness, especially the one with George Smathers. The President was too often inattentive to legislative needs, out enjoying himself when he should have been giving vital support to those trying to round up the votes and move bills through committees. "While we could understand in ourselves the need in that terribly demanding job for the President to be able to remove himself," said Charles U. Daly, "and admired the way he did that and the joy he took in life . . . it complicated our job."[25]

One Kennedy aide, Fred Holborn, points out that the real "Kennedy legislators" did not arrive until the Johnson sweep over Goldwater. Having said that much, he agrees with the consensus view that patience was an attribute the President lacked, and legislation frequently required close mothering and some active trading before it could be achieved.[26] But Kennedy tended to dislike having to spend the time it took to deal with all the parties involved. He thought one explanation was enough. When matters seemed to have reached a dead end, he preferred to drop them. Unlike his successor he had a great "sense of distance" from Capitol Hill.[27] His taste was prey to powers that knew how to take advantage.

Nobody had become more potent than Kerr of Oklahoma, whose rise to power in the absence of Johnson's leadership won him the reputation as the "uncrowned King of the Senate." He was a self-made multimillionaire, one of the Hill's wealthiest men, whose father had been a tenant farmer in what was then Indian territory. Kerr, sixty-six in 1962, had made his fortune in oil and natural gas. After serving as Oklahoma's governor, he had gone on to the Senate. Whereas Hubert Humphrey was the man to see to find out what was going on, Kerr was the one who could get things done. A chairman of no single committee, he was a key member of several.[28] Twice he demonstrated his power by defeating the administration's Medicare bill and frustrating the desired legislation on taxes and trade. He had also been instrumental in thwarting the liberal filibuster that had opposed the establishment of a communications satellite corporation as a private enterprise. Robert Kerr was clearly the man to deal with. Somebody dubbed him as "the new wagon master of the rocky road to the new frontier."[29] He had no hesitation about saying that you couldn't get a tax bill unless he got his judge, and Bobby Kennedy later said that Kerr's "only interest was money and advancing his own and his friends' economic well-being." But the President admired his strength and ability to be so blatant about what he wanted.[30] Kennedy's cultivation of Kerr was one time when he could not be faulted for aloofness.

On October 29, 1961, *Air Force One* delivered the President to Kerr's "Ker-Mac" ranch at Poteau, Oklahoma. The "ranch" that Kennedy found was more like a modern barony, as big and grandiose as its owner. It stood on a fifty-two-thousand-acre plot that overlooked a river valley. The house, furnished in Chinese elegance at the desire of Kerr's wife, had fourteen thousand square feet, three kitchens, nine bedrooms, eleven baths, and, for the grandchildren, a playroom outfitted as a ship. Kerr himself had rejuvenated the land with rich grasses, and so he was able to accommodate his two thousand Black Angus cattle.[31]

Quite a spectacle, having the President of the United States out there in rural Oklahoma, and Bob Kerr appreciated the opportunity fully. He made Kennedy a captive of presentations by district and division chiefs of the Corps of Engineers, who displayed models and charts to explain the progress made on the Arkansas River Navigation Project. The President was surely less than enthralled. "Kerr was just glorying in this," recalled Edwin Bayley, who was with the President's entourage; "he's that kind of guy . . . for the benefit of his home audience, making him do tricks."[32] Kennedy then had dinner with the Kerr family, which included the Senator's three sons and their wives, his daughter, and her husband.[33] "And Kennedy had to stay there and eat with the family, and they couldn't even have a drink," continued Bayley. The presidential party remained overnight at the ranch. While he was there, of course, the Chief Executive, the "leader of the free world," had to open a new highway there, "which didn't need opening, and go look at all of Kerr's cows, and then hang around with that family, with whom he had about as much in common as nothing. All this to butter him up. And I could see it wasn't going to do any good anyway, Kerr being that kind of arrogant guy."[34]

But Kerr's power did do Kerr some good. The following year, the Kennedy administration recommended $66.1 million for Oklahoma water development and $9.5 million in government loans and grants under the Area Redevelopment Act to build twin lodges at Lake Eufaula. That allocation was twelve times greater than any other ARA grant.[35] The trade bill did pass, and so did the tax bill with the investment credit write-off, but the "uncrowned King of the Senate" died on New Year's Day, 1963, and he was no longer open for business.

"Solutions" were usually illusory. Ongoing matters continued to preoccupy the Kennedy White House in a way that tended to confirm the insolubility of world politics. If anything the globe had become an even more dangerous place than Kennedy had found it in January 1961. Arms limitations and Berlin continued to remain constant preoccupations, their solutions elusive. Movement toward some kind of modification in each area was made even more difficult by the different interests within the Atlantic community. The allies had their own ideas of how far Washington should, or would, go toward guaranteeing European security.

Berlin, of course, would not disappear as either an area of conflict or symbol of East-West differences. By the summer of 1962 the question seemed to be threatening whatever equanimity had been reached. On June 18, through Georgi Bolshakov, the President received a new Khrushchev warning about pressures against the city. American insistence on occupation rights was still a thorn (a "bone in his throat," he had called it). A peace treaty would ultimately have to be signed, the relations between the USSR and the German Democratic Republic "normalized."[36]

For a while, as unpublicized talks continued between Dean Rusk and Andrei Gromyko, some optimism seemed warranted. But as the summer progressed, positions appeared to harden. There was still no room to negotiate. Since the previous fall the President had begun exchanging correspondence with Khrushchev; there was now the possibility of adding "hot-line" communications between the Oval Office and the Kremlin. At his news conference of July 23, however, all Kennedy could say was that he and Khrushchev "understood each other, but we differ." Then he repeated his fear of miscalculation by pointing out the "danger of governments getting out of touch with each other."[37] One month later he cautioned against assuming that the crisis seemed to be "blowing up towards a cold winter of some sort." He expressed instead the hope that he might talk with Khrushchev if the Soviet leader came to the United Nations that fall.[38] When the time for that possibility neared, Rusk conducted an off-the-record "backgrounder" and told the press that there was a fifty-fifty chance of Khrushchev coming to New York. That still left no realistic hope for a settlement. The Russians were holding to their "free city" proposal, the question of access rights was as difficult as ever, and tolerating American troops in West Berlin no more bearable.[39]

Berlin, then, remained the focal point for any military move Moscow might try to justify in case of a showdown. Within the city itself, as Lyndon Johnson found during his visit after construction of the wall, the overwhelming view was "to regard the present crisis as being essentially a confrontation of power between the Soviet Union and the United States." What a prolonged division might mean for morale was another matter. "Virtually every Berliner with whom we talked," reported Johnson, "has a story about families torn apart and unable to obtain information about the fate of loved ones who may be no more than a few blocks away."[40]

No single issue commanded as much of Kennedy's attention. All other global irritations were peripheral, all related, and each and every one a test of whether the Soviets would somehow use that situation as a device for dissolving Western commitments to the city. Russian motivations were beside the point. The political and military factors were paramount. There could be no retreat from that point. Such matters as steel prices, the fluctuations of the domestic economy, and increasing civil rights pressures were insignificant when measured against the survival factors that Kennedy kept watching. Clearly the impasse would not be broken over Berlin itself. Strength, then, had to come from repairing other weaknesses in America's global position. Meeting them one by one, from Latin America to Southeast Asia, Africa, the subcontinent of India, and the Middle East, along with making some progress on arms control, might at least bring piecemeal progress. Kennedy's inaugural warning that his mission would not be completed in the first one thousand days was becoming something of an understatement.

Kennedy had also become convinced about the necessity of achieving sociopolitical solutions for the problem of revolutionary subversion by, as Schlesinger has written, "taking the human base away from the guerrillas."[41] Guerrilla warfare, he told members of the Foreign Service Institute, was the "most ancient form of warfare." But it had become more important than ever, and its significance was going to grow. "This is not merely a military effort," he explained to the group when it gathered on the South Lawn during the summer of 1962, "but it also requires . . . a broad knowledge of the whole development effort of a country, the whole technique of the National Government to identify themselves with the aspirations of the people."[42] The attorney general, possibly even more interested in the tactic than his brother, also derided the notion that the system of government did not matter as long as it was anti-Communist.[43] If it had not been for such efforts, Bobby later told John Bartlow Martin, Venezuela would have been taken over and Caracas run by the Communists.[44] The President himself added the military emphasis when he told a veterans' meeting that summer that the United States was concentrating "on developing our special forces, which are well suited to assist those governments in maintaining their position against the threats of guerrillas and insurgents."[45] As a direct result of the realities encountered at the Bay of Pigs, the administration had strengthened its capacity for dealing with what Kennedy became increasingly convinced would shape the nature of future warfare.

Once again, but this time for a new administration, Dr. Killian came to Washington. The man who had most recently been Eisenhower's science adviser now became chairman of Kennedy's reconstituted intelligence unit, the Foreign Intelligence Advisory Board. Replacing the defunct OCB, its major function was to bring together experts in various forms of covert operations. Kennedy told Killian of his particular interest in making the most of U-2 spy planes.[46]

In addition to the MIT president, the new board had high-caliber specialized talent. Only one member, Clark Clifford, was suspected of having been named for political reasons, but anyone aware of the regard Kennedy had for the Washington attorney would have known that his presence had a more serious purpose. William O. Baker of Bell Telephone Laboratories and Polaroid's Edwin Land brought expertise in the field of electronics. General James Doolittle, the hero of the air war against Tokyo, had since become associated with Space Technology Laboratories. The others, including Harvard historian William Langer, Gordon Gray, Robert B. Murphy, and J. Patrick Coyne, who served as the board's executive secretary, had strong intelligence and diplomatic backgrounds. As they got into their work, they could see, as Clifford later told Larry Hackman, "that in some instances in the foreign intelligence field, you had the feeling that you were in a ball park and a ball had been hit out to midway left-center field, and the center fielder and the left fielder would both go for it and crash and the ball would fall to the ground. Other times—and some dramatic instances—a ball would be hit out to left center field and each would think that the other was going to get it and the ball would fall on the ground again."[47]

Told that there had been inadequate consultations between the National Security Council and the CIA, Kennedy had to be talked out of changing the name of the intelligence agency. He also wanted to drop Bissell and Dulles right away, but the board cautioned against both moves. Within a few months both Bundy and the President advised Bissell that he would have to resign, "which did not surprise me or in any way outrage me," he recalls. "I thought it was more or less to be expected." After a "decent interval" he finally resigned, on February 17, 1962. By then Dulles was already gone, having left at the end of September.[48]

Kennedy then gave the directorship to John McCone. Clifford denies published reports that the job had been offered to him, but the President did consider giving it to Bobby. The attorney general feared it would be impolitic. An agency so dear to the hearts of conservatives would be better off in the hands of a Republican, and, in any event, best not headed by the President's brother.[49] But the choice of McCone created some doubts.

Mostly the move was defensive. McCone was a self-made businessman from California and one of the architects of the agency. Having a conservative Republican and cold-war hard-liner meant that the CIA would be in the custody of someone highly acceptable to those most eager to see it strengthened. He was also a good manager; but perhaps just as important was McCone's continued relationship with Dwight Eisenhower, in whose administration he had served as chairman of the Atomic Energy Commission. His critics, however, remembered him as the man who had fought vehemently against trying to negotiate a nuclear test ban treaty. He had also been a partisan of Lewis Straus, whom liberals had managed to prevent from confirmation as Eisenhower's secretary of commerce. "A real alley fighter, you know," was the way Roger Hilsman recalled McCone. "A very rich man, a very militant, anti-Communist, Republican. A shipbuilder and all the rest of it. So we thought, everybody thought on Capitol Hill and in the administration, we were in for trouble."[50]

Intelligence operations were expanded. The FIAB, principally concerned with oversight and technical expertise, concentrated largely on communications and satellites. The Agency for International Development often worked closely with the CIA. The AID mission, as in Southeast Asia, were often heavily infused with intelligence operatives. Edwin Bayley thought that about "half the Saigon mission was CIA," but there was resistance and only mixed success when the President tried to rein in the agency by placing country units under the responsibility of the local ambassadors.[51] Under the direction of the National Security Council the CIA rapidly expanded its counterinsurgency capabilities, especially in Latin America, Africa, and the Far East.

Unlike AID, however, the Peace Corps resisted CIA involvement. Bayley, who became director of public information for the Corps, has told of Sargent Shriver's efforts to keep his staff "clean." Those suspected of having any intelligence connections were weeded out. "And we were very serious; we said it openly; we would screen out any person connected with the CIA just as we would screen out a Communist. . . . We considered them about in the same class as far as the Peace Corps was concerned. . . . Now, whether the CIA got to anybody afterwards or not, I don't know. But we tried to do that. Anybody found with that connection, out they went." Shriver took up the matter personally with the President, who appreciated the probable consequences of having the Peace Corps considered just another CIA front.[52]

The Cuba Study Group thought covert actions needed better monitoring and should not be left to the whims of the CIA. "It's time we take the bucket of slop and put another cover on it," said the report.[53] The result was the creation of the Special Group for Counterinsurgency with General Taylor as its chairman. The mechanism was a direct outgrowth of the search for ways of dealing with global Communist subversion and insurrection, it was hoped with better interagency coordination. Subsequent directives made its objectives more specific and extensive. One came from the President's desire to "give utmost attention and emphasis to programs designed to counter indirect communist aggression" through police assistance programs, and "military, police, intelligence and psychological measures."[54] Their responsibilities were also extended to "support both the training and active operations of indigenous paramilitary forces."[55]

Whatever the formal lines of command, the President was in close touch with their proceedings. "It is also well known that President Kennedy often dealt directly with subordinate officials rather than going through channels and Robert Kennedy was also active in this field,"

U. Alexis Johnson has testified. "You always had the feeling when dealing with Bobby that he was the fearless watchdog in behalf of the President. He had enormous possessive pride in the President and was looking after the President's interests in a way in which he felt that the President could not do."

Johnson, who later chaired the Special Group (CI) had experiences with the attorney general that were hardly easygoing. Bobby "would bore in with some lower officials of the government who would perhaps not answer his questions satisfactorily, grab on to a problem, and figuratively shake the unfortunate official who might be making a presentation, and then leave." The bureaucracy was slovenly, and the shaking often accomplished a useful purpose. But, Johnson went on, "I felt that he tended to forget that he was not just Bobby Kennedy, but that he was the attorney general, and a more junior official of government was at a very serious disadvantage in dealing with him." On one occasion, when an AID official's response was unsatisfactory, "Bobby got up and slammed his chair on the floor and stalked out of the room, slamming the door." Johnson's experiences with the younger brother led him to request being relieved as the group's chairman.[56] The passion of both Kennedy brothers in the counterintelligence enterprise came under heavy criticism in later years after congressional hearings and documentation verified the pattern of activities that ranged from Southeast Asia to Africa and Latin America.

Still, if Kennedy was reacting with ever greater concern to "wars of national liberation" as the military threat to modern civilization, he was also responding "from long and firmly held views that were fundamental to his political philosophy.[57] The nonexistence of an "international Communist conspiracy," whether a monolithic force or the product of competing Marxist systems, was not a gamble that any President (and certainly not a Democrat in the 1960's) could afford to take. Recognizing that objective opens the way for understanding the Kennedy behavior toward Cuba and Castro after the Bay of Pigs. Highlighting the relationship was the project known as Operation MONGOOSE (a deliberately misleading CIA cryptogram) that began in November of 1961 and lasted until the resolution of the Cuban missile crisis. The campaign's basic justification was the need to conduct a "secret war" against "their" secret war. During that period, before it was succeeded by a stepped-up program, it mostly remained devoted to intelligence-gathering. Although one of its purposes has been described as the creation of "internal dissension and resistance leading to eventual U.S. intervention," sabotage was limited to, as General Lansdale put it, "blowing up bridges to stop communications and blowing up certain production plants." The guidelines were that the actions "must be inconspicuous."[58] It became the CIA's largest single clandestine program.

A collateral campaign consisted of continued efforts to assassinate Castro. A congressional committee investigating such plots calculated that eight attempts were made from 1960 through 1965. When interviewed in 1964, Attorney General Kennedy repeatedly denied any knowledge of the plots. If the CIA had engaged in such activities, he said, "they wouldn't have done it without telling me."[59] That essentially became the heart of the Kennedy defense: The administration never authorized assassinations and had no information that any were attempted; any such acts must have been carried out by overenthusiastic intelligence agents who thought they had White House clearance.[60]

Richard Helms, Bissell's replacement, later insisted that he had all the authority he needed. Assassination, he said, was "not part of the CIA's position" and not part of its "armory." But no "member of the Kennedy Administration . . . ever told me that [assassination] was proscribed, [or] ever referred to it in that fashion." When asked whether the President had been informed of any assassination plots, Helms said that "nobody wants to embarrass a President of the United States by discussing the assassination of foreign leaders in his presence." He was continually pressed, however, to do what he could to bring down Castro. Bobby Kennedy was especially vehement, without actually saying that he wanted Castro killed. Bissell had also experienced such demands. "That pressure was exerted, all right," he said. "I felt that pressure, mainly from Bobby, and I was in a sense sympathetic to it; and I was trying my best to conform to it."[61] The intelligence community's explanation was simple: It does not act unilaterally on something like assassinations. That sort of program could not have been pursued without "strong pressure and specific direction from the White House."[62]

Bobby, of course, had been told in May of 1961 about the Rosselli and Giancana efforts that predated the Bay of Pigs, but the information had included the "understanding that the assassination plan aimed at Castro had been terminated completely."[63] If the attorney general knew about that level of activity, didn't his brother? That the whole enterprise was on JFK's mind is clear from conversations he had with reporter Tad Szulc and George Smathers. In November 1961 he raised the point with Szulc and when the newsman said he did not think the United States should have anything to do with political murders and that at any rate it would not alter Cuban policy, the President said that he agreed. Several days later he told Dick Goodwin that "we can't get into that kind of thing, or we would all be targets."[64] He also talked about it with George Smathers, and the Florida senator later discussed that conversation in an oral-history interview.

Smathers would not be the most credible witness about a Kennedy involvement, especially with Castro. In the days when both were young congressmen before Smathers was elected to the Senate in 1960, they were close friends. On the subject of Castro and Cuba, Smathers recalled: "I don't really believe that the President, after a while, put too much credence in what I had to say about Cuba and Latin America because he thought I had oversold myself, for political reasons, and, second, having traveled as I had in Latin America from 1947 up to 1960, I had met all the dictators," he later acknowledged. "So I think this sort of made him draw back from me with respect to the problem of Cuba and Latin America." Finally, long after the Bay of Pigs, at the President's request, "we didn't talk about Cuba." When, however, Smathers tried to raise the subject at dinner in early 1962, Kennedy angrily smashed his fork down on the plate, cracking it, and said, "Now, damn it, I wish you wouldn't do that. Let's quit talking about this subject."[65]

Sections of the interview can be used either way, to link the President to the assassination attempts or to exonerate him, and Smathers offers enough for each side. But Smathers also said that he never did give the green light and that the CIA probably acted without his knowledge. Kennedy, he claimed, later told him, "I've got to do something about those bastards." Smathers described him as "furious," as believing that such agencies should be stripped of their exorbitant power. The question about killing Castro really came down not to whether it was good or bad, but "whether or not the reaction throughout South America would be good or bad." Smathers started to say he himself had not thought it a bad idea at all, and then caught himself. Finally, he explained, he came around to the view, as presumably did the President, that it would be a negative move "particularly where it could be pinned on the United States."

It is doubtful that Jack Kennedy would have confided in Smathers. Smathers talked too freely, gave too many interviews, gossiped, threw around his importance and connections too openly. What is convincing about Smathers, however, and what does make his testimony useful, was his ability to upset the famed Kennedy "cool" with a matter that obviously rankled.

Nowhere was the pressure for "getting even" for the Bay of Pigs disaster greater than within the military and intelligence establishments. "They wanted to prove they could conduct this kind of activity effectively," recalled Roswell Gilpatric, a member of the Special Group (CI).[66] Helms repeatedly told Senator Frank Church's committee that "Those of us who were still [in the agency] were enormously anxious to try and be successful at what we were being asked to do by what was then a relatively new Administration. We wanted to earn our spurs with the President and with other officers of the Kennedy Administration."[67] One of those who testified, Defense Secretary McNamara, acknowledged that "We were hysterical about Castro at the time of the Bay of Pigs and thereafter, and that there was pressure [from President Kennedy and the attorney general] to do something about Castro."[68] Adolf Berle testified on Capitol Hill on May 14 and found that the "real drive there was to put in troops." Most expressed sorrow that it had not been done earlier. Berle may be suspected of having heard what he wanted to hear, but he also reported in his diary right afterward that the climate at that point was somewhat better than it had been earlier. Only a few days before, he wrote, we "were within a hair's-breadth of a straight war operation . . ."[69]

The atmosphere was sufficiently volatile to alarm Mike Mansfield, the Senate's majority leader. The air was full of jingoism, bitterness, and frustration over the inability to bring down Castro, and anxiety about unleashing full American might. Mansfield sent a long, carefully modulated letter to the President, arguing that "the courageous thing to do and the sensible thing to do" would be not yielding to "the temptation to give vent to our anger at our own failure." That would only strengthen Castro's position with his own people, "jeopardize our relations with much of Latin America and do further damage to our position throughout the world." Instead American force should be used prudently. It should be saved for clear-cut security threats. That could include a move to take over our naval base at Guantánamo, or "the establishment of Soviet missile or any other kind of base *for Russian forces* in Cuba, provided," Mansfield added, "we are seriously re-evaluating our own base-policies on the rim of the Soviet Union." The key, however, was restraint. Intervention would only lead to "a long drawn-out guerrilla war with substantial casualties and great costs. When it is over we will have to install some kind of government in Havana and prop it up with a costly aid program for a long time to come." We might even, he pointed out, "have to reinstate the sugar quota."[70]

Operation MONGOOSE was, first of all, designed to bring down Castro. He had to be harassed, monitored, discredited, and removed. The ulterior motive behind Kennedy's sponsorship of MONGOOSE was both cynical and pragmatic, involving as much the granting of illusory power as actual authority to the Pentagon and intelligence communities. As with Congress itself they constituted a force that contained implicit power and threats. Kennedy viewed them as a bureaucracy that posed a potential albatross for civilian government. During the summer of 1962 his friend Paul Fay discussed with the President Fletcher Knebel's novel, *Seven Days in May,* which described an attempted military takeover in the United States. He told Fay the work of fiction was not farfetched. "It's possible," said Kennedy. "It could happen in this country, there would be a certain uneasiness, but the conditions would have to be just right." If there were too many Bays of Pigs, "it could happen." And then he added, "But it won't happen on my watch," falling back on an old Navy term.[71] Indeed, after the Bay of Pigs, after the restraint of overt military intervention in Laos, Jack Kennedy was hardly the favorite President of the uniformed services. Moreover, as David Detzer has observed, "Generals do not like to kowtow to men the same age as majors or lieutenant-colonels."[72] Graham Allison has put it another way. "Were the organizations on top of which the President was trying to sit going to drag the country over the nuclear cliff in spite of all his efforts?"[73] His elevation of General Curtis LeMay as Air Force chief of staff not long after the Cuban mishap was part of the appeasement of the military hard-liners. Personally he despised LeMay. Everytime he had to see the general, Roswell Gilpatric has recalled, "he ended up in sort of a fit. . . . The subject of LeMay's continued tenure came up frequently when McNamara, the President, and I were talking about military personnel. And it was no surprise or secret about the problems that LeMay presented, but the alternatives were so much worse." He also became disenchanted with Lyman Lemnitzer and finally did replace him as chairman of the Joint Chiefs of Staff with one of his more trusted generals, Maxwell Taylor.[74] Nor, of course, did Kennedy ever overcome the feeling that he had suffered bitterly at the hands of the CIA during the sequence of events that culminated on the Cuban beaches. It was nevertheless safer to make some accommodations by giving them a little latitude. For such things as convincing Congress of the need for military appropriations, in particular, the brass was absolutely essential. Like the powers on Capitol Hill, they were another establishment a President had to handle.

"Kennedy," said General Lansdale, who took over the operational end of MONGOOSE, "distrusted the CIA and believed that someone from outside the Agency was required to oversee major covert action programs."[75] The proposal was drawn up by three of the President's people —Lansdale, Dick Goodwin, and Bobby. The Special Group (CI) then expanded itself to create the SG (Augmented), which approved the

MONGOOSE plans, and the President directed that they be "kept closely informed" of the operation.[76] Richard Helms later pointed out that "the mechanism was set up . . . to use as a circuit breaker so that these things did not explode in the President's face and that he was not held responsible for them."[77]

In reality the White House held the leash on MONGOOSE. Lansdale's function included full coordination of the enterprise with the State and Defense departments. The "augmented" portion of the Special Group was achieved by the addition of General Taylor and the attorney general. Fifteen members in all, they would gather in the morning, with the original CI group gradually leaving as the day progressed, until, as Thomas Powers has written, "the three members of the Special Group for overseeing covert operations would hold its meeting, with the result that John McCone, beginning in November 1961, and the other Special Group members would sometimes spend six or seven hours in a stretch in three successive meetings dominated by one priority: getting rid of Castro."[78]

When the Church Committee held its hearings, there were some very striking insights into their actual operations. One aspect was the activism of Bobby, who, as can be recalled, had been almost totally uninvolved in the Bay of Pigs planning. Now the attorney general became the chief cheerleader, speaking in the name of the White House and exhorting them on to action, somehow protesting too much all the time about their lack of productivity while never specifying exactly what they could do.

That January in his office at the Justice Department Robert Kennedy said that "a solution to the Cuban problem today carried top priority in the U.S." Government. Only the day before, he said, the President had indicated to him "that the final chapter had not been written—it's got to be done and will be done." They were told, according to notes recorded by Helms's executive assistant, that "No time, money, effort— or manpower is to be spared."[79] Helms testified that Bobby continued to press for action through constant phone calls to various members of Task Force W (which had been set up in Florida to carry out the Cuban operation), and Gilpatric agreed that Bobby was the "moving spirit," whose role was "principally to spur us on, to get going, get cracking." Neither he nor McGeorge Bundy remembered the attorney general being anything but vague about actual operations, and certainly neither associated him with any comments suggesting murder, but Gilpatric was clear about Bobby's desire to "limit the Castro regime's effectiveness." Bundy agreed that both "from the President in his style and from the Attorney General in his style [there was an effort] to keep the government active in looking for ways to weaken the Cuban regime."[80] Almost a year went by, however, and the accomplishments were negligible, so in early October the attorney general told the SG (A) that he would personally chair their meetings. On the sixteenth of that month he let Helms know that the President was unhappy, that nothing much was happening.[81]

That was true. Nothing much had been accomplished. That was the fact despite the creation by Task Force W of establishments in Miami and Washington that included some four hundred Americans, a small navy, an air force, fifty proprietary fronts, and two thousand Cuban agents, all at a cost of over fifty million dollars a year.[82] Firm restrictions had been drawn, bizarre plans vetoed within the SG (A). Lansdale himself contributed thirty-three planning task ideas. One involved the notion of incapacitating Cuban sugar workers by using chemical warfare during the harvest season. Nonlethal chemicals would temporarily put them out of commission for a twenty-four to forty-eight-hour period "without ill effects" but with reduced production.[83] Lansdale turned down a proposed "Operation Bounty." That idea would have created "a system of financial rewards, commensurate with position and stature, for killing or delivering alive known Communists." Cubans would be informed by leaflets, delivered by airdrops, that the bounties would range from $5,000 for an informer to $100,000 for government officials. To denigrate Castro in the eyes of the populace, however, his head would be worth just two cents.[84]

But the schemes that did survive were ordered cut back by the SG (A) and the effort limited mostly to intelligence-gathering.[85] According to the testimony of the executive assistant to William Harvey, the idiosyncratic character who headed Task Force W, the group was forced to give "specific detailed plans for every activity carried out by the task force."[86] Powers has stated the situation accurately by writing that "the result was a logjam between the Kennedys, who continued to press for action, and the CIA, which peppered the SG (A) with proposals but couldn't get them approved."[87]

Just before the discovery of missiles in Cuba, MONGOOSE had begun a more ambitious phase. General Taylor had informed the President that Castro was not likely to be brought down without direct U.S. military intervention. On August 23, Bundy issued NSC Memorandum #181, which called for the immediate implementation of MONGOOSE Phase B, which meant accelerating the sabotage program and provoking incidents designed to produce tensions between Cubans and Soviet military personnel. That thereby put into effect John McCone's idea of creating a wedge between Castro and the "old" Communists.[88] Bob Kennedy, later reviewing that phase, said "we were making more of an effort through espionage and sabotage in the last—August, September, or October. It was better organized than it had been before and was having quite an effect. I mean, there were ten or twenty thousand tons of sugarcane that was being burned every week through internal uprisings and plus—"[89] It all went as far as landing agents on Cuban soil just before the presidential blockade in October, but MONGOOSE went out of business and the SG (A) was abandoned at the end of the month.

There was, of course, a fine line between authorizing such covert actions and maintaining control in the interest of broader objectives. In the case of Castro the Kennedys must have been astonishingly naive not to have known that pressing the CIA to effectuate his "removal" hardly referred to dumping him by sending in Mayor Daley to arrange an election. They were well aware of the Rosselli–Giancana enterprise. Their desire left neither of their deputy directors of planning with much doubt about what they were after. Within the SG (A) there was much talk about restraining some of the more ludicrous schemes, modifying sabotage, and prohibiting an invasion, but the only mention of the word *assassination* came on August 10, 1962, when Robert McNamara raised that as an option, and then the words "including liquidation of leaders," which appeared in Lansdale's memorandum of the meeting, were quickly expunged at William Harvey's insistence.[90] Whether done explicitly or implicitly, it is impossible to absolve the Kennedys of responsibility for the attempts on Castro's life.[91]

Like MONGOOSE, the Alliance for Progress was inspired by Castro. The objectives were similar—merely to immunize Latin America against revolutionary fervor, as Kennedy himself stated that goal on several occasions. At a dinner for his friend Smathers in March of 1962, he referred to the Alliance as a program "which I believe can successfully counter the Communist onslaught in this hemisphere." However, the Alliance was far more open than MONGOOSE in its means.

It later became fashionable to claim that the Alliance had, in effect, merely extended what had begun during the final Eisenhower year and was formalized by the Act of Bogotá. The claim has some validity. The Eisenhower initiative also involved the concept of social reform. In comparison with the *Alianza,* however, its scope was limited and emphasis on structural changes muted. The Kennedy program stressed long-term economic development along with social reforms and inter-American cooperation, in order to ameliorate instability, and Latin America's gross social and economic inequities, which bred radical solutions. Edwin Martin, who became Kennedy's Assistant Secretary of State for Inter-American Affairs, later pointed out that "if there were not a Communist ideology to exploit these problems, something else would take its place."[92] Kennedy hoped to reconcile the region's established authorities to the need for reform. The bait would be a half billion dollars in American assistance. Thus, Kennedy's effort to reorder at least part of the world was by peaceful means.

A slow start and resistance to change by entrenched interests and cultural patterns was expected, and nobody thought the *Alianza* could achieve its goals overnight. However, many in Washington tended to dismiss the plan as a "romantic change" to decorate the New Frontier's international facade.[93] Adlai Stevenson's ten-nation tour of the continent during the spring of 1961 revealed gloom wherever he went, with the exception of those quarters where there was hope of exploiting United States fear of Castro in order to attract more American dollars. But efforts to undercut Castro himself, Chester Bowles later warned Dean Rusk, "may in fact breathe new life into his movement, and that in the process we may compromise the essential elements of the Alliance for Progress itself."[94]

Competition for American dollars also inspired complaints that Washington was ignoring some of those trying to comply with the ideals while helping the undeserving. "Despite US calling for structural reforms," said a diplomatic cable to Rusk from Bolivia, "it is [the] first country to violate its own policy by giving massive aid to countries doing nothing [to] effect necessary reforms. Other countries which have done nothing to meet these requirements are much better financed by US than Bolivia."[95] São Paulo labor circles doubted that the Brazilian government under President Goulart, despite all the personal wooing by Kennedy, would ever voluntarily implement effective reforms. Most of those in government were wealthy men unlikely to loosen their own pocketbooks. So, Rusk was warned, only "massive continuous pressure from the U.S. on the Brazilian elite can possibly force the latter to make *effective*, as distinguished from *paper*, reforms."[96] To the discomfort of the State Department, however, the *Alianza* was too often being referred to as "the United States aid program for Latin America," and Undersecretary of State George Ball cabled embassies to remind them that the whole enterprise required institutional and structural changes carried out "by the Latin American countries themselves." Such improvements had to go "hand in hand with the use of increased amounts of external assistance."[97]

When President Kennedy visited with President Mateos in Mexico, he received a tumultuous welcome. "I've never seen anybody making such an impression on the people of another country—anytime, anywhere," remembered Ambassador Thomas Mann. His smile was light, his wit and grace charming, and his words were what the people wanted to hear. They were suffused with the social justice rhetoric rarely heard from American leaders.

Jackie spoke in Spanish, and her remarks brought tears. She was talked about for weeks afterward. Together, the President and the First Lady were able to reach the Mexican people as personifications of what the *Alianza* was supposed to mean. "New factories and machinery mean little to the family without a home, to the student without a meal, to the farmer who even gives up hope of finally owning the land that he tills," said Kennedy at a luncheon.[98] He signed an agricultural agreement with Mexico, and spoke at a housing project in the capital.

But in July, a Sherman tank given to Peru via the American military assistance program ripped open the Peruvian presidential palace's iron gates. Seventy-three-year-old Manuel Prado y Ugarteche and his constitutional government were deposed by the military. Prado's regime had maintained strong support from the Kennedy administration, and the coup was a direct slap in the face to the aims of the *Alianza*. The Kennedy administration responded by canceling military assistance and eighty-one million dollars in aid. Diplomatic relations were suspended. Meanwhile, American corporations with Peruvian investments totaling almost eight hundred million dollars protested against Washington's "hard line." The White House heard complaints from Peter Grace, president of W. R. Grace and Company, and from Americans with mining interests in the country. The junta began to gain popular acceptance by virtue of its new strong authority, and in the face of a promise of "clean" elections for the following June, there was little that Kennedy could do but to live with the situation.

Kennedy was left feeling that the direction of the Alliance was right but that the operation was flawed. David Bell thought he had come to agree that "foreign aid was a more limited tool and could be counted on to achieve a less rapid and more limited result than he may have thought at the outset."

The Alliance brought about few changes. New Castros were kept from power, but the deterrents were military, the coups as frequent as ever (if not more so), and American intervention was both overt and covert. Usually interference was prompted by the twin objectives of containing communism and making Latin America safe for investors. And investments were considered to be essential. The continent was burdened with the heaviest annual population growth of any region, 2.8 percent. Even the *Alianza*'s hope for a two and a half percent gross national product growth would have needed doubling before it could accommodate that birth rate.[99] As two students of the program later concluded, "The Alliance provides additional justification for disillusionment."[100]

By the summer of 1962 Kennedy and his administration had achieved one significant diplomatic success. Indonesia's president, Achmed Sukarno, a character considered by Kennedy as little better than a loathsome demagogue, was kept from forcibly taking over West New Guinea. One hundred and fifty thousand square miles of wilderness territory, populated by Stone Age Papuan tribesmen, it had been retained by the Dutch after Indonesian independence. For Sukarno, taking over the land represented nationalistic satisfaction and a third-world attack upon lingering colonialism. And there was no doubt that he had the means to accomplish just that without much trouble. The American dilemma, and the problem for Kennedy's diplomacy, was to somehow retain loyalty to the Netherlands without alienating Sukarno and losing him to the Communist bloc. A Marxist Indonesia would well negate the struggle to keep Laos and South Vietnam free from communism. With guerrilla fighting taking place in West New Guinea, Kennedy was determined to press the Dutch for a quick settlement before Sukarno succumbed to the temptation. The rationale for doing something about the situation was simple, as Robert W. Komer of the NSC staff put it to the President: "Why spend billions containing Communist pressures on the mainland while leaving the Communists a free hand in the rich archipelago behind?" An incentive for America's ally to go peacefully was the possible Indonesian grant of concessions to Dutch corporations that had been ousted when the East Indies became an independent nation.[101] For Sukarno the infusion of capital, even from the hated colonialists, would be welcome.

Patience was rewarded with at least Washington's primary goal, but the route was painfully slow and irritating. Instrumental in pushing the negotiations and applying pressure on the Dutch were Howard Jones, the American ambassador in Djakarta, and Averell Harriman, who took over the State Department's Far East desk in the fall of 1961. At a lower echelon the problem was assigned to George McGhee, the undersecretary of state for political affairs. "Although we had little sympathy for Sukarno or his objectives," McGhee has pointed out, "it seemed to be in the Dutch interest, as well as the general interest, that the Dutch withdraw."[102] America's NATO ally was not allowed to forget that there was but one graceful solution to that problem, while Sukarno was carefully distracted from compulsiveness or tying himself to the Chinese Communist camp. When Kennedy faced newsmen at a State Department briefing late in the spring of 1962, he said with candor: "I would like to see the United States stay out of some of these fights, but it is a luxury we cannot afford."[103] Meanwhile as guerrillas continued to fight in the area (also called West Indria), a veteran negotiator, Ellsworth Bunker, responded to George Ball's request that he serve as a mediator in behalf of the United Nations. The day-to-day work was done on an estate near Middleburg, Virginia, under the constant surveillance of the President and the secretary of state.[104] As is the usual case in such talks, progress was unsteady.

The final impasse was broken when the Dutch yielded to Indonesian demands for assurances, and an agreement came a little more than a month after the Laotian solution at Geneva. On August 15 the UN was given administration of the territory by a provision for a formal transfer to the international body until it could be turned over to Indonesia four and a half months later. However a stipulation to permit the Papuans to determine their own independence was, unfortunately for the natives of that primitive area, up to Sukarno's good intentions, and that settlement brought strong criticism as a capitulation. Predictably Sukarno was impatient. As Warren Cohen has written, the Dutch were "merely spared the humiliation of turning the land directly over to the Indonesians."[105]

The Indonesian settlement had been reached and only the formal signatures remained to be added when Kennedy prepared for a White House meeting involving other victims of international politics, the Palestinian refugees. The years since Israel's creation by the United Nations had virtually institutionalized their displacement. From the spring of 1961, when UN debates over the issue had again exposed American vulnerabilities in the area, the administration had searched for ways to restore some balance to Middle East policy. After a mid-August weekend spent mainly at the Johns Island, Maine, home of the former boxing champion, Gene Tunney, Kennedy settled down in the Cabinet Room on the fourteenth with a representative group from the White House, State, Defense, and the American mission to the UN. The question of Israel and the refugee problem monopolized the agenda.

Eight men, including the President and his secretary of state, as well as the American ambassador to Israel, Walworth Barbour, were facing a question less immediately explosive than several other trouble areas, but as with so many of the world's difficulties, equally defiant of a ready solution. For Washington the domestic political dimension had, perhaps, been the most problematic. A recurring dichotomy was the preoccupation of State Department planners with the multitude of geopolitical interests, while White House political advisers worried about pro-Israel pressures at home. One veteran of Arab–Israel negotiations who was present in the Cabinet Room that afternoon recalled those influences with some bitterness by repeating the State Department canard that "in any administration, the President is the desk officer for Israel." Mike Feldman, another member of the group, was described as "the assistant desk officer," and by Robert Kennedy, in a subsequent oral-history interview, as a good man who had a single-minded concern for the welfare of Jews.[106]

All that was unfair to Feldman. His prepresidential service with Kennedy had been as a valued assistant on many legislative matters, but his ethnic identification also gave him another vital function. Under Kennedy he was expected to be as much in touch with the Jewish constituency as was Maxwell Rabb under Eisenhower. During the spring of 1961 the President had turned to Feldman for some kind of formula that could represent an American initiative capable of moving toward a resolution of the Middle East impasse. That meant contending with the refugees.

Feldman's basic problem, however, was that Kennedy aimed at proving that an American President, even a Democratic one, could pursue an "evenhanded" Middle East policy. Since the birth of Israel the outstanding humanitarian tragedy had been the dislocated refugees, some 1.2 million by 1961, who lived in the adjacent areas of Jordan, Syria, Lebanon, and the Gaza region of what was then the ephemeral amalgam of Syria and Egypt known as the United Arab Republic. As Dean Rusk explained the situation when interviewed in 1981, "Some of us thought that the refugees ought to be given a chance to make their own personal choices about what they wanted to do in the longer run. We began to get grandchildren of refugees, and things like that. The prospect for refugee existence was very poor."[107]

The issue was far from the only one dividing Israel from her Arab neighbors, and perhaps not even the most significant, but certainly the most emotional. Phillips Talbot, who was with the State Department team in the Cabinet Room that August 14, has recalled that "the very refugee centers and their schools were becoming focal points for a very strong mood of discontent with the existing situation."[108] The search for a solution had an obvious humanitarian appeal, which carried great weight with all those in that room. For American foreign policy, moreover, an opening would have created the hope of stability for the incendiary region adjacent to Suez and the world's major oil sources. For Kennedy and his administration the political breakthrough would have been significant; and for that very reason the coming congressional elections encouraged further caution. Even failed American efforts would not be in vain: responsibility for continuing tensions could thereafter be attributed to stubbornness by the principals rather than American indifference to humanitarian needs.[109]

Within the Jewish state the specter also involved Soviet exploitation that, as in the Congo and elsewhere, constantly hovered over any efforts at problem-solving. The Russians had been initial supporters of Israel's right to statehood; their fellow-travelers in the United States had co-opted Zionism with their own political pitch. But long since then, taking along a substantial number of American radicals (many of them Jewish) the Russians had gone over to the Arab side. Palestinian refugees, hitherto ignored and pawns of efforts to forge an elusive pan-Arab movement, had replaced European Jews as the chief victims of "imperialism." The injustice seemed even more blatant when in April of 1961 the General Assembly defeated an effort to give the United Nations custodial rights over properties left in Israel by the refugees. Especially galling to the administration in Washington was the bitter remark by Saudi Arabia's Ahmed Shukairy that only the Russians gave a damn about what happened to the dispossessed. That comment, which coincided with the Bay of Pigs landing, was quickly followed by his charge that Kennedy only cared for Cuban refugees.[110]

Kennedy, in fact, had come to the presidency with less of the oratorical posturing in behalf of Israel expected from Democratic candidates. He had accepted advice to soft-pedal the usual rhetoric.[111] A campaign address before the Zionist Organization of America turned out surprisingly successful precisely because it failed to pander to the cause of Zionism with the usual clichés. Instead Kennedy proposed extending friendship "for all people in the Middle East" and promised that the "authority of the White House be used to call into conference the leaders of Israel and the Arab States to consider privately their common problems . . ."[112] "It was one of the most successful things I've ever seen," recalled a prominent American Jewish leader who had been an international president of B'nai B'rith. Seated next to him in the hall was Rabbi Abba Hillel Silver, a disciple of Louis Brandeis and veteran American Zionist. The Cleveland rabbi, who hardly ever had a good word for Democrats, said to his companion, Philip Klutznick, "Is this man for real? . . . This is the best speech I've ever heard on this subject."[113]

During Kennedy's first spring in office, those within the State Department most concerned with that troubled region worried about the consequences of a forthcoming informal meeting between the President and Israeli Prime Minister Ben-Gurion, one that took place not at the White House but the Waldorf-Astoria. They succeeded in getting the President to attempt to mitigate any affront to Arab sensitivities by having him sign identical letters of reassurance to five Middle East leaders. Promising American support for the UN's Palestine Conciliation Commission's efforts to rectify the refugee situation, it went on to pledge that the question would be resolved "on the basis of the principle of repatriation and compensation for property." That bit of diplomacy, which was consistent with the best traditions of surreptitious State Department overtures to the Arab world while the White House more openly performed its domestic political rituals, was unmasked when a copy leaked in Jordan was reprinted in *The New York Times*.[114] Kennedy soon heard some angry words from American Jewish leaders who had been prominent in his campaign against Nixon. He finally complained to McGeorge Bundy that the "reaction has been so sour I would like to know whose idea it was, what they hoped to accomplish and what they think we have now accomplished."[115] But he could hardly pawn off on State what the world had a right to regard as a presidential initiative.

And, more vigorously than any American President, he had undertaken to make some dent in the impasse. He called in Feldman and asked the lawyer to develop some kind of plan for bringing together the Israelis and Egypt's Gamal Abdel Nasser, then president of the United Arab Republic. He began to soften Nasser through private correspondence, which seemed to pave the way in Cairo for a more sympathetic reception to the American plan that finally did emerge. That was one bonus that came from the Kennedy–Nasser exchange.[116] But the plan itself that received a serious hearing and began to form the basis for a possible solution was, technically, the product of the UN's Palestine Reconciliation Commission and its special representative.

The commission consisted of Turkey, France, and the United States. Of the three only the U.S. cared much about making some real headway. The French, moreover, were still at the tail end of their pro-Israel period and had little incentive for upsetting the status quo. Then it was decided to exert the commission's role through the appointment of a special representative; he would also be an American, which meant Washington would pull the strings of what was ostensibly a UN operation. President Kennedy accepted the recommendation of Dean Rusk that the assignment be given to Dr. Joseph E. Johnson, the president of the Carnegie Endowment for Peace.

Johnson was a Harvard Ph.D. who had taught history at Williams and

Bowdoin. Since World War II he had been closely associated with Rusk. Tall, graying, and immensely dignified, at the age of fifty-one he was the Hollywood stereotype of a professor. Motivated by the humanitarian objective, he undertook his mission with passports from both the U.S. and the UN, and was conscious of his role to fulfill the world organization's obligation under General Assembly Resolution 194 (III), paragraph 11. That 1948 resolution provided for the right of refugees wishing to return to their homes to be able "to do so at the earliest practicable date, and that compensation should be paid for the property of those choosing not to return and for loss of or damage to property which, under principles of international law or in equity, should be made good by the Governments or authorities responsible." The Conciliation Commission was also thereby instructed to facilitate their "repatriation, resettlement, and economic and social rehabilitation."[117]

Johnson thus went forth into a situation loaded with cultural antagonisms, politics, and mutual suspicion. Illustrative of the Arab–Israeli difficulties is the confidential recollection of a senior American diplomat of what happened just before the expiration of the British mandate in Palestine when the Zionists accepted a monthly immigration figure of twenty-five hundred. "That's impossible," replied the head of the Arab delegation. "They would only bring in twenty-five hundred pregnant women, and that would make five thousand." Wisely, with that kind of climate, Johnson's version of shuttle diplomacy led to his assumption that it would be best to work out a formula without requiring each side to formally express a public commitment.

He set out for Israel with Dag Hammarskjöld's reminder that the country was a "secular theocracy." Everywhere he went, he was asked whether he was Kennedy's emissary. "Ben-Gurion asked me that question," he recalled. What about Golda Meir, then the Israel foreign minister? Had she raised the same question? "I'm not sure she was bright enough to," Johnson said. "She's not my favorite." That view was one of the few points of agreement he had with Feldman, who found Meir tough and difficult as a personality.[118] But Johnson was able to relate to Ben-Gurion, who "was really a very smart guy," and also worked closely with the Israeli UN delegate, Gideon Raphael. "I saw every American ambassador in the field," Johnson explained. "I saw some of the French. I paid courtesy calls rather than anything else. They couldn't be less interested as far as I could see at that time." He talked to the Arab leaders on that first trip. Finally his tentative draft of a plan provided for voluntary repatriation, with each refugee to be given a choice of country. About one in every ten, it was assumed, would choose Israel, and they should be prepared to accept up to 200,000. Each man and woman would be given the opportunity for a completely confidential interview, such as in a confessional booth, and asked for their preference. "But then we ran into the political obstacle on the Arab side," volunteered Dean Rusk. "We knew—we had strong reason to believe—that if any such attempt were made to poll these people that the word would be passed around that you've got to say that you've got to go back to your home in Palestine or you'll have your throat cut, and therefore there was no free choice as far as the refugees were concerned."[119] For their part the Israelis feared the creation of a fifth column that could jeopardize their internal security.

Johnson returned to the Middle East in the spring of 1962 and continued his discussions.[120] Shown a draft of his proposal, with its history of the refugee situation as a legacy of the first Arab–Israel war, the "Arabs raised a stink," Johnson recalled, "and I thought some of their stink was justified. . . . and the Arabs asked that it be modified, and I did modify it; used language that I still think is very fair language. But the Israelis then raised absolute hell." The "hardest task," he added, "and the one I spent my most time on, was negotiating with the U.S. Government," and that involved working closely with the State Department to make the plan more palatable to the Arabs.

When Johnson arrived at the Cabinet Room that August 14—his first meeting with the President—Kennedy had already had his fill of the conflicts. "Dr. Johnson," he told him, "I never want to go through an experience such as I went through last fall," a sentiment shared by the members of the American delegation to the UN.[121] Before the assembled group the President thanked Johnson for his sacrifice in having undertaken the mission, and then listened as the draft plan was spelled out, but said little. Then, as Feldman recalled, "with his peculiar knack of being able to reach into the future," he guessed that both the Arabs and the Israelis would find political objections. Johnson was more optimistic. If handled correctly, if implemented without a public pronouncement, both sides might well agree. "Well," responded the President, "I guess our only chance with the Israelis at least is to get it presented favorably." Turning to Feldman, he said, "How about you going over and getting them to accept it?" As Feldman later remembered that meeting:

> We then discussed briefly the need for secrecy in the mission. We didn't want anybody else to know about the plan, least of all would we want the Arabs to know that we were talking to the Israelis without talking to them. I raised the question as to whether or not it would not be useful, however, if somebody did not talk to Nasser at the same time I was talking to Ben-Gurion, particularly if the Israelis were going to take it.

If the Israelis were going to accept, then it was the general feeling there, and this included the President, that it would be important that we get the acceptance of Nasser as quickly as possible. He was the key on the Arab side. We considered sending people over to wait in Cairo. And when they got a signal from me they'd go and talk to Nasser. It was eventually decided, however, that we wouldn't send anybody special over for that purpose but instead we would rely on our ambassador. [John S.] Badeau was ambassador then. And he would await a signal from me. And we had a prearranged method of communication under which when he got the word he could go in and talk to Nasser and see whether Nasser would agree. . . . basically [the plan] called for the Israelis taking those who, under free choice, chose to come to Israel, and the Arabs taking those refugees who, under free choice, chose to go to their countries. This sounds like a good plan but to an old politician like the President . . . he immediately could see all the gimmicks in it. Free choice is a pretty good word, but he said, "It's a free choice for who?" That's about how it worked out. [122]

Feldman traveled to Israel under the cover story that he was a guest of the Weizman Institute of Science, but when he got down to discussions with Ben-Gurion and Mrs. Meir, he found confirmation of Kennedy's doubts. "He was really remarkable," he recalled, noting their argument that the Arabs could persuade the refugees to return to Israel and their objection to not being able to impose a limitation. That was all right, Feldman in effect then cabled Washington, because the Johnson Plan did not require Israel to take more than they could readily absorb. Besides, it seemed logical to the Israelis that the Arab governments were capable of making their own contribution to the cause of repatriation. But there was a by-product in the discussions that was peripherally related to the refugee question, really an attempt to make the Israelis more amenable.

That was approval of an American sale of Hawk antiaircraft missiles, which the government then in Tel Aviv had been urging from Washington for a long time. The offer was made through Feldman on August 19, even before his cable that informed Dean Rusk about Mrs. Meir's claim to have obtained "concrete evidence" that Egypt was being supplied with guided missiles "which they had purchased from West German sources at a cost of 250,000,000 pounds sterling." Subsequent cables alleged that the Soviets themselves were charged with having supplied Egypt with the weapons. The American ambassador to Lebanon, Armin Meyer, later offered that explanation to the government in Beirut to justify the American sale. Without any mention of the *West German* sources, a subsequent State Department summary of foreign and press reaction to the Hawk decision, dated October 1, 1962, repeated explanations made on Israeli radio that *"Soviet** arms supplied to the Middle East might upset the balance of armaments in the region."[123]

Kennedy covered his diplomatic flanks. Worried about mollifying the British, who had a competitive antiaircraft system, the Israelis were told that they had the choice of whether to buy the Hawks from Washington or the Bloodhounds from London.[124] At the same time, steps were taken to make certain Nasser was not caught off guard. Anticipating the adverse reaction of the Egyptian president, the State Department sent Robert C. Strong, of the Office of Near Eastern Affairs, to join Ambassador Badeau in breaking the news. Nasser's response was predictable, but more satisfactory was his gratification at the diplomatic courtesies.[125] King Hussein of Jordan, not a friend of Nasser's, was meanwhile reassured that Kennedy's new influence with the Cairo government would benefit the long-run interests of that Hashemite kingdom so close to Israel.[126] Kennedy's delicacy in dealing with the situation had also minimized the sort of bitterness that could have been expected from the region's press. Nevertheless suspicions were far from eliminated. Talbot thought that the Hawk sale, coinciding with the Johnson Plan overtures, "made the Arabs feel that the negotiations were in part an excuse to provide for the further arming of Israel."[127] On September 26 the administration made public its plan to sell the missiles.

The Johnson Plan and the sale were inextricably linked, but the exact degree of mutual dependence could never be determined. Robert Komer, who was involved in deliberations over the plan, remains unclear about that relationship, conceding only that "it may have had a minor contributory effect" and that the Israelis had made "crystal clear" that nobody else had missiles with the capability of the Hawks.[128] A much more confident, and somewhat bitter, explanation has been offered by Ambassador Badeau. "It was done," he has said, "because the Congress was facing the first election . . . after Kennedy had been elected and individuals who were contributors to the campaign funds of various candidates withheld their contributions in that summer along into August and said, 'You don't get this until we know what you are going to do for Israel.' " Once Kennedy had the evidence to justify the sale militarily, he was able to go ahead with the commitment, which was why Feldman's cables from Tel Aviv detailed that the Egyptians had already received missiles.[129]

But the fate of the Johnson Plan itself was another matter. Johnson's

*Emphasis supplied

staff estimated that it would cost about one and a third billion dollars, a figure regarded as somewhat high by the State Department.[130] Furthermore the Israelis had already emphasized to Feldman the unacceptability of not having a ceiling on the number of admissions. Hopeful as he was, Feldman nevertheless cabled Rusk from Tel Aviv about his concern at "Ben-Gurion's evident attempt [to] place conditions on his acquiescence and put us in [a] position of seeking prior commitments from Nasser. This would be inconsistent with the Johnson Plan and unacceptable to us."[131] The Israelis held out for Nasser's commitment to agree to permit refugees so inclined to settle within the United Arab Republic and "not to direct propaganda to the refugees urging repatriation but should permit them to express preferences without danger of being considered a traitor."[132] Mrs. Meir feared that failure of the plan would give the Arabs an opportunity to claim that the Israelis had no desire to accommodate the refugees. Feldman pointed out that her desire to have it go ahead via a motion in the General Assembly would be "contrary to the basic assumptions by Johnson that the only way to begin the process of elimination of the refugee problem was by doing it without seeking the commitment of anyone."[133] Meanwhile, and not surprisingly, one Arab country after another issued public words of discouragement, saying in effect that the matter was up to Israel and that Israel must accept the burden for repatriation and resettlement.

When, at the United Nations, Meir saw Johnson's version as modified by the State Department, she became furious. That was not what she had originally seen in Tel Aviv. It was totally unacceptable, just as Kennedy had predicted. To merely poll the refugees while removing Israeli control over who could enter the country could not be tolerated. Meir cited a resolution passed in the Knesset that "there can be no returning the Arab refugees to Israeli territory and the only solution to the problem is their settlement in the Arab states."[134] The plan was dead.

Feldman later recalled that some sixty-two changes had been made after the original draft. Johnson, angry that Feldman had shown the working plan to the Israelis prematurely, points out that "the document as originally proposed gave the Israelis an unbeatable veto on any possible refugee on security or any other grounds—how many were coming and all the rest of it." Feldman at first thought that Johnson had made the changes on his own. "I later found out that the State Department had gotten together with Johnson while I was in Israel to, as I saw it, make the plan slightly more favorable to the Arabs, because on the basis of my cable they had concluded that the Israeli government would hold still for it."[135] An embittered Johnson gave up his seventeen-month effort at the end of January 1963 and returned to the Carnegie Endowment.[136] Dean Rusk, reflecting on the failure, has observed that "the feelings on both sides were so strong and so deep that the governments in the area were unable to make the concessions necessary to make peace and remain in power."[137]

The plan was quietly put aside. As of a 1978 review the actual document remains classified, consigned to government archives and the UN. From time to time the State Department attempted its revival by tying its acceptance to American aid. But Kennedy reluctantly let it remain at rest, its demise serving as evidence to the Israelis of a friendship that Kennedy had formed.

Nowhere perhaps did that closeness become more emphatic than at a meeting between the President and Golda Meir at Palm Beach on the morning of December 27, 1962. By then the second Cuban crisis had ended, and the foreign minister was lavish in her praise of how it had been handled by the President, clearly implying that the experience ought to promote understanding of her own security problems. She explained that Israel was aware that the Egyptians had been getting more arms from the Russians, and that the flight of Soviet-supplied TU 16s from Egypt to drop bombs in Yemen had reminded her country what they were capable of doing. With German help, she added, the Egyptians had been building surface-to-surface missiles since 1960. After listening carefully to her concern for maintaining the balance of power in the interest of a free world, Kennedy explained the American need to preserve Israel's position in the Middle East. Then he went beyond direct assurances given by any previous President. He said that it was quite clear that the U.S. would rush to Israel's support in case of an invasion. According to a State Department summary of their conversation, Kennedy also told her that the United States "has a special relationship with Israel in the Middle East really comparable only to that which it has with Britain over a wide range of world affairs." But while acknowledging that the Johnson Plan was dead, he said, "we should keep on trying" and suggested that he "would like now to see if we can make some progress on refugees and maintain our friendship with Israel without constantly cutting across other interests in the Middle East."[138] When Prime Minister Ben-Gurion heard about Kennedy's comment, he was "deeply grateful." He thoughtfully added, however, that Israel must nevertheless rely upon itself.[139]

The situation in the Middle East remained essentially unchanged. The displaced continued as hostages of each side's political needs. No progress had been made toward recognition of Israel's right to exist, and grievances remained for the subsequent creation of the Palestine Liberation Organization to provide a semblance of Arab solidarity. Kennedy's legacy in dealing with the region, however, was to enhance American influence while leaving the Israelis with a firmer commitment than ever before.

10

"To Resist the Tide"

The spring of 1962 was a political turning point for Kennedy's presidency. His popularity had been holding at more than seventy percent. He seemed secure and virtually immune from serious challenges. Surveys about probable contenders for the Republican nomination in 1964 were hardly more significant than the usual exercises in speculation. However, since December there were signs of trouble with the downhill movement of the stock market. In April came further shocks to the economy and greater hostility from big business than Kennedy had ever experienced. At that time, with the full support of Arthur Goldberg, Bob McNamara, the Justice Department, and much of the apparatus that the federal government made possible, Kennedy reacted more precipitously than he had ever permitted himself to do. He forced Roger Blough's United States Steel Corporation to rescind recently announced price increases.

Blough himself had been all too willing to benefit from the administration's efforts to hold down wages by convincing the steelworkers to restrain their demands. Much of that work had involved the personal efforts of Arthur Goldberg, and his good offices were at stake. Goldberg had convinced David McDonald and his union that they would be better off in the long run by cooperating to secure a noninflationary settlement.

In his meetings with the President and Goldberg, Blough never uttered a word about a commitment to reciprocate by not raising prices. He remained silent, encouraging the government to assume cooperation. Any explicit departure from independent pricing, maintained Blough, a graduate of Yale Law School, would have violated the antitrust laws' prohibitions against price-setting.[1] There was, then, no actual agreement.

Shrewdly the corporation's board chairman had played along, gotten his way, and then suddenly confronted the President in April with the information that steel would be going up by six dollars a ton. If Blough had been patient enough to wait until the summer, if he had let some more time pass after the wage settlement, Kennedy told Charles Bartlett, "he could have had his price increase and there would have been no trouble." He was not outraged that U.S. Steel had raised its prices—it had not done so since 1958 and was entitled to an increase—but it "was just the juxtaposition of the increase and the settlement."[2] Also, by not having acted to counter Blough, Kennedy would have lost a labor secretary and all that that would have implied about union support. Goldberg, angered at the assumed damage done to his credibility, regarded the Blough move as a double cross and wrote out his resignation. "You kept silent, and silence is consent," he later rebuked Blough. "One thing you owe a President is candor."[3] Goldberg was prepared to tell the world that Blough had misled the President.

"Isn't this a hell of a note?" said Kennedy to his labor secretary when Blough walked out of the Oval Office with his bombshell. "What if we roll them back?" Goldberg rescinded his resignation and teamed up with Clark Clifford to meet with the corporation's officers. U.S. Steel's ability to sustain the increase became impossible when Inland Steel refused to go along, and McNamara and the Defense Department redirected the government's purchases. By that weekend the nation's largest steel producer capitulated by rolling back its prices. The administration had its victory. "They fucked us, and we've got to try to fuck them," Jack Kennedy had told Ben Bradlee.[4] Liberals were pleased that the rapacity of the nation's third largest corporation had been thwarted, and labor pique turned into applause for a President who had upheld the "public interest." The final irony may have been that Kennedy may not have "fucked" steel at all but that insufficient demand, rather than the government's pleas, had kept Inland from going along. The "evidence seems strong," concluded Grant McConnell in his study of the controversy, "that considerations of the market largely determined the ending of the steel crisis," and so there is reason to doubt that the price would have held in any case.[5]

That was a moot point, however, because the affair complicated the relationship between Kennedy and business. The antagonism seemed to have been confirmed by the President's widely quoted comment that his father had always told him that "all businessmen are sons of bitches." Kennedy judiciously tried to correct that story by saying he had actually been more selective. He had merely said that "all steelmen are sons of bitches." Bradlee reported that the President told him that he said "sons of bitches, or bastards, or pricks. I don't know which. But I never said anything about *all* businessmen." He explained that he had also called Reston, but the *Times*'s correspondent "didn't have the guts to change the original story."[6]

Much of the press comment was critical, and so were most Republicans. With reason many regarded it as a troubling example of unwarranted exercise of power by the federal government against private enterprise. They overlooked how Blough had used government for his own advantage. Barry Goldwater expressed that sort of myopia when he said that "when we have a President who takes it upon himself to set prices in this country, then I suggest that every man, woman and child knows what we are up against. We need no longer hold back and be careful about what we say about our opposition."[7] Two early-morning (one at 3:00 A.M.) calls on reporters by FBI agents attempting to establish a price-fixing conspiracy were also widely reported and widely condemned.[8]

All this combined with heavy reportage of Billy Sol Estes's activities involving manipulation of federal support programs. The dealings of the Texas financier were, Kennedy suspected, being used to taint the Democrats and by extension the administration. On May 9 the President told his regular news conference that he was reading the papers more but "enjoying it less—and so on, but I have not complained nor do I plan to make any general complaints. I read and talk to myself about it, but I don't plan to issue any general statement on the press."[9]

That vow came to an abrupt end when the *New York Herald Tribune* carried an editorial depicting Pierre Salinger saying to Kennedy, "Mr. Khrushchev said he liked your style in the steel crisis." The White House thereupon announced that it had suspended all twenty-two copies of its *Tribune* subscription.[10] Actually, of course, copies of "the Trib" continued to be available in the White House,[11] and the gesture was, according to Sorensen, later considered a mistake.

But the accelerating stock market decline was viewed as one result of his action against steel. At a dinner for the White House Correspondents and News Photographers Association, the President poked fun at both himself and the situation by saying that he had a few "opening announcements," and among them was the following:

First, the sudden and arbitrary action of the officers of this association in increasing the price of dinner tickets by $2.50 over last year constitutes a wholly unjustifiable defiance of the public interest. If this increase is not rescinded but is imitated by the gridiron, radio, TV, and other dinners, it will have a serious impact on the entire economy of this city![12]

Kennedy was resigned to what he considered the scapegoating of the administration. He insisted that the economy was "rising, unemployment is down, the prospects in this month are good, and, therefore, I think that the stock market will follow the economy."[13] More bitterly he complained that when the market went down, it was called the "Kennedy stock market," and when it went up "it's the free enterprise system."[14] But Wall Street prices, which had been weakening since December, long before the confrontation with Blough, tumbled severely on May 28. In one of the wilder trading days in market history the overinflated prices collapsed. The downward spiral lasted three days. Thirty-five million shares had changed hands, the greatest volume in a generation; the Dow Jones average had gone from 611.78 to a low of 563.24.[15]

At noon on the day the market broke, the President got on the phone with Bob Lovett. He wanted to know two things: What did Lovett think was happening? Should he issue a statement and try to do something through the Treasury?[16] At an emergency White House meeting the next day Kennedy considered several possible alternatives, including "quickie" tax cuts.[17] Four days later Lovett came in. By that time the market had recovered. Now the discussion centered on long-term palliatives, and the two men talked about the adverse effects of excessive taxation of the accumulation of savings and venture capital. Lovett's concern about the stifling of effective production had led him to prepare two illustrations of active corporate cases in which excessive income taxes had discouraged the construction of additional plants. The lesson was clear: Taxation had prevented capital formation, and that had crippled investments. Such burdens had to be lifted. The realities of finances had to be explained to businessmen. If only they could be weaned away from fear of spending as threats to the budget, and therefore to the economy, they might realize the stimulative possibilities for the economy, enjoy the profits, and the government might even have enough income to narrow the deficits. At the same time, there were encouraging signs that the business world was sufficiently anxious about the situation to downplay worries about the budget.[18]

Kennedy became convinced that with the right approach, at the proper forum, he might make some headway. With a commencement address already scheduled for Yale University on June 11, he decided that that would be an appropriate time and place. He asked the council to compile a list of "twenty myths," and they were turned over to Sorensen. But the actual drafting of the speech, Heller recalls, was characteristic of the Kennedy White House. "A lot of people got into the act."[19]

As usual the primary responsibility for the finished product was Sorensen's. But Schlesinger "had a considerable run at it, and it had its contributions from Galbraith as well. Members of the council made their own suggestions, and additional comments were solicited from Treasury. As the work progressed, Kennedy kept in close touch with Sorensen and offered further guidance. But what was quite unusual was that the President "rewrote a considerable chunk on the plane between Washington and New Haven," remembers Heller. "He had in his hand the report from the Bank on International Settlements and something from *The Wall Street Journal* and some other things, which he inserted into the speech, late, late, late into the game. I would think that at least a quarter of it grew out of that plane ride. So it was very, very much Kennedy's heart and soul on economics."[20]

That Yale address lamented the burdens on the nation's economy that were caused by conventional notions. Kennedy pleaded for "not labels and clichés but more basic discussion of the sophisticated and technical questions involved in keeping a great economic machinery moving ahead."[21] "The myth persists," he argued, "that Federal deficits create inflation and budget surpluses prevent it," and he pointed to the postwar surpluses that had failed to prevent inflation while stability had not been upset by recent deficits. "Obviously deficits are sometimes dangerous—and so are surpluses."[22] It was a myth to believe "that government is big, and bad—and getting steadily worse," when in fact it was growing less rapidly than the economy as a whole. In relation to the problems of federal fiscal policy, the budget "is not simply irrelevant; it can be actively misleading. And yet there is a mythology that measures all of our natural soundness or unsoundness on the single simple basis of this same annual administration budget."[23] The real need was for high employment with a steady expansion of output, stable prices, and a strong dollar. He closed with words from Thomas Jefferson: "The new circumstances under which we are placed call for new words, new phrases, and for the transfer of old words to new objects."[24]

The President was, of course, preaching heresies, pure Keynes. But few businessmen were buying his advice. They were clinging to the fiscal orthodoxy of balancing budgets not by stimulating through pump-priming but by reduced spending. Their thinking was complex, far from monolithic, but while they favored the tax credit for depreciating capital outlays and endorsed the trade bill so tariffs could be lowered, they remained strongly antiadministration and hostile to a tax cut that might lead to higher deficits.[25]

Kennedy and his advisers were puzzled that so few seemed able to grasp what was in their own interest. Sorensen despaired that much could be done about the situation. "Nor can we discharge every appointee that comes under attack, withdraw our legislative program, relax our enforcement of the law or join the Republican Party," he wrote in a memorandum for the President. But that, in effect, "is what many of these business critics are asking."[26]

In the spring and summer a "Kennedy market" had been bad enough; before the fall congressional elections a "Kennedy recession" could be even more serious.[27] There was much uncertainty about what had caused the slump, but Gallup surveys showed nothing else cited as frequently by the public as Kennedy's action against U.S. Steel. Although sixty-five percent continued to reject the idea that the President was antibusiness, by August the weakened economy had resulted in a loss to his popularity, which dipped below seventy percent.[28] The immediate need was to educate as many businessmen as possible as to Kennedy's true attitude and to win their confidence—and investments—in the economy.

Douglas Dillon had already decried the "misconception that the Kennedy Administration is pursuing overall anti-business policies."[29] But the effort to cultivate business confidence and influence its thinking then became a full-fledged campaign. Meetings were scheduled with commercial leaders. Just about every member of the Cabinet and sub-Cabinet worked at lining up contacts. The President himself hosted seventeen bankers and executives at a White House luncheon on July 12.[30]

Sorensen then sent memoranda to the heads of twenty-four departments and agencies informing them that he was compiling a list of major actions undertaken or proposed by the administration "which might be termed 'pro-business' or 'pro-free enterprise.'" Within twenty-four hours he wanted them to respond with additional items showing what their units were doing. The request brought a flow of paper from every department, specifying their initiatives: how Defense was instituting cost-cutting that would ultimately reduce tax burdens through a three-billion-dollar reduction over a three-year period; how two thirds of the Justice Department's antitrust legislation had been spurred by complaints from businessmen themselves; how, by establishing a Communications Satellite Corporation, the President had recognized the importance of the private sector; and reports of speeches, meetings, and briefings of newsmen representing financial publications. Secretary of Commerce Hodges had the additional idea of suggesting that "it might not be a bad idea to let the business community know the number of businessmen that are serving in this Administration. We are all familiar with the typical businessman's attitude that Schlesinger-Galbraith and company are running the country. I rather suspect," he added, "that there are many more businessmen appointed by this Administration than educators."[31] Sorensen prepared Kennedy for a Thursday morning Cabinet meeting by warning that "business criticism of this Administration had intensified to a level justifying the concern of every Cabinet member because of its unfavorable effect on the political climate in general, including the businessman's own willingness to invest."[32]

Later that day the President went to the home of Felix Frankfurter. The associate justice, with one month left before retirement after twenty-three years on the Supreme Court, was recovering from a recent hospitalization. Frankfurter and the Kennedys had had an old relationship. While still on the faculty of the Harvard Law School he had suggested that Joe Junior study under Harold Laski at the London School of Economics, and that later led to Jack's brief stay there. Now, together with Dean Acheson and Schlesinger, the President paid his respects.

Kennedy wanted to hear more from the justice himself about comments that had reached him through Bundy about the administration's failure to "educate" the public. Frankfurter welcomed the President's interest, and said he was concerned that not enough was being done about promoting better understanding of the fundamental purposes of democracy. Words were meaningless. Only the "evocative" powers of a great teacher could make the principles governing the nation live again. The justice could hardly have been more direct: Kennedy had somehow not conveyed the basic values of the American system.

The President agreed that communication was a problem that he also found perplexing. But, he pointed out, this was no longer the 1930's. Federal functions were different. FDR's New Deal had been able to offer legislation with direct benefits to various groups of people. They were concrete, understandable in personal terms, not merely reforms that were abstractions to workers. The only New Frontier initiative that came close to matching that kind of thing was medical care. Government had, in its need to deal with so many different things, become much more complex. Acheson agreed with the President, and added the observation that domestic and foreign affairs were increasingly independent and involved. What did the balance-of-payments problem mean to the worker asked to temper his wage demands?

That kind of argument strained Frankfurter's patience, and he digressed into a favorite area, the function of a President who also happened to be a Democrat. A Democratic President really doing his job, he argued, was not going to have good relations with business. At that point Kennedy interrupted by saying that he had come to that conclusion himself and asked Frankfurter why he thought so. Because, replied the justice, the major purposes of a Democratic President were beyond the experience of businessmen and were therefore apt to create doubt and suspicion. To accomplish his goals a Democratic President had to direct funds, goods, and people to concerns that relate to human life and had little to do with economic values. That should compel the President to be a "molder of American life," and a strong Democrat was likely to do so in ways that seemed alien, if not frightening, to businessmen. Kennedy "listened very attentively and sympathetically," according to a summary of their conversation, and Frankfurter was also impressed that his words received such careful attention.[33] He was, alas, a voice from the past, and this was, after all, the New Frontier. To govern and to rejuvenate the economy Kennedy could not afford to alienate the private sector.

The Business Council did come out in favor of a a tax cut, Heller discovered when he met with them in mid-July. That was good; that was movement in the right direction; they were coming around to an understanding of Keynesian economic gospel. Moreover, the cut they wanted was one that would be both immediate and permanent.[34] Perhaps the private sector was showing signs of connecting with the administration.

But trepidations continued within the White House. Sorensen reminded Kennedy that he himself had cautioned against overreacting at the time of the Berlin crisis. Now, in dealing with the economy, it was essential to avoid a similar temptation.[35] The President meanwhile kept close watch over the various aspects of the international financial situation, including a run on the dollar and a fifty-million-dollar gold loss to England. After a meeting with Bill Martin, Gardner Ackley, who had replaced Kermit Gordon on the CEA, came away from the Federal Reserve chairman and noted in a personal memorandum that "once again, the balance of payments is the key to everything else."[36] By the second week in August the decision was made to act before the elections by requesting a tax cut.

Economic data showed little to make such a move urgent. If anything, preliminary figures already in for July indicated improvements in unemployment and production. But Walter Heller pointed out that not only would such a request "take out advance insurance against a 'Kennedy recession,' " it would also "give Democratic congressional candidates a more activist economic policy to brandish in the 1962 elections."[37]

The result was the President's report on the economy, delivered over national television on August 13. "The single most important fiscal weapon available to strengthen the national economy," he declared, "is the Federal tax policy," and promised that such a bill would be introduced into the new Congress at the start of 1963.[38] Three months later, with the congressional elections over, he addressed the Economics Club of New York. This time, with rhetoric full of traditional homilies to "free enterprise," he called for making the kind of cuts that would stimulate private investments and "reduce the burden on private incomes and the deterrents to private initiative which are imposed by our present tax system." He had hoped to present his message "in an atmosphere of a balanced budget," but the need for stepped up spending for nuclear and conventional forces as well as the space program had ruled that out.[39]

Those who had been most impressed with the Yale speech now led the disenchanted. Galbraith quickly called it the most "Republican speech since McKinley."[40] Both Schlesinger and Sorensen agreed that he had fallen back on conservative clichés and given his worst performance. Kennedy phoned Heller right afterward and said, "I gave them straight Keynes and Heller, and they loved it," which brought Sorensen's subsequent comment that "it sounded like Hoover, but it was actually Heller."[41]

Kennedy had come down on the side of what he thought was politically feasible. His liberal critics were overlooking facts of life that included the following: 1) the President's own skepticism about the efficacy of federal economic programs; 2) the narrowness of his election, which discouraged innovations; 3) the absence of an economic crisis sufficiently distressing to the middle classes to create a constituency for more expansive government policies; 4) the precariousness of the congressional liberals, who were once again vulnerable against a combination of Republicans and southern Democrats; 5) control of key committees in the hands of the most powerful fiscal conservatives on the Hill; 6) Kennedy's personal sympathy with the aims and problems of most businessmen. Finally Kennedy had to contend with the continued independence of the Federal Reserve Board, which could pursue monetary policies potentially counterproductive to the enthusiasts urging economic expansion. With the additional pressure of the Business Advisory Council, which declared its own independence and began to call itself simply the Business Council, Kennedy, like Eisenhower before him, gave reassurances that the interests of commerce were not being neglected by the White House.

Reform was the key word. Everybody wanted reform. What they meant was another matter. To businessmen *reform* meant reducing rates. To others that meant adjusting the tables to mitigate some of the more obvious inequities. Wilbur Mills, chairman of the Ways and Means Committee, held out for his own pet changes. More eager to stimulate the economy than to tinker with anything that might provoke even more opposition, Kennedy vacillated. Finally Kennedy had to agree that "reforms" had to be part of the package that was submitted in January.[42]

Kennedy himself remained uncertain about the political consequences of cutting taxes while submitting a budget with a projected deficit of $11.9 billion. Fiscal conservatives were upset by such "irresponsibility." Conflicts slowed matters down some more, and when the economy then began to improve, the whole issue seemed less urgent. The legislation remained locked up in the Eighty-eighth Congress until September. At that point the House finally produced a bill, but one that was cleansed of most "reforms." When the presidency came to its abrupt end in November, the Senate Finance Committee had yet to act.

As the corporations themselves had begun to recognize, they were about to become the prime beneficiaries. The bill that the administration got behind by the summer of 1963 had abandoned most reforms, thereby caving in to pressures for various interest groups, and held out potential annual gains of $2.6 billion from the rate cuts, $1.5 billion from new depreciation allowances, and another $1.3 billion from a new investment tax credit. Bernard Nossiter has pointed out how fine all that was as far as Kennedy was concerned, because it suited his probusiness attitude.[43] But that was incidental when considered alongside his objective of promoting economic stimulation and also having a major tax bill to show before 1964. Sheer productivity had its attractions, especially for an administration that had vowed to "get America moving again."

Kennedy had well understood Frankfurter's warning about the "money powers." The justice, in his own later recollection of their conversation, recalled that the President had called that group his most important problem.[44] The administration's predicament was also labor's. Heller reported that AFL-CIO leaders were watching "the spectacle of the Administration's economic troops marching off to fight the problems of the balance of payments, inflation, and economic growth with undisguised dismay." They were worried about getting "the dirty end of the stick—big cuts for the fat cats, some crumbs for the little folk, and no reform."[45] But labor had nowhere else to go, and at least Kennedy had neutralized much of the business community.

Whether they really were sons of bitches was mostly irrelevant. As Charles Bartlett has recalled, Kennedy liked many of them as individuals, but as a group "I don't think [he] had an enormously high opinion of most businessmen." He had "an enormous sense of their selfishness." He could understand that; he didn't expect more, but he didn't really crave their company."[46] Later Bobby Kennedy told an interviewer that "more was done for business in the United States during the last three years than has ever been done for business."[47]

11

"Signing on for Civil Rights"

The civil rights movement helped elevate Jack Kennedy to Lincolnesque proportions. In reality the drive for racial equality overwhelmed him, forced him to amend his political calculations, and weakened the pragmatic coalition he had been working to harmonize. If, as Bobby has recalled, life would have been simpler in the White House without the Russians, it would have also been convenient had the drive for a "second reconstruction" not matured during his brother's brief presidency.

Nothing else had the potential for being so divisive. The impatience of young activists, black and white, and their allies willing to give financial and personal assistance had followed the South's "massive resistance" against the Court's desegregation orders during the fifties. At a time of cold war and social and economic realignment, the campaign to overturn the symbolic and concrete obstacles to an integrated society not unnaturally turned to Kennedy for inspiration and help.

He had already signaled the possibility of change. It could, he had suggested, come without a revolution; it would be legitimate; a new president would be more sensitive. He had campaigned as a full supporter of civil rights. The party's civil rights plank, which had been written by Chester Bowles at the request of Democratic Party Chairman

Paul Butler, had made that a clear commitment. The "moral and political leadership by the whole Executive Branch of our Government" was pledged behind efforts to do whatever may be necessary, including requesting new legislation, to wipe out literacy tests and poll-tax requirements for voting. Discrimination in jobs and federally assisted housing would also be ended. "Above all," said the platform, "it will require the strong, active, persuasive, and inventive leadership of the President of the United States."[1]

Afterward, when the campaign progressed, Kennedy changed that emphasis. During his September speaking tour when he concentrated his efforts in small towns and agricultural centers, the subject hardly came up. Then there was a significant switch. He began to talk about what could be accomplished by "executive action." He made that point again when interviewed on *Meet the Press* in mid-October; and, as political scientist John Hart writes, he "had begun to realize the practical and political problems of implementing the civil rights plank in the party platform and had changed his campaign statements accordingly," and that campaign theme set the tone for the presidency.[2] Left behind was any hint of legislative action, including the position he had been forced into supporting during the August rump session by the shrewd Republican attempt to divide the vulnerable Democrats along North–South lines. He had also responded to that move by asking Emanuel Celler, the chairman of the House Judiciary Committee, and Senator Joseph Clark of Pennsylvania to draft possible legislation. All that was now part of the former strategy.

The new position was also more personally compatible. Kennedy's own attitude resembled the outlook of most liberally educated middle- and upper-class Americans, and that held for those in the Civil Rights Division in the Justice Department as well. Along with them, Kennedy recognized the barbaric aspects of racial injustice, but it was an appreciation that remained as removed from personal experience as the poverty that Jack Kennedy had confronted while campaigning in West Virginia. The desperation itself was not felt, and the moral fervor of a Martin Luther King, Jr., left him cold. There remained the illusion that progress would come at the pace that he and his peers thought was reasonable. Ingrained in his education was the traditional view of how the South had been thrown into chaos during the dark days of "Black Reconstruction." Historian David Donald was present with Kennedy at one of Bobby's Hickory Hill "seminars" when the President participated in an after-dinner discussion of the subject. He told the historian that he was "determined to go down in our history books as a great President," and was curious about the ways to do so. But during that talk he showed no awareness of the more recent literature that showed the self-serving character of what had been depicted as the evils of "Black Reconstruction."[3]

Socially as well as politically Jack Kennedy was closely attuned to the South. He had developed personal ties with Governor John Patterson of Alabama. There were other friends, such as Bob Troutman of Atlanta, the Battles of Virginia, and, of course, there was always George Smathers. He also worked at cultivating Harry Byrd, and however "uncivilized" he considered Jim Eastland, he tried to keep an easy relationship with the chairman of the vital Senate Judiciary Committee. Kennedy's Florida friend helped serve as a link with other southern senators. When Smathers afterward spoke out against a Kennedy endorsement of a civil rights bill, he was promptly called to the White House, where he found the President in a bathrobe and slippers. He pulled from his pocket a newspaper clipping of the speech and said to Smathers, "You really took my jock off." Smathers explained that the Florida electorate had left him no choice but to speak out.[4]

Kennedy's personal distaste, then, was only vaguely related to his perceptions of what could be and what ought to be done. The situation was not as simple as the moralizers seemed to be preaching. Southern society had developed along those lines. It was doubtful, as Eisenhower had certainly believed, that the federal government could really force change without flirting with the possibility of further bloodshed and without, as the abolitionists had learned a century and a half earlier, creating an even more oppressive counterreaction. That was the last thing the President wanted. It would also certainly jeopardize the already fragile coalition that he was attempting to hold together among the liberals and old New Dealers from the North and the powerfully based southern wing of the party on Capitol Hill. They had the obvious ability to retaliate by denying him certain key pieces of legislation: the Trade Expansion Act, the tax bills, Medicare. Anything else that came out of the White House that could ultimately provide tangible economic assistance to poor blacks and whites alike was also vulnerable if he gave the segregationists a club they could hold over his head.

To civil rights activists and those taking the historical view that justice was long overdue, especially since the Supreme Court had long since spoken, such detachment and reasoning was lofty, insensitive. Considerations involving Capitol Hill politics and provoking hatred from racists were illegitimate and immoral. The lawbreakers were being permitted to get their own way. Of the man whose tone en route to the White House had promised so much, more was expected. NAACP Director Roy Wilkins, one of the movement's more seasoned and moderate leaders, thought Kennedy himself was morally convinced about the need for justice, but that his background hindered his ability to understand the depth of racial injustice.[5] He did not want to get involved with legislation. He hoped the matter would work itself out.[6] "In 1961," one recent historian has written, "the Kennedys saw the struggle against racism as a conundrum to be managed, not a cause to be championed."[7] Kennedy's whole effort, said Congressman Hale Boggs, another close southern ally, "was to temper conditions, to overcome disagreements, to unite the nation. . . . He had a thorough understanding of the difficulties that confronted the smaller southern communities and so on. He understood this perfectly. His whole approach was one of understanding and sympathy, and yet, once he had decided on a course of action, he never hesitated."[8]

That so much exploded while he was in the White House was no coincidence of history. The civil-disobedience campaign that mounted during the spring of 1961 drew its strength in no small part from an underlying confidence that there was a man in the White House who would sooner or later have to respond with the full power of federal authority. Letters from the Congress of Racial Equality to Kennedy, the Justice Department, and the FBI warned of the coming Freedom Ride campaign to defy laws preventing integrated transportation. So far there were no replies.

In early May two busloads of blacks and whites left Washington, D.C., and headed toward Montgomery, Alabama. Riders were beaten and run out of town; jails were filled; the government's tolerance of how much it could withstand without using troops was being severely challenged, and it was not always clear whether federal laws were involved. Activists planned ways of provoking the Kennedy administration into becoming their ally.[9] The failure of the federal government to act when there was no violence reinforced violence as the only way to get action.

Violence reached its ugliest point when an impassioned mob savagely attacked a Greyhound bus at Anniston, Alabama, smashing windows, slashing tires, and menacing the lives of the passengers. After the bus managed to escape with the aid of local police, it was pursued by gangs in cars. When the slashed tires went flat about six miles outside Anniston, the stranded bus was at the mercy of the local citizens. Someone then threw an incendiary bomb into a window. Others held the doors shut, preventing riders from leaving the smoke-filled vehicle until it became obvious that the bus was about to explode. As they rushed out, just before the bus burst into flames, they were beaten by the mob. The local hospital refused to treat the wounded, so they had to be rushed to Birmingham by a caravan of armed cars. By that time another bus, this one a Trailways, pulled into Anniston. Eight local whites rushed inside and demanded that the black students move to the rear section. When that order was refused, they and white Freedom Riders were set upon and beaten. A retired schoolteacher who had tried to talk the mob out of violence was clubbed over the head and left with permanent brain damage. Finally, when the Trailways bus reached Birmingham, they were again attacked by a gang that had spent hours awaiting their arrival. The police headquarters was just two blocks from the terminal, but even though they and everyone else knew exactly what was about to happen, they failed to intervene until after the passengers were mauled. "The reporters knew that they were coming. Everyone knew they were coming," recalled Burke Marshall.[10] The governor, John Patterson, urged that they get "out of Alabama as soon as possible." A few days later Birmingham's police commissioner, Eugene (Bull) Connor, had the students driven at midnight to the Tennessee border, about 150 miles away. But they were determined to reach their goal. Then after returning to Birmingham with the assistance of a southern black civil rights worker, they were unable to find a bus driver willing to take them on to their goal, the state capitol at Montgomery.[11] "After all," Bobby Kennedy argued over the telephone with the Greyhound bus dispatcher, "all these people have tickets and are entitled to transportation to continue the trip or project to Montgomery."[12] Finally on May 20, with the assistance of additional volunteers, twenty-one Freedom Riders left for Montgomery. When they arrived, they were immediately plunged into an unrestrained mob.

The situation was brutal, and inexcusable. Elementary rights and protections were being withheld. The whole notion that such outrages required no additional legislative protection from the federal government was being severely tested. Burke Marshall confronted the President with the problem on a Sunday morning that May. Together with the Deputy Attorney General Byron White, he told Kennedy that federal police action could no longer be delayed.

They had their breakfast just off the President's bedroom. It was the first time the problem of serious racial disorders had been taken to him directly. Kennedy listened to descriptions that included evidence of KKK involvement and efforts to get local judges to issue restraining orders, but, the President was told, there was no precedent for such a suit. "My first impression of him from that meeting," Marshall later said, "was just of a tuned-in intelligence. I mean a real intelligence at work on gathering all this data and understanding it, weighing it, and accepting it. I mean not complaining about the governor or complaining about the mob or complaining about the biracial group or the situation, but simply taking it all in and accepting it as the facts that he had to face."[13] He never did eat that breakfast. The Justice Department could obviously no longer just stand by.

The attorney general continued to make the series of phone calls that he had begun after the Anniston and Birmingham incidents. Several went directly to John Patterson, but the governor was clearly trying to avoid a direct conversation with Bob Kennedy. The attorney general did get some help from Senator Eastland, who at least promised protection for riders reaching Jackson, Mississippi.[14]

The President then decided to send his own representative, John Seigenthaler, to Montgomery to work things out with the governor and his people. At that point Patterson accepted responsibility for providing police-escort protection for the buses, a decision that may well have been prompted by appeals from Alabama businessmen fearful that the disorders would have economic consequences. But Seigenthaler, a Tennessee newspaperman who had been associated with Bob Kennedy since Teamster investigation days, himself became a victim of brutality. While trying to protect a black woman, he was attacked in the street, knocked unconscious, and left on the ground for twenty-five minutes before being taken to a hospital, where he recovered. The President then directed his brother to take whatever action was appropriate and necessary. Section 333, Title 10, of the U.S. Code empowered him to act in order to suppress any unlawful combination or domestic violence depriving citizens of constitutional rights.[15]

On May 20 the President issued a public statement that expressed his "deepest concern." He called upon responsible local officials to "exercise their lawful authority to prevent any further outbreaks of violence," and asked all sides to avoid additional provocations.[16] Finally, that evening Bobby got a call from Governor Patterson, who insisted that there was no legal authority for sending in U.S. marshals. Besides, he argued, outside help was not necessary. The situation could be controlled locally. The attorney general then asked how come those people happened to have been beaten in Montgomery, and the governor replied that it was hard for a small police department to control two or three thousand people. "Well," said the younger Kennedy, "it's obvious that you do need outside help," a point that Patterson continued to resist. Moreover, calling out the National Guard would be embarrassing. "I will have to take steps to defend myself politically," he told the attorney general. Bobby sympathized with that argument but insisted that additional protection had become necessary. He was going to send in marshals under the supervision of Byron White, and he hoped that they would have the governor's cooperation. "You are going to have to paddle your own boat and I have to look out for myself," he told Patterson.[17] The attorney general then announced that the Justice Department would seek to enjoin the KKK and the National States Rights Party from any further interference. Deputy Attorney General White and his contingent would be sent to Montgomery "to assist state and local authorities in the protection of persons and property and vehicles."[18]

It was as much as he could do, but understandably not enough for the more extreme militants. Yet the dilemma posed the larger question of how openly and vigorously the federal government could respond to each instance of violence, whether or not the activists were being deliberately provocative. Neither were the activists happy that the President was then also contemplating the ramifications of the violence upon his forthcoming meetings with De Gaulle, Khrushchev, and Macmillan. The potential for embarrassment in Europe was enormous. "Tell them to call it off," he told Harris Wofford. "Stop them." Wofford replied, "I don't think anybody's going to stop them now."[19] But the attorney general asked for a "cooling-off period." "We've been cooling off for 100 years," responded James Farmer, the executive director of CORE. "If we got any cooler we'd be in a deep freeze."[20] Bobby Kennedy's assistant, Joe Dolan, agreed with the request, but urged one further step. Going into the Deep South with integrated groups was bad enough, but "when some of the white passengers are females and some of the negro [sic] passengers are males," the situation poses a "violation of the ultimate southern taboo and it would appear that if the freedom riders want progress rather than bloodshed they should make this small concession even if only temporarily to southern mores and folkways."[21] The idea of a "cooling-off period" in itself received wide support from leading newspapers, but Martin Luther King, Jr., preferred to call it a "lull."[22] On June 5 King urged the President to issue a "second Emancipation Proclamation."[23]

Other political hesitations from Washington increased the discontent among leading activists about the quality of the President's support for their drive. He refused requests from CORE and Dr. King to personally welcome the Freedom Riders back to Washington.[24] When he returned from Europe, he also turned down a suggestion from Wofford and Marshall that his report to the American people on June 6 include "a few stout words" about the racial and constitutional crisis.[25] Suspicions were even increased when Bobby met with some of the younger civil rights leaders on June 16 and tried to convince them of the limitation of further demonstrations. Instead they should exert their efforts through the power of the ballot box. Educating southern blacks about the importance of voting and getting them to register should be given top priority as the best way to achieve long-term changes. Their efforts would also be given financial support by such philanthropic organizations as the Field and Taconic foundations. Dr. King, who was at that meeting, believed that the attorney general had guaranteed "all steps necessary to protect those rights in danger," and that included safeguards against reprisals from southern whites. To the more skeptical, however, it was only, as Harvard Sitkoff puts it, a "clever ploy by the Administration to increase Negro voting strength in preparation for Kennedy's 1964 re-election bid, and to 'get the niggers off the streets.' "[26]

Yet, with the support of the Justice Department and such federal judges as Frank Johnson of the Middle District of Alabama, progress was made through executive action. Judge Johnson enjoined the KKK, the National States Rights Party, and the police of Birmingham and Montgomery from interfering with interstate travel. Through vigorous efforts by the attorney general, the Interstate Commerce Commission finally issued an order ending segregation in interstate bus terminals.[27]

All in all, through executive leadership the Kennedy Justice Department compiled an impressive record in attempting to enforce court orders and existing legislation. The Civil Rights Division brought over forty-two suits in four states to secure voting rights for blacks. Through the Voter Education Project promoted by the administration, 688,800 blacks were qualified to vote between April 1, 1962, and November 1, 1964. Kennedy also supported the anti–poll tax amendment, which cleared the Congress in September of 1962 and was ratified within two years as the Twenty-fourth Amendment. As one student of black voting in the South has pointed out, "Whereas the Eisenhower lawyers had moved deliberately, the Kennedy–Johnson attorneys pushed the judiciary far more earnestly."[28]

Executive action worked in other ways as well. In addition to the appointment of Robert Weaver, the administration placed forty blacks in important posts during its first two months. Later that year Thurgood Marshall, who had argued the school segregation case of Topeka, Kansas, before the Supreme Court, was placed on the Second Circuit of Appeals in New York.[29] Weaver later recalled that such appointments were "symbolic of this concern [with equal employment opportunities] as well as the evidence of the political power of and the importance of the Negro in America."[30] By an executive order, issued in early March of 1961, Kennedy created the President's Committee on Equal Employment Opportunity, thereby superseding two largely ineffectual committees. The effort at revitalization was made more effective by placing the committee under the chairmanship of Vice-President Johnson, who worked closely with a competent staff and forged a close involvement with the Labor Department.[31] Kennedy was clearly trying to delay any possible requests for legislation until as late in his first administration as possible.[32]

To critics, of course, executive action was pitifully inadequate and unresponsive. Roger Wilkins, a nephew of the civil rights leader who was currently with the administration's foreign aid program, complained in 1962 that "this Administration seems to be using appointments and the achievement of voting rights as an excuse for doing little or nothing else. Presidential indifference is the unkindest cut of all."[33] In an oral-history interview the leading civil liberties lawyer and ADA founder, Joseph Rauh, Jr., deplored the failure to call for legislation.[34] At the time the Kennedy administration was formulating its strategy, however, remarkably few of its well-wishers, from the Southern Regional Conference to Roy Wilkins and Dr. King himself, advocated going beyond vigorous enforcement of the laws already on the books. Indeed, Harris Wofford authored the preinaugural memorandum that argued the need for confining requests for new legislation to simply asking for an extension of the Civil Rights Commission.[35]

The political considerations that guided this approach were made all the more obvious by calls for White House initiatives that came from such Republicans as Senators Jacob Javits of New York and Everett Dirksen of Illinois. They and their colleagues were fully aware (as they had been during the special session in August) that they were simply trying to embarrass Kennedy and the Democrats.[36] Getting through an extension of the Civil Rights Commission itself was hard enough; when that was finally achieved, it was limited to a two-year reprieve.[37] Indeed, civil rights legislation that was introduced during that first year by a number of senators simply died in Eastland's committee.[38] In 1962 Mike Mansfield tested the possibilities in the form of a literacy bill to guarantee voting registration rights for those who had completed at least a sixth-grade education. Not only were there not enough votes to break a filibuster, but there was little public support as well. Kennedy spoke out for it during a press conference in May, saying he was amazed that anybody could question the bill's constitutionality, but the administration sidestepped giving it serious support.[39] *The New York Times*'s correspondent described the vote on cloture to break the filibuster as one that "had all the conviction of a professional wrestling match: everybody played his role for the crowd, but nobody got hurt."[40] As Carl Brauer has pointed out, it became more judicious for Kennedy to consider economic assistance, just as FDR had concluded, as a better way to approach the problems of blacks.[41]

By the fall of 1962, and with congressional elections near, the President had yet to apply that "stroke of a pen" to sign the order for open occupancy in housing. Clearly within the authority of executive action, it had become his most specific contradiction between promise and performance. Criticism was combined with ridicule. The mails brought "pens for Jack" to the White House. Within the executive branch itself Weaver, Wofford, and Lee White worked to get one signed. Bobby was ambivalent; so in a sense was Sorensen, torn between his moral conscience and political calculations. Several samples of the proposed order were drawn up. But the President continued to hedge, succumbing as much to congressional pressures as on the question of legislation, once again yielding to such political advisers as O'Brien and estimates of Capitol Hill realities. In October 1960 Nick Katzenbach, then in charge of the Justice Department's Office of Legal Counsel, drafted an order to effectively end federal loans or grants for restricted housing.[42] Assistant Special Counsel Lee White, however, virtually ruled out any such move just a few days later when he sent the President a compilation with thirteen possible civil rights measures. In it he referred to the chairmen of the housing committees of each chamber of Congress. Both were from Alabama, and, White noted, "Sen. [John] Sparkman and Cong. [Albert] Rains are, of course, strongly opposed to any Housing order. And quite clearly the bill to create Dept. of Urban Affairs would be lost if order issued—it is already in trouble, however, and on the civil rights issue." Earlier the President's reason for the delay had been predicated on the need to get his housing bill.[43] Once that had gotten through in June, he feared that signing the executive order would so offend Sparkman and Rains that his hoped-for Department of Urban Affairs would never win approval, especially since it was widely assumed that it would be headed by a black man, Robert Weaver. But Weaver, White now advised, "much prefers the order to the Dept. if he must choose between them."[44] When the President met with the members of the Civil Rights Commission on November 22, he advised that he might well sign the order soon. He also told them it would be a topic for discussion at Hyannis Port over the Thanksgiving Day weekend. One member of the commission, Father Theodore Hesburgh, sensed that he was ready to act but had been talked out of it by his advisers.[45]

Indeed, as the President met that holiday weekend with Bobby and others from Justice, as well as Budget Director David Bell, the housing order was on the top of their agenda. They sat in the living room overlooking the lawn. Outside, despite the falling rain and the important matter under discussion, Bobby spent much of the time playing touch football. When the President needed him, he called "Hey, Bobby," through the window, and the attorney general would come in, "give his remarks on whatever we were talking about, and then he would go out back with his children in the cold rain." Burke Marshall concluded that it was the first time "any President got advised by an attorney general on an important matter like this when the attorney general was just dripping wet in an old sweater, coming in from playing touch football in the rain."[46] The conversation centered far more on the reasons for further delay than on finally acting to fulfill the campaign pledge. It was, at that point, full of traps. The draft had even gone beyond what had originally been promised. There were questions of doubtful constitutionality, and, of serious concern to Kennedy, possible consequences upon the economy. Considering it all, the President joshed Ted Sorensen about who had put "the stroke of a pen" words into his mouth. The star Kennedy speechwriter denied that it had been his doing. It must be, the President responded dryly, that nobody had written it.[47]

Kennedy's Gallup poll showed his level of approval at seventy-seven percent, near his all-time high.[48] The civil rights conflicts were in the relative "lull" Dr. King had talked about, and The Washington Post was running a series of articles on the reduced importance of race as an issue in southern politics.[49] Even the urging of Charles Abrams, the president of the National Committee Against Discrimination in Housing, that the lack of much opposition at the moment made it a good time to sign the document, had its corollary. That also implicitly acknowledged the absence of an important, strong constituency constituting a threat. Between that Thanksgiving meeting and July 5 of the following year, the matter came up only twice at presidential news conferences, and each time the discussion was perfunctory. Asked on January 15 about his campaign promise, Kennedy explained that "we are proceeding ahead in a way which will maintain a consensus, and which will advance this cause."[50] On July 5 a reporter wanting to know why he had not acted after seventeen months in office was told that it would be announced "when we think it would be a useful and appropriate time."[51]

Later that summer, and especially in the early fall, the issue that would not go away engulfed the Justice Department and this time the President himself. Martin Luther King's desegregation campaign in Albany,

Georgia, had failed to achieve its objective. The organizers were out-maneuvered by the city's police chief, who averted a repetition of the Alabama violence and filled the jails with relatively quiet efficiency, blatantly violating constitutional rights. Kennedy's desire to have a moderate candidate for Georgia's governorship, Carl Sanders, elected that fall added to his normal reluctance to intervene.[52] That made it all the more surprising when he did speak out at a news conference on August 1, and in a manner that drew praise from civil rights supporters, including Dr. King, who wired his appreciation at the "directness of your statement to [sic] Albany crisis."[53] His remarks had not been pitched in moral tones, just simple, easily understandable logic. Kennedy said he could not understand why it was that the U.S. Government could sit down with the Russians at Geneva but that Albany's city council was unwilling to "do the same for American citizens."[54] The Justice Department then entered an injunction hearing as *amicus curiae* (friend of the court), and that was quickly followed by a suspended sentence and freedom from jail for Dr. King.[55]

But the turning point in Jack Kennedy's personal remoteness from the civil rights movement came with the often described efforts of a black man, James Meredith, to join the student body of all-white "Ole Miss," the University of Mississippi at Oxford.[56]

Meredith had the full force of the law on his side. His application for admission had been filed the day after Kennedy's inauguration as President; then he experienced evasions and harassment. Finally, on September 13 Supreme Court Justice Hugo Black, a native of Alabama, ordered no further interference with the courts. An unyielding Governor Barnett, naturally playing to the Mississippi electorate, responded with "We will not surrender to the evil and illegal forces of tyranny."[57] Having come this far, Meredith was determined to go ahead. In the process he gave Bob Kennedy and Burke Marshall some last-minute consternation by his plans to celebrate his arrival at the campus by driving up in his new gold Thunderbird. Fearful that nothing would better provide further grist for racists eager to exploit black stereotypes, Meredith was talked out of that bit of entertainment with the help of comedian Dick Gregory and others who were reached by Marshall.[58]

The President had hoped to make himself as invisible as possible. As Sorensen advised, "There are too many questions you should neither evade nor answer directly."[59] There was also Kennedy's fear that a full-blown black revolt could be sparked if Meredith were murdered.[60] In reality, however, Jack Kennedy was far from detached. The log of his taped telephone conversations relating to Meredith shows twelve recorded calls, seven with Governor Barnett.*[61] After Oxford, as Schlesinger has written, "the Kennedys began to understand how profoundly the republic had been trapped by its history."[62]

For Jack Kennedy the experience was personally devastating, exasperating, and an exercise in dealing with the irrational. He issued a proclamation calling on obstructionists to cease their activities and disperse peaceably. Hundreds of marshals were dispatched to the site, and they were reinforced by federalizing the Mississippi National Guard and the deployment of U.S. troops to the Millington Naval Air Station at Memphis. If needed, they could quickly be flown down to Oxford.

Barnett, meanwhile, was engaging in political theatrics despite the risk of provoking violence. Bobby Kennedy found himself in a ridiculous discussion over the governor's request to permit Meredith's admission only if Barnett could be photographed having to "forceably" yield to marshals with drawn guns. How many should actually be drawn? How many marshals should simply have hands on holsters in the ready position? During one of his painful conversations with the governor the President turned away from the phone and said to Bobby, "You've been fighting a sofa pillow all week."[63] Finally Barnett agreed to a "sneak" registration, trying to get Meredith in with a guard of marshals on Sunday, when traffic around the campus should be light.

That Sunday night the President delayed making his televised report to the nation on the Oxford situation until he could assume that Meredith had been safely escorted onto the campus. Unfortunately his words misled both himself and the troops near Memphis. He talked as though it had all been accomplished: Meredith had been registered, the National Guard had not been needed, and Ole Miss had upheld its "great tradition."[64] As he learned immediately afterward, however, that was far from true. Even as he talked, the mob had gone into action. Marshals were attacked with bottles, bricks, everything the crowd that had awaited Meredith's arrival could get their hands on. Tear gas and bullets responded in exchange. Meanwhile, at the military base near Memphis the soldiers were grossly unprepared for the emergency. The President's speech had lulled them into believing that all had gone peacefully.

In Washington the attorney general, now desperate, kept calling the Pentagon, only to be repeatedly told that the troops would be leaving in "twenty minutes." Meanwhile the marshals were besieged; several were wounded and required hospitalization. One man needed surgery because

*There were twenty conversations between the attorney general and the governor from September 15 through September 28.

a bullet had penetrated his neck and severed an artery. On the campus General Edwin A. Walker stood erect, silent and defiant, his commanding figure alone inciting the mob. Two people were killed, one a foreign correspondent. While all this was happening, the Army was taking forever to arrive, one delay after another impeding their ability to be of much use. Angrily the President appealed to the commander: "People are dying in Oxford. This is the worst thing I've seen in forty-five years. I want the military police battalion to enter the area. I want General Billingslea to see that this is done."[65]

Kennedy was furious. He had taken Barnett's word that troops would not be needed. He had been too optimistic, too careless; they should have been sent in sooner. Even after they finally arrived, the melee continued on through the night. Not until the next morning was Meredith registered.

The episode was an educational one for Jack Kennedy. He had tried to reconcile differences, to understand Barnett's political concerns, and in the end had been deceived. Politically it was not as damaging in the South as it might have been, possibly because of the speech itself or the late arrival of the troops. Kennedy came out of the affair looking like a moderate, having acted with force when that was clearly the only option.

There was still the housing order. His hoped-for reorganization plan, which would have created a Department of Urban Affairs, had been defeated in February, and the absence of the "stroke of the pen" had become an embarrassment. Having acted in Mississippi, having had his hand forced, he was ready to issue the order before the congressional elections. Now, however, protests were coming from a different direction. Northern Democrats, some of the liberals, were urging delay until after the voting. Their pleas mounted by August, and were strongest from legislators with middle-class and Roman Catholic constituents. The White House heard from people like Martha Griffiths and Pat McNamara of Michigan, Leonor Sullivan of Missouri, and Byron Rogers of Colorado. Lee White said that "there were an awful lot of people running for re-election who let it be known to the White House that, if the President signs that Order, tell him he'd better plan on someone else representing my district beside[s] me."[66]

When it came, the announcement was made at a pre–Thanksgiving Day news conference. It was also the second of three opening statements, sandwiched in, as Sorensen later noted, between revealing that the Soviets were withdrawing their bombers from Cuba and the fact that hopeful news was coming about the border conflict between China and India. And it was limited, avoiding constitutional problems and affecting only conventional mortgages. It placed housing facilities already under construction at the hands of the "Housing Agency and other appropriate agencies to use their good offices to promote and encourage the abandonment of discriminatory practices that may now exist."[67] With that out of the way the President left the next day for his holiday weekend at Hyannis Port. By then most people were praising his handling of the missile crisis in Cuba.

The housing order had left a thirst for something more meaningful. Joe Rauh, Jr., promptly told Kennedy that it was an "historic step on the road to equality" even though its coverage was inadequate. For all the "deep gratitude and admiration" the civil rights movement now felt toward Kennedy, symbols were no longer enough. There could be no legislation for desegregating schools, equal job opportunity, doing away with literacy tests for voters who should be able to qualify automatically, or ending discrimination in public accommodations unless the Senate changed Rule XXII. Unless that were modified to lower the voting requirement for ending filibusters from two thirds to three fifths, such reforms would never have a chance.[68]

But Kennedy would not budge. Liberals pleaded with him to join the fight in the Senate. They tried to move him by convincing Lyndon Johnson, but the vice-president preferred to remain out of that battle.[69] Kennedy had gone about as far as he was then inclined. He was not about to mess himself up with the Congress. Much of his key legislative requests remained bottled up on the Hill. If symbols were important, symbols would have to suffice.

So he did those things that demonstrated toothless advocacy. He went to Howard University and attended a luncheon of a black women's sorority and talked in platitudinous terms about all children being able to develop their talents.[70] Two days later his State of the Union Message confined civil rights to one brief paragraph about the right to vote, at the same time noting that 1963 was the centennial of the Emancipation Proclamation. He followed that up by holding a large Lincoln's Birthday reception in the White House on the evening of February 12 after a meeting with the Civil Rights Commission. Before going to the pool the President spent about a half hour mingling with the largest gathering of blacks ever entertained in the White House. Carl Brauer has noted that the occasion "marked the culmination of an important trend established by Kennedy—the granting of full social recognition to blacks by the nation's President."[71]

The Emancipation Proclamation came up again, but this time more publicly, on the last day of February. Departing somewhat from the administration's civil rights strategy, Kennedy sent a special message to

Congress that, while still containing limited provisions, did call for legislation. The voting-rights laws that had been passed earlier should give greater enforcement powers to referees appointed to oversee the registration process. He also held that completion of a sixth-grade education should negate the need for a literacy-test qualification. But instead of asking for an outright ban on segregated educational facilities, he said he would recommend giving technical and financial assistance to facilitate school districts with the desegregation process. Nor did he ask for any legislation in the fields of employment or public accommodations, but, declared "For the first time, the full force of Federal executive authority is being exerted in the battle against racial discrimination."[72]

The message sent, the point was made. Black leaders were to be mollified; along with them, liberal Democrats inside and outside of the Congress, who had been calling for legislation. Potential Republican opponents, especially someone like Rockefeller, would be kept from criticizing the administration for having failed to act.[73] But the administration's follow-up with Congress was delayed and halfhearted. Meanwhile eight senators introduced their own bills. Most were stronger than Kennedy's request, but Democratic liberals waited for presidential leadership to set the pace.[74]

Then came April and the start of Dr. King's campaign to desegregate Birmingham. Events soon forced the President to stop equivocating. King, wanting to regain prestige lost after failure at Albany and to maintain his credibility in the face of increasing competition from other black leaders, had also decided that the time had come to force Kennedy's hand. And he aimed at Birmingham, the largest segregated city in the country. It had given up its International League baseball team rather than permit it to play against integrated clubs. Within the city blacks were still relegated to a traditional Jim Crow role that was almost entirely unaffected by the federal laws and court decisions of the preceding thirteen years. It was the perfect spot for King to choose, and in running head-on against Bull Connor, the police chief, he could have asked for no better luck. Connor's police provoked rather than controlled. Random arrests were made at even the appearance of a black person carrying a sign. Mass arrests and resistance became the characteristic approach of the law-enforcement agency. On and on it went, through the jailing of hundreds, including King. On the third of May, a Friday, the brutality went beyond mere mass arrests. Connor's police charged into a crowd that had found refuge in a park opposite a Baptist church. They flailed out with nightsticks, police dogs, and high-pressure fire hoses. The President watched it all on television, as did the rest of the country. The next morning Kennedy received a twenty-member ADA delegation. He told them that what he had seen made him sick; he wished he could do something, but what? The police had broken no federal laws, because there was no such protective legislation to break.[75]

What happened next in some ways illustrated the *ad hoc* style of the Kennedy operation. Something had to be done. Bobby sent Burke Marshall to Birmingham. What Marshall found was hardly encouraging. Not only would the white leaders not talk to King, Marshall reported back, but "They wouldn't talk to anybody that *would* talk to him."[76] And after all those weeks of demonstrations King had no clear idea of his own objectives. What would he settle for? What would satisfy his followers? He had provoked and agitated Connor, but not until pushed by Marshall did he hold a meeting to clarify the movement's goals. "Well," said Marshall, "they came up with some demands, requests. They came up with a program at least; it was directed at the large downtown stores, principally on the fact that the lunch counters were closed to Negroes and that there were no Negroes employed in other than janitorial capacities." Since segregated lunch counters turned out to be the principal grievance, and there was no legal remedy, that made things even more sensitive. And something had to be done, given the emotional pitch; that emotion was aimed at President Kennedy. Why wasn't he doing something? The best recourse, the one with the most emphatic power to resolve the issue, was to appeal to the collective strength of the businessmen who operated the department stores that had lunch counters. Marshall was amazed at how much the ordinary people of Birmingham looked to the financial leaders for guidance about such matters. "And they all talked about power structure, or the big mules," he remarked, "or some phrases like that about very powerful businessmen in a very remarkable way—remarkable how much these people didn't have a mind of their own."[77]

On their own, however, the businessmen were most vulnerable. Or they feared their vulnerability, which was just as bad. The risk of provoking social and economic reprisals was just too great. White Birmingham businessmen who had participated with the Senior Citizens Committee (a power structure designation, which had nothing to do with the elderly), to explore ways of achieving an amicable solution, were publicly labeled "weak-kneed quislings." One store that was suspected of being owned by a member of the committee had its window smashed. The KKK held a Saturday night rally and called for the turning in of credit cards from stores whose officials participated.

The committee itself spoke for the major employers of the area and, in some cases, for the local outlets of chain stores. They included top executives of U.S. Steel's Tennessee Coal and Iron Division, the largest employer in the area; the Alabama Power Company; the First National Bank of Birmingham; Vulcan Materials Company; Woodward Iron Company; as well as the telephone company. They were the ones most directly affected by the business slump associated with the disorders. Department-store sales had dropped ten percent during the four weeks before May 4, and some of the smaller establishments were hurt even harder. Since the Freedom Rides had begun, investments in Birmingham's new plants and expansion had dropped by half.[78]

While Burke Marshall shuttled back and forth between meetings with the white leaders, businessmen, and blacks, the Kennedy administration made a concerted effort to telephone members of the Senior Citizens Committee. The President himself probably made several calls, as did each member of the Cabinet. "It obviously had an effect on these men personally," said Marshall, who was at the scene. Appropriately enough, the decisive meeting was held at the Chamber of Commerce. "There were fire engines going by all the time, outside, sirens screaming; reports would come in from the police chief and the sheriff that they didn't think they could handle the situation for more than a few more hours. It was very tense."[79]

The resolution was an accommodation with the blacks that affected most lunch-counter space and black employment. The fear of reprisals, however, remained great. For self-protection the committee issued a statement that explained that a "minority" had disagreed with the decision.[80] After that the provocations continued; there was little semblance of peace in Birmingham. Dr. King's brother's home was bombed, as was the motel used by the civil rights leaders. Kennedy went on television to deplore the continuing violence. He also announced that Marshall and Joseph Dolan were about to return to the city, and that Defense Secretary McNamara had been instructed to alert units of the armed forces trained in riot control to be ready at bases in the Birmingham area. Preliminary steps had also been taken for federalizing the National Guard.[81]

Nevertheless the Birmingham settlement, enforced by the "power structure," held. But then another unwitting ally of Dr. King, the new governor, George Wallace, did his part to provoke a federal response. Wallace had come into office pledging resistance to desegregation. If he also wanted a showdown, he was about to get it when a federal district court ruled in behalf of admitting black students to the University of Alabama at Tuscaloosa. For the Kennedys that suggested a replay of Ole

Miss, and they were not about to let that happen. Bobby went down to Montgomery with Marshall and Ed Guthman to talk to the governor in person.

They found Wallace playing his version of Ross Barnett's game. The Alabama governor was more interested in tape-recording their office conversation so he could play back his defiant words for his own political value. He was also obvious about hoping for his chance to confront federal troops.[82] The delegation from Justice left perplexed about what the governor would actually do.

Once again the Kennedy administration turned to business leaders. Those with useful contacts helped to compile an "Alabama Notebook," which had lists of key companies and officials. The commercial leaders in turn requested Wallace's commitment for a peaceful resolution, and he made so many promises along those lines that the Kennedys were finally confident he would do better than Barnett.[83]

However Wallace had his show. He stood at a lectern in bright sunlight, his feet carefully placed within white semicircles that were painted on the ground so the cameras could show him in the most flattering pose for that time of day. Before Wallace stood Nick Katzenbach with the court order for the students' admission. Each man had his say, their statements entirely predictable: Federal orders would be enforced, and Wallace was unyielding. Then they parted, and each went his own way. From Washington the President federalized the National Guard, and, in Tuscaloosa, Katzenbach escorted the students to the dormitories.[84]

Only a few hours later the President spoke to the nation. No other Chief Executive had ever talked that way about human rights in America. It was also the most eloquent speech and close to being the most spontaneous. His prepared remarks were not completely typed until just a few minutes before he went on the air. "And the President, it didn't faze him a bit," recalled Burke Marshall. Bobby remembered that the whole thing "took place over a period of forty-five or fifty minutes. The President and I sat, and he made notes because he was going to do it extemporaneously. He wrote down all those notes; and just as he was leaving the room, Ted Sorensen came in with the draft. That's why he did the end part extemporaneously."[85]

There was, however, nothing extemporaneous about the decision to speak to the nation and announce the submission, finally, of an omnibus civil rights bill. The argument had reached the point where reservations about the legislative consequences for the rest of Kennedy's program had become moot. The only details that were needed involved the resolution of the Alabama affair; aside from that he knew what he had to say. "The decision to ask for legislation," Sorensen has said, ". . . was a very, very important decision for him, of course. He knew that it would tie up the Congress for the rest of the year, at least; he knew that it would make some other legislation impossible; . . . and he knew how much was riding on it for him, politically and historically. He knew all of that."[86]

Bobby had heard much of the frustration firsthand in the Kennedy New York City apartment at 24 Central Park South on May 24. A three-hour meeting with black artists and writers brought together by James Baldwin confronted him with their impatience at explanations of legal limitations. Baldwin, who had written a prophetic New Yorker article that was later published in book form as The Fire Next Time, was especially vehement, even suggesting that the President of the United States personally escort the two students into the University of Alabama. The attorney general's explanations about the legal system, about presidential prerogatives and limitations, carried little weight. He and they were talking about two different things. He, as the nation's highest law-enforcement officer, was trying to explain how "the system" had to respond to the crisis: litigation, legislation, enforcement of existing laws through the FBI. They, emotional, exasperated by explanations of why things could not be done despite the obvious need, were impatient with further rationalizations that impeded immediate results. "The meeting shattered them all," wrote Schlesinger, in the best account of the event.[87]

At that point the problem had the active concern of Lyndon Johnson. Outwardly his relations with the President were cordial; Jack Kennedy was even deferential, careful to heed all formalities and courtesies due to Lyndon. The Kennedy–Johnson sniping had been carefully kept below the surface, largely confined to the staff level, and of course to the tensions that existed between the vice-president and the attorney general. Jack Kennedy's awareness of how hard it would be to contain Johnson's energies had been an additional consideration in giving him some important and desired assignments.

But beneath the surface the stress was there, as it would be with two such men brought together by a shotgun marriage.

Johnson had requested not to be consulted about the Ole Miss affair, but now, with the President directing the preparation of civil rights legislation and contemplating how to present it to the nation, he was beginning to churn up. The program was being prepared. He had read about it in the papers, but, as he said to Ted Sorensen when he got on the phone to have his say on Monday, June 3, "I've never seen it. Hell, if the vice-president doesn't know what's in it, how do you expect others to know what's in it?"[88]

Johnson had been wound up, and now he was unwinding, finally saying what was on his mind, getting through to the President via Sorensen. Homework, he said, had not been done on the legislation, public opinion, congressional leaders, or the bill itself. The approach was all wrong. Three or four months of debate would be touched off and only result in having the President's program killed and "inflam[ing] the country and wind[ing] up with a mouse." Not that legislation should be avoided; the South may be lost anyway. But there were ways of going about it, ways of getting Dirksen to come through with Republican support and move the legislation. "Hell," Johnson argued, "Javits gets Humphrey souped up; they put on a few terrible demonstrations; we get a civil war going on in the South; they move Kennedy in, and they cut off the South from him, and they blow up the bridge. If I were Kennedy, I wouldn't let them call my signals. I'd pass my program, make them stand up and vote for it." How to handle it? Lyndon, the master of the Senate, was now letting it all out as Sorensen listened patiently, saying very little but remaining polite.

"While I was doing that," the vice-president went on, "I'd put the Republicans on the spot, making them buy my program. Or if they want more, just let Dirksen say just how much he wants. And I would try to call in my southern leaders that got Lockheeds around the country and others and say, 'Now, here we've either got to do it in the streets or in the courts, and they are going to do it in the streets. I can't sit idly by, and what do you recommend, Senator?' Let them chew on it a day or two, because this world wasn't made in a day." Let them know they would get their contracts. If they knew that, they would vote for the bill. "That's the loudest language the President can speak," Johnson said. "Do you follow me?"

"I sure do," said Sorensen.

And the country needed the planes. "We have the leadership of the world because we took the air away from Hitler," explained Lyndon. "And we had it ever since we took it away from him. My judgment is we ought to keep the leadership in aviation.

"The only person that's hurt by this is the President and the Democratic Party. If he does this now, he's played right into the Republicans' hands. They've done exactly what they wanted to do. I told the President at that time that Rockefeller was going to out-Negro our administration, just like he out-Negroed Averell Harriman. He's going to lay it on to us, and they are going to try to make them take a position in between the Negro and the South. But we ought to do it our way instead of their way. We got a little pop gun and I want to pull out the cannon. The President is the cannon. What the Negroes want to know is [that] the President's own heart is on their side. I believe that they believe that he is. They believe the attorney general is. They believe I am. I think they believe me. But I just want to convince them to be sure they believe it. And then I would get some support."

What the blacks really needed was the moral commitment. That would do a lot more than any bill. Their goals were not really going to be achieved by legislation, said Johnson; maybe they'd be helped by "a little thing here, an impact area or vote or something. I think the Negro leaders are aware of that. What Negroes are really seeking is moral force, and [to] be sure that we are on their side, and make them all act like Americans." And making a speech from Washington would not be the way to do it. One thing blacks and whites in the South had in common was doubt that the government was really on the side of the Negroes. "The whites think we're just playing politics to carry New York. The Negroes feel, and they are suspicious, that we are just doing what we've got to do. Until that is laid to rest, I don't think you are going to have much of a solution." The President shouldn't make that speech from Washington. If he made a commitment in Jackson, Mississippi, "it would be worth a hell of a lot more than it would in Harlem."

Here's how it should be done, Johnson told Sorensen. He knew because he'd been doing it himself. "I've been into North Carolina this year at Jefferson. I've been into Florida. Neither place would allow Negroes to come. I said I'm going to come and I'm going to talk about their constitutional rights, and I want them on the platform with me, and if you don't let them come, I'm not coming, period. By God they put them in both places, right on the platform and right eating with us. The first time George Smathers ever had dinner with them in St. Augustine, but we had them." The President could do the same, in North Carolina or someplace. He, too, should be there and have the local leaders on the platform while saying those things. He should go to Texas and have Governor John Connally with him, and go to San Antonio and be introduced by Henry Gonzalez. San Antonio would be a perfect place. Johnson had taken UN observers down there, and they were amazed to find that in America it was possible to see fifty high school bands with Negroes, Mexicans, and whites all marching down the same street. "They saw fifty thousand people, like a football stadium, and they just saw black, brown, white, and everything in San Antonio. I think television ought to see that. I think that that's the place for him to make a Gettysburg speech." Without all this, without demonstrating the moral support, without giving out the contracts and jobs they wanted, nothing would be accomplished. "You ought to get your tax bill passed, instead of killed," Lyndon warned. "This Kennedy program oughtn't go down the drain. I'm afraid that that's what will happen if you send this up here."[89]

When Kennedy spoke on the eleventh, he faced the cameras from his desk in the Oval Office. A strong moral commitment dominated the message. The nation, he said, faced a "moral crisis as a country and a people." This cannot be the land of the free "except for the Negroes." "The heart of the question is whether all Americans are to be afforded equal rights and equal opportunities, whether we are going to treat our fellow Americans as we want to be treated." And then, in an especially moving passage, he said, "We cannot say to 10 percent of the population that you can't have that right; that your children can't have the chance to develop whatever talents they have; that the only way that they are going to get their rights is to go into the streets and demonstrate. I think we owe them and we owe ourselves a better country than that."[90]

His substantive achievement, however, was the announcement that he would be sending the Congress an omnibus civil rights bill. Novel to such measures that had already been introduced by Republicans and Democrats was a request for protection of individual rights to have access to public facilities. In February he had talked about public accommodations; but now he was taking the important step of actually proposing federal legislation for the right of all Americans to be "served in facilities which are open to the public—hotels, restaurants, theaters, retail stores, and similar establishments." And that was not all: The federal government would participate more fully in lawsuits to end segregation in public education, and there would be more protection for voting rights. The outstanding omission, however, was any request for banning discrimination in employment, the long-sought-after Federal Employment Practices Commission. But others had already included that protection in previously introduced bills, and the President now endorsed that concept when he submitted his own legislation on June 19. Altogether, his commitment was irreversible. He was now more interested in sending up legislation that could be enacted than in political ploys.[91]

Later that same night, Medgar Evers, the NAACP field secretary in Mississippi, was killed by a sniper outside his home. Three months later four little black girls died in Birmingham when their church was bombed on a Sunday morning. Dozens of others attending their Bible class were also injured.[92] The Kennedy brothers were now anxious to get on top of that situation, to prevent a new orgy of conflict. They thought of rushing Douglas MacArthur to the scene, but the general was eighty-three and of dubious value at that point, so they turned to a former West Point football coach, one who had made his name with the Academy's great teams, Earl Blaik. Along with Blaik, they added ex–Secretary of War Kenneth Royall, a well-connected southerner. The two men went to Birmingham, talked to the contending groups, and finally succeeded in setting up a fifteen-member biracial committee to preserve law and order.[93]

He had also seen in Birmingham, Blaik later told the President, a bumper-sticker with the double entendre of "Kennedy for King—Goldwater for President."[94]

Kennedy's apprehensions about the political consequences were beginning to be borne out. With the momentum building up in the South, Gallup polls began to reflect the decline. The first survey taken after the speech showed thirty-six percent believing he was pushing integration too fast; eighteen percent not fast enough; and thirty-two percent "about right." One month later forty-one percent said "too fast."[95] His popularity in April, never having fully recovered from the stock market slump and the steel price controversy, had been sixty-six percent; now it continued downward: August, sixty-one percent; September, fifty-three percent.[96] Another Gallup report released on August 18 justified his rising concern about George Romney, the automobile executive who had recently become Michigan's governor. Southern voters were preferring Goldwater over Kennedy by fifty-four to thirty-eight, but it was even more important that Romney also had a lead over Kennedy in the South. Romney's margin was less than Goldwater's, by seven percent, but unlike the senator from Arizona Romney's support had a wider geographical distribution.[97]

Having risked his popularity, having weakened his legislative prospects, Kennedy worked all the harder to at least secure his civil rights bill. He overcame his qualms about cajoling legislators and lobbied vigorously. He got together with leaders from various sectors of the society. During one three-week period he met with some sixteen or seventeen hundred businessmen, lawyers, church groups, women's groups, labor leaders, educators, and most of the governors. He met with the Business Council, too. Lyndon Johnson, overcoming his own hesitations about the ability to get it through, pitched in and was especially effective in persuading groups of lawyers.[98] Civil rights leaders and liberal lobbyists also did their part.

The President had touched the most sensitive vein in American society. As an aide advised Hubert Humphrey, the Democratic Senate whip, "Republicans are flirting with the possibility of being cool or even hostile to the civil rights program in the belief that they have already lost the black vote and have a chance of taking the Southern vote. There is also a suggestion of hostility toward the civil rights program among suburbanites who fear an encroachment on their housing."[99] Just before Kennedy delivered his televised speech, he notified Dwight Eisenhower in order to explain what he was about to do and requested his support. The former president said he favored voting rights, but told Kennedy that a "whole bunch of laws" would not solve the problem.[100] On June 22, one day before leaving for a ten-day European trip, the immediate objective was the organizing of a massive lobbying effort behind the bill as he received twenty-nine black leaders in the White House. He heard some complaints from them about the absence from the bill of a fair employment provision. Johnson was there, and he suggested that they should go ahead and try to drum up some real support.[101] Kennedy, however, offered a word of caution: Continued demonstrations could offend representatives from small states, and their votes were essential.[102] That placed the President on the defensive, for he thereby appeared hesitant about the practical wisdom of staging a giant civil rights rally in Washington itself.

Kennedy was, in fact, skeptical about the value to his legislation of the "march" being planned for August 28. The polls had shown that the public was not receptive to further demonstrations. Violence could be counterproductive, and his personal participation would be a serious gamble. He would leave himself open to embarrassing criticism from some of the more militant speakers. Any messy development in a throng of a quarter of a million would immediately become the fault of his presidency. He had endorsed their right to gather, lauded their objective of trying to arouse the nation to the legislative need, and was making every effort to corral all possible supporters, but he could do no more.[103]

"How can our country endure when we legislate on the basis of threat and intimidations from mobs?" was Richard Russell's rhetorical question to former Senator William Knowland. "The President's action implicitly approving these demonstrations and those that are threatened against the national Congress is the most startling position of a Chief Executive of this nation of which I have any knowledge."[104] Others virtually panicked at the thought of hordes of blacks running amok in the nation's capital. There might be "two or three hundred thousand Negroes, in violation of the law, swarm[ing] over the Capitol grounds and into all Committee rooms, offices, etc. If Kennedy permits that to happen," worried Senator A. Willis Robertson of Virginia, "my guess is that the people in the North and other sections who don't endorse priority in jobs and everything else for the non-whites will not endorse Kennedy for reelection in November 1964."[105] Oil magnate H. L. Hunt of Texas was particularly upset. He wrote to Robertson and others about the "Kennedy threat."

Hunt's letter to Harry Byrd was especially impassioned, the agitation of a man who feared the specter of his country being overwhelmed by revolutionaries. These were, he wrote, "unusual times" and the question was nothing more or less than "saving our freedom." Physicist Edward Teller had told him that "there is no chance to get the Kennedy's [sic] out unless they are defeated in 1964." And to beat them the Republicans must produce a candidate "as strong or stronger than Goldwater." That could only be done by moving some of the southern electoral votes into the Democratic column. That prospect "would add great strength to the Republican ticket in certain Northern states which Republicans might not otherwise carry. If this situation develops, the Republicans would not have to carry nearly as many southern states as would otherwise be required for Kennedy to be defeated." A "few Southern statesmen" would have to announce they were switching parties to get the movement going.[106]

Meanwhile, within the New Frontier itself, there was increasing anxiety that any Republican but Rockefeller might be able to win the South in 1964.[107] In Austin, Texas, on July 19, Governor John Connally went on statewide television to respond to the Kennedy civil rights program and denounced the administration for not permitting the states to make their own progress.[108]

One month later the largest of all demonstrations formed before the Lincoln Memorial. Masses of people covered all the land around the reflecting pool. The crowd, more white than black, heard singer Joan Baez, who sang "We Shall Overcome," and then teamed up with Peter, Paul and Mary in a stirring rendition of Bob Dylan's "Blowin' in the Wind." Dylan himself sang about the death of Medgar Evers. And they heard Odetta and spirituals from Mahalia Jackson. Then, of course, there were the speeches. John Lewis, a young black activist, remained militant even after his speech had been toned down. The high point came when Dr. King said, "I have a dream that one day . . . When we let freedom ring, when we let it ring from every village and every hamlet, from every state and every city, we will be able to speed up that day when all God's children, black men and white men, Jews and Gentiles, Protestants and Catholics, will be able to join in the words of that old Negro spiritual 'Free at last! Free at last! Thank God almighty, we are free at last!' "[109]

Before lunch that day the President presided over a full-scale meeting on Vietnam, which had caused considerable dissension among his own chiefs. Then he left for the mansion at 1:40 and did not return to his office until 4:25. One aide, who specialized in intergroup relations in the capital, said the TV set was on in the Oval Office, but had no idea of whether the President was actually there and watching. Still, that gap of almost three hours in the appointment calendar coincided almost perfectly with the speechmaking schedule around the reflecting pool.[110] When it was all over, and the affair had concluded smoothly, the President received the organizers and was photographed with them at the White House.

The civil rights bill still had many obstacles to overcome. Several committees were involved, the Commerce Committee for the interstate aspects of the public accommodations title, and, of course, the Judiciary Committee of each chamber. Manny Celler should certainly be no trouble, but Jim Eastland was another matter, and that posed the problem of cloture even if it could be brought to the floor. Key Republicans, Ev Dirksen, Charlie Halleck, would obviously have to be brought around. But, as the President had feared, a deep-freeze had restricted the flow of other legislation. The presidency and the Congress were in a virtual deadlock. When a vote came up for a new authorization for the Area Redevelopment Act, the House, acting on the day after Kennedy's June 11 speech, defeated the bill by five votes. Its enactment in 1961 had been by a comfortable 251–167. An analysis of the two votes showed that the main differences came from switches by twenty Republicans and nineteen Democrats. The most significant indicator, however, was that all but one of those who reversed themselves were from border or southern states, and their ranks included major beneficiaries of ARA allocations.[111] A Congressional Quarterly survey published in late July showed that not only were routine appropriation bills being held up, but that thirty-eight percent of the administration's proposals had not even been taken up by either house.[112]

And so it went. Equal-rights legislation had created a great fog over Capitol Hill. The Kennedy presidency had become controversial, and there was no way of returning to the politics of conciliation with die-hard segregationists and conservatives. An administration that had temporized, weighed the arithmetic of Capitol Hill and the mood of society, had in effect been driven to take a firm ideological stand. If Kennedy could win in 1964, he would have to be lucky enough to have Goldwater rather than Romney, and the President was so aware of that that he lost no opportunity to mention Barry's name as being in the lead. Romney's respectable acceptance below the Mason–Dixon line and favorable standing through most of the country had begun to make him appear as a potentially stronger national candidate than Nelson Rockefeller, who was also beginning to pay the political price for his divorce and quick remarriage. As to Romney, Jack Kennedy said to his friend Red Fay, "You have to be a little suspicious of somebody as good as Romney. No vices whatsoever, no smoking and no drinking. Imagine someone we know going off for twenty-four or forty-eight hours to fast and meditate, awaiting a message from the Lord whether to run or not to run. Does that sound like one of the old gang?"[113]

12

"The Cuban Missile Crisis"

There was hardly anyone unaffected by the Cuban missile crisis. Kennedy impressed more than a handful of those who saw him up close during those days with his self-control, his ability to converse without betraying the slightest bit of anxiety. On the afternoon of Monday, October 22, just before he went on television to announce the quarantine of Cuba, he received the prime minister of Uganda, Milton Obote. The President kept his usual charm, behaved courteously, patiently engaged in a forty-minute conversation, and then walked his visitor out to the West Wing. That evening when he turned on his television set, Obote was astonished. Nothing about his own visit had hinted what was really on the President's mind, and it was an experience he never forgot.[1]

Obote would have found it similarly hard to understand that he was dealing with the same man who, that weekend, had suggested to Mrs. Kennedy that she and the children ought to consider staying close to the underground shelter that was available in case the First Lady had to be evacuated. "No other decision in his lifetime would equal this," Sorensen has written.[2] At least a dozen times during the crisis the President lost his famous "cool."[3] In much of America people either braced themselves for disaster, while others rushed to remote fallout shelters or went on mindless shopping expeditions to stock up for an unknowable future. What do you do when the holocaust is just around the corner? After the speech Columbia University Professor Richard Neustadt wrote to Sorensen about how his own students had received the telecast. "This time," explained Neustadt, "these kids were literally scared for their lives and were astonished, somehow, that their lives could be risked by an *American* initiative. In short, what they have heard and said *ad infinitum* about hazards in our era suddenly came *home* to them; for the first time, apparently, awareness of the real world got transferred from their heads to their guts."[4]

If individual responses tended toward the irrational, retrospective views of what it was all about suggest that leaders were not much more secure. On the day the President announced his quarantine—as he preferred to call the blockade—his friend, British Ambassador David Ormsby-Gore, sent a secret telegram to London saying he could "not believe that the missiles so far landed contributed any significant military threat to the United States."[5] Openly at the White House, Ormsby-Gore showed his doubts by prodding for release of the evidence.[6] Schlesinger's early account explains that the photographic findings detected "Ilyshin-28 jet aircraft able to deliver nuclear bombs," and from then on the word *nuclear* was used as though such warheads were in fact installed.[7] Nevertheless there never was any evidence of the delivery of nuclear warheads. There were intermediate- and medium-range ballistic missiles as well as the Il-28s and Russian personnel, and American intelligence showed without doubt that the Soviets were sufficiently prudent to keep Cubans far from the weaponry. Marine Corps General David Shoup made the point that there was nothing new and alarming about the situation. We had been living under the threat of ICBMs for some time.[8] Sorensen himself has said that "the United States was already living under the shadow of Soviet missiles which could be launched from Soviet territory or submarines, and, therefore, there was no real change in our situation which required any kind of drastic action," and that appraisal was shared by the President and his defense secretary. On the first day of the deliberations of what later became known as the Executive Committee of the NSC (ExCom), McNamara sounded very much the same way. "A missile is a missile," he has been quoted as having said. "It makes no difference whether you are killed by a missile fired from the Soviet Union or from Cuba."[9] Dean Acheson disagreed with such analyses. He feared the great accuracy possible from "short-range missiles located about ninety miles from our coast" as opposed to "long-range ones located about five thousand miles from our coast." When sent to brief De Gaulle, the French president asked a question for which Acheson was unprepared. "Suppose," said De Gaulle, "they don't do anything—suppose they don't try to break the blockade—suppose they don't take the missiles out—what will your President do then?"[10] And suppose the Russians responded in other ways that seemed entirely logical: They retaliated for the quarantine by a blockade of West Berlin, or struck at the American Jupiter missile sites in Turkey? We couldn't give up the Jupiters under threat. But, Kennedy had to contemplate, was it rational to flirt with nuclear war just to preserve antiquated Jupiters that he had already thought ought to be removed? Why in the world did Khrushchev himself take the gamble of placing readily identifiable military hardware within such easy range of American surveillance?

One theory, advanced by the Turkish ambassador to the United States, was that Khrushchev was inadequately informed about American politics. He did not know the difference between a congressional election and a presidential election year in the manner of domestic responses and thought the government would be in the same disarray in the former as in the latter. Therefore he could begin the placement of the weapons, have the sites constructed, ready the storage bins for future delivery of nuclear warheads, and no alarm would be raised until after the November elections. By then the Americans would be unable to act without leaving themselves open to retaliation.[11]

But there was also the possibility that Moscow's move may have been aimed at trying to force a quid pro quo that would get the Americans to remove their missiles from Turkey. Perhaps it was still another test of Washington's capacity to react decisively and fulfill her global pledges. Graham Allison, in a sophisticated study of decision-making, suggested that the administration's announcement that the much-publicized "missile gap" was nonexistent had actually encouraged Kremlin efforts to overcome American strategic capabilities by installing the missiles.[12] Writing before the world learned about the post–Bay of Pigs efforts to bring down Castro, Allison dismissed the hypothesis that they were placed on Cuban soil to defend the country against American attack. "No amount of conventional arms in Cuban hands could defeat a major American attack in Cuba," he pointed out. ". . . by moving offensive strategic missiles into Cuba, in the face of the President's firm warning and the Soviets' solemn promises, the Soviet Union assumed risks manifestly out of proportion to the objective of Cuban defense. . . . Cuban defense might have been a subsidiary effect of the Soviet gamble but not its overriding objective."[13] Another student of the affair, Herbert S. Dinnerstein, thought Khrushchev was trying to have Cuba "perform the same function as a base for his missiles that U.S. bases within bomber range of the Soviet Union had performed for the United States since 1948." Had he succeeded in Cuba, the interests of Soviet nuclear parity would have been advanced "by almost a decade."[14] However neither Robert McNamara nor his deputy, Roswell Gilpatric, saw it that way. They held to the Jupiter missile theory. McNamara, said Gilpatric, regarded it more "as a tactical move by Khrushchev rather than a grand strategy, an operation of grand strategy. And I think he believed that."[15]

The "experts" were not very clear—nor could they be. They would have had to acknowledge the repeated American threats to Cuban security. Accordingly the Russians transported the equipment to the island in major part to satisfy Cuban demands for at least symbolic, if not more substantial, evidence that Moscow was willing to protect their nation from the U.S. Whether or not it was most convenient, Castro was in the Soviet camp. Moscow had its own nuisance clients to support, its own need to demonstrate credibility as a protector. They would give Castro what he wanted, but all the while keep Cuban hands far from the firing mechanisms. At the same time, Russian interests would be served by having nuclear missiles on the island. Castro had initiated the request, but, as he later told Herbert Matthews, Khrushchev's choice of making them nuclear was to serve Russian and not Cuban interests. "We felt that we could not get out of it," the Cuban dictator also told a French correspondent. Accepting them as part of the security package would also certify Cuban solidarity with the Soviet bloc.[16]

Raúl Castro had gone to Moscow in July and expressed Cuba's concern that the United States was going to invade. Frantically he asked for help. Before that month was over, Khrushchev, who had raised the possibility of placing missiles there as early as April, decided to grant the request. The move would have the additional advantage of giving the Soviets some leverage for dealing with the Americans on the unresolved question of Berlin.[17] On September 2 Cuba's minister of industries, Ernesto (Che) Guevara, was in Moscow. In connection with his visit, the Russians justified the arms buildup by saying they were supplying Cuba with "armaments" and "specialists for training Cuban servicemen" in view of certain threats from "aggressive imperialist quarters with regard to Cuba." As long as such threats continue, they then warned, all of "Cuba's true friends have every right to respond to this legitimate request."[18]

None of this had anything to do with increased American vulnerability to Soviet attack, and Kennedy knew it. Nevertheless it did not mean that the administration could tolerate discovering that the Russians had equipped Cuba with missiles that could be construed as "offensive." Michael Mandelbaum, in his study, *The Nuclear Question,* has made the point that "the practical distinction between 'offensive' and 'defensive' armaments is difficult to draw, and the principle of deterrence further blurs the line between the two."[19] As long as Kennedy could argue that Soviet military support was "defensive" in nature, his political position was secure. As Bobby Kennedy later told an interviewer, "they weren't posing any threat, really. I don't see what the problem was—the Russians in Cuba. I mean, I'd rather have the Russians running the SAM [surface-to-air missiles] sites than the Cuban [sic] running them."[20]

On September 6 Sorensen was called to the Russian embassy in Washington and told by Ambassador Anatoly Dobrynin that nothing would be done to aggravate the international situation before the congressional elections.[21] There were other disclaimers from Moscow, both public and in the form of a personal message to Kennedy from Khrushchev that no surface-to-surface missiles would be placed on Cuba.[22] Kennedy's assurances, however, did not rest on such sources alone. On September 19 the United States Intelligence Board, which coordinated all intelligence activities, unanimously approved an estimate that the Soviets were not about to convert Cuba into a strategic base equipped with offensive weapons.[23] Almost one month later, on October 13, Dobrynin, who later claimed that he did not know what was going on, assured Chester Bowles that the Soviet Union was not shipping offensive weapons into Cuba and was fully aware of how risky that would be.[24]

By the time Kennedy heard from Bowles, Soviet duplicity had already been exposed and Kennedy's hand forced. He now had to act. He had many reasons for believing that war would not come unless he overplayed his hand. ". . . Khrushchev had never for a moment considered choosing war," Schlesinger has written in his biography of Robert Kennedy. He has also cited the comment from Khrushchev's memoirs that "It would have been preposterous for us to unleash a war against the United States from Cuba. Cuba was 11,000 kilometers from the Soviet Union. Our sea and air communications were so precarious that an attack against the U.S. was unthinkable."[25] Khrushchev's own explanation, in view of what is now known about Operation MONGOOSE, seems credible: "We stationed our armed forces on Cuban soil for one purpose only: to maintain the independence of the Cuban people and to prevent the invasion by a mercenary expeditionary force which the United States was then preparing to launch."[26] There is, moreover, every reason for believing that Kennedy was reasonably confident that that was the case.

Not until 1965, with the publication of the *Penkovsky Papers,* did the public realize anything about the man who may well have been the most useful spy for America in the Soviet Union. He was undoubtedly among the "number of well-placed and courageous Russians" referred to by CIA Director Richard Helms publicly in 1971 who had helped the U.S. in identifying Soviet weapons in Cuba during the crisis.[27] The CIA's intelligence expert during the missile uproar, Robert Amory, has been even more explicit: "Well, all I can say is he provided us with uniquely valuable stuff that beautifully complemented the material we were getting from photographs. In other words, it gave us the detail and enabled us then to interpret our photographs better, and the photographs gave us the things to ask him as questions that he could put [to] his technical friends. And a combination of a highly placed spy and this capacity to look down on the whole Soviet Union put us in the securest possible position and had an awful lot to do with the 1962 missile crisis."[28]*

Even if he had been one hundred percent certain that the Russians were not about to go to war and that the missiles represented no more threat to American security than the Jupiters in Turkey did to the Russians, Kennedy had to act—and act publicly. His only option was to move prudently, to maneuver between his own military—who as usual would come down on the side of force—and the delicacies involved in getting Khrushchev to respond acceptably. Following the introduction of Soviet personnel and equipment that summer Kennedy's own Republican opposition had gone all-out to make Russian support for Castro a campaign issue for the congressional elections. Not only had the GOP campaign committee announced that Cuba would be "the dominant issue of the 1962 campaign," but several individuals had gone public with inflammatory statements. Homer Capehart, up for reelection to the Senate from Indiana against challenger Birch Bayh, had produced banner headlines by calling for an immediate American invasion.[29] Another Republican, Senator Kenneth Keating of New York, who was not up for reelection that year, started as early as August 31 to make public charges about the vulnerability of Cuba to becoming a Soviet base. By his own count Keating went on to make at least twenty-five statements on the subject. Gradually he became more specific. On October 10 he took the Senate floor to report that "construction has begun on at least a half-dozen launching sites for intermediate range tactical missiles," with the "power to hurl rockets into the American heartland and as far as the Panama Canal Zone."[30] Only a week before Keating's evidently informed

---

*During the height of the crisis, Penkovsky was arrested in the Soviet Union and later executed.

remarks, the Congress had passed a joint resolution that expressed American determination "by whatever means may be necessary, including the use of arms, . . . to prevent in Cuba the creation or use of an externally supported military capability endangering the security of the United States." The resolution had been initiated by Senator Dirksen and, in the House, Charles Halleck, as members of "the joint Senate-House Republican leadership." Modeled on the Formosa Resolution of 1955, it was passed overwhelmingly by the Democratic-controlled Congress.[31]

Kennedy, meanwhile, had worked hard in September to support Democratic candidates by both denying the presence of "offensive" weapons and promising that in any case their installation would not be permitted. In a press conference on the thirteenth he denied that the weapons being received by Cuba were potentially hostile. He also vowed that "If Cuba should possess a capacity to carry out offensive actions against the United States, that the United States would act. I've also indicated that the United States would not permit Cuba to export its power by force in the hemisphere."[32]

A significant source was Kennedy's own CIA director, John McCone. Since August 10 McCone had feared that incoming reports were showing the installation of offensive MRBMs designed for Cuba by the Russians, but his own subordinates felt it lacked documentary credibility.[33] McCone himself later said that the "majority opinion in the intelligence community, as well as State and Defense, was that this would be so out of character with the Soviets that they would not do so. They had never placed an offensive missile outside the Soviet's own territory." Almost everybody, then, assumed the buildup was defensive. "I was not persuaded about that," McCone said, "because Cuba, being an island, such defensive mechanism could be destroyed momentarily by low-flying airplanes that could come in under radar, and with a very few well-directed rockets could destroy the very intricate radar control mechanism of a surface-to-air missile site."[34]

McCone took his suspicions to the President. They met on August 22, with McNamara and Rusk also present. McCone's zealous anticommunism had weakened his own credibility, and he had little documentary evidence. His warnings were, ironically, viewed as self-serving as those of the anti-Castro Cubans.[35] Such persistence in trying to alert Kennedy has actually led to the suspicion (probably unfairly) that McCone had fed information to Keating (who never did reveal his sources), thereby hoping to force attention.[36] Meanwhile the Defense Department made its own efforts to extract information from the New Yorker, but with no success. Ros Gilpatric concluded that he must have been getting his material from some Florida newspapermen.

Special daily intelligence reports on Cuba began five days after McCone's meeting with the President. Dean Rusk also tried to get the other members of NATO to join with the U.S. in "certain measures designed to bring certain pressures upon the Castro regime."[37] On August 31 Kennedy was told of "hard" intelligence reports about the installations of SAMs, the introduction of substantial numbers of Soviet personnel, and missile-equipped torpedo boats, but there was no evidence of offensive ballistic missiles. The President then gave his assurances and promises to act if necessary. In mid-September, Rusk made a personal appeal to the NATO council, hoping to at least prevent the members from permitting their ships to carry goods to Cuba. But the reaction was disappointing, even in the face of American threats to close U.S. ports to "all ships of any country that is carrying arms to Cuba."[38]

By Monday evening, October 15, developments in Cuba had been clarified. Photographs taken during a U-2 reconnaissance flight over western Cuba by Major Rudolph Anderson showed a launching site for Soviet MRBMs being built in an area fifty miles southwest of Havana, at San Cristóbal. Other pictures showed additional sites for intermediate-range missiles at Guanajay and Remedios. Their range was twice that of the MRBMs, about two thousand miles. Missile erectors were in position, as were shelter tents for fifty-foot-long ICBMs. Clearly visible at Guanajay was a storage site to receive nuclear warheads, but there was no evidence that the equipment itself had arrived.[39] Then began the critical thirteen days.

The President saw the pictures for the first time at about nine that Tuesday morning. He was still in his dressing gown going through the morning newspapers and having his coffee when Mac Bundy walked in with the evidence. Bundy assured Kennedy that it was conclusive: the images shown by the amazingly detailed high-altitude photographs were clear about what the Russians were doing. One way or another they would have to go, the President said, and directed Bundy to institute low-level photographic flights. He called Ken O'Donnell into his office, showed him the U-2 pictures, and said, "We've just elected Capehart in Indiana, and Ken Keating will probably be the next President of the United States."[40] When Bobby saw the evidence, he said, "Can they hit Oxford, Mississippi?"[41] They had been "taken." All the Russian assurances were worthless. Kennedy asked Bundy to round up every top responsible official for a meeting later that morning.

It began as an ad hoc group in response to a specific emergency.

Present were those in key positions from the military, intelligence, public information, State, and Defense. The President opened the sessions acting as the chairman. From time to time Robert Lovett and Dean Acheson came in as consultants. Whenever he could get away from New York without arousing too much suspicion by leaving his UN post, Stevenson joined them. In usual attendance were the vice-president, Bob Kennedy, McNamara, General Taylor, Bundy, McCone, Gilpatric, Ed Martin, U. Alexis Johnson, Douglas Dillon, Sorensen, George Ball, Llewellyn Thompson, Dean Rusk, Paul Nitze, O'Donnell, and Don Wilson, the deputy director of the United States Information Agency. They constituted what was later formally designated as the Executive Committee of the NSC.

McCone provided the group with running accounts of the CIA's latest surveillance reports and photos. One of the great problems in watching the pictures was knowing whether the nuclear warheads had arrived. "In other words," Ed Martin has said, "if they had the missiles in place and the heads were there then you had certain risks of retaliation, perhaps even unauthorized from the Soviet Union, that did not exist if the heads were not there or if the missiles weren't in a position to fire."[42] At least they had the luxury of a few days' leeway before there was real danger, but exactly how many was uncertain. Suddenly Jack Kennedy knew that it was less important to be tough than to be prudent.

At that first meeting the President had little of his famed coolness. He appeared "very clipped, very tense," Gilpatric has noted. "I don't recall a time when I saw him more preoccupied and less given to any light touch at all. The atmosphere was unrelieved by any of the usual asides and changes of pace that he was capable of. He seemed to believe that the Soviets meant business in the most real sense, and this was the biggest international crisis he'd faced."[43]

The sessions went on for two weeks. Most were held in George Ball's conference room at the State Department. Ball's office served as their administrative headquarters. "We ate up there as well as in the Conference Room," Martin recalled, "for three nights running on beef sandwiches and a glass of milk sent in from a nearby restaurant."[44] It was hard to tell when one meeting ended and the next began; they just flowed into each other, often depending on when officials could leave their regular duties inconspicuously. Wives were supposed to be kept from knowing about what their husbands were doing through some of those late-night sessions, but some were surely informed, undoubtedly to relieve domestic strains. The President himself told Jackie. After the first few meetings he yielded the chair to Bobby—he had to fulfill previous speaking commitments, again so suspicions would not be aroused. Moreover he soon learned that his absence encouraged greater spontaneity among those in attendance, avoiding some of the "group-think" atmosphere that had characterized the Bay of Pigs discussions.

At about five that first afternoon the President gave an off-the-record talk to some eight hundred editors in the State Department auditorium. When a question turned to Cuba, he was noticeably hesitant about saying much. He simply commented that the matter was not on as direct a collision course as Berlin, where the positions were irreconcilable. But he did drop a clue that became obvious only later. It was in the form of a Robert Graves translation of a poem by a bullfighter, Domingo Ortega:

> Bullfight critics ranked in rows
> Crowd the enormous Plaza full;
> But only one is there who knows—
> And he's the man who fights the bull.[45]

The question, of course, was how to fight the bull. From the outset the President had several considerations governing the circumstances under which the weapons were to be removed. The ExCom had to give him a clear consensus. He wanted no resentment about failure having been caused by the rejection of specific suggestions. After the Bay of Pigs and the cancellation of the air strikes, and after the limited response to Laos, he was conscious of a disgruntled military. He repeatedly asked them tough questions, testing how well they understood the implications that were involved.[46] That Tuesday he had received a "top secret report for the President only" from the U.S. Intelligence Board Watch Committee that told him of their conclusion that "no Sino-Soviet Bloc country intends to initiate direct military action in the immediate future."[47] But he had been deceived before, both by his own intelligence sources and by Soviet assurances. Late Thursday evening the President told them, "Whatever you fellows are recommending today, you will be sorry about a week from now."[48]

All week, through the hours of meetings, listening to McCone's latest estimates, wondering about the nuclear storage bins and how much time they had, positions fluctuated. The division between "hawks" and "doves" (the terms were first applied during discussions of this particular situation) was fluid for the most part. Nor was it always clear which course was most dangerous. Acheson and Max Taylor thought an air strike, or even an invasion, had fewer dangers than what McNamara suggested right at the outset: a blockade. Confronting Soviet ships on the high seas threatened a potential head-on U.S.–Russian risk to a far greater degree than a "surgical" operation. For the most part that was the view of the Joint Chiefs. David Detzer has written that "The generals tended to see the Cuban missiles as a military problem—not a diplomatic or political or a psychological one." They urged hitting all Cuban airfields and radar installations to support the strikes at the missile sites.[49] Should planes be sent in, however, the lives of Soviet technicians might be involved. Khrushchev might then lose his options. Bobby listened to their proposals, then passed a note to the President that said, "I now know how Tojo felt when he was planning Pearl Harbor."[50] Indeed, it was Bobby this time who cautioned moderation. Later that week he made his persuasive comment that the United States would be guilty of creating a "Pearl Harbor in reverse" by going on the attack, which Acheson considered "a thoroughly false and pejorative analogy."[51] But Bobby was right. What were they talking about? What were the legal implications? What international laws had been violated by either the Russians or the Cubans? There was never any question that Havana had wanted the help from Moscow.

Bobby revealed the President's preference. The blockade option offered the best opportunity for the United States not to appear to be the aggressor—and for Khrushchev to make his choices as well. All the while, of course, the American military would prepare for the worst. Strategic Air Command planes circled the globe in their most extensive alert in history. The 1st Armored Division, with fifteen thousand men, four tank battalions, and six mechanized infantry, was ordered to the East Coast to get ready for a possible invasion of Cuba. American civilians were evacuated from the naval base at Guantánamo, on the Cuban coast, and 379 people were flown in six planes to Norfolk, Virginia. Missiles were readied for firing. Polaris submarines began to move toward the Soviet Union.[52] McNamara ordered four tactical squadrons placed at readiness for an air strike. While all this was happening, George Ball and Gilpatric joined McNamara and Bobby in arguing for the quarantine. By the time the President returned from a speaking engagement on Wednesday night, Ed Martin had drafted a four-page memorandum outlining the choices. But he still lacked a consensus.

By Thursday the balance seemed fairly secure on the side of the quarantine, but on Friday morning the Joint Chiefs resumed their pleas for an air strike or invasion. General Taylor took the lead.[53] That day the President had to leave for a speaking tour to Cleveland and Chicago. Before flying off, he called in Bobby and Sorensen and told them he was impatient and discouraged. He was counting on them "to pull the group together quickly—otherwise more delays and dissension would plague whatever decision he took," Sorensen later reported.[54]

Bundy had also discussed the situation with the President. Then, after Kennedy left, Bundy said he was speaking for himself and explained that his own preference was for "decisive action with its advantages of surprise and confronting the world with a *fait accompli.*" Acheson, Dillon, and McCone seconded that position, and General Taylor said that it was "now or never for an air strike." At that point the attorney general made his Pearl Harbor comment, and the remark was prefaced with the statement that he had also spoken to the President that morning. He argued that a sneak attack would be a departure from the American tradition; we had not done that in 175 years. Thousands of lives would be lost, Cuban as well as Russian. Whatever action taken should compel the Russians to remove their missiles, but it should also permit them room to maneuver. Schlesinger has quoted Bobby as later explaining that "I said I just did not believe the President of the United States could order such a military operation. I said we were fighting for something more than just survival and that all our heritage and our ideals would be repugnant to such a sneak military attack." Bobby's words were most effective, but, as Schlesinger points out, "the record suggests that its impact was not spontaneous."[55] The die-hards were not ready to capitulate.

In the Midwest the President stopped over at Springfield to lay a wreath on Lincoln's tomb. In Chicago he campaigned for Sidney Yates's election to the Senate and spoke before Mayor Daley's Cook County Democrats. He was also greeted by large crowds, and there were posters urging him to show "less profile and more courage."[56] On Saturday morning he was at the Sheraton-Blackstone Hotel when, at about 10:00 A.M., he received a call from Bobby. The decision, he was told, was up to him: it could no longer be left to a committee. He had to return to Washington immediately.[57]

Salinger explained to the press that the President had a cold and would not be able to complete his speaking engagements. Kennedy then called Jacqueline, and told her he wanted her and the children nearby.[58] "When our plane landed at Andrews Air Force Base outside Washington," Larry O'Brien has written, "I flew with Kennedy on the helicopter back to the White House. He sat staring silently out the window, chin in hand, obviously in deep thought."[59] Shortly after 1:30 P.M., the helicopter landed on the South Lawn, and the President went directly to the pool for a swim. Bobby joined him there and talked to his brother from the edge of the pool. At 2:30 P.M. they walked into the Oval Office, where a formal gathering of the NSC, meeting #505, then went on for over two and a half hours.[60]

The advisers who had been at George Ball's conference room shifted to the White House. "We went in personal cars from the State Department to the meeting to avoid a conspicuous line of black Cadillacs outside," remembered Ed Martin, who drove over to 1600 Pennsylvania Avenue alone in a small Hillman Minx convertible.[61] Adlai Stevenson was also present, having flown up from New York the day before.

The meeting began with McCone's briefing. There was still no evidence of storage bins for nuclear warheads. But photographic evidence had clearly established "the presence in Cuba of Soviet strategic missiles, including mobile missile launchers and missile sites under construction."[62]

The advocates of military action made their final try. General Taylor resumed his support for Bundy's proposed air strike, and he was joined by Dillon and McCone. Then Stevenson, who had missed most of the sessions, spoke out. He opposed the air strike, as of course had Bobby, McNamara, and Ball. But the atmosphere became tense, all eyes on the UN ambassador as he pursued another possibility. The blockade was essential. For a final settlement, however, he suggested that the naval base at Guantánamo and the Turkish and Italian missile bases be traded for the missiles on Cuba. The island itself should be neutralized, its territorial integrity guaranteed, and United Nations inspection teams sent to all three countries to supervise compliance. At the very least there must be no quarantine without the prior backing of the Organization of American States. If necessary it should be limited to weapons only and not include petroleum, oil, and lubricants, which were so essential to Castro.[63]

Several of the others quickly pounced on Stevenson's comments. Kennedy, somewhat surprised at the vigor of Adlai's advocacy, also rejected his position. It would place the U.S. on the defensive instead of indicting the Soviets. They were the ones guilty of blatant duplicity. Only as recently as Thursday, Andrei Gromyko had paid a call at the White House as a courtesy to the President before returning to the USSR and had denied the existence of offensive weapons. Backing down in the way Stevenson suggested would also confirm European suspicions that America would not defend them in a crunch.[64]

At somebody's suggestion a straw vote was taken, and that showed eleven in favor of a quarantine and six holding out for a strike. The President kept his own preference hidden, although his inclination was obvious almost from the start. He and Sorensen and Bobby went out to the second-floor balcony afterward. There Kennedy told them that the situation was playing into the hands of the Republicans. Their warnings on Cuba will have been confirmed, and the Democrats would once again be vulnerable to charges of softness on communism—after the Bay of

Pigs especially, "soft" on Castro as well. Others would simultaneously call them the "war party" and charge them with endangering the security of the country. Either way they would be damned. Then the President said (Sorensen thought "somewhat ruefully"), "Well, I guess Homer Capehart is the Winston Churchill of our generation."[65]

The military had their usual choice of accommodation to the Commander in Chief's decision or resigning. Their unhappiness with the choice was no secret. Bobby later reported that General LeMay was so bitter that he talked about going ahead and bombing them on Monday anyway. Admiral George W. Anderson, the chief of naval operations, was later removed by Kennedy for continuing to complain about being "sold out."[66]

By that evening word was out in the nation's capital that something was about to happen. A Virginia newspaper contemplated a possible connection between the President's "cold" and the activity at the Norfolk Navy Yard. Kennedy made a personal appeal to *The New York Times* not to tip off the Russians in advance, but the paper did report that unusual troop movements probably pertained to Cuba.[67] The President gave Jackie the choice of taking the children closer to the fallout shelter or remaining with him in Washington, and she chose to stay in the White House. Kennedy also received a suggestion from Robert Lovett that Stevenson should be bolstered at the UN, and John McCloy was called home from Europe to help "stiffen" Adlai.[68]

To whatever degree the President may have been tantalized by the idea of a quick air strike to achieve a *fait accompli,* it was dispelled that Sunday morning when the head of the Tactical Air Command advised that there could be no guarantee of protecting the United States itself from retaliatory missiles.[69] By noon that day, after he had attended mass, the President made his final decision. He arrived at the White House at 10:50 A.M. and remained there all day. At midafternoon he met again with the NSC. This time it was a matter of checking out the approaches to America's allies. Acheson was dispatched to see De Gaulle. Ed Martin was sent to Mexico City, where the OAS diplomats had gathered to talk about the Alliance for Progress.[70] Lyndon Johnson was briefed by Bundy late that afternoon, and the vice-president, unhappy about the decision, commiserated with Richard Russell.[71] Johnson and the President then spent most of the evening reviewing the international situation, while Ted Sorensen worked on the speech for Monday evening.

Before the President's 7:00 P.M. announcement a lot of people were still trying to figure out what was happening. All over the world American armed forces were on the alert. One hundred and eighty naval vessels were deployed into the Caribbean, and a B-52 bomber force went into the air fully loaded with atomic weapons. Imposing a blockade did not mean the ships would stop and submit to inspection, or that they would turn back. An air strike—or an invasion, or both—might still be necessary. The objective remained to get rid of the missiles already in place. That was what the President tried to explain when he met with congressional leaders just before going on television.

That encounter, Bobby has written, was the most stressful of all the meetings.[72] Richard Russell, already tipped off by Lyndon Johnson, was as unhappy as the vice-president. He insisted that physical removal of the missiles would be less dangerous, and now was joined in that view by Bill Fulbright. The President "didn't seem to appreciate the suggestion," remembered the Arkansas senator. "It occurred to me then, and I suggested this would be more provocative to the Russians, more likely to escalate into war than if you attacked Cuba itself." What if the Russian ship doesn't turn back? Fulbright asked the President. We would have to escort it into port. What if it resists? We would have to sink it. No matter what their arguments, it was too late. Of course, they were unaware of Kennedy's reason for believing that he had chosen the least provocative route.[73]

One suggestion that Kennedy did accept came from Ormsby-Gore. The English ambassador pointed out that placing the blockade intervention line at eight hundred miles from Cuba, which was designed to keep outside the range of MIG fighters, would not give the Russians much time to make their decision. "Why not give them more time," Ormsby-Gore pointed out, "to analyze their position?" Kennedy accepted that point promptly. He called McNamara and ordered the line shortened to five hundred miles.[74]

Also that day intermediate-range missiles were spotted being moved past the British embassy in Havana. At 6:00 P.M. Rusk summoned Soviet Ambassador Dobrynin to the State Department, and forty-six ambassadors of allied and friendly countries were given a mass briefing in the auditorium. Ed Martin, George Ball, and Alexis Johnson met in Ball's conference room with Walter Lippmann, Joe Alsop, Scotty Reston, and Al Friendly of The Washington Post to explain what was happening.[75] Since noon the world had been alerted that the President would speak that evening.

The speech was crisp, not truculent, but deliberate and clear. He announced that "unmistakable evidence has established the fact that a series of offensive missile sites is now in preparation on that imprisoned island." Additional sites were yet to be completed, but those ballistic weapons already installed constituted a direct threat to most of the major cities of the Western Hemisphere. Moreover, he charged that the transformation of Cuba into a strategic base "constitutes an explicit threat to the peace and security of all the Americas, in flagrant and deliberate defiance of the Rio Pact of 1947." He called it a "deliberately provocative and unjustifiable change in the status quo which cannot be accepted by this country, if our courage and our commitments are ever to be trusted again by either friend or foe." The quarantine will be imposed to check against the further buildup of all offensive military equipment, and close surveillance of Cuba will continue. Any missile launched from there will be regarded "as an attack by the Soviet Union on the United States, requiring full retaliatory responses upon the Soviet Union," he announced, and urged Khrushchev "to halt and eliminate this clandestine, reckless, and provocative threat to world peace and to stable relations between our two nations." "Our goal," he concluded, "is not the victory of might, but the vindication of right."[76]

"We went to bed that night," wrote Bobby afterward, "filled with concern and trepidation, but filled also with a sense of pride in the strength, the purposefulness, and the courage of the President of the United States."[77]

Tuesday came, and the world was still there. In St. Augustine, Florida, Jack's Aunt Loretta, a sister of Joseph P. Kennedy, sent a telegram to Evelyn Lincoln: "Have just returned from Mass at the oldest Cathedral in our country. Praying for America and our President."[78] From Jackson, Mississippi, Bobby received a wire from Ross Barnett: "Disregard verbiage in previous telegram. Mississippians join in a firm stand in the Cuban situation. Efforts to stop all communistic attempts to destroy our American heritage and constitutional government should have the positive support of every American and likewise attention of our full military forces if necessary."[79] Gallup surveys taken that day showed that eighty-four percent of Americans favored the blockade with just four percent opposed. One in every five thought that World War III would result. Political analyst Samuel Lubell also found three out of every five Americans believing that "some shooting" was inevitable.[80] Meanwhile there were no signs of a Soviet move on Berlin; in fact no evidence existed of Khrushchev's belligerence. Bobby met with Dobrynin and pointed out how much more moderate the President's response was than the suggested reactions of some senators. Dobrynin was very concerned and stuck to the contention that there were no nuclear missiles on Cuba. Bobby left him with the statement that "the President felt he had a very helpful personal relationship with Mr. Khrushchev," and while they had vast areas of disagreement, "he did feel that there was a mutual trust and confidence between them on which he could rely."[81] In New York, with Republican John McCloy at his side in the UN, Adlai Stevenson went on the offensive against the Soviet delegate, Valerian Zorin, before a special meeting of the Security Council. He cited the OAS resolution, together with its request for action from the Security Council.[82] During that morning's ExCom meeting intelligence brought fresh information about a heavy Soviet flow of coded messages to their ships headed toward Cuba. All that was certain was that the vessels were right on course. McCone also reported that Soviet submarines were on their way to the Caribbean. After that meeting, back in his office, the President talked about Barbara Tuchman's *The Guns of August.* "The great danger and risk in all of this is a miscalculation," he said, "a mistake in judgment." Neither side wanted war, but such things as "security," "pride," or "face" could force nations into disaster. All that could bring an escalation into armed conflict, which, Bobby has written, "was what he wanted to avoid."[83]

That disaster was avoided. They came to the brink, almost "eyeball-to-eyeball," but finally found a way out. Harriman had indicated that Khrushchev was behaving like a man eager to avoid trouble. Still, with two Russian ships heading toward the blockade line, a holocaust was possible. Bobby described his brother: "His hand went up to his face and covered his mouth. He opened and closed his fist. His face seemed drawn, his eyes pained, almost gray. We stared at each other across the table. For a few fleeting seconds, it was almost as though no one else was there and he was no longer the President. Inexplicably, I thought of when he was ill and almost died . . ."[84] But at 10:25 A.M. a message arrived that Russian ships had "stopped dead in the water." In all, fourteen of the ships had stopped or turned back that day, and most of those that were continuing were tankers.

Despite the advice of those who wanted to intervene, the tankers and a passenger ship were let through. The President weighed the improbability that they were carrying anything vital. Meanwhile he was in constant touch with Khrushchev through a series of daily communications. On Friday, October 26, largely as a demonstration to Khrushchev, a vessel was stopped—an American-built Liberty ship under Lebanese registry that was headed toward Cuba under a Soviet charter from the Baltic port of Riga, the *Marcula.* The President himself selected that one to make his symbolic point. It was boarded by an armed party from two destroyers, the *John Pierce* and the *Joseph P. Kennedy, Jr.* As anticipated, it contained no weapons and was allowed to go on.[85]

Kennedy followed up the interception with the following message to Khrushchev: "If the Soviet Government accepts and abides by your request that 'Soviet ships already on their way to Cuba . . . stay away from the interception area' for the limited time required for preliminary discussion you may be assured that this government will accept and abide by your request that our vessels in the Caribbean 'do everything possible to avoid direct confrontation with the Soviet ships in the next few days in order to minimize the risk of any incident.' "[86]

The blockade was working because each side wanted it to work. But that did not solve the questions of the missiles and the Il-28s still in Cuba, and aerial reconnaissance was showing that work to get them ready was going ahead quickly. At the UN that Thursday evening Adlai Stevenson ripped into Zorin without mercy.

"Do you, Ambassador Zorin," Stevenson asked, "deny that the U.S.S.R. has placed and is placing medium- and intermediate-range missiles and sites in Cuba? Yes or no? Do not wait for interpretation. Yes or no?"

"I am not in an American court of law," said the Russian, "and therefore do not wish to answer a question put to me in the manner of a prosecuting counsel. You will receive the answer in due course in my capacity as representative of the Soviet Union."

"You are in the courtroom of world opinion right now," Stevenson shot back, "and you can answer 'Yes' or 'No.' You have denied that they exist—and I want to know whether I have understood you correctly."

Zorin: "Please continue your statement, Mr. Stevenson. You will receive the answer in due course."

"I am prepared to wait for my answer until hell freezes over, if that is your decision," was Adlai's dramatic response. "I am also prepared to present the evidence in the room."[87]

At last Adlai Stevenson had impressed Jack Kennedy. It was excellent theater, and before a global television audience. "I never knew Adlai had it in him," said the President. "Too bad he didn't show some of this steam in the 1956 campaign."[88]

Friday brought important new developments. That was the day Bartlett passed along Khrushchev's assurances that came from Georgi Bolshakov. It was also the day when Aleksander Fomin, a counselor at the Soviet embassy, invited ABC's State Department correspondent, John Scali, to lunch. Fomin had had an important message to pass on through Scali, whom he had met several times before. Would the Americans be prepared to issue a public pledge not to invade Cuba in exchange for removing the missiles? Fomin, it was assumed, spoke with the authority of a man who was, in addition to being a colonel in the KGB, a personal friend of Khrushchev's. "Would you," he asked Scali, "check with your high State Department sources?"

At the UN, Zorin approached Secretary-General U Thant with a similar proposal, and Cuban delegates were suggesting the possibility of dismantling the bases as part of a bargain. Meanwhile in Washington, at about the time Scali was reporting his information, the State Department had been alerted to receive a long message from Khrushchev himself.[89] The Chairman wanted to reassure Kennedy that the missiles were not "offensive," but conceded that debating that point would be fruitless. "If assurances were given by the President and the government of the United States that the U.S.A. would not participate in an attack on Cuba and would restrain others from actions of this sort, if you would recall your fleet, this would immediately change everything. . . . Let us not only relax the forces pulling on the ends of the rope; let us take measures to untie that knot. We are ready for this."[90]

At that night's late ExCom meeting the analysis of all the day's events encouraged optimism. A breakthrough finally seemed possible. Just at that point it all seemed to collapse, however, because Saturday morning brought a new message from Khrushchev. As it came in by radio, it was obviously far different from the earlier one, much colder and more formal. A new kind of exchange was now being proposed: removal of the American Jupiter missiles from Turkey as a swap for the Cuban dismantlement. The Russians would also offer a nonaggression package to Turkey. That new difficulty combined with other developments on that October 27. J. Edgar Hoover reported that Soviet personnel in New York were destroying all sensitive documents, possibly in preparation for war. Also a U-2 pilot, flying one of his several reconnaissance missions over Cuba, was shot down by a SAM missile and killed. By that Saturday, Walt Rostow later remembered, the Kennedy government was within hours of taking the missiles out from the air.[91]

The Jupiter affair was later obscured by much misunderstanding. The President had never ordered their removal. They were obsolete, useless as offensive weapons, and highly vulnerable. Placing fifteen such missiles in Turkey was done as much to bolster America's NATO ally psychologically and politically as for military reasons. The agreement to install them had been made by the Eisenhower administration in 1959, but not until Kennedy was in power were they actually put in place. Kennedy had explored the matter and found that since under the original agreement the Turks owned the missiles and the United States the nuclear warheads, it was not that simple to remove them.[92] It would involve

Turkish domestic political sensitivities as well as the reactions from other NATO members to such a unilateral act by the United States.

On the day the Khrushchev suggestion about the Jupiters was received, the CIA quickly cabled the State Department with a survey analyzing the probable impact elsewhere to a U.S.–Soviet deal pertaining to the "obsolete Jupiter system."[93] George McGhee had earlier taken up the matter while in Ankara, and later reported to the President that in his opinion "the Turks would not agree to the removal of the MRBMs without some compensation or stronger pressures than would be justified at that time."[94] Moreover, even if their removal had been ordered, doing so now under duress would be far more complicated politically both in the United States and within the NATO command.

At 4:00 P.M. that Saturday the President requested that U Thant be informed that "a number of proposals have been made to you and to the United States in the last thirty-six hours. I would appreciate your urgency ascertaining whether the Soviet Union is willing immediately to cease work on these bases in Cuba and render the weapons inoperable under UN verification so that various solutions can be discussed."[95] But within the ExCom patience had just about expired. Bobby Kennedy has written that there was "almost unanimous agreement that we had to attack early the next morning with bombers and fighters and destroy the SAM sites."[96] The President also ordered twenty-four troop-carrier Air Force Reserve squadrons into active duty.

But then he held back. Most of all Kennedy wanted to give Khrushchev additional leeway. He felt that his Soviet counterpart was under pressure from his own hawks. "It isn't the first step that concerns me," he said, "but both sides escalating to the fourth and fifth step—and we don't want to go to the sixth because there is no one around to do so. We must remind ourselves we are embarking on a very hazardous course." He warned that it was important to avoid humiliating Khrushchev, pointing out that the U.S. would have to deal with him on many other issues later.[97] To some colleagues, however, especially within the military, "the President had cracked and folded."[98] Yet on that day Khrushchev was warned that Cuba might be invaded within two or three days.[99]

It was Bobby, then, supported by Sorensen, who suggested that Khrushchev's second message be ignored as though never received, and that the American response should revert to Friday's position. Nobody was quite ready to account for the two different overtures from Moscow, whether the second was as genuinely Khrushchev's as the first, or whether Kremlin hard-liners had superseded the Chairman afterward.

One suggestion holds that the second letter was actually drafted earlier and held for a Saturday morning release in New York while the first was composed by Khrushchev *later*, after Friday's events, and immediately transmitted while the second was still making its way through the bureaucratic pipeline.[100] Later Foy Kohler, writing from the American embassy in Moscow, informed Dean Rusk of the explanation that was circulating through the Soviet capital. According to that theory the Friday letter had been written and transmitted over the wires by Khrushchev personally without any consultations. When the other leaders later heard about his action, apparently the same night, "long meetings and heated discussion ensued, leading to [the] despatch that came on Saturday."[101]

The Kennedy response drafted by Bobby and Sorensen then achieved its purpose. Over the President's signature, it gave assurances against an invasion of Cuba. There was, however, no direct pledge about the Jupiters. Much more generally, the letter simply said that "the United States is very much interested in reducing tensions and halting the arms race; and if your letter signifies that you are prepared to discuss a detente affecting NATO and the Warsaw Pact, we are quite prepared to consider with our allies any useful grounds."[102] Bobby Kennedy then met Dobrynin at the Justice Department. He told the Russian ambassador that there could be no quid pro quo under threat or pressure. "However," Bobby later quoted himself as having said, "President Kennedy had been anxious to remove those missiles from Turkey and Italy for a long period of time. He had ordered their removal some time ago, and it was our judgment that, within a short time after this crisis was over, those missiles would be gone."[103]

No bargain had been signed, no promises given. But a lawyer-like understanding was reached. Together with the letter, it was clear. They would be removed, as they were the following April (to be replaced by much more potent Polaris submarines).

By nine o'clock that Saturday morning Khrushchev's response began coming in. From the very first paragraph the positive tone was clear. What was much more explicit was the information that he had given instructions to his officers "to take appropriate measures to discontinue construction of the aforementioned facilities, to dismantle them, and to return them to the Soviet Union."[104] Khrushchev's major problem during the days to come was with an infuriated Castro, angered that Moscow had made the agreement without any consultation. Two days later the Kennedy administration ordered the termination of Operation MONGOOSE.

On Monday the President telephoned General Eisenhower with a complete briefing. The ex-president advised, according to his notes of their conversation, that *"the Government should by all means hold the initiative that it had finally seized when it established the quarantine."* After their talk Eisenhower promptly called John McCone to "give him the gist of the conversation, particularly about the reservations that I thought should accompany any all-out promise of ours." In other words McCone, "who is normally my contact with the President on matters involving national security," should be in a position to monitor further arrangements that Kennedy might make.[105]

Appropriately, Dean Acheson wrote to Kennedy that day, "Only a few people know better than I how hard the decisions are to make, and how broad the gap is between the advisors and the decider."[106]

The impact of the missile crisis on the congressional elections, which took place while the process of dismantling was being monitored, was hard to distinguish. Birch Bayh squeaked past Homer Capehart by just 10,944 votes, or 50.3 percent of the total. Richard Nixon, who had supported the quarantine but had renewed the issue of communism during the campaign, lost the gubernatorial race to incumbent Pat Brown, thereby removing him from serious consideration as a Kennedy opponent in 1964. In Massachusetts there was more direct (but not surprising) satisfaction. Ted Kennedy, who had received surreptitious assistance from the presidential staff, was elected to the Senate. Having easily defeated Edward McCormack in September's Democratic primary, he had no trouble turning back his Republican challenger on November 6—George Cabot Lodge, the son of the man Jack Kennedy had defeated for his Senate seat in 1952. Overall, however, the party balance remained about the same. Republicans gained two in the House, and Democrats four in the Senate. The state house lineup was exactly the same. Lou Harris informed Kennedy that local issues had been more significant than the international crisis.

Resolving the missile crisis had prevented a Soviet-operated offensive base from being established in Cuba, while the terms of the settlement had protected the island from an American invasion. Castro was embittered by the Russian deal with Washington, undoubtedly regretting that he had permitted Cuba to become so dependent upon Moscow. Apart from that, the situation remained unchanged. Havana was still convinced that the Cuban revolution could be made secure only by undermining hostile neighbors.

The United States had more reason than ever to view Cuba with suspicion. By the spring of 1963, Kennedy was following a dual policy with regard to Castro. One involved resumption of the harassment: with Operation MONGOOSE disbanded and the SG (A) abolished, a Cuban Coordinating Committee was established within the State Department. Together with the Standing Group, their mission was to find new ways of bringing down the regime. The President also approved of a new sabotage program. However, the objective of the renewed covert activities was somewhat more modest: merely to "nourish a spirit of resistance and disaffection which could lead to significant defections and other by-products of unrest." By October, a series of operations was approved by the Special Group. They were designed to carry out acts of sabotage against such targets as an electric power plant, an oil refinery, and a sugar mill. Before the month was over, twenty-two specific targets were designated.[107]

Even earlier in 1963, before the Special Group made its relatively conservative recommendations, the CIA had resumed plotting against Castro personally. Under the leadership of agent Desmond Fitzgerald, assassination operations continued through a Cuban intimate of Castro's named Roland Cubela, who was protected by the CIA code name of AM/LASH. For all of this, as Bissell maintains, "There's awfully little evidence, believe me," [of White House complicity or knowledge].[108]

Only later, in May of 1963, did the CIA produce an evaluation that agreed with the sentiments that Tad Szulc and Mike Mansfield had expressed much earlier: "the odds are that upon Castro's death, his brother Raúl or some other figure in the regime would, with Soviet backing and help, take over control." It went on to warn that "if Castro were to die by other than natural causes the U.S. would be widely charged with complicity even though it is widely known that Castro has many enemies."[109] But the AM/LASH involvement continued into Johnson's administration despite that memorandum. As in so much of the relationship between the government's use of intelligence operations and subsequent actions, night does not always follow day.

The other part of Kennedy's revised two-prong approach to Castro was much more intimately tied to the President and his administration. Superficially it was the exact contradiction of the first. If the regime could not be brought down, it might at least be yanked out of the Soviet orbit. Among the background papers prepared by the CIA for the NSC meeting of April 23 was the projection that "Cuba will continue to be an economic burden to the USSR, policy differences with Moscow will persist."[110] Therefore, even while the administration's authorized program of harassment was under way, sub rosa attempts were being made to explore the possibility of an accommodation.

Bundy himself had proposed that to Kennedy as early as January 4.

But an actual concerted effort did not take place until the fall. Bill Attwood, working for Adlai Stevenson at the U.N., heard from the Guinean ambassador to Cuba that Castro was looking for a way to get out from under Khrushchev. Attwood had first met Castro by interviewing him for six hours in 1959. When Attwood received confirmation of interest in exploratory talks from the Cuban ambassador to the UN, he relayed the information to the State Department and argued for the wisdom of persuading Cuba to adopt a policy of non-alignment.[111] He then began a series of talks with the ambassador, Carlos Lechuga, which continued into November. On the eighteenth of that month, Attwood called a member of Castro's staff in Cuba with the information that the United States wanted preliminary negotiations to be held at the UN. Bundy told Attwood that the President wanted a personal conference to "decide what to say and whether to go or what we should do next."[112]

But Attwood never did get to deal directly with Kennedy on the matter. Interviewed in 1980, Attwood said, "I saw Castro last October and saw him two years before and he keeps referring to that little period and how he was on the other end of the phone." With all the clandestine activities going on against him, how did Castro think he could get through to Kennedy? "He read a lot about them," Attwood replied. "He understood that these things were being done by a police or a Secret Service bureaucracy. I think he probably felt that Kennedy was not fully in control of the CIA."[113]

13

"Friends and Allies"

One of the more remarkable attributes of Jack Kennedy was that despite cold-war tensions and endless conflicts at home, he managed to remain in close touch with the details of life around him. The President asked probing, personal questions to get the latest gossip. He constantly seemed eager to hear what others were doing, to know about their love lives, marriages, and plans.

A woman who worked for magazines and covered the White House beat observed that he was surrounded by "layers and layers of people."[1] He was happiest and relaxed most easily in the company of good friends. During his lifetime his reputation as a womanizer was mostly confined to the West Wing staff itself, or to the newspaper people who passed along rumors that never reached typewriters. The revelations of subsequent years gave the public some entertainment. The golden boy in the White House was suddenly transformed into a Lothario, and the portrait was not easily contradicted.

But we are dealing with a man whose zest for life was more complex than that. With everyone, male and female, he gave the impression that the crises were but inevitable interruptions, not excuses to stop having a good time. One of his British friends, Lord Longford, has written that

"It is one thing to learn to charm, another to inspire. In Britain Anthony Eden did the first, Sir Winston Churchill (once the war came) did the second. Jack Kennedy did both."[2]

Kennedy's women, real or imagined, tended to overshadow his male relationships. The man Ben Bradlee has called the "world's champion male chauvinist pig" had a durable following of varied and loyal hangers-on. Power fosters that attraction, certainly, but with Jack Kennedy the magnetism was often overwhelming.

Lem Billings entered Jack's life at Choate and never left. He remained a bachelor and seemed to have subordinated his life to his friend. Members of the President's staff thought of him as "a handy old piece of furniture." He was helpful to have around. One reporter was surprised to find him alone in the mansion with a pregnant Jackie, but Billings, he thought, was "a drag."[3] Billings never did leave JFK's circle, and afterward continued to serve the Kennedys from Steve Smith's New York office. He outlived Jack by nearly two decades and preserved the kind of loyalty that was also kept by a very different sort of personality, Dave Powers.

Dave, the poor boy from the Charlestown docks, became the court jester and servant of Kennedy's mature years, filling the President's idle moments with Irish jokes, baseball lore, and displaying his remarkable talent for statistics of all sorts, from batting and pitching records to voting. As Clem Norton once remembered about the Kennedy–Powers relationship, "He gets a kick out of Dave. If Dave wasn't there, he'd send for him so he could look and see he was sitting there."[4] "I remember Kennedy and Powers sitting nude at poolside, and Powers telling the President one wild Irish joke after another," Traphes Bryant has written. "Strangely enough, most of his favorite jokes seemed to be about death and funerals and drunken Irish wakes."[5] Powers forever after worshiped the Kennedy monument that he retained in his mind, and, as curator of the Kennedy Library in Boston, remained reverential.

When Jack socialized, however, it was with such banker friends as Charles Spalding and Jim Reed, or his close English companion, David Ormsby-Gore. Joseph Kraft, the newspaper columnist, has pointed out that the people around him were pretty much layered and structured and not just a conglomeration of all who were close. Kraft would have thought it most unlikely to have been included at dinner with the John McCones and the Ormsby-Gores.[6]

More often such writers as Kraft would have been assigned to a different category, the company of journalists. Bill Walton was among them, but political success augmented such holdovers as the Krocks,

Bartletts, Grahams, and Alsops with other prominent writers. Still, Mary McGrory, one of the more perceptive writers, quickly learned that his company was not to be taken for granted. One either informed or amused him. If you did neither, she concluded, "he would turn you off very easily."[7]

Kennedy's infatuation with the press had its obvious practical value, but he also genuinely enjoyed their company. He carefully kept up with their bylines, and followed their publications. Pierre Salinger had to remind him that it might be a good idea to cultivate some of the more anonymous wire-service reporters. Kenny O'Donnell, hard-boiled and pragmatic, considered his boss and the press office sadly out of touch with the way Americans got their information. "Why do you sons of bitches listen to *The New York Times* and believe it?" he asked at one point. "The guy in Iowa, Kansas, or Nebraska never saw *The New York Times*, never heard of *The New York Times*, doesn't care what Scotty Reston writes."[8]

And the managers of the nation's fourth estate fell for Jack Kennedy. They enjoyed his intelligence; most of all they liked his candor and good humor. Ronald Steel points out that "Few Presidents had ever had a more adoring press corps."[9] Nor had so many socialized so much with a President. Kennedy dined not only at Joe Alsop's, but at the homes of such other journalistic luminaries as columnist Rowland Evans and Ben Bradlee, then the head of *Newsweek*'s Washington bureau. Not surprisingly there were some adverse cosequences. Charles Roberts of *Newsweek*, for example, complained that the President "tried a little too much to be buddy-buddy, played favorites a little."[10]

The dean of them all, Walter Lippmann, experienced the sting of presidential disfavor. The nation's most eminent political journalist had been slow to warm to Kennedy, gradually abandoning his doubts because of the impressive confidence the swiftly rising young senator had managed to inspire among the Cambridge academic community. But then after the West Virginia primary he annoyed the candidate by suggesting that he take second place on a ticket headed by Adlai Stevenson. After the Bay of Pigs, but before the presidential trip to Europe, Lippmann was interviewed on television and chided Kennedy for failing to lead the public by not educating them about what he was trying to do. The administration, Lippmann remarked, was "like the Eisenhower administration thirty years younger." The President himself didn't complain, but General Clifton called CBS and, as Lippmann remembered it, "protested violently about the whole thing."[11] Lippmann had often been invited to White House receptions to impress visiting heads of state.

Periodically the President had him in for a private lunch, usually with Bundy or Schlesinger.[12] Nevertheless, after the comment about Eisenhower, Lippmann understood that any real relationship "was over." That didn't end his access to the White House, but later meetings were more professional and superficial.[13]

Play remained a strong part of the President's personality. The Kennedy White House has since been depicted as a virtual mecca of debauchery, where indeterminate numbers of young beauties hid until Jackie left and then cavorted with the President, joining him for nude swims and experiencing the joys of the mansion's bedroom.

One woman finally remarked that "If all women who claimed privately that they had slept with Jack had really done so, he wouldn't have had the strength left to lift a teacup."[14] Truth became impossible to distinguish from fantasies. Actress Jayne Mansfield, a sex symbol who died in 1967, claimed she spent three romantic years with JFK. His fondness for show business glamour inevitably linked the Kennedy name with such other starlets as Rhonda Fleming, Angie Dickinson, Kim Novak, and Janet Leigh. All such liaisons supposedly occurred during the White House years, with perhaps the most captivating rumor of that period linking him with Marilyn Monroe. She sang for the President at a Madison Square Garden forty-fifth-birthday gala. *Time* magazine showed her at the microphone wearing a metallic, tight gown that voluptuously celebrated every curve of her body. The caption then noted that the appearance had taken place at a party for the President, but failed to inform readers that she was singing in the presence of thousands at the giant indoor stadium in New York City.[15] It is improbable that the JFK–Marilyn Monroe relationship went beyond that.

Jack had learned a number of things from his father, and one of them was how to conduct affairs with propriety. Products of their respective times, neither father nor son regarded women with the seriousness that he reserved for men. Barbara Ward was very close to the mark when she told Elspeth and Walt Rostow that Kennedy "had little empathy for the trained, intelligent woman—he may have, but my impression is he hadn't. I think the coolness was mutual," she said, and, after some reflection, added, "I never felt that people of my type would ever have very much influence or play very much part."[16]

Two male friends from Capitol Hill who saw the President frequently were favorite companions, Frank Thompson, Jr., of New Jersey and Congressman Torby Macdonald. Torby, Jack's old Harvard friend, had developed with JFK a closeness that shared not only similar tastes and thoughts, but women as well. Both had had affairs with Joan Lundberg

Hitchcock, a West Coast beauty.[17] Jack and Torby had on occasion teamed up with the same woman to form a *ménage a trois.* "To some extent, the way Torbert was about women, Jack Kennedy was the same way," explained one of Macdonald's close friends. "Only more so," she added, "because he had the advantage of a tremendous amount of money, so he could spend any amount he wanted to."[18]

For almost two years Jack became involved with the beautiful and talented sister of Ben Bradlee's wife. For a good part of his life, as far back as his senior year at Choate, Kennedy had crossed paths with Mary Pinchot. At the school she had been taken to a dance by a Choate sophomore, Bill Attwood. Jack and the journalist, who also became Kennedy's ambassador to Guinea, never forgot how he immediately spotted "the best" and kept cutting in.[19]

Mary *was* "the best," beautiful, talented, wealthy, and, as it turned out, she had an impressive political pedigree. Her father was Amos Pinchot, who had helped build Teddy Roosevelt's Progressive Party in 1912. He was also a founder of the organization that led to the establishment of the American Civil Liberties Union and was a member of its board. A brother of Amos, Mary's uncle, was Gifford Pinchot, the conservationist hero of the progressive era and a two-term governor of Pennsylvania. The Pinchots, who had their homestead in Milford, had amassed a fortune from the dry-goods business.

Jack and Mary probably saw each other again while she was at Vassar, when he dated some of her classmates. Five years later they came together at the charter conference of the United Nations at San Francisco while Jack was covering the event for the Hearst papers and Mary was there as the bride of Cord Meyer, Jr., who was an assistant to the American delegate, Harold Stassen. Meyer, the bright young man with such promise, then pioneered the United World Federalist movement. Later, having had his fill of coping with the persistence of nationalism, he went to work for the CIA. Twelve years after their marriage, and partly because of his preoccupation with the agency, they were divorced.[20] Mary had earlier discovered her artistic talents and went on to become an abstract painter. She became the companion of Kenneth Noland, who was still in the "struggling artist" stage of his career. When Kennedy became President, her presence at the White House was not unusual.

She was there, and her name recorded on the official guest list, at a dinner on March 15, 1961, given in honor of Prince and Princess Stanislaus Radziwill. The President also dined with her at the Bradlee home, and she was also with him, although not officially listed, during a birthday cruise down the Potomac in 1963. They got together socially at Joe Alsop's Georgetown home as well. In September of 1963, on the first leg of a trip that ultimately took him as far as the West Coast, Mary Meyer and Toni Bradlee flew with the President to the Pinchot estate in Milford. He delivered a little eulogy to the family and unveiled a plaque that marked the dedication of the property for conservation studies.[21] That he and Mary were at least good friends was far from a secret.

Kennedy first tried to make love to Mary in December, but her relationship with Noland was still too strong. That condition then changed, and by January she began to share the President's bed. From then on they had brief, private interludes, but the liaison was durable and lasted for the rest of Kennedy's life.

All the time they must have delighted in planting deceptive hints among their friends. Preserving their privacy became most important, especially since he was the President of the United States. But Mary had the very human compulsion not to let it all pass without the rest of the world one day finding out that she and Jack Kennedy were lovers. She confided in two married friends. Mary recorded that time of her life by making notations in the margins of her sketchbook. Someday her two children would know that she had been loved by the President of the United States.

Mary felt that her love was reciprocated. At least one unidentified source who knew them both has been quoted as saying that Jack probably did love her. She had become "the secret Lady Ottoline of Camelot."[22]

She also told one of her two friends that Jack felt "no affection of a lasting kind for his wife."[23] But Jack Kennedy had found an outlet both sexually and intellectually with Mary. He could enjoy life with her. He could talk in ways she understood, and their trust was mutual. Jacqueline was often gone from the White House for one reason or another, either traveling or at the Kennedy country house, so Jack and Mary had their opportunities and, given the natural limitations of his situation, their moments of freedom. In July 1962 Mary surprised him with some joints of marijuana. Together they smoked two, and he reportedly told her that it was not at all like cocaine. "I'll get you some of that," he then volunteered. The incident, moreover, took place just a few weeks before the convening of a White House conference on drug abuse.[24] The cocaine story was given to the press after her death by one of her confidants, a former *Washington Post* editor, James Truitt.[25]

Their relationship covered the greater portion of his time in office, and there is every reason for believing that she was an important support. She understood all about the pompous asses he had to put up with. When he was with her, the rest of the world could go to hell. He could laugh with her at the absurdity of the things he saw all around his center of power. He could tell her how ironic it was that one of the most segregationist of southern senators had a black mistress. He could talk about the ridiculous bright boys he himself had enlisted, but who took themselves so seriously. Every time he thought he might someday retire to the life of a college professor, he imagined himself swamped by a bunch of pedantic intellectuals.[26] He already had his fill of them. They used the word *liberal* so much that it made him gag. They could turn out some pretty good speeches, with some lofty phrases and ideas, but they were also out of this world. Only Sorensen had his feet on the ground. Ted knew what it was all about. Next to Bobby he had the best instincts. But imagine stiff, proper Ted if he could see the President now with Mary? She surely heard about the good laugh the President had when one of his bright boys walked into the Oval Office and seriously told him that Rusk should be replaced after the reelection and that State should be given to Bobby.[27] Bobby—imagine that! Wasn't that a shit! Didn't he have enough trouble with nepotism as it is, especially with Teddy getting a Senate seat? That, of course, was something he couldn't do much about. The Ambassador had put his foot down. Jack and Bobby had gotten what they wanted. Why not let Teddy have his turn?[28]

Mary was always interested in the city of Washington, and she must have heard him go on about how he would like to live there after the presidency was all over. He had even discussed with Bill Walton the strategy of having Walton buy a home in the District as a cover for his own intended postpresidential use. He might then be able to spare time for overseeing the rehabilitation of Pennsylvania Avenue. He cared a lot about that. The main boulevard of the capital city of the world's leading power was a disgrace, full of dilapidated buildings, and restoration was long overdue. Ever since his days as a young congressman on the District of Columbia Committee he had become far more of a Washingtonian than a Bostonian.[29]

About half a year after finally really getting to know Mary, he began to tape White House meetings and telephone conversations. Ike had certainly done that (even his NATO headquarters had been wired!), and it wasn't a bad idea. If he wanted to do some postpresidential writing, he would then have a rich fund of material. He and Sorensen might even collaborate on his memoirs. He'd do some writing or teaching, or something like that. Maybe Phil Graham could get him the presidency of *The*

Washington Post, or maybe it would be great to be the youngest living elder statesman.[30] He had already mentioned to George Smathers that maybe the Senate could pass a bill that would make every former president an honorary member.[31] That would give him a forum. But he certainly did not want to become a secretary of state.[32] As a former chief executive he would hardly want to be a waterboy to a future president. Even Rusk—proper, cool, and very patient—was frustrated. He had told him he couldn't afford to remain on after one term.[33] He might get McNamara to take over, and that would give him a stronger man at State, anyway, maybe one who could finally take control of the Department. But, boy, was he glad he hadn't gone along with Stevenson. That would have been impossible.

Just before Christmas of 1962, the President was interviewed on television about his first two years in office. He told ABC's Bill Lawrence that "the problems are more difficult than I had imagined they were." There were important limitations. "We are involved now in the Congo in a very difficult situation. We have been unable to secure an implementation of the policy which we have supported. We are involved in a good many other areas. We are trying to see if a solution can be found to the struggle between Pakistan and India, with whom we want to maintain friendly relations. Yet they are unable to come to an agreement. There is a limitation, in other words, upon the power of the United States to bring about solutions."[34]

However intractable the President was finding the world, the search for solutions went on. Self-determination for the Papuans was impossible, and finding a formula for Palestinians was equally elusive, but they were merely peripheral to the long-run goals. The West New Guinea dispute had been resolved without either a war or Indonesian absorption in a Communist bloc. In the Middle East, while the Johnson Plan was given a prudent burial and political kinships had tightened the military bond with the Israelis, at least somewhat of a better dialogue had been opened with the other side as well. Private communications begun with Nasser during that period were in effect a prelude to the Begin–Sadat détente. And into 1963 the search went on.

At home, civil rights upstaged everything else. Men and events superseded long-range planning. The calmer international atmosphere after Cuba II helped shift attention to the battles in the streets of Birmingham. Finally the political fallout became inconsequential. As he himself put it, the chips would have "to fall where they may."

That was pretty much how it was with international events. It is hard to see their relationship to the coming presidential campaign. Berlin was certainly unaffected, as was the Congo, where in fact the administration had to contend with greater dissatisfaction over its policy of backing the UN's opposition to Moise Tshombe's secessionist province of Katanga. Some of the strongest dissent over that policy came from among the ranks of Kennedy's own northern Democrats. The increased expectation that a nuclear test ban might be possible was a direct legacy of the missile crisis and the cool heads that finally prevailed there. In South Vietnam the administration was getting into its quagmire for several reasons, none having to do with immediate election strategy: 1) the commitment had been made, and reinforced since the Eisenhower period; 2) the mandarin style of President Diem and his Catholicism, virtually negating his ability to relate to the Buddhists; 3) the militance of the government's opposition that finally led to monks burning themselves alive, raids on their pagodas, and a revolt of the generals, all of which finally led to the administration's conviction that Diem had to go.

It is significant that his three most memorable speeches of 1963—the one at American University on June 10, his civil rights report to the American people the very next day, and his *"Ich bin ein Berliner"* remarks on June 26—came not only during the same month but were closely related to the accident of events rather than to any strategy for accomplishing New Frontier objectives. In each case he had been pushed.

The vital thing for Kennedy, however, and the point that made his final imprint possible, was how he responded to the choices that conditions had created. That drive during those final months seemed to have obtained its fuel from circumstances. Possibly Kennedy needed to become the statesman for world peace because civil rights was an albatross with both the electorate and with the Congress, and as leaders will, he had to provide the counterbalance where the President has the best forum to influence his own popularity: the world stage. A specific speech, such as the one in West Berlin, would have served that need as a collateral purpose, but in each of the initiatives, as with civil rights, the relationship between the requirements of statecraft and political expediency is hard to prove.

Certainly that was true in moving toward a nuclear test ban treaty. The combined quest for arms limitation and solving the nuclear dilemma may well be considered among Jack Kennedy's most consistent goals. The resolution of the missile crisis did not clear all the obstacles. There remained questions of inspection, both for scientific reasons and for writing a treaty acceptable to the Senate. Ardent nationalists could be expected to wave their flags even harder, as though eager to invite disaster.

The way had to be cleared, but the desire was there, and that momentum led directly to Kennedy's American University speech and, finally, to the treaty itself. Khrushchev's amenability was evident in the same communication that announced his agreement to withdraw the missiles. "We should like to continue the exchange of views on the prohibition of atomic and thermonuclear weapons, general disarmament, and other problems relating to the relaxation of international tension," he wrote at that time.[35] The Soviet attitude was anticipated by the NSC's Planning Committee, which stated in its own report of October 29 that, with the missile crisis ending, "it is conceivable that Khrushchev himself may wish to move forward towards a détente on Berlin and to leave behind him some achievement in the field of arms control and disarmament."[36] Within the next week, the weight of world pressures to do something was shown by two General Assembly resolutions in which the UN called for the cessation of all nuclear tests and for a comprehensive treaty.[37]

At the end of November, Kennedy received a White House visit from Anastas Mikoyan, the first deputy chairman of the Soviet Council of Ministers. Sorensen has reported that the Russian official liked the spirit of the President's statements and felt that their two countries should begin the process of negotiating on all outstanding questions.[38] What Kennedy essentially told Mikoyan, as Walt Rostow remembered, was, "Look, this is an awfully dangerous world. I didn't think you would do this and you obviously didn't think I would react as I did. This is too dangerous a way for us to go on."[39] Khrushchev followed through with his letter of December 19, in which he told Kennedy that the "time has come now to put an end once and for all to nuclear tests, to draw a line through such tests."[40] When the President met in his office with William C. Foster, the director of the Arms Control and Disarmament Agency, he emphasized that he wanted a test ban treaty for two reasons: its impact on the arms race and Communist China.[41] When he then brought up the issue before the National Security Council, he tailored his emphasis to that particular audience. He told them that he had CIA support for believing that such an agreement would reduce the chances of Chinese Communist emergence as a nuclear power. His exchange of correspondence with Khrushchev had confirmed that the Russians were also convinced about the importance of a test ban to the world situation. He said nothing more specific about how and why Peking would be affected, nor did he quote from his exchanges with Moscow, but he left no doubt that the Russians were thinking along the same lines.[42]

Kennedy's Arms Control and Disarmament Agency (a creation of his presidency) had been studying the question of a test ban control since the previous spring. Its feasibility related to matters of inspection to guard against Soviet cheating, and there was little doubt that the suspicions that existed on Capitol Hill and within the Pentagon directed the President toward a limited treaty rather than something more comprehensive. "Perhaps we should take a new look at this *limited* test ban," Adrian Fisher, Foster's deputy, recalls Kennedy as having urged. "Perhaps that would be better than nothing." But as Fisher then also pointed out, "in terms of the President's own thinking, his concentration was primarily on the comprehensive ban, but he focused on the limited a lot." Kennedy pointed to the demand for on-site inspection, which was strong within Congress, and wondered "why can't we agree that we don't need on-site inspection," that there were in existence sufficient means of detecting violations.[43]

That would have cleared the way to a treaty, but Kennedy's soundings of key powers on Capitol Hill revealed the expected suspicion and resistance. Conversations with Henry Jackson of Washington, who had a great deal of influence with his colleagues on military matters, had been most discouraging.[44] "I have serious doubts that we will ever be able to persuade Russia to agree to a foolproof system of inspection," insisted Richard Russell.[45] Thomas Dodd of Connecticut, the rabidly anti-Communist Democrat, complained to Fisher that the draft of a limited test ban as drawn up by the Arms Control and Disarmament Agency lacked proper safeguards against Soviet cheating.[46]

Nevertheless, slowly, the President pushed the matter. On January 22, 1963, after having been further encouraged to go ahead by Ormsby-Gore, Kennedy explained that he wanted the Atomic Energy Commission to defer any planned underground tests for a few weeks while talks could take place in New York between Foster, his Soviet counterpart, and the British ambassador. But those conversations went nowhere, and Kennedy told the AEC to go ahead with its underground tests. Nor did February bring any kind of breakthrough when the Eighteen Nation Disarmament Conference resumed its sessions in Geneva. The Soviets had accepted the idea of on-site inspections and having unmanned seismic stations on their territory, but the U.S. insisted on no fewer than eight annual inspections to be made on Russian soil. On February 21 the AEC accordingly requested approval for a new series of atmospheric tests. After momentarily asking for such plans to be deferred, the administration thought it would be best to indicate quite openly the preparations for their resumption. Dean Rusk suggested to Bundy that "if the fact that we are getting ready to test becomes known, this might do more to spur on the test ban negotiations than would any indication of concern about Soviet complaints about these preparations."[47] On May 6 Kennedy authorized June 1, 1964, as the readiness date for a new series to be conducted in the Pacific.[48]

When he heard that *Saturday Review* editor Norman Cousins was going to Russia, Kennedy suggested that he visit Khrushchev to sound him out on the testing question. Cousins met the Chairman at a Black Sea resort and quoted his reaction as follows: "I know that three inspections are not .necessary, and that the policing can be done adequately from outside our borders. But the American Congress has convinced itself that onsite inspection is necessary and the President cannot get a treaty through the Senate without it. Very well, then let us accommodate the President." Khrushchev also lamented to Cousins about the American misconception that he was an absolute dictator "who can put into practice any policy I wish. Not so," he explained. "I've got to persuade before I can govern. Anyway, the Council of Ministers agreed to my urgent recommendation," but the Americans were still holding out for eight inspections.[49]

The breakthrough was not ideal, but it was within the realm of what Kennedy thought could be achieved. His major personal initiative came with a speech at the John R. Reeves Athletic Field on the campus of American University in Washington, D.C., on June 10, 1963. Not since Eisenhower back in 1953 had an American President taken that kind of step to allay cold-war frictions. This, though, was a decade later. Knowledge and anxieties about nuclear fall-out had increased vastly. Kennedy's American University speech remains a landmark in the history of post–World War II Soviet–American relations. Ever since the missile crisis, Rostow has noted, he had been waiting to deliver that kind of speech. His major points added up to a significant desire to turn away from the cold war:

1) The United States wants "Not a Pax Americana enforced on the world by American weapons of war."

2) The stockpiling of "billions of dollars [of] weapons acquired for the purpose of making sure we never need to use them is essential to keeping the peace," but it "is not the only, much less the efficient, means of assuring peace."

3) "Let us reexamine our attitude toward the Soviet Union. It is discouraging to think that their leaders may actually believe what their propagandists write."

4) The American people should be warned about falling "into the same trap as the Soviets, not to see only a distorted and desperate

view of the other side, not to see conflict as inevitable, accommodations as impossible, and communication as nothing more than
an exchange of threats."

5) ". . . both the United States and its allies, and the Soviet Union
and its allies, have a mutually deep interest in a just and genuine
peace and in halting the arms race."

6) "For, in the final analysis, our most basic common link is that we
all inhabit this small planet. We all breathe the same air. We all
cherish our children's future. And we are all mortal. . . . We must
deal with the world as it is, and not as it might have been had the
history of the last 18 years been different."

7) "Our primary long-range interest in Geneva, however, is general
and complete disarmament—designed to take place by stages,
permitting parallel political developments to build the new institutions of peace which would take the place of arms. . . . The one
major area of these negotiations where the end is in sight, yet
where a fresh start is badly needed, is in a treaty to outlaw nuclear
tests. The conclusion of such a treaty, so near and yet so far,
would check the spiraling arms race in one of its most dangerous
areas."

He also announced some specific steps: the arrangement for a direct
Moscow-to-Washington line—the so-called "hot line," "to avoid on each
side the dangerous delays, misunderstandings, and misreadings of the
other's actions which might occur at a time of crisis"; Khrushchev and
Macmillan had agreed with him to open high-level discussions in Moscow soon "looking toward early agreement on a comprehensive test ban
treaty"; the United States would not conduct nuclear tests in the atmosphere as long as other states refrained from doing so. "We will not be
the first to resume."[50]

The hot line was the culmination of a step first proposed by the
Russians. Their idea, as expressed more than a year earlier, was a direct
telephone link between the Kremlin and the White House, but Kennedy
had discouraged that as failing to address itself to the reality that the
difficulty was "comprehension rather than communication." Finally, ten
days after the American University speech, the two nations signed a
memorandum of understanding that provided for a private teletype link.
The hot line was operable before the end of the summer of 1963.[51]

Kennedy emphasized the importance he placed on the nuclear test
negotiations by assigning the task to the most experienced of all American diplomats, Averell Harriman, a move that also left the Russians with
no doubt about his intentions. Khrushchev told Harriman that he

thought Kennedy had made "the greatest speech by any American President since Roosevelt."[52]

If the Russians were now hopeful, and if Kennedy thought he could make a breakthrough, others within the administration continued to view the enterprise with skepticism. Walt Rostow worried that Moscow was trying to take the West off guard and thereby diminish its unity. After all, Laos and Vietnam were still unresolved situations, Russian troops remained in Cuba, and too much had been invested in a link with the West German government to risk a superficial détente.

On July 24, while the Harriman negotiations were taking place, Dean Rusk and John McCone briefed Dwight Eisenhower. They told him that Khrushchev's revised attitude probably came from the Sino–Soviet rift plus Moscow's eagerness to limit defense spending. Furthermore the Russians could afford a standstill in nuclear development because they had perfected a method of underground testing not detectable by radioactive fallout. Eisenhower supplied the thought that any future American need to break the treaty might have to involve compromising intelligence sources to prove Russian deceit.[53] Once more, informing Eisenhower was an appropriate step. Kennedy was not about to repeat Woodrow Wilson's error in making the Treaty of Versailles a partisan accomplishment. The American delegation invited to Moscow for the signing included both Republican and Democratic senators. Two other members of the GOP who were asked to go along were Everett Dirksen and Bourke Hickenlooper, the party's ranking member on the Armed Services Committee. Both declined, pleading the desire to maintain their independence.[54]

Finally, on August 5, the treaty was signed in the Kremlin. The signatories were bound "to prohibit, to prevent, and not to carry out any nuclear weapon test explosion, or any other nuclear explosion at any place under its jurisdiction or control (a) in the atmosphere, beyond its limits including outer space, or underwater including territorial water or high seas, or (b) in any other environment if such explosion causes radioactive debris to be present outside the territorial limits of the state under whose jurisdiction or control such explosion is conducted." The inspection issue was sidestepped. Clandestine tests could, after all, be detected in the environment without on-site verification. Furthermore the treaty gave all signatories the right to withdraw by giving a three-month notification if it decided that its supreme interests were being jeopardized.[55]

Three days after the signing in Moscow, Kennedy sent the treaty to the Senate for ratification. The message clearly revealed his uncertainty about its prospects. He emphasized that the risks of rejection outweighed those of agreement on limitations. America already had sufficient strategic forces to "deter or survive a nuclear attack," and the treaty would not reduce that capacity. Moreover, it was a limited step, one that would not in itself diminish the need for an adequate military arm. Nor would it negate underground testing or do anything about the existing stockpiles of nuclear weapons. "On the other hand," he warned the Senate, "unrestricted testing—by which other powers could develop all kinds of weapons through atmospheric tests more cheaply and quickly than they could underground—might well lead to a weakening of our society." Thereby, of course, he raised the specter of nuclear proliferation. And if that alone were not sufficient grounds to attempt limitations, it would inevitably go a long way toward doing something to minimize the dangers of radioactive fallout.[56]

Securing ratification was another matter. The Foreign Relations Committee then held two weeks of hearings. Dr. Edward Teller, who was in close touch with elements of the far Right, was an especially vigorous opponent. Teller testified by calling it "a step away from safety and possibly . . . toward war," and also sent scores of letters to various members of Congress. "We may now be involved in another move which will make [the American disadvantage] permanent and which in the field of missile defense may give added opportunity to the Russians."[57] Teller's position was strongly backed by leading individual and organizational spokesmen for the military, including former chiefs of staff Arleigh Burke, Arthur Radford, and Nathan Twining. Their ranks included defense contractors.[58] "The right-wing crowd has really been moving into gear on the Test Ban Treaty," Hubert Humphrey's administrative assistant wrote to Ken O'Donnell. "Fulton Lewis, Jr., has had two or three major newscasts. H. L. Hunt has made a large amount of money available to the campaign."[59]

Meanwhile Kennedy worked behind the scenes to mobilize support, laboring to focus pressures on Capitol Hill through the formation of a bipartisan group that called itself the Citizens Committee for a Nuclear Test Ban.[60] Finally the Foreign Relations Committee reported out the treaty in early September, and then it received a big boost on the Senate floor from Republican Minority Leader Everett Dirksen, which helped turn the tide. Still, attempts were made to scuttle the ban by the old ploy of adding crippling amendments. One that was introduced by Barry Goldwater sought to condition its ratification on a complete UN-inspected Soviet withdrawal from Cuba. The final vote, however, on September 24, was a one-sided eighty to nineteen, well above the required two-thirds majority. Of the nineteen dissenters, ten were from the South.[61]

Several developments had occured to make the treaty possible. A key change was a shift of public opinion. By September, polls were showing popular approval reaching the eighty percent level, a development not unrelated to the twin impact of the President's American University speech and the publicity being given to the fallout peril.[62] Somewhat to his surprise Kennedy discovered that for himself on the day after the Senate had acted. He was on the western speechmaking swing that had begun the day before at the Pinchot estate in Pennsylvania. That Wednesday he spoke at the Yellowstone County Fairgrounds at Billings, Montana, and included in his remarks satisfaction over the news from Washington. He thanked the two Montana senators, Mike Mansfield and Lee Metcalf, and paid tribute to the "able support" given by Ev Dirksen. His remarks were greeted with cheers and applause.[63] For the rest of that trip, in Great Falls, at the electric generating plant in Hanford, Washington, the Mormon Tabernacle in Salt Lake City, he endorsed the treaty with pride.

Nevertheless Kennedy was attacked by those who felt that it did not go far enough. It had made too many concessions to hard-liners.[64] Especially disliked was the continuation of underground testing, and that was suspected by some critics as a way for the United States to surreptitiously gain an advantage. The President had nevertheless moved from the edge of disaster to a first step in the process of rationalizing both the cold war and the nuclear threat. He had had to accommodate himself to the Joint Chiefs, whose support was grudging at best, and to all those ready to accuse him of trusting the Russians too much. Few first steps ever take one all the way home. Justifiably, no other accomplishment ever gave him greater satisfaction.[65]

The Congo also became the immediate object of Kennedy's attention right after the missile crisis. Kennedy's Congo policy had run afoul of America's NATO allies, caused dissension within the State Department, and provoked the hostility of certain American conservatives who viewed Tshombe's "break-away" province in almost romantic terms. They could sympathize with his resistance to central government authority, or to surrendering control over the mineral riches of Katanga to the legatees of the dead Lumumba, who had been killed before the CIA could quite accomplish the job themselves. They also saw Tshombe as the best hope for a strong economic and political pro-Western bastion in Africa. There could also be no fear of his slipping into the Communist bloc. George Ball, who emerged as the State Department's chief Congo strategist, described a potentially independent Katanga as "a kind of enclave of colonialism, dominated and financed by white elements" that had no character as a political entity.[66] The more Kennedy pursued his policy, the greater his support for UN efforts to restore order, the firmer became the opposition both in America and Europe.

Kennedy's course in dealing with that troubled newly independent nation resembled many of his other responses. He zigzagged, perhaps bending to the political resistance in and out of Congress, and didn't always have sufficient clarity about how he hoped to achieve his goal. Still his basic assumptions never changed. Supporting the central government in Leopoldville against its various rivals was an opportunity for the United States to pursue an African policy that appealed to the anticolonialists. While the momentary threat of Soviet influence in the area was undoubtedly exaggerated, failure to bring Katanga into line would concede victory to the copper-mining interests and their mercenaries. They would run Tshombe as a neocolonialist agent, and that in the long run risked creating an opening for Soviet exploitation of "Western imperialism." In the aftermath of the chaos left by the Lumumba murder Kennedy and the UN worked to prop up the government of Cyrille Adoula. Adoula was a forty-year-old labor leader who had little going for him except his intelligence, evident competence, and—of appeal to Kennedy—some familiarity with American history. He had no regional or tribal backing and lacked faithful followers. His only real power—the force that got him elected and supplied the necessary apparatus to keep him in power—was the CIA.[67]

The American intelligence establishment centered in Leopoldville was another thing Kennedy had to deal with. Under CIA Station Chief Lawrence Devlin, they were a formidable government in their own right. Their "Binza boys," named after a suburb of Leopoldville, constituted the corps of Congolese who had disposed of Lumumba. As Richard Mahoney has observed in his careful study of the situation, "To dislodge or dispossess the Binza boys would have been extremely difficult and would have involved a struggle not only in Leopoldville but in Washington as well," and that was something Kennedy would not do.[68]

Opposed to backing the central government were a number of right-wing groups in America. Pro-Katangese lobbying in the U.S. was powerful and well financed. Marvin Leibman, who had organized the Committee of One Million for the China Lobby in behalf of Chiang Kai-shek, shrewdly equated Tshombe and his followers with the recent Hungarian resisters to Soviet rule by setting up an organization called the American

Committee for Aid to Katanga Freedom Fighters.[69] Even more important was Michael Struelens, a Belgian who organized a well-financed and highly effective pro-Katanga lobby. At one point Struelens ran a full-page ad in *The New York Times* that proclaimed Katanga as "the Hungary of 1961." Struelens's money also helped win the active support of Senator Thomas Dodd. The Connecticut Democrat, who has been described as a "Spellmanite type of Irish politician"—one more like Joe Kennedy than Jack Kennedy—was the subject of the President's comment that the "highest-paid white mercenary of all was not in Katanga but right here in Washington as a ranking member of his own party."[70] Dodd was too important on Capitol Hill for the Justice Department to give him any trouble; besides, doing so would only galvanize conservative opposition to the administration. Such others on the Right as William F. Buckley, Jr., Richard Nixon, Barry Goldwater, and the John Birch Society also took up Tshombe's cause.

So did Arthur Krock. The former Kennedy family intimate supported Dodd's attempt to have Tshombe come to the U.S. so that he could testify before the senator's committee. Kennedy held fast against granting a visa. When Krock then accused the administration of denying Tshombe his right to be heard, Kennedy countered with a proposal. Since Krock belonged to the all-white Metropolitan Club in Washington, Kennedy jocularly suggested that "I'll give Tshombe a visa and Arthur can give him dinner at the Metropolitan Club."[71] Kennedy eventually confronted Dodd with the administration's knowledge of the financial ties with Struelens, but that was part of an attempt to neutralize the senator rather than to prosecute.[72]

Supported most firmly by his ambassador to Leopoldville, Edmund Gullion, Kennedy never departed from the essential objective of getting Katanga to reintegrate itself with the central government. Their additional influence would also help safeguard whatever inclination Leopoldville might have toward the Communist bloc. All of this meant American support for the UN's peacekeeping effort, first under Secretary-General Dag Hammarskjöld, and then, after his death in a plane crash, under his successor, U Thant. It was, as Mahoney has written, "the most sustained and exacting effort by an American administration to foster peaceful change in the African environment," but as the UN effort became more active in its attempt to subdue Katanga, the international organization came under fire for having exceeded its peacemaking mandate. Kennedy persisted, however, through months of attempts to bring the major rivals together, in his policy of trying to identify the U.S. with the nonaligned powers. All of this ran contrary to Soviet aims of keeping Africa an area of turmoil and a source of potential danger.[73]

By the time the missile crisis had ended, Kennedy realized that something had to be done quickly. An attempt to bring Adoula and Tshombe together in late 1961 had ended on a reneging of the agreement on the part of the Katangan leader. There was also fear that Adoula himself would not last much longer. At Dodd's request Kennedy sent Undersecretary of State for Political Affairs George McGhee to the scene to counterbalance Gullion's more determined anti-Katanga position. In August of 1962, after further Tshombe–Adoula talks broke down, U Thant sponsored a "Plan of National Reconciliation" that provided for a federal constitution for the Congo. But that, too, was evidence of UN actions for Washington's desires. U Thant's association with the plan was only nominal. McGhee himself later said that the "actual plan was largely worked on in the [State] Department, quite a lot in my office, with representatives of the French and British and the Belgian governments present."[74] At the end of October, McGhee reported back to the President in the White House.

Adoula's position was more precarious than ever. His government was relying on the UN to compel Tshombe to follow the reconciliation plan, but Tshombe only delayed and continued to resist. Meanwhile the UN's own military forces, largely manned by Indian contingents and officers, needed bolstering. Kennedy then directed that more assistance be given to the Congolese army through air transportation. He also approved a contingent plan for training their forces and making more equipment available.[75] In mid-December, General LeMay reported for the Joint Chiefs and recommended that the U.S. implement a military assistance program to revitalize the UN's political and military efforts. Since the existence of a pro-Western regime continued to be jeopardized by failure to solve the Katanga problem, the American role should be to furnish whatever forces were required to tip the balance of power decisively in favor of the UN forces.[76] At the same time, CIA alerts from Leopoldville warned that withdrawing those UN forces would only open the way for political exploitation by African radicals.[77] At an NSC meeting on December 17 Kennedy authorized informing U Thant that the United States was ready to supply additional airplanes and equipment. The President also emphasized that Tshombe's ability to hold out against a new UN effort, even though reinforced by an American air squadron, would raise the possibility of further actions in view of the requested military appraisal.[78]

Meanwhile Kennedy sent an eight-man military mission to Leopoldville to assess the UN's needs.[79] But Kennedy soon heard that Tshombe was raising new conditions and Adoula and the UN were refusing to talk to him. From the American point of view, George Ball was advised, it was worth "taking large risks to settle the situation in an acceptable manner in the next two weeks." Tshombe should be left without any doubt that his failure to negotiate would be followed by the UN's resumption of war "with all-out U.S. support."[80]

Kennedy then moved to resolve as cleanly as possible a situation that had threatened to become another Laos or South Vietnam. In January, UN forces, led by two Indian generals and fully equipped militarily by the U.S., advanced on the Katangan city of Kolwezi. The Indians had proceeded on their own timetable in the invasion of Katanga and had already crossed a key river. They pressed on, and resistance evaporated. From that point, with reconciliation a hopeless prospect and backed by the Kennedy administration, they marched into Kolwezi in late January and ended Katangese resistance. The troops were personally greeted by Tshombe, and two and a half years of attempted suppression had finally been completed.[81] "Now that the UN Forces have occupied Kolwezi," Kennedy wrote to McGhee on January 21, "and Katangese secession is over, I think a little sense of pride in our achievement in the Congo so far is in order, even though there is still hard work to be done."[82]

"President Kennedy could have stopped it," Gullion said in a 1964 interview. "I think that the decisive thing . . . is the role not merely of abstaining from condemning the UN during its period of operation but the fact that they were actively sustained. The statements from the White House at that time, on which the President must have been consulted, were in that sense deploring fighting but supporting the UN."[83] Sixteen years later Gullion added that "Kennedy, I think, risked a great deal in backing this operation, backing this whole thing. I don't know to what degree he shared the trepidations of the State Department about the excessive use of force by the UN. Obviously he wanted this success to be got as cheaply as possible—by diplomatic means, if possible; if it came to force, by the least effusion of blood."[84]

The final irony, of course, was that Adoula's regime continued to be shaky throughout 1963, posing additional problems for Kennedy, and the following year Tshombe returned in triumph as prime minister not of Katanga but of all of the Congo. He didn't last long, but his subsequent exile was sweetened by his possession of considerable wealth.[85] For the Kennedy administration, however, a solution had been found, and one that had the additional virtue of representing successful enforcement of UN authority. The exercise of power, nevertheless, including the way the international organization had been used, raised troubling questions about cold-war policies.

Kennedy's final June was memorable. On the tenth he had spoken at American University and announced the forthcoming nuclear test ban talks, and only one day later the cause of human rights got his full endorsement in a dramatic speech to the nation. Eleven days later, on Saturday, June 22, he met with Dr. King and the large contingent of civil rights leaders. That same evening the President left for Andrews Air Force Base to begin his flight to West Germany, the start of a crowded, ten-day European trip.

The timing could not have been better: Kennedy was the hero of the missile crisis, the champion of equality at home, and the foremost world leader in the service of democracy, the containment of communism, and —with the new hope for doing something about the nuclear specter— the goal of world peace. From the Russian side, too, tensions seemed reduced. The President's briefing book advised that Khrushchev's current concern was that East Germany, with its escape routes sealed off, should now concentrate on internal stabilization. No challenges were expected from Moscow in the near future.[86]

The President made the trip without Jackie, who was entering the seventh month of pregnancy. For the most part he was accompanied by Rusk, Bundy, Sorensen, Salinger, Powers, and O'Donnell. In West Germany, Ireland, Great Britain, and Italy, of course, there were the American ambassadors and local officials. But the outstanding quality about those ten days was the overwhelming way that the President was received. It was as though he was a new prince of peace and freedom.

That was certainly true in West Germany. He arrived in Bonn on Sunday and was greeted at Wahn Airport by Chancellor Adenauer. That morning, Kennedy attended mass at the famed Cologne Cathedral, which was surrounded by an enormous crowd of Germans waving tiny American flags. As he proceeded during the next few days, accompanied by George McGhee (whose Congo mission had been followed by an ambassadorship to Germany), the crowds became even larger and more enthusiastic. At a news conference he held in Bonn late Monday afternoon, a reporter called attention to the different tone of remarks made by Kennedy and the chancellor. Adenauer "seemed to be concerned mostly with your concern to defend Europe, while you were concerned with new approaches or approaches to a new peace. Has this difference manifested itself in your private talks with the chancellor?" he was asked. Of course not, said Kennedy. Adenauer was only quoting from the American University speech. Their objectives had no major differences. German desires for reunification were like those expressed by any divided country. But, he added, "there is no immediate solution." Aside from questions of relevance to the German Federal Republic and NATO, reporters kept returning to questions that related to the American University speech.[87]

When Kennedy reached West Berlin on Wednesday, he was hailed as a savior of Germany. No conquering hero had ever received a more enthusiastic reception. He toured much of the city that morning, the cheering crowds lining his route. There were estimates that claimed that perhaps half of the city's two and a third million people saw him that day, and that may well not be an exaggeration.[88] What he heard and what he saw undoubtedly made an enormous impact on him emotionally. From Checkpoint Charlie after leaving the Brandenburg Gate, he looked across the barrier into East Berlin and surveyed the great contrast between the democratic and the Communist sectors of the city. That undoubtedly contributed to his high point of emotion at the Rudolph Wilde Platz outside the Shöneberger Rathaus, West Berlin's city hall. Here was Kennedy the politician, telling the crowd what it wanted to hear, almost as though he were campaigning for reelection, and being swept along with the enthusiasm. His remarks were so intemperate that, as O'Donnell and Powers have written, they risked undoing "all of the success of his appeal for peace and understanding with the Soviets . . ."[89]

He combined both defiance and appeal to pride. "Two thousand years ago the proudest boast was 'civis Romanus sum,' " he said right after his introductory comments. "Today, in the world of freedom, the proudest boast is 'Ich bin ein Berliner.' " Then came the rhetorical challenge: "There are some who say that communism is the wave of the future. Let them come to Berlin. And there are some who say in Europe and elsewhere we can work with the Communists. Let them come to Berlin." He went on to tell them that they lived "in a defended island of freedom, but your life is part of the main," and, at the conclusion, declared that "All free men, wherever they may live, are citizens of Berlin, and, therefore, as a free man, I take pride in the words 'Ich bin ein Berliner.' "[90] An official of the German government said afterward that no Berlin crowd had ever responded as warmly and as emotionally as they did to Kennedy that day, not even to Hitler at the height of his power.[91] He had indeed come perilously close to a complete contradiction of his own movement toward détente. The heart had obviously turned the head.

Nor was the rest of the journey much less emotional or sentimental. He went on to Ireland. He visited New Ross and spoke at the quay from which his great-grandfather, Patrick Kennedy, had sailed to America more than a century earlier. If he had not left New Ross, Kennedy told them, "I would be working today over there at the Albatross Company," and he pointed at a fertilizer plant across the river.[92] That afternoon everybody who claimed some connection with the Kennedy clan rushed to meet the President at the old homestead near Dunganstown. A much more poignant moment came on Saturday, in England, before he dined with the Prime Minister and his wife at the Macmillan country home, Birch Grove. At the Chatsworth estate of the Duke and Duchess of Devonshire, the President paid his only visit to the grave of his sister Kathleen. She had been married to the duke's older brother, Billy Hartington, and her death in an airplane crash in 1948 came only four years after Billy was killed in the war. Jack and Kathleen had been very close, especially during their months together in Washington before she went off to Europe. He kneeled and prayed. His sister Jean then placed a fresh bouquet of red and white roses beside the headstone, which was inscribed: "Joy she gave—Joy she has found."[93]

From England, Kennedy went to Italy, landing at Milan's Malpensa Airport, and spending some time there before going on to Rome so that the new pope, Paul VI, could be coronated. Pope John XXIII had died on June 3. When Kennedy was received by the new pope on Thursday morning, he did not kneel before the pontiff and kiss his ring. "Norman Vincent Peale would love that," he told Ken O'Donnell. "And it would get me a lot of votes in South Carolina."[94] Kennedy, of course, had not even undergone that ritual before Cardinal Cushing; now he had a better excuse: He was there as a head of state and not as a visiting Roman Catholic. Nothing, however, matched the excitement and enthusiasm shown when he reached Naples that same afternoon, the final day of the trip. The uproar was spontaneous and frenzied. Crowds rushed into the path of the President's car, screaming, swarming all over. It was the noisiest demonstration of the entire European tour. Naples was also the poorest city he visited. By the time that day was over and Kennedy and his party were airborne toward Washington, it was also obvious that no President since Wilson and FDR had so touched the European people.

14

"Twilight"

The presidential summer retreat that year was not at Hyannis Port but at the nearby Squaw Island cottage that he rented from his father's friend Morton Downey, the tenor. There, just a few miles to the west of the family compound, was the possibility of more seclusion for himself, Jackie, and the children.

While Jackie was there, she had to be rushed to the nearby Otis Air Force Base Hospital for an emergency cesarean operation. The President heard the news while meeting with his Citizens Committee for a Nuclear Test Ban. By the time his plane landed at Otis at 1:30 that afternoon, their baby had already arrived. Five weeks premature and weighing just four pounds, ten and a half ounces, he had to struggle against a burden not uncommon among infants born so early, hyaline membrane disease. A coating of the air sacs was making breathing so difficult that although he seemed to be doing well at first, emergency assistance soon became necessary. He was rushed from Otis to the Children's Hospital Medical Center in Boston and placed in a chamber where oxygen was administered under pressure. But the infant, who was baptized as Patrick Bouvier Kennedy before leaving Otis, still couldn't overcome the condition. At 4:04 A.M. on August 9, just thirty-nine hours after his birth, his heart gave out under the strain.

The President was with his wife almost constantly during those hours. After the death he stayed at Squaw Island with Caroline and little John until their mother returned from the hospital. Patrick was originally buried near the President's birthplace, at Holyhood Cemetery in Brookline. O'Donnell and Powers have written that "The loss of Patrick affected the President and Jackie more deeply than anybody except their closest friends realized."[1]

By the late afternoon of Monday, August 12, the President was back in the Oval Office for a meeting on the situation in the Far East. With the ratification of the test ban treaty at the center of his attention, and with Cuba remaining as a potentially vulnerable spot politically, there were new dangers to his position emanating from deteriorating conditions in South Vietnam. After a long period of relative stability, one in which Kennedy had been able to maneuver between those advocating stronger American commitments to the government in Saigon and others, such as Averell Harriman and Chester Bowles, who had opposed any major involvement, the "limited partnership" with Diem was becoming less tenable. North Vietnamese support for the Vietcong had been stepping up. By the end of 1962 there was a tenfold increase in the number of Americans killed and wounded over the previous year. In December, Mike Mansfield had gone there at the President's request and in effect confirmed what such American correspondents as David Halberstam and Neil Sheehan were filing from the war zone. Just as had the French, Mansfield warned, the United States was in danger of being sucked into a futile conflict. "It wasn't a pleasant picture I depicted for him," said the senator afterward.[2] Diem had resisted having American combat troops. He did not want the U.S. to take over his war and his country. Moreover, he continued to defy the Kennedy administration's insistence that he make internal reforms.

Kennedy's "limited partnership," as General Taylor called the enterprise, was characteristic of his approach. He increased the level of American "advisers," and the numbers of helicopters and other equipment. The CIA, under Station Chief John Richardson, worked actively to provide intelligence support. Diem meanwhile adopted the strategic-hamlet program of Sir Robert Thompson. Thompson, a British counterinsurgency expert, had experimented with the plan in Malaya and the Philippines. In South Vietnam, it was hoped, the guerrillas could in effect be starved out by preventing peasant villages from becoming sanctuaries, and that meant regrouping the villages into hamlets under the protection of the army with such barriers as moats and stake fences. At the same time, the number of Americans there under the Military Assistance and

Advisory Group headed by General Paul Harkins escalated to some eleven thousand by the end of 1962.[3]

Later on it would become almost inconceivable to realize that the Vietnamese situation did not capture major attention from the American press until after the start of 1963. Only then did stories from that part of Southeast Asia command steady front-page coverage. Nor was it at the center of the President's own interest. Such matters as the Congo, Berlin, and Cuba had taken far more of his time.

In December, in addition to the Mansfield trip and the gloomy dispatches about the Diem government's inability to make much progress, further discouragement came from a State Department intelligence report. There was, in short, little room for optimism. Instead of giving more emphasis to nonmilitary means of counterinsurgency, reorganizing his government, and sharing some of his authority, Diem was moving too slowly in that direction and relying too much on the strategic-hamlet program and military measures. The adjustments he had been tentatively making in response to Washington's pressures had slowed down the Vietcong somewhat, but neither had their forces weakened nor the "national liberation war" abated. The guerrilla force was estimated at about twenty-three thousand elite fighting personnel, in addition to another 100,000 irregulars and sympathizers. The enemy still controlled about one fifth of the villages, had varying degrees of influence among an additional forty-seven percent, and was thought to be dominant over some nine percent of the population. Furthermore, "Viet Cong influence has almost certainly improved in urban areas not only through subversion and terrorism but also because of its propaganda appeal to the increasingly frustrated non-Communist anti-Diem elements," reported Roger Hilsman in an intelligence memorandum to Dean Rusk.[4]

There was increasing internal discontent among important military and civilian officials, who were participating in plots to overthrow Diem. If the fight against the Communists should deteriorate much further, Hilsman also warned, a "coup could come at any time."[5] Diem himself had been responding by turning inward and relying more on his brother, Nhu. "The two men," George Herring has written, "personally controlled military operations in the field and directed the strategic hamlet program, and they brooked no interference from their American advisers."[6] Nhu's wife had become the government's chief spokesman. Her insensitivity to the Buddhist critics of the Catholic family oligarchy ruling the government gradually brought increasing unpopularity to the regime.

Kennedy meanwhile feared the consequences of negotiating an American way out. His position had not altered from the off-the-record press briefing he gave on August 30, 1961, in which he said, "It is probably true in hindsight that it was not wise to become involved in Laos, but how do we withdraw from South Korea, from Viet-Nam. I don't know where the non-essential areas are. I can't see how we can withdraw from South Korea, Turkey, Iran, Pakistan. Over-extended commitments is a phrase with a lot of appeal, including to some at Harvard."[7] Holding fast in each area had long since become a test of American credibility. To yield in one would mean signaling susceptibility to withdrawal everywhere. As late as September 9, 1963, he was asked by David Brinkley on an NBC television program whether he subscribed to the domino theory. "I believe it," he replied. "I think that the struggle is close enough. China is so large, looms so high just beyond the frontiers, that if South Viet-Nam went, it would not only give them an improved geographic position for a guerrilla assault on Malaya, but would also give the impression that the wave of the future in southeast Asia was China and the Communists. So I believe it."[8]

At the start of the year Roger Hilsman and Michael Forrestal went to Saigon for the President. Kennedy wanted still another view. This time he knew it would come from two critics of Diem. Considering their outlook, a glowing report would have relaxed him.

Forrestal and Hilsman had separate sessions with Diem and his brother. From Diem, Forrestal heard about the importance of strength rather than reforms for maintaining loyalty from the peasants. The long conversation left the American visitor convinced that the South Vietnamese president was not only immovable but had rationalized the rule exerted by his own family as one that was consistent with the family structure of the society itself. Forrestal left without many doubts that Diem was a serious obstruction to any kind of settlement. Hilsman himself was an experienced guerrilla fighter. During World War II he had served with the famed Merrill's Marauders in Asia and with the Office of Strategic Services. When he met with Diem's brother, he thought that Nhu had been on drugs. He seemed devious, unattractive, harsh, and very explicit about his own ambitions. He also boasted about his connections with the northerners and some of their leaders. His attitude toward the problem of relocating the peasants in the delta was far more brutal than Diem's. Nhu also supported the use of chemical warfare and defoliants. Both Americans, Hilsman explained afterward, discovered that the war was "a fraud, a sham. The American military are still chasing Viet Cong and advising the Vietnamese to chase Viet Cong. They're not adopting the program the President has recommended, our own military are not. Diem has turned the strategic hamlet-program over to Nhu, who's taken the title, the name of it, and nothing else. And in fact, what Diem signed, what we persuaded him to, had not been adopted."[9]

Their report was less critical than Mansfield's, but still disturbing. Conceding that some progress had been made over the past year, it pointed out that the negatives were still "awesome." Even the officially supplied figures were disturbing. Despite U.S. urgings, it said, "there is still no single country-wide plan worthy of the name but only a variety of regional and provincial plans," and they seemed to be "both inconsistent and competitive." The strategic-hamlet program was mostly a sham, "inadequately equipped and defended," or "built prematurely in exposed areas." But the real question Forrestal and Hilsman raised was "whether the concentration of power in the hands of Diem and his family, especially Brother Nhu and his wife, and Diem's reluctance to delegate is alienating the middle and higher level officials on whom the government must depend to carry out its policies." The government had to be pushed harder for an overall plan.[10]

Meanwhile the Joint Chiefs of Staff came up with a plan for the possible withdrawal of American advisers starting in late 1963 and ending in 1965.[11] It was, however, one plan among many, and Kennedy's own reevaluation of the situation offered little evidence for believing that he was ready to negotiate and begin pulling out. He knew that falling back would leave him wide open to American conservatives. "If I tried to pull out completely now from Vietnam," he explained to Mansfield, "we would have another Joe McCarthy red scare on our hands, but I can do it after I'm reelected. So we had better make damned sure that I *am* reelected."[12]

Then came a sharp setback, an entirely new phase, and the upgrading of the war on the President's list of priorities. On May 8 a crowd gathered in Hué to celebrate the anniversary of Buddha's birth was fired into by government troops. Protesting against religious persecution and demanding a reversal of such policies, Buddhist priests went on hunger strikes. Far more startling to the world was the subsequent photograph of a monk seated in the middle of a downtown Saigon street totally enveloped in flames. That picture of his self-immolation in protest against the government became the most graphic evidence of the dissension. It was only the first in a series of such suicides and helped raise new questions about the entire American commitment.[13]

The division within Kennedy's administration was centered around whether or not support for Diem should be withdrawn. Those who argued against undermining the regime held that there was no adequate replacement in sight. Meanwhile Kennedy had sent several emissaries to Saigon to try to get Diem and the Buddhists together, but each side was immovable. When Ambassador Frederick Nolting's tour of duty expired that summer, the President replaced him by sending Henry Cabot Lodge, Jr., to Saigon.

Why Lodge? He spoke French, he had had experience in international affairs as Eisenhower's representative to the United Nations, but most of all, as Dean Rusk's biographer explains, Kennedy was persuaded by his secretary of state that "Lodge was to the Republican Party of 1963 what Dulles had been in 1950: the personification of its liberal internationalist wing. . . . Rusk sought to coopt part of the Republican Party, to outmaneuver . . . Goldwater . . ."[14]

Actually the Lodge appointment was entirely consistent with Kennedy's placement of people like John McCloy and John McCone in positions of potential partisan conflict. In his 1964 interview Bob Kennedy explained that "Lodge was interested in going someplace where there was a difficult problem, they needed somebody who would work with the military, spoke French, had some diplomatic experiences. So he fitted into it."[15]

The most intriguing possibility eventually raised is that Lodge was sent to effectuate the overthrow of Diem by working with the generals who hoped to bring about a coup.[16] Lodge has explained that Kennedy was very much disturbed by the picture of the monk on fire. He talked about the overall reportage of what was going on in Saigon and said that the Diem government was entering a terminal phase. The American embassy had also had poor press relations. "I suppose that there are worse press relations to be found in the world today," Lodge remembered that the President told him, "and I wish you would take charge of press relations." As far as helping to overthrow Diem, Kennedy said that the "Vietnamese are doing that for themselves and don't need any outside help."[17]

Almost immediately after that, Diem helped to speed his own downfall. Just before Lodge's arrival, in complete contradiction of a promise made to Ambassador Nolting, Nhu's American-trained Special Forces went on a rampage against Buddhist pagodas in Hué, Saigon, and other cities. More than fourteen hundred Buddhists were arrested. Right after that American intelligence also reported that Diem was actively engaged in trying to work out a deal with the Hanoi regime of North Vietnam.[18]

If Lodge had been sent with an understanding that he might have to support the generals wanting to get rid of Diem, his actions appeared to confirm that purpose. He showed as little outward support toward the South Vietnamese president as possible, disassociating himself almost completely.[19] On August 24, with Kennedy at Hyannis Port and, "by a strange coincidence, most of the other senior members of the administration" out of town for the weekend, word arrived that South Vietnamese generals knew that Ngo Dinh Nhu was negotiating with the Communists. The information was relayed to Washington via long-distance telephone by Admiral Harry Felt.[20]

Quickly on that Saturday, after a series of consultations and telephone calls—including to the President, Forrestal, and Hilsman—Harriman sent a cable to Lodge in the name of the State Department. Its message was clear: The U.S. could no longer tolerate a situation where power remained in Nhu's hands. "We wish to give Diem reasonable opportunity to remove Nhus, but if he remains obdurate, then we are prepared to accept the obvious implication that we can no longer support Diem. You may also tell appropriate military commanders we will give them direct support in any interim period of breakdown central government mechanism." Lodge cabled back that it was most unlikely that Diem would get rid of both his brother and sister-in-law and that Nhu was in control of the combat forces in Saigon. "Therefore," he replied, "propose we go straight to Generals with our demands, without informing Diem. Would tell them we prepared to have Diem without Nhus but it is in effect up to them whether to keep him."[21]

For a time it almost seemed that it was the American State Department, in the absence of Dean Rusk, Robert McNamara, John McCone, or McGeorge Bundy, that had undertaken its own coup against those who continued to believe that there was little choice but to back Diem. General Maxwell Taylor first heard about the cable when Ros Gilpatric called him that evening at Fort Myer with the information that clearance from the President had already been obtained and that, in Rusk's absence, George Ball had consented while playing golf. Gilpatric has since observed that "I frankly thought it was an end run. I didn't see why it had to be done Saturday night with the President away, with Rusk away, with McNamara away, Bundy away. I was suspicious of the circumstances in which it was being done. . . . In other words the Defense and military were brought in sort of after the fact."[22] To General Taylor it seemed somewhat of a *fait accompli.* Even if Diem wanted to comply, the telegram to Lodge was obviously an open encouragement "to plotters to move against him at any time."[23]

Mike Forrestal agrees that the circumstances indeed were suspicious.

Harriman had originated the cable. The senior diplomat, by then under-secretary of state for political affairs, wanted to take advantage of the weekend conditions because he knew how much trouble he would have getting support if everybody were present.[24] Still, the most important—and often the least noticed element—was the endorsement that came from the President himself, not at the center of action in the Oval Office, but at the other end of a wire in Hyannis Port.

But there was no immediate result. The cable had advised the Voice of America radio people to publicize only that part of the message that would prevent the Vietnamese army from being associated with any plot. Hilsman tried to work that out by briefing a news correspondent so the information could be fed to the Voice, thereby maintaining the usual procedure according to which the propaganda network operated. But the people who actually made the broadcast failed to check their instructions with a telegram sent to guide them. The entire story then went out on the airwaves, "not only," as Hilsman wrote, "that the United States had proof that the Vietnamese Army was innocent of the assault on the pagodas and that Nhu's secret police and Special Forces were to blame," but about the threatened sharp American reduction of aid to Diem.[25]

At a meeting in the embassy in Saigon, Lodge was furious. "Jack Kennedy would never approve of doing things this way," he shouted. "This certainly isn't his way of running a government."[26]

When the President returned from the Cape and met with his staff that Monday, he found more opposition to the Harriman cable than he had evidently expected. "And so the government split in two," the attorney general later said. "It was the only time really, in three years, the government was broken in two in a very disturbing way."[27] In Saigon the generals were unable to get the backing of key army units and remained uncertain, despite CIA assurances, of what American intelligence would do, and withheld any actions.[28]

When the coup came, it resulted from the appropriate opening, which was a combination of the muffled hand from Washington and changed circumstances in Saigon. In the interim Kennedy's customary indecision made the entire process seem more diabolical than it was. First of all the failed move of August provided an opportunity to reassess the situation. At the end of the month Lodge cabled that there was "no turning back" from the overthrow. American prestige was already too committed.[29] Kennedy sent him a personal and private message that pledged his full support to enable his ambassador to "conclude this operation success-fully," and, with the clear memory of what happened at the Bay of Pigs, added, "I know from experience that failure is more destructive than an appearance of indecision."[30] On September 2, after De Gaulle had criticized the American involvement in Vietnam, Kennedy was interviewed by Walter Cronkite on a CBS television news program. At that point, in response to a question about Diem changing his pattern, the President answered in a manner that has too often been quoted incompletely. What he said at that point was: "We hope that he comes to see that, but in the final analysis it is the people and the government itself who have to win or lose this struggle. All we can do is help, and we are making it very clear, but I don't agree with those who say we should withdraw. That would be a great mistake."[31] It was not immediately evident that, in reality, he was talking just as much about the Vietnamese choice of a leader as about the American commitment. On the same day that he talked to Cronkite, Kennedy called Hilsman and asked whether his undersecretary of state had done any thinking about "selective cuts in aid that would not hurt the war effort but still make Diem and Nhu understand that we mean business."[32] Encouragement was also given to Senator Church's threat to introduce a resolution calling for the suspension of aid to South Vietnam unless it ended its repressive policies.[33] During this period, however, the President had no way of knowing that things in Saigon would be better without Diem. But his hand was being pushed. An Alsop story in *The Washington Post* on September 18, evidently based on interviews with Diem and Nhu, gave further information about their dealings with Hanoi.[34] Reacting to such stories, Kennedy sent McNamara and General Taylor to Saigon. Once again Diem was immovable, contending that the war was going well, pointing with pride to favorable results from just completed rigged elections, and, as McNamara wrote, offering "absolutely no assurances that he would take any steps in response to the representations made to American visitors. . . . His manner was one of at least outward serenity and of a man who had patiently explained a great deal and who hoped he had thus corrected a number of misapprehensions." The McNamara–Taylor report, however, cautioned that it was not the time to take the initiative in trying to change the government. "Our policy should be to seek urgently to identify and build contacts with an alternative leadership if and when it appears." Mainly the suggestion of the mission was to apply selective pressures on the regime.[35]

On October 2 the White House announced that a thousand men would be withdrawn by the end of the year. Gilpatric later stated that McNamara did indicate to him that the withdrawal was part of the President's plan to wind down the war, but, that was too far in the future.

They were still, at that moment, deeply divided about what to do about the internal situation in Saigon.³⁶ At just that point the recall of John Richardson, the CIA station chief who was close to the regime, seemed to be another signal, although it may not have been intended for that purpose.³⁷ Still, it is hard to believe that the move, along with the talk about reductions of American aid to the government, lacked the purpose of giving further encouragement to the anti-Diem generals.

During a series of meetings that were held from August 23 through October 23 between Lodge, General Harkins, and the anti-Diem plotters, including Duong Van Minh (Big Minh), there was agreement on what had to be done: The U.S. agreed that Nhu had to go and that the disposition of Diem ought to be left to the generals. There could be no American help to initiate the action, but support would come during the interim period in case of a breakdown of the central government's mechanism. What was also clear was that if they did not get rid of the Nhus and the Buddhist situation were not redressed, the United States would end economic and military support.³⁸

Lodge later reported that he had advised the President "not to thwart" a coup. That act, rather than initiating one, would have constituted interference.³⁹ Yet even at that point Kennedy wavered, suffering a recurrence of earlier doubts. He told Bundy that the U.S. should be in a position to blow the whistle if it looked as though the coup was failing.⁴⁰ Bundy cabled Lodge that there should be no American action that would reveal any knowledge that a coup was even possible. The "burden of proof" must be on the plotters "to show a substantial possibility of quick success; otherwise we should discourage them from proceeding since a miscalculation could result in jeopardizing U.S. position in Southeast Asia."⁴¹ Indeed, the Americans in Saigon behaved as though things were normal.

On the morning of November 1 Admiral Felt paid a courtesy call on Diem at the presidential palace. In the afternoon Diem called Lodge to ask about the American attitude toward the coup. Lodge was evasive, but admitted he was worried about Diem's personal safety. That night, the president and Nhu escaped from the palace to a hideout in the Chinese quarter of Saigon. From there Diem contacted the generals and asked for safe conduct back so he could make a graceful exit from power. On his return, however, according to a prearranged plan, he and his brother were shot and killed by Big Minh's personal bodyguard.⁴²

The news of Diem's death outraged Kennedy. General Taylor wrote that he "leaped to his feet and rushed from the room with a look of shock and dismay on his face which I had never seen before."⁴³ George Smathers remembered that Jack Kennedy blamed the CIA, saying "I've got to do something about those bastards"; they should be stripped of their exorbitant power.[44] Mike Forrestal called Kennedy's reaction "both personal and religious," and especially troubled by the implication that a Catholic President had participated in a plot to assassinate a coreligionist.[45] Every account of Kennedy's response is in complete agreement. Until the very end he had hoped Diem's life could be spared.

It has now become clear that however futile his efforts Kennedy tried to prevent the murder. He told Francis Cardinal Spellman that he had known in advance that the Vietnamese leader would probably be killed, but in the end he could not control the situation.[46] At least one attempt, and possibly three, came from a direct attempt to communicate with Diem by using a personal emissary, someone completely loyal to Jack Kennedy, someone totally without any other obligation, his intimate friend, Torby Macdonald, the Massachusetts congressman.

As far as is known, there are no written records. It was completely secret. Mike Forrestal remembers briefing Macdonald for the trip.[47] Torbert Macdonald, Jr., recalls that his father told him about it.[48] The congressman's widow is certain that he made at least three trips to Saigon for the President.[49] Torby's closest friend during his final years, who desires to remain anonymous, has a photograph of him posing before the ancient temple at Angkor-Wat in Cambodia, indicating that he went through that country while traveling to South Vietnam as a private citizen.[50]

Macdonald himself explained why Kennedy sent him. The President had begun to develop personal sources of information from FBI men who were bypassing J. Edgar Hoover and going directly to him. Some CIA people were following a similar route and avoiding the Agency. By that time the President was learning. When he first came into office, he had been intimidated by the Pentagon and the CIA, but he had begun to find out how to get around them. When he heard that Big Minh and his group were planning to assassinate Diem, he wanted to make a direct contact. He was hesitant about using the embassy in Saigon because he could not trust his own people there. Nor did he have enough confidence in Lodge, who had maintained a distant relationship with Diem. Finally, there was no South Vietnamese he could trust. So he called on Torby, who then carried the President's personal plea, which was to get rid of his brother and take refuge in the American embassy. As Macdonald later explained it, he told Diem: "They're going to kill you. You've got to get out of there temporarily to seek sanctuary in the American embassy and you must get rid of your sister-in-law and your brother." But Diem refused. "He just won't do it," Macdonald reported to the President. "He's too stubborn; just refuses to."[51]

Diem's death preceded Jack Kennedy's by just three weeks. What JFK would have done about American involvement in South Vietnam can never be known for certain. It is probable that not even he was sure.

Ken O'Donnell has been the most vigorous advocate of the argument that the President was planning to liquidate the American stake right after the completion of the 1964 elections would have made it politically possible. The withdrawal of those thousand advisers, he said, was but a first step in that process.[52] At the time the Joint Chiefs asked for an increase of American strength to seventeen thousand, Kennedy told his military aide, Ted Clifton, that he would go along with the request but had warned that he would approve no more.[53]

At that moment Kennedy could not have anticipated the shape of either the domestic political climate or the situation in Southeast Asia. Still, for him to have withdrawn at any point short of a clear-cut settlement would have been most unlikely. As Sorensen has said in an oral-history interview, Kennedy "did feel strongly that for better or worse, enthusiastic or unenthusiastic, we had to stay there until we left on terms other than a retreat or abandonment of our commitment."[54] The remarks he had planned to deliver at the Trade Mart in Dallas on the afternoon of November 22 contained the following statement of purpose: "Our assistance to these nations can be painful, risky and costly, as is true in Southeast Asia today. But we dare not weary of the test."[55] "I talked with him hundreds of times about Vietnam," said Dean Rusk, "and on no single occasion did he ever whisper any such thing to his own secretary of state." In addition, and what was more important, Rusk pointed out, was that a decision in 1963 to take troops out in 1965 following the election of 1964 "would have been a decision to have Americans in uniform in combat for domestic political reasons. No President can do that and live with it."[56] When Ken O'Donnell was pressed about whether the President's decision to withdraw meant that he would have undertaken the escalation that followed in 1965, the position became qualified. Kennedy, said O'Donnell, had not faced the same level of North Vietnamese infiltration as did President Johnson, thereby implying that he, too, would have responded in a similar way under those conditions.[57] As Bobby Kennedy later said, his brother had reached the point where he felt that South Vietnam was worth keeping for psychological and political reasons "more than anything else."[58]

The day Diem died, the President canceled his plan to fly to Chicago for the Army–Air Force football game. He spent the late afternoon going over the situation in Saigon with Secretary Rusk and his closest advisers from Defense, the military, and intelligence. Shortly after six he was airborne via helicopter and arrived at the new Kennedy country home in Atoka, Virginia, thirty-five minutes later.

Jackie and the children were already there, enjoying what was only their second weekend at the thirty-acre estate near Rattlesnake Mountain. Glen Ora had been abandoned because the lease had expired, and the new country home became mostly Jackie's. The President went there on some weekends starting in late October.[59]

There can be little doubt that the strains of their relationship were healed by the infant's death. At a party for their tenth anniversary on September 12, some of the change was visible. "This was the first time," Ben Bradlee noted, "we had seen Jackie since the death of little Patrick, and she greeted JFK with by far the most affectionate embrace we had ever seen them give each other. They are not normally demonstrative people, period."[60]

It is all too often true that healing is but momentary when basic differences remain. Among the more serious causes of their marital problems was her almost total isolation from his political existence. When, that fall, his schedule became frenetic once again, Jacqueline felt the burden of her isolation even more deeply with the memory of Patrick still so fresh in her mind. Political obligations were once again coming first.

There were presidential trips to various parts of the country. In late September he planned a western swing to boost conservation, but also to bolster loyal Democrats in the area. In Texas factional differences were also requiring presidential attention. Liberals there had only recently formed a coalition that included Mexican-Americans, blacks, and organized labor, while conservatives were veering toward Republicanism. Governor Connally's criticism of the administration's civil rights proposals was partly motivated by his efforts to keep the conservatives loyal. But the governor's positions were also being vehemently denounced by Ralph Yarborough, the state's liberal senator and political opponent of both Connally and LBJ.[61] Johnson had long since been arguing that the President had to go to Texas.

Fortunately his improved physical condition made the new burdens more tolerable. "He was in the best health since I had known him,"[62] Dr. Travell has recalled. His physique had shown a remarkable change from the sallow, sickly-looking young man. He never looked or felt better in his life. Dr. Kraus was making his White House visits at the rate of somewhat less than once a month. The President's experiences with illness had even encouraged his administration to spur a fitness program, which received much national publicity especially when fifty-mile hikes became somewhat of a rage in early 1963. Even when he had had his limitations, he had managed to do what was necessary, but at least he was in better shape for the new challenges.

And his schedule was correspondingly heavy. That was a period of endless meetings and consultations devoted to civil rights, the tax bill, ratification of the test ban treaty, and developments in Saigon. Before he went off on that western trip, when Mary Meyer made the first stop with him at the Pinchot estate, he had also delivered a major address before the Eighteenth General Assembly of the United Nations. The speech was a vigorous endorsement of his desire to "make the world safe for diversity," urging that "people must be free to choose their own future, without discrimination or dictation, without coercion or subversion," and it was received with enthusiasm by just about every delegation.[63]

Diversity, however, had also come closer to home. Four days after his UN appearance the public heard that Jacqueline had decided that she needed a change. She planned to accept an invitation from Greek shipping magnate, Aristotle Onassis, to travel aboard his yacht, the *Christina*. Onassis himself had made the suggestion to Jackie's sister, Princess Radziwill, who was with him in Athens when the baby died. Lee then telephoned the invitation to the First Lady.[64]

That gave the President a new set of political worries. However sympathetic the public might be to the grieving mother in need of a vacation, there were disturbing implications. The most obvious, of course, was knowledge that she was going off on a pleasure cruise for over two weeks without him, and leaving her two children behind. A potentially more serious concern was a conflict-of-interest implication. A man like Onassis not unnaturally had had many dealings with the government, both directly or through companies that he controlled. For some years the government had been trying to sue him for fraud in connection with using surplus American ships without paying taxes. His present hospitality could be interpreted as a form of bribery. Not long after Jackie returned, a Senate subcommittee heard testimony about the trouble a journalist had encountered when during her trip he tried to get data about federal payments to Onassis. The newspapers carried his explanation that the only reason he could offer for the obstruction was because "figures high in the Administration were accepting hospitality from Mr. Onassis."[65] Ultimately Onassis paid a seven-million-dollar fine instead of facing a court trial in the United States, but Jacqueline's new friend remained a questionable associate for a First Lady.[66]

Then, of course, there was the matter of how the public would react to her behavior. Jackie was the only unescorted woman aboard the *Christina*, and Onassis the only unescorted man.[67] Kennedy tried to ameliorate that somewhat by asking Franklin D. Roosevelt, Jr., and his wife to go along with them so the trip would have more "respectability."[68]

The voyage itself attracted close newspaper coverage in the United States. Much of it emphasized the luxurious world on the lavish yacht, with its sumptuous food and drink. Readers were able to follow her visits through the Aegean, where the vessel stopped at Lesbos, Crete, and the Ionian Sea island of Scorpios, which Onassis owned. She visited the temple of Apollo at Delphi, and then, with Lee Radziwill, was a guest of King Hassan II of Morocco and toured the market at Marrakech.[69]

As it turned out, JFK's worries were excessive. As one of her biographers has noted, "Jackie had become, to her public, just what her father had said she had been to him—'all things holy.' "[70] Still, Kennedy took no chances. When her plane arrived at Washington on October 17, unlike his previous practice when she returned from trips, he was at the airport with both children. They had a family reunion.[71]

Subsequent events that came after his death would, of course, tempt one to read too much into the trip. But the President, who had spent the two weekends of her absence with the children at Atoka (according to the White House appointment calendar), was clearly sensitive to the implications. Jacqueline's personal secretary, Mary Gallagher, has made much of clues she saw immediately afterward that a significant relationship had been established. There were exchanges of gifts and thank-you notes, but such courtesies were routine. In a more suggestive manner she also adds, "I recall that when she got back, she asked me to record Onassis's winter address in my address book—on avenue Foch in Paris —and also his address in Athens on Vasileous Georgious-Glyfada. I mailed a letter to his Athens address."[72]

While Jackie was gone, the President signed the nuclear test ban treaty. During the days after her return his paramount interest was in getting the civil rights proposals over the hurdles so it could come to a vote, which meant extricating it from the committees and then obtaining cloture to override the inevitable filibuster. It had long since become clear that little else of importance could move on Capitol Hill until southerners first had their chance to record their opposition. "After the civil rights vote they will be freer, having gotten their *agin* on the record," Bobby Kennedy was advised.[73]

The central figure on the Hill in all this was not a southerner at all, but, as Lyndon Johnson had advised, Ev Dirksen, the Republican minority leader. His influence was essential in order to line up enough Republican votes so that a filibuster could be stopped. Even before Kennedy's proposals had been received in the Senate, Mike Mansfield had begun negotiations with the Republican counterpart. A common front with the man from Illinois as its centerpiece was regarded as the key to cloture. On June 13 Dirksen agreed to cosponsor a bill with Mansfield that would include all Kennedy proposals except those relating to public accommodations.[74] Manny Celler's Judiciary Committee, meanwhile, was drafting a bill that went beyond the administration's requests, granting stronger enforcement provisions for the public accommodations section. They were so strong that, in two days of testimony in mid-October, the attorney general advised that they be toned down because they might not be wise legally or politically.[75]

Late in October the President visited his father's house at Hyannis Port. Then, as the Chief Executive got into the helicopter, preparing to leave with Dave Powers, the Ambassador sat on the porch in his wheelchair, as he always did, waiting for the departure of the whirlybird that carried his son. When they looked back at the crippled man, Powers saw tears in the President's eyes. "He's the one who made all this possible," Jack said, "and look at him now."[76] That was their last meeting.

By the time the President returned to Washington, plans had already been completed for the Texas trip. On Wednesday, October 23, Lyndon Johnson telephoned Governor Connally with the news and some of the details. The next day Adlai Stevenson reached Dallas to speak at the Sheraton-Dallas luncheon commemorating United Nations Day. Even before his arrival right-wing forces had been agitating. Their main event was a counter "celebration" called United States Day, and General Edwin A. Walker was the main speaker. Stevenson also found a mass of handbills with President Kennedy's photograph and the message: WANTED FOR TREASON. When the UN ambassador began to speak, some in the mob became incensed. One woman screamed, and two men spat in his face. Somebody else hit him on the head with a sign. Only intervention by the police got him out of there safely.[77] "Actually," Stevenson then wrote to his friend Agnes Meyer, "I never had a warmer or more enthusiastic reception anywhere, and the idiot fringe was small if vocal and violent." He added that U Thant had forwarded the assurance that "the United Nations has never had better advertising, especially in that opaque area where little light penetrates."[78]

Stevenson also wrote to Ken O'Donnell about the President's "gloomy conclusion that the idiot fringe is in fact 'winning their fight in Dallas.' On the contrary," he added, "my guess is that the President will have an enthusiastic and sincere reception."[79]

There was also more reassurance from Capitol Hill. On the twenty-ninth Celler's House committee approved their civil rights bill by a vote of 20–14, with all but one of the southerners going along. That Saturday, Nick Katzenbach was at the Army–Air Force football game in Chicago with Ev Dirksen. The Senate minority leader told the deputy attorney general that the civil rights bill would find its way out to the Senate floor, and that was good news. The President knew that Dirksen was a man who kept his word. Eighteen days later, on November 20, a bipartisan bill, which was stronger than the administration's earlier requests, was formally reported out, but Howard Smith's Rules Committee had yet to clear it for floor action. The next day, however, Dirksen said he expected that Congress would be ready to act in a few months.[80]

On the morning of Wednesday, November 20, Kennedy had breakfast with a group of legislators and members of his staff. He mentioned the forthcoming flight to Texas scheduled for the next day. Hale Boggs told him that he was about to go into "a hornet's nest." The President replied, "Well, that'll add interest."[81]

At 11:05 A.M., November 21, *Air Force One* took off in the direction of San Antonio. Jackie was also on board. Whatever else those Texans might have to say about their President, they would at least see for themselves that he was a family man. "In San Antonio," John Connally later testified, "she was rather stiff, I thought, rather unused to this. She had not been traveling much and campaigning much with the President and she was not noticeably ill at ease at all, but nevertheless, reserved, quiet and perhaps a little bit . . . apprehensive about this whole thing. . . . Not apprehensive in the sense of being fearful of violence, but just not being used to it."[82]

San Antonio gave them a spectacular turnout. Crowds containing large numbers of Mexican-Americans cheered, jumped, and waved placards at the President and the First Lady. JACKIE, COME WATERSKI IN TEXAS! urged one, and others offered more of a regional flavor with such hand-lettered messages as BIENVENIDO, MR. PRESIDENT. Everywhere the motorcade went, as the President sat in the Commander in Chief's seat at the right rear of the limousine and his wife to his left, there were more signs, more enthusiasm. WELCOME, JFK could have been the title of the occasion. And, of course, in a car behind them Congressman Henry Gonzalez, the city's favorite Texan, shared some of the glory with the visiting President. The presidential motorcade also visited the new Aero-Space Medical Health Center at the nearby air base, which Kennedy then dedicated with a tribute to the scientific breakthroughs bound to result from medical space research.[83]

At 3:23 the presidential motorcade went to Kelly Air Force Base. Lyndon Johnson and Lady Bird made the trip in a separate limousine with Governor and Mrs. Connally, and then they flew in *Air Force Two* to Houston, where they landed first so they could join the reception committee welcoming the First Family. The motorcade then regrouped. Now it was Congressman Albert Thomas's turn to share the spotlight with the President. At 4:50 the caravan reached the Rice Hotel.

The President and his wife made an unscheduled visit at the Rice to a meeting of the League of United Latin American Citizens. His brief comments were almost entirely devoted to associating what he was trying to accomplish through the Alliance for Progress with FDR's Good Neighbor Program of the 1930's. Jacqueline, however, now warming to the trip and encouraged by the enthusiasm, took advantage of the opportunity to offer a few comments in Spanish, stumbling only slightly.[84]

At the same hotel that evening the President attended a testimonial dinner for Congressman Thomas. The Democrat, who had been in the House since 1937, was regarded as one of the more powerful figures on Capitol Hill, and the President lauded him as one of the "most remarkable members of Congress." Thomas's most notable recent accomplishment was having Houston become the headquarters for the new space center that would engineer the moon-exploration program.

When the dinner was over, the Kennedys flew to Carswell Air Force Base at Fort Worth, and arrived at their suite in the Texas Hotel shortly after 11:30 P.M. It rained the next morning, but a crowd had assembled across the street from the hotel, and Kennedy went across the street in good campaign fashion. When they expressed disappointment at the absence of the First Lady from his side, he explained that "Mrs. Kennedy is organizing herself. It takes longer, but, of course, she looks better than we do when she does it."[85] At a breakfast in the Texas Hotel of the Fort Worth Chamber of Commerce, the President began his remarks by saying, "Two years ago, I introduced myself in Paris by saying that I was the man who had accompanied Mrs. Kennedy to Paris. I am getting somewhat that same sensation as I travel around Texas. Nobody wonders what Lyndon and I wear."

His more serious remarks reminded the businessmen what the administration had been doing for them, Fort Worth, and the defense of the United States. General Dynamics, located in their city, would soon be producing the new tactical fighter experimental (TFX) plane, for which the Australian government had already placed $125 million worth of orders. "In all of these ways," he told the breakfast gathering, "the success of our national defense depends upon this city in the western United States, 10,000 miles from Viet-Nam, 5,000 or 6,000 miles from Berlin, thousands of miles from trouble spots in Latin America and Africa or the Middle East." He reminded them that Texas was fifth among the states in total dollars' worth of military procurement, with a value of nearly $1.25 billion. Furthermore his administration had increased the U.S. defense budget by over twenty percent during the past three years. They enjoyed what they heard. He didn't sound radical at all.[86]

The next stop that morning was nearby Dallas, where he was scheduled to cultivate that city's business establishment at the Trade Mart. Before leaving Fort Worth, he said he wanted to have the limousine's bubble-top removed if the weather cleared.

Motorcades were useful for getting close to the people, and riding in an open car would do much to make the most out of that opportunity. From the outset of planning for the trip, Dallas had been regarded as the most important stop. The city was the state's most important commercial center and the heart of Texas power.

Texas was increasingly hostile toward the administration. From 1961 through 1962, thirty-four threats on Kennedy's life had been compiled by the Secret Service from that state alone.[87] The center of the Lone Star State's extremism was also thought to be in Dallas. That was the city where Lyndon Johnson had been attacked by a fierce crowd during the 1960 campaign, and Adlai Stevenson had been a victim only a few weeks earlier. Not only right-wingers constituted the threat and made the atmosphere foreboding, but the Secret Service had also identified as potentially dangerous several other categories: the far Left, anti-Castro Cubans, Puerto Rican nationalists, black militants, as well as the usual assortment of those who were recognized as mentally disturbed. Still, no extensive investigation had ever been done in Dallas, and both Miami and Chicago were considered potentially more dangerous places for a presidential visit.[88]

During the days before Kennedy's arrival, the militants of the Right had begun to flood the city with hate posters and leaflets. On that Friday morning, The Dallas News carried a full-page advertisement sponsored by "America-Thinking Citizens of Dallas." Kennedy and his administration were charged with ignoring the Constitution, scrapping the Monroe

Doctrine in favor of the "Spirit of Moscow," and being "soft" on Communists, fellow-travelers, and ultra-leftists.[89]

Still, the trip could hardly have been avoided. The assumed most likely complication would come from unruly mobs, and there would be embarrassing heckling and ugly signs, little that the Secret Service would be unable to handle in their primary function of protecting the President. Moreover, it was 1963. Teddy Roosevelt had been wounded by a bullet during his Bull Moose campaign. FDR was almost hit in 1932 by a bullet that killed Mayor Anton Cermak of Chicago, and Harry Truman's temporary residence at Blair House once became the target of Puerto Rican nationalists but no President had been killed since McKinley in 1901. There was no way Kennedy could preserve his political credibility by avoiding a state with twenty-five electoral votes. Moreover, it had gone for him narrowly in 1960 and, with the bitter feud that aligned Connally and LBJ against Senator Yarborough added to the controversies the administration itself had sparked, Texas was far from a sure bet in 1964. If Connally and Johnson thought his visit would serve their purpose, Kennedy had enough reasons of his own for going.

Not the least of which was the President's continued eagerness to convince businessmen that he was on their side, as he had tried to do that morning in Fort Worth. Not only would going through downtown Dallas in a motorcade display his own confidence and defy intimidation, but going on from there to the Trade Mart to give a probusiness talk to the state's commercial leaders would be important for his purpose. Before he flew to Texas, Kennedy told the governor that "If these people are silly enough to think that I am going to dismantle this free enterprise system, they are crazy." Connally himself later explained that aside from the need to enhance his own standing in the state, Kennedy's main reason for making the trip was to raise money.[90]

The major question, then, was whether the itinerary should be publicized. Word that he would be coming first appeared in the city's local papers on September 13. The route itself was based on the one normally used for parades through the downtown district. Leading it through Dealey Plaza was not decided until November 15. Three days later local papers showed the exact route. There had been some suggestion that the precise plan not be made public, but Kennedy's own staff rejected it. And it made sense to tell people where they could see the President. After all, it was important to attract the largest possible crowd.[91]

The President and his entourage took off in *Air Force One* from Fort Worth at 11:20 A.M. The weather was clearing, which meant there would be no bubble-top between himself and the crowds. "Our luck is holding," he said to Connally. "It looks as if we'll get sunshine." It was a perfect autumn day. The sunshine was brilliant, and the temperature was at sixty-eight degrees.

The city's leaders threw a little ceremony at the airport for the First Family, and Jackie received a bouquet of roses. At a nearby security barrier a crowd estimated at four thousand had gathered. They were obviously friendly, much like the people he had seen in San Antonio, Houston, and Fort Worth, so he spent a few minutes walking along the fence and shaking outstretched hands. Then it was time to line up the motorcade.

The first two cars contained Dallas police officials and Secret Service agents. The third limousine was the President's. He took his usual right-rear seat alongside his wife. Connally sat on the jump seat immediately in front of the President, and Nellie Connally took the one opposite Jackie. Both had their backs turned toward the First Family. Behind their car was a long line of additional limousines: Vice-President and Mrs. Johnson, Senator Yarborough, the President's physician, Dr. Burkley; and then congressmen, local dignitaries, photographers, reporters, and members of the White House staff. At about noon the motorcade left Love Field and began to follow its route toward the Trade Mart.

Along the edges of the city the reception continued as friendly as before. As the motorcade neared downtown, the crowds at the curb became larger. Still, there were no indications of trouble, just one fellow who held a sign that said, KENNEDY GO HOME. The President caught a glimpse of it, and asked Connally whether he had also. "Yes," said the governor, "but we were hoping you didn't."

"Well, I saw it," said the President. "Don't you imagine he's a nice fellow?"

"Yes," agreed the governor. "I imagine he's a nice fellow."[92]

One sign, carried by a little girl, said, PRESIDENT KENNEDY, WILL YOU SHAKE HANDS WITH ME? Kennedy stopped the motorcade, granted her request, and the limousine was immediately mobbed while Secret Service men worked frantically to keep the crowd at a distance. The President paused again when he saw a Roman Catholic nun with a group of schoolchildren. Each time more well-wishers surrounded his car.

The crowds became still more dense when the cars turned into Main Street and moved westward toward Dealey Plaza. Now people were everywhere, waving from office buildings, filling the streets, cheering, defying all the apprehensions about what sort of greeting the President would get in Dallas. The governor turned to tell him that the city's businessmen would have to be impressed by the remarkable reception, and Kennedy's face showed his appreciation.

At the corner of Main and Houston, the motorcade made a ninety-degree turn to the right and headed north to where the Texas School Book Depository overlooked Dealey Plaza. As they approached Elm Street, Mrs. Connally said to Kennedy, "Mr. President, you can't say Dallas doesn't love you," and he answered, "That's obvious." Then the motorcade turned sharply to the left to resume its westward course toward the Trade Mart via the Stemmons Freeway. The time was 12:30 P.M. The President was waving to the crowds, who were about to be left behind, and the limousine was nearing the triple underpass to get to the freeway. Suddenly, as the papers reported the next day, there were three shots. The President clutched his neck with both hands and slumped down in his seat. One bullet had passed through his throat, another shattered his skull. Instinctively Jacqueline turned around and rose as though to climb over the trunk of the car, her knees on top of the backrest of the rear seat, as though she was trying to retrieve some of the pieces that had been blown away. Mrs. Connally later recalled that she heard the First Lady say, "I have his brains in my hand." Governor Connally had also been hit, seriously but not mortally, by a bullet that went through his body from his back.

The driver suddenly pulled the limousine out of the motorcade line. As Nellie Connally later told it, "and we must have been a horrible sight flying down the freeway with those dying men in our arms. There was no screaming in that horrible car. It was just a silent, terrible drive."[93] In an emergency room at Parkland Hospital, the President was pronounced dead at one o'clock. Jacqueline Kennedy, no longer wearing the pillbox hat that she had worn earlier in the day, walked beside the bronze coffin as it was taken to a waiting hearse. Her raspberry-colored suit was coated with her husband's blood.

Few deaths have ever shocked so much of the world. He had been the President for 1,037 days. At 2:15, twenty-four-year-old Lee Harvey Oswald, an employee of the book depository who had a Russian-born wife and had recently returned from a long stay in the Soviet Union, was arrested in a movie house. Before his apprehension he killed a police officer, J. D. Tippit, on a Dallas street. Aboard the presidential plane, ninety-nine minutes after Kennedy's death, President Lyndon B. Johnson was sworn in by Judge Sarah T. Hughes of the Northern District of Texas. Mrs. Kennedy stood to the left of the new President.[94] Two days later, while grieving throngs in Washington were lined up for a view of the former president's coffin in the Capitol Rotunda and while practically everyone else in the nation watched on television, Jack Ruby's gun appeared in full view of the cameras and Oswald was killed at point-blank range in the basement of the Dallas police station. "Jack, you son of a bitch!" said a policeman who instantly recognized the nightclub operator.[95]

It took hardly any time at all for the world to doubt that Lee Harvey Oswald, firing from the sixth-floor window at the southeast corner of the Texas School Book Depository, had acted alone and sent two bullets into the President. As early as December 2 the United States Information Agency reported the widespread belief that the assassination resulted from a conspiracy. Guesses were that it was the work of any number of people who may have been politically motivated: rightists, leftists, racists, or Zionists.[96] A Gallup survey published that same week found that only twenty-nine percent of Americans thought Oswald had been a lone killer. Fully fifty-two percent figured that it was the work of a group.[97]

Those suspicions were never satisfied. President Johnson acted quickly to constitute a special commission under the chairmanship of Chief Justice Earl Warren. Less than a year after the assassination (because speed was thought to be important), the Warren Commission delivered its report. The conclusion was explained in a simple statement that said, "The Commission has found no evidence that anyone assisted Oswald in planning or carrying out the assassination."[98]

Any expectations that the skeptics would be convinced were quickly demolished as a band of "assassination entrepreneurs" went to work. The Warren Commission's own credibility was lacerated by Edward Jay Epstein's study of its methods and procedures. Once the commission had lost its authority, the enterprise was open to anybody. Investigators pursued theories that suggested that there had been two Oswalds, that shots had come from a forward direction located on a grassy knoll to the right of the motorcade, and, more bizarre, a conspiracy that had resulted in the secret alteration of the President's body "between the time of his murder and the time of the autopsy, which began some six and a half hours later and thirteen hundred miles away, at Bethesda, Maryland." The official autopsy, then, was of a body that "was a medical forgery." Such alterations "suppressed evidence of shots from the front."[99] That the President was killed by a conspiracy was suggested by accounts that linked Oswald to the CIA, the hatred for Kennedy by frustrated anti-Castro Cuban exiles, and the vehement pursuit by the Justice Department of organized crime. Jack Kennedy's relationship with Judith Campbell was cited as another obvious link to criminals.[100]

The most credible recent critique of the judgment that Oswald had acted alone came in 1979, and that was the product of a two-and-a-half-year congressional examination of the deaths of both President Kennedy and Martin Luther King, Jr. Under the chairmanship of Representative Louis Stokes of Ohio, the Select Committee on Assassinations rested its findings very heavily on acoustical studies of a tape-recording inadvertently made through an open microphone on a Dallas police motorcycle and on the organized-crime relationship. The testimony of two acoustical experts swayed the committee from a fifty-fifty sort of verdict to the finding of a "ninety-five percent" probability of a plot. Even then the committee's conclusion was guarded: Oswald was involved, and his motivation was political; the evidence was circumstantial. In a key passage the report said that "The scientific evidence available to the committee indicated that it is probable that more than one person was involved in the President's murder. That fact compels acceptance. And it demands a reexamination of all that was thought to be true in the past. Further, the committee's investigation of Oswald and Ruby showed a variety of relationships that may have matured into an assassination conspiracy. Neither Oswald nor Ruby turned out to be 'loners,' as they had been painted in the 1964 investigations. Nevertheless, the committee frankly acknowledged that it was unable firmly to identify the other gunman or the nature and extent of the conspiracy."[101] In 1980 the FBI issued a twenty-two-page report that denigrated the key acoustical evidence used by the Stokes Committee. The bureau's own laboratory analysis showed that the findings of the committee and its scientific consultants were "invalid."[102]

Although two decades have passed, there is still no tangible evidence that demonstrates that however flawed the Warren Commission's investigation may have been, its conclusion was wrong. A British investigator who had theorized that the body in Oswald's coffin was really the corpse of a Russian agent sent to kill the President was disappointed in October of 1981 when he finally got his desire to have the grave opened. It revealed the remains of Lee Harvey Oswald, after all.[103] Other conspiracy buffs are likely to meet with similar discouragement, but that will not be much of a deterrent. A bibliography listing books and articles on the subject provided with the Stokes Committee report contained about one thousand titles.[104] A commercially published comprehensive historical and legal bibliography put out by the Greenwood Press of Westport, Connecticut, in 1980 requires 442 pages.[105]

Most difficult to accept is that Lee Harvey Oswald, who, not long before, had tried to kill General Edwin A. Walker by firing a bullet into his home, may have acted as much on his own as the young man who so nearly murdered Ronald Reagan and the two women who menaced Gerald Ford. Almost as much disbelief accompanies the simple explanation that Jack Ruby killed Oswald for any reason other than personal agitation over the death of the President. Ruby's role has been central to conspiracy theories. In 1979 David Belin, one of the Warren Commission lawyers, explained very convincingly the improbability that Ruby's motive was anything other than his own revenge for JFK's death. Their encounter in the basement of the Dallas police department, wrote Belin, was a happenstance "that changed the course of history."[106]

The assassination was irrational, but many refused to believe that it was anything other than rational. It was hard to accept the senseless death of one who had come to symbolize youthful leadership. Moreover, it was the first of that decade of political murders, and a president had not been killed for over a half century. Therefore, as Ellen Goodman has pointed out, it came with the surprise and shock no longer possible when John W. Hinckley, Jr., nearly killed President Reagan.[107]

By November 1963 JFK was no longer the great architect of national pride as in the days right after his inauguration, but, rather, a controversial president. Liberals had reasons for immediately assuming that he must have been killed by right-wing fanatics, and conservatives were sure that the murderer came from the Left. An era of distrust of the nation's intelligence services, both the FBI and the CIA, reinforced theories of either organizational motivations or actions by "uncontrollable" individual agents. The frustrations and anger of Texas oil men, segregationists, mobsters and anti-Castro Cubans provided other suspects. The proximity of the Kennedy killing to the Diem murder even suggested to some a Vietnamese connection. Without much logic, there were those who, like Lyndon Johnson, thought they detected the dirty work of Fidel Castro; others suspected the Kremlin. The world was so complex that the simplest explanation became the most difficult to accept, and John Kennedy would have understood that.

Epilogue

The John F. Kennedy who became President was the survivor of what had been a "brutal filter." To become worthy of his father, he had overcome the natural inhibitions of his personality. He had endured persistent pain and escaped a premature death sentence. The public view of Jack was as a "golden boy," but the original "golden boy" for the Kennedys was Joe Jr., the "lost prince," and the second son had surmounted a multitude of barriers to become a worthy replacement.

Joseph P. Kennedy, the former ambassador, had done his work behind the scenes, but in significant ways he was as much a liability as an asset. Jack had to get there by his own wiles, and he had few illusions about the process. He is not known to have said so directly, but he would have agreed with the fiery, red-bearded spoilsman of gilded age New York, Roscoe Conkling, who reminded reformers that "parties are not built up by deportment, or by ladies' magazines, or gush!" Those who thought Kennedy cynical and crafty had a point, but in his pursuit of goals he could be as cautious and indecisive as anyone else.

Jack Kennedy never thought of the world as a moral place, which is what he had in mind when he said that "life isn't fair." All of life was a test, each new obstacle a trial. His escapades, his sexual adventures, were respites from constant crises, and were moreover as much a privilege of aristocracy as any other symbol of rank. Yet there was a great dichotomy between the playboy and the somber, quiet desperation that characterized his discipline and determination to meet challenges. He was forever meeting challenges. They were the aspirations of an aristocratic responsibility, a burden especially great for one first establishing the claim to such credentials.

If he was to become that leader, an American Churchill, perhaps, the tests would be crucial. All of his trials had been won by small margins. At the head of the government the latitude would not be much greater. He saw the world as the battleground of a civil war between the extremes of Right and Left. He asked for sacrifices, and that distinguished him from his Democratic and Republican rivals.

It was the missionary approach, the sailing-against-the-wind romanticism that conveys a masculine, messianic quality and portrays the stakes as choices between freedom and slavery, between extinction and survival. Implicit throughout, and sometimes specified, was whether this challenge—to him the highest calling—was within the ability of a democratic society forced to compete with the single-minded, efficient, centrally directed advantages inherent in totalitarianism. This basic Kennedy preoccupation foreshadowed his subsequent global policies. Always it was the exporting of democracy, at once doubting its ability to resist the forces of evil and, at the same time, remaining convinced that it represented the preferred choice among the options available to man.

Just as it has often been suggested that only Nelson Rockefeller's heritage made him a Republican, and that his true place and certainly his more likely means of fulfilling political ambitions would have been as a Democrat, so may it be said that Jack Kennedy was a Democrat by culture and geography only. Having come to power by that route, his only way to move ahead was by mobilizing the remnants of the New Deal, trying to resurrect and reorder that coalition through a style that fused moderation with idealism.

He was, as Presidents tend to be, primarily interested in global affairs. Kennedy's belief in democratic self-determination was backed up by an extensive American military commitment. His infatuation with paramilitary operations, counterinsurgency, and inability to rationalize intelligence operations made a mockery of rhetoric that appealed to reason. Subsequent revelations about secret wars did much to establish JFK as a man who had actually brought international tensions to their most dangerous moments. His constant need to demonstrate toughness had helped to manufacture potential disasters everywhere. In Southeast Asia, in particular, he left behind a prescription for even greater disasters to come.

He "stood up" to Khrushchev but capitulated to Congress. He followed a domestic course that precluded battling for the fulfillment of the economic and social welfare needs of the Democratic Party's postdepression constituency. His effectiveness on Capitol Hill was limited, and he even appeared submissive. He had vowed to "get America moving again" but failed to deliver in key ways.

Glamour overshadowed quality. JFK appeared too handsome, too witty, too intelligent; Jackie was too beautiful, too cultivated, and much too elegant. So was Sorensen's lofty prose, which began to seem like the tinsel wrapped around an artificial world that posed as a modern Camelot.

Kennedy had struggled to reach the top. Once there he paused, looked at the barriers to further progress, and, rather than press forward with his momentum, accommodated himself to the new realities. Where others may have seen opportunities, he found that the much-advertised "corridors of power" were really Byzantine labyrinths. His assessment argued for caution, for harnessing resources to fight the real battles some other day. Explanations for the meagerness of output held that he needed more time and more support from Capitol Hill and the American public. If he developed more popular strength and could be reelected decisively in 1964, unlike the narrow victory of 1960, he could then go on to reach those "new frontiers." He was, they reasoned, learning and growing as he went along.

Like Adlai Stevenson, however, John F. Kennedy attracted architects more impressed than he by the efficacy of new designs. Also, as in Stevenson's case, they were convinced that a man so civilized, so quick to grasp the intricacies, would surely adopt their view of an America less preoccupied with the powerful and more concerned with the displaced. Their confidence in his growth largely spoke for their own commitment to his leadership. As with Stevenson, Kennedy enchanted not only those who worked on his New Frontier but a generation of young people who found themselves similarly inspired by a man who seemed convinced that democracy and quality were not incompatible. From them Kennedy derived much of his political and quantitative strength. In turn he told them what they wanted to hear. Kennedy "did not ride the tide of intellectualism," Arthur Schlesinger, Jr., wrote to a critical Alfred Kazin in 1962, "he drew it with him." He knew how easily women could be seduced, and he understood that men were not very different. He dazzled a generation of intellectuals accustomed to having a "nitwit" in the

White House, and when they recovered from his charm and reviewed the era, they resented the deception.

They had been used. His thousand days led to the nightmare years that followed. The rage that destroyed neighborhoods and the endless search for the "light at the end of the tunnel" only resulted in an "age of disillusionment." And Jack Kennedy, to whom the torch had been passed, became the orphan of failure. At best he was an "interim" President who had promised but not performed. He was rejected along with his era.

Memories, however, are notoriously short. The point has been made many times before, but it is worth repeating: If Kennedy was a "cold warrior," who was not in his day? Who, that is, among those who could have plausibly risen to the presidency? He believed that strength was the most effective producer of reason, and that has yet to be disproved. He saw the world as a dangerous place, and reacted accordingly. If he had not, his inevitable replacement would have been someone who would have promised to really get tough. When the course gave signs that it could be altered, Kennedy responded accordingly and tried to lead toward a more rational accommodation. He convinced much of the world that his purpose was peace. His American University speech and the test ban treaty were bold moves for those cold-war years, and they began a round of arms limitations agreements and more dialogue that at least psychologically (an element that cannot be minimized) seemed to move the world away from having to think the unthinkable. At his death he was involved in sounding out a new, saner relationship with Cuba. The face that he put on the national purpose through such programs as the Peace Corps and the Alliance for Progress, whatever their limitations, was at least consistent with the idealism much of the world preferred to associate with America.

That was strengthened by his identification with the civil rights movement. There, too, he was cautious; but, finally caught up in a revolution against the great cancer in American life, his Justice Department worked to enforce the laws already passed. The President withheld the full power of the Executive Office for too long. There were, as usual, too many reasons for delay. He had to be pressed too hard, but when the time came, he provided the leadership that the struggle for equality had always needed from the White House.

When President Johnson faced the nation in his first address after the assassination and said, "Let us continue," the meaning was clear. Almost despite himself, defying his own calculations, at his death Jack Kennedy had already become identified with the universal aspirations that are elusive to so many. Had he been given more than a thousand days, there is no telling how far he might have gone in that direction. Much depended on what he thought the American people would accept.

He was, finally, a moderate conservative and a rational idealist. Above all Jack Kennedy, trained to be a politician, was a politician. His self-discipline, combined with hereditary assets, had taken him far. His life, his rise to power, and the White House years reflect his struggle to govern in a democratic society. During his brief period in the White House he established a new style and tone for the presidency, one that evoked national pride and hope. That made his limitations all the more painful.

Notes

Key to Abbreviations

Columbia–OH	Columbia University Oral History Research Office, New York, New York
DDRS	Declassified Documents Research System Carrollton Press–U.S. Historical Documents Institute, Inc., 1911 Ft. Myer Drive, Arlington, Va. 22209
DNC	Democratic National Committee
FDRL	Franklin D. Roosevelt Library, Hyde Park, New York
JFKL	John F. Kennedy Library, Boston, Massachusetts
JFKL–OH	John F. Kennedy Library Oral History Collection
LBJL	Lyndon Baines Johnson Library, Austin, Texas
NSF	National Security Files
NYT	*The New York Times*
POF	President's Office Files
RFK Papers	Papers of Robert F. Kennedy, John F. Kennedy Library

Chapter 1

1. Theodore H. White, *In Search of History—A Personal Expedition* (New York: Harper & Row, 1978), p. 524.
2. Robert Frost, *Complete Poems of Robert Frost* (New York: Holt, Rinehart and Winston, 1964), p. 467.
3. Richard Cardinal Cushing, JFKL–OH (E. M. Kennedy interview).
4. Leonard Reinsch, JFKL–OH (Charles T. Morrissey interview).
5. Adlai Stevenson to Theodore C. Sorensen, December 30, 1960, Sorensen Papers, Box 62, JFKL.
6. Walter Lippmann, JFKL–OH (Elizabeth Farmer interview).
7. John Kenneth Galbraith to John F. Kennedy, January 9, 1961, Galbraith Papers, Box 76, JFKL.
8. Pierre Salinger, *With Kennedy* (Garden City, N.Y.: Doubleday, 1966), pp. 108–109.
9. John F. Kennedy, *Public Papers of the Presidents 1961* (Washington: U.S. Government Printing Office, 1961), pp. 1–3.
10. Thomas C. Patterson, "Bearing the Burden," *Virginia Quarterly Review,* 54 (Spring 1978), p. 204; cf., Henry Fairlie, *The Kennedy Promise* (Garden City, N.Y.: Doubleday, 1973), p. 143; Louise FitzSimons, *The Kennedy Doctrine* (New York: Random House, 1972), p. 13.
11. John B. Sheerin, "President Kennedy's Foreign Policy," *Catholic World,* February 1961, p. 262.
12. Jack Bell, JFKL–OH (Joseph O'Connor interview).
13. Eleanor Roosevelt to JFK, January 25, 1961, POF, Box 32, JFKL.
14. *NYT,* January 21, 1961.
15. *New Republic,* January 30, 1961, p. 4.
16. *NYT,* January 22, 1961.
17. Ibid., p. 3.
18. Ibid.
19. Kay Halle, JFKL–OH (William McHugh interview).
20. Carlos Baker, ed., *Ernest Hemingway, Selected Letters: 1917–1961* (New York: Scribner's, 1981), p. 916.
21. Kay Halle, interview, August 18, 1981, and JFKL–OH (William McHugh interview).
22. White House Appointment Book, JFKL.
23. Typescript of Remarks, POF, Box 136, JFKL; *NYT,* January 15, 1960.
24. H. L. Tinker, "Jack Kennedy's Challenge," *Choate Alumni Bulletin,* January 1947, p. 21.
25. *Lawrence* (Mass.) *Eagle,* February 8, 1946.
26. John F. Kennedy, "When the Executive Fails to Lead," *The Reporter,* September 18, 1958, pp. 14–17.
27. Ben Bradlee, *Conversations with Kennedy* (New York: W. W. Norton, 1975), p. 140.
28. Chester Bowles, JFKL–OH (Robert Brooks interview).
29. Lyndon B. Johnson, Office Diary, July 9, 1960, Box 1, LBJL.
30. *NYT,* July 14, 1960.
31. Ibid.
32. David Garth, interview, April 2, 1981.
33. John Bartlow Martin, *Adlai Stevenson and the World* (Garden City, N.Y.: Doubleday, 1977), p. 527.
34. John Sharon, Columbia–OH (John Luter interview).
35. Charles Spalding, JFKL–OH (John F. Stewart interview).
36. *NYT,* July 14, 1960.
37. James Rowe, interview, January 9, 1981.
38. Walter Jenkins, interview, June 26, 1980.
39. Confidential interview.
40. William Attwood, interview, September 11, 1980.

41. Newton Minow to JFK, December 10, 1962, POF, Box 123, JFKL; John Sharon, Columbia–OH (John Luter interview); William Attwood, Columbia–OH (Kenneth S. Davis interview).
42. Black Notebook III, Box 1, Krock Papers, Seeley Mudd Library, Princeton University.
43. Joseph P. Lash, *Eleanor: The Years Alone* (New York: W. W. Norton, 1972), p. 289.
44. William Attwood, *The Reds and the Blacks* (New York: Harper & Row, 1967), p. 5; W. Willard Wirtz, Columbia–OH (John Luter interview).
45. David Garth, interview, April 2, 1981.
46. William Attwood, interview, September 11, 1980.
47. Russell Hemenway, interview, May 18, 1979.
48. Barbara Ward Jackson, JFKL–OH (Walt W. and Elspeth Rostow interview).
49. John Kenneth Galbraith to JFK, June 1, 1960, POF, Box 29, JFKL.
50. Carmine Gravel, JFKL–OH (John F. Stewart interview).
51. Paul David, *Presidential Election and Transition, 1960* (Washington: Brookings Institution, 1961), p. 9.
52. Walter Johnson and Carol Evans, eds., *The Papers of Adlai Stevenson,* 8 vols. (Boston: Little, Brown, 1972–1979), v. 7, p. 528.
53. Dean Acheson, JFKL–OH (Lucius Battle interview).
54. Marie B. Hecht, *Beyond the Presidency* (New York: Macmillan, 1976), pp. 144–145.
55. David E. Koskoff, *Joseph P. Kennedy* (Englewood Cliffs, N.J.: Prentice-Hall, 1974), p. 429.
56. *NYT,* July 5, 1960.
57. Ibid.
58. Ibid.
59. Janet Travell, *Office Hours: Day and Night* (New York: World Publishing Company, 1968), pp. 332–333; *NYT,* July 5, 1960.
60. Janet Travell, JFKL–OH (Theodore C. Sorensen interview).
61. William Walton, interview, January 15, 1981.
62. R. Sargent Shriver, interview, January 14, 1980.
63. Dr. Hans Kraus, interview, December 8, 1980.
64. Edward M. Kennedy, ed., *The Fruitful Bough: A Tribute to Joseph P. Kennedy* (privately printed, 1965), p. 141.
65. Merle Miller, *Plain Speaking: An Oral Biography of Harry S Truman* (New York: Berkley Publishing, 1973), p. 187.
66. Herbert E. Alexander, *Financing the 1960 Election* (Princeton, N.J.: Citizens' Research Foundation, 1965), p. 17.
67. W. A. Swanberg, *Luce and his Empire* (New York: Scribner's, 1972), pp. 410–414; Koskoff, *Joseph P. Kennedy,* pp. 420–432.
68. Kennedy, ed., *Fruitful Bough,* pp. 127–128.
69. Charles Spalding, JFKL–OH (John F. Stewart interview).
70. Richard J. Whalen, *The Founding Father: The Story of Joseph P. Kennedy* (New York: New American Library, 1964), p. 450.
71. Kenneth P. O'Donnell, interview, December 4, 1976.
72. Arthur M. Schlesinger, Jr., *Robert Kennedy and His Times* (Boston: Houghton Mifflin, 1978), p. 193.
73. Lloyd K. Garrison, interview, June 19, 1974.
74. Theo Lippman, Jr., *Senator Ted Kennedy: The Career Behind the Image* (New York: W. W. Norton, 1976), p. 13.
75. Robert F. Kennedy, JFKL–OH (Arthur M. Schlesinger, Jr., interview).
76. Pierre Salinger, JFKL–OH (Theodore H. White interview).
77. Arthur M. Schlesinger, Jr., *A Thousand Days* (Boston: Houghton Mifflin, 1965), p. 58.
78. *NYT,* July 17, 1960.
79. Anne Hodges Morgan, *Robert S. Kerr: The Senate Years* (Norman: University of Oklahoma Press, 1977), p. 188; Walter Jenkins, interview, June 26, 1980.

80. Myer Feldman, JFKL–OH (Charles T. Morrissey interview).
81. Theodore C. Sorensen, interview, April 27, 1977.
82. Joseph Alsop to Lyndon B. Johnson, March 1964, and Alsop to Johnson, March 25, 1964, Johnson Papers, Box 78, LBJL; Theodore H. White, *The Making of the President 1964* (New York: Atheneum, 1965), p. 408.
83. Schlesinger, *Robert Kennedy*, pp. 207–208.
84. Clark Clifford, JFKL–OH (Larry Hackman interview).
85. Arthur Krock, *Memoirs: Sixty Years on the Firing Line* (New York: Funk & Wagnalls, 1968), p. 362.
86. Lyndon B. Johnson, Office Diary, July 13, 1960, Box 1, LBJL.
87. Ibid.
88. Ibid.
89. Evelyn Lincoln, *My Twelve Years with John F. Kennedy* (New York: McKay, 1965), p. 161.
90. Harris Wofford, *Of Kennedys and Kings: Making Sense of the Sixties* (New York: Farrar, Straus & Giroux, 1980), pp. 53–54.
91. Bobby Baker, *Wheeling and Dealing: Confessions of a Capitol Hill Operator* (New York: W. W. Norton, 1978), p. 124.
92. Lady Bird Johnson, interview, June 25, 1980.
93. Baker, *Wheeling and Dealing*, p. 126.
94. Ibid., p. 126.
95. Walter Jenkins, interview, June 26, 1980; Lyndon B. Johnson, Office Diary, July 14, 1960, Box 1, LBJL.
96. Lincoln, *Twelve Years*, pp. 164–165.
97. Alfred Steinberg, *Sam Rayburn: A Biography* (New York: Hawthorn Books, 1975), p. 330.
98. Hale Boggs, JFKL–OH (Charles T. Morrissey interview).
99. Steinberg, *Rayburn*, p. 330.
100. Arthur J. Goldberg, interview, March 10, 1981.
101. Robert F. Kennedy, JFKL–OH (Arthur M. Schlesinger, Jr., interview).
102. Arthur Goldberg, interview, March 10, 1981; Robert F. Kennedy, JFKL–OH (Arthur M. Schlesinger, Jr., interview).
103. Lyndon B. Johnson, Office Diary, July 14, 1960, Box 1, LBJL.
104. Robert F. Kennedy, JFKL–OH (Arthur M. Schlesinger, Jr., interview).
105. Walter Jenkins, interview, June 26, 1980.
106. Robert F. Kennedy, JFKL–OH (Arthur M. Schlesinger, Jr., interview).
107. *NYT*, July 16, 1960.
108. Clark Clifford, JFKL–OH (Larry Hackman interview).
109. Edwin Bayley, JFKL–OH (Larry Hackman interview).
110. G. Mennen Williams, JFKL–OH (William W. Moss interview).
111. *NYT*, July 16, 1960.
112. Johnson and Evans, eds., *Stevenson*, v. 7, pp. 540–541.
113. *NYT*, July 17, 1960.

Chapter 2

1. Martin, *Stevenson and the World*, p. 533.
2. Clark Clifford, JFKL–OH (Larry Hackman interview).
3. C. G. B. to Marjorie Griesser, July 19, 1960, James Warburg Papers, Box 21, JFKL; Martin, *Stevenson and the World*, pp. 530–531.
4. Richard Russell to Billy F. Bennett, July 25, 1960, Russell Papers, Box I. C. 2, Richard B. Russell Memorial Library, University of Georgia.

5. Telegrams, JFK to Richard Russell, July 14, 1960, and Russell to Kennedy, July 15, 1960, Russell Papers, Box VI. 26 and Box I. C. 2, Russell Library, University of Georgia.
6. Lash, *Eleanor*, p. 296.
7. Adlai Stevenson to Eleanor Roosevelt, August 7, 1960, Eleanor Roosevelt Papers, Box 4437, FDRL; Martin, *Stevenson and the World*, p. 531.
8. Lawrence Fuchs, JFKL–OH (John F. Stewart interview).
9. William Walton, interview, January 15, 1981.
10. Adlai Stevenson, Memorandum of Conversation with Mrs. Roosevelt, August 15, 1960, Stevenson Papers, Box 797, Princeton, and Mrs. Roosevelt to Mary Lasker, August 15, 1960, POF, JFKL.
11. Eleanor Roosevelt to Ruth Field, August 1960, Stevenson Papers, Box 797, Princeton.
12. Adlai Stevenson, Memorandum of Conversation with Mrs. Roosevelt, August 15, 1960, Stevenson Papers, Box 797, Princeton.
13. Arthur M. Schlesinger, Jr., to JFK, August 30, 1960, Stevenson Papers, Box 798, Princeton.
14. News Releases, Democratic National Committee, October 5 and 10, 1960, Stevenson Papers, Box 789, Princeton; Transcript of Remarks to the Liberal Party, September 14, 1960, Pre-Presidential Papers, Box 911, JFKL.
15. Michael J. Kirwin, JFKL–OH (Tristram Coffin interview).
16. Theodore C. Sorensen, *Kennedy* (New York: Harper & Row, 1965), p. 148.
17. Claire Sterling, "The Vatican and Kennedy," *The Reporter*, October 27, 1960, pp. 26–27.
18. Koskoff, *Joseph P. Kennedy*, p. 385; Robert F. Kennedy, JFKL–OH (Anthony Lewis interview).
19. Vito Nicholas Silvestri, "John F. Kennedy: His Speaking in the Wisconsin and West Virginia Primaries 1960," unpublished Ph.D. dissertation, University of Indiana, 1966.
20. Andrew R. Baggaley, "Religious Influence on Wisconsin Voting, 1928–1960," *American Political Science Review*, March 1962, p. 70.
21. Robert F. Kennedy to A. Willis Robertson, August 31, 1960, Robertson Papers, College of William and Mary.
22. Theodore H. White, *The Making of the President 1960* (New York: Atheneum, 1961), p. 106.
23. Chalmers Roberts, *First Rough Draft* (New York: Praeger Publishers, 1973), p. 176.
24. White, *Making of the President 1960*, p. 101.
25. Ibid.
26. Ibid.
27. Memorandum, April 8, 1960, Robert F. Kennedy Papers, Box 7, JFKL.
28. John F. Kennedy, *John Fitzgerald Kennedy: A Compilation of Statements and Speeches Made During His Service in the United States Senate and House of Representatives* (Washington, D.C.: U.S. Government Printing Office, 1964), p. 1,115.
29. *Washington Post*, May 6, 1960.
30. Sorensen, *Kennedy*, p. 193.
31. Marshall Frady, *Billy Graham: A Parable of American Righteousness* (Boston: Little, Brown, 1979), p. 443.
32. Brooks Hays, JFKL–OH (Warren Cikins interview).
33. *Time*, September 19, 1960, p. 23.
34. *NYT*, September 8, 1960.
35. James Wine, JFKL–OH (John F. Stewart interview).
36. John Cogley, JFKL–OH (John F. Stewart interview).
37. Deane Alwyn Kemper, "John F. Kennedy Before the Greater Houston Ministerial Association, September 12, 1960: The Religious Issue," unpublished Ph.D. dissertation, Michigan State University, 1968.
38. John Cogley, JFKL–OH (John F. Stewart interview).

39. Kemper, "Houston Ministerial Association," pp. 159–160.
40. Sorensen, *Kennedy*, pp. 189–190.
41. William V. Shannon, *The Irish in America* (New York: Macmillan, 1963), p. 402.
42. John W. Turnbull, "The Clergy Faces Mr. Kennedy," *The Reporter*, October 13, 1960, p. 33.
43. Kemper, "Houston Ministerial Association," pp. 39–40.
44. James Wine, JFKL–OH (John F. Stewart interview).
45. John Cogley, JFKL–OH (John F. Stewart interview).
46. A reasonably accurate version of his remarks is included as an appendix in White, *Making of the President 1960*, pp. 391–393.
47. DNC, Remarks of Senator John F. Kennedy, September 12, 1960, Pre-Presidential Papers, Box 911, JFKL.
48. John Harllee, JFKL–OH (Charles T. Morrissey interview).
49. Patricia Barrett, *Religious Liberty and the American Presidency: A Study in Church-State Relations* (New York: Herder & Herder, 1963), pp. 24–25.
50. DNC, News Release, October 21, 1960, Stevenson Papers, Box 789, Princeton.
51. Sidney Kraus, ed., *The Great Debates* (Bloomington: Indiana University Press, 1962), p. 367.
52. *NYT*, September 28, 1960.
53. Myer Feldman, JFKL–OH (Charles T. Morrissey interview); Howard K. Smith, Columbia–OH (John Luter interview).
54. John Kenneth Galbraith to Lou Harris, September 27, 1960, Galbraith Papers, Box 74, JFKL.
55. Kraus, *Great Debates*, p. 369.
56. Ibid., pp. 370, 399.
57. DNC, News Release, October 21, 1960, Stevenson Papers, Box 798, Princeton.
58. Kraus, *Great Debates*, p. 417.
59. Richard Nixon, *RN: The Memoirs of Richard Nixon* (New York: Grosset & Dunlap, 1978), p. 221.
60. *NYT*, March 21, 1962.
61. Peter Wyden, *Bay of Pigs: The Untold Story* (New York: Simon and Schuster, 1979), p. 67.
62. David Wise and Thomas B. Ross, *The Invisible Government* (New York: Bantam Books, 1965), p. 362.
63. Archibald Cox to Richard Goodwin, October 19, 1960, DNC Files, Box 199, JFKL.
64. Richard Goodwin, interview, May 22, 1981.
65. Cf. Wyden's *Bay of Pigs*, pp. 65–67, which accepts Goodwin's explanation.
66. Richard Goodwin, interview, May 22, 1981.
67. Chester Bowles to JFK, October 17, 1960, DNC Papers, Box 198, JFKL.
68. *NYT*, October 22, 1960.
69. Harry F. Byrd to James F. Byrnes, August 25, 1960, Byrd Papers, Box 242, University of Virginia.
70. Richard Russell to Reverend Thomas M. Less, September 29, 1960, Russell Papers, Box I. C. 2, University of Georgia.
71. Charles J. Bloch to Richard Russell, July 27, 1960, Russell Papers, Box VI. 19, and Ross R. Barnett to Russell, August 16, 1960, Russell Papers, Box VI. 26, Russell Library, University of Georgia; Joint Statement by Senators James O. Eastland and John Stennis, August 19, 1960, McCormack Papers, Box 102, Boston University.
72. Robert F. Kennedy to R. Sargent Shriver, August 4, 1960, RFK Papers, Box 1, JFKL.
73. Roy V. Harris to Richard Russell, August 24, 1960, Russell Papers, Box VI. A. 10, Russell Library, University of Georgia.
74. Harris Wofford, JFKL–OH (Berl Bernhard interview).

75. *NYT,* September 21, 1960.
76. G. Mennen Williams, JFKL–OH (William W. Moss interview).
77. Rowland Evans and Robert Novak, *Lyndon B. Johnson: The Exercise of Power* (New York: New American Library, 1966), p. 301.
78. *NYT,* July 31, 1960.
79. Lyndon B. Johnson, Office Diary, August 9, 16, 18, 19, 25, 26, 1960, Box 1, LBJL; Wofford, *Kennedys and Kings,* p. 60.
80. Orville Freeman to JFK, August 15, 1960, Pre-Presidential Papers, Box 540, JFKL.
81. Richard Russell to James B. Burch, November 9, 1960, Russell Papers, Box 1. C. 2, Russell Library, University of Georgia.
82. Richard Russell to Harvey J. Kennedy, November 17, 1960, Russell Papers, Box 1. C. 2, Russell Library, University of Georgia.
83. Carl M. Brauer, *John F. Kennedy and the Second Reconstruction* (New York: Columbia University Press, 1977), pp. 40, 43.
84. Wofford, *Kennedys and Kings,* p. 58.
85. Memorandum, Civil Rights Section, to Bobby Kennedy, Larry O'Brien, Steve Smith, and Dan Martin, RFK Papers, Box 2, JFKL; *Washington Post,* August 4, 1960.
86. Wofford, *Kennedys and Kings,* pp. 14–15.
87. *NYT,* October 26, 1960.
88. Wofford, *Kennedys and Kings,* p. 16.
89. Harris Wofford, JFKL–OH (Berl Bernhard interview).
90. Hubert Humphrey to Richard Russell, October 26, 1960, Russell Papers, Box VI. 10, Russell Library, University of Georgia.
91. R. Sargent Shriver, interview, November 19, 1976.
92. Wofford, *Kennedys and Kings,* p. 21.
93. Harris Wofford, JFKL–OH (Berl Bernhard interview).
94. David L. Lewis, *King: A Critical Biography* (New York: Praeger Publishers, 1970), p. 129; Harris Wofford, JFKL–OH (Berl Bernhard interview).
95. Robert F. Kennedy, JFKL–OH (Anthony Lewis interview).
96. Jean Stein and George Plimpton, *American Journey: The Times of Robert Kennedy* (New York: Signet, 1972), p. 90.
97. Cf. Richard Russell to Robert F. Kennedy, November 8, 1960, Russell Papers, Box VI. 25, Russell Library, University of Georgia.
98. *Newsweek,* November 14, 1960, p. EE–9.
99. Leo Damore, *The Cape Cod Years of John Fitzgerald Kennedy* (Englewood Cliffs, N.J.: Prentice-Hall, 1967), p. 219.
100. *NYT,* November 9, 1960.
101. Ibid., November 10, 1960.
102. Herbert S. Parmet, *Jack: The Struggles of John F. Kennedy* (New York: Dial Press, 1980), pp. 91, 510–511.
103. Damore, *Cape Cod,* p. 230; Sorensen, *Kennedy,* p. 230; Schlesinger, *Thousand Days,* p. 125.
104. David, *Presidential Election,* p. 151; John Hart, "Kennedy, Congress, and Civil Rights," *Journal of American Studies,* August 1979, p. 170.
105. Henry Brandon, JFKL–OH (Joseph E. O'Connor interview).

Chapter 3

1. Roswell Gilpatric, JFKL–OH (Dennis J. O'Brien interview).
2. Richard M. Rovere, "Letter from Washington," *The New Yorker,* December 24, 1960, p. 52.
3. Clark Clifford, interview, April 18, 1980.

4. Edward McCabe, Columbia–OH (Paul Hopper interview).
5. Adam Yarmolinsky, "The Kennedy Talent Hunt," *The Reporter,* June 8, 1961, p. 24.
6. R. Sargent Shriver, interview, April 18, 1980.
7. Adam Yarmolinsky, JFKL–OH (Daniel Ellsberg interview).
8. Albert Wohlstetter to Deirdre Henderson, November 15, 1960, and Abram Chayes to Henderson, December 6, 1960, Henderson Papers, JFKL.
9. Myer Feldman, JFKL–OH (Charles T. Morrissey interview).
10. Robert F. Kennedy, JFKL–OH (John Bartlow Martin interview).
11. *NYT,* December 10, 1960; Arthur Goldberg, interview, March 10, 1981.
12. *NYT,* December 19, 1960; Drew Pearson to Robert F. Kennedy, December 5, 1960, RFK Papers, Personal Correspondence, Box 1, JFKL.
13. Richard Russell, Draft Statement, December 1960, Russell Papers, Reasley File, Box XXI. 7, Russell Library, University of Georgia.
14. Richard Russell, Memorandum of Conversation, December 1, 1960, dictated December 15, 1960, Russell Papers, Box I. C. 2, University of Georgia.
15. Clark Clifford, JFKL–OH (Larry Hackman interview), and Clifford on *Bill Moyers Journal,* National Educational Television, March 6, 1981.
16. Schlesinger, *Thousand Days,* p. 142.
17. *NYT,* December 24, 1960.
18. Robert F. Kennedy, JFKL–OH (John Bartlow Martin interview).
19. Ibid.; Wofford, *Kennedys and Kings,* p. 77.
20. Robert F. Kennedy, JFKL–OH (John Bartlow Martin interview).
21. Clark Clifford, JFKL–OH (Larry Hackman interview).
22. R. Sargent Shriver, interview, April 16, 1980.
23. Albert Gore, *Let the Glory Out: My South and Its Politics* (New York: Viking Press, 1972), p. 147.
24. *NYT,* December 2, 1960.
25. Arthur Goldberg, interview, March 10, 1981.
26. William McCormick Blair, Columbia–OH (John Luter interview).
27. Robert F. Kennedy, October 1, 1962, RFK Personal Correspondence, Box 4, JFKL.
28. Schlesinger, *Robert Kennedy,* pp. 222–223.
29. Dean Acheson, JFKL–OH (Lucius Battle interview).
30. Walter Lippmann, JFKL–OH (Elizabeth Farmer interview); Ronald Steel, *Walter Lippmann and the American Century* (Boston: Little, Brown, 1980), p. 523.
31. J. William Fulbright, JFKL–OH (Pat Hopt interview); *NYT,* November 30, 1960.
32. *Kansas City Star,* December 1, 1960.
33. Schlesinger, *Robert Kennedy,* pp. 222–223.
34. J. William Fulbright, telephone conversation, July 1, 1981.
35. Interoffice Memorandum, November 29, 1960, Russell Papers, Box 11, Russell Library, University of Georgia.
36. Robert A. Lovett, JFKL–OH (Dorothy Fosdick interview).
37. Adlai Stevenson, Notes for Talk with Kennedy, December 8, 1960, Stevenson Papers, Box 789, Princeton.
38. John Sharon, Columbia–OH (John Luter interview); Wofford, *Kennedys and Kings,* p. 83; *NYT,* December 9, 1960.
39. Richard Russell to Charles Rowland, December 17, 1960, Russell Papers, Box I. C. 2, Russell Library, University of Georgia.
40. James Warburg to Matthew Robinson, November 11, 1960, Warburg Papers, Box 42, JFKL.
41. Whalen, *Founding Father,* p. 462; Kenneth P. O'Donnell and David F. Powers, *"Johnny, We Hardly Knew Ye": Memories of John Fitzgerald Kennedy* (Boston: Little, Brown), p. 229.
42. *NYT,* November 15, 1960.
43. Ibid., November 22, 1960.
44. Ibid., November 25, 1960.

45. Ibid., November 26, 1960; Stephen Birmingham, *Jacqueline Bouvier Kennedy Onassis* (New York: Grosset & Dunlap, 1978), p. 89; Maud Shaw, *White House Nannie* (New York: New American Library, 1966), p. 78.
46. *NYT,* November 28, 1961.
47. Ibid., December 3, 1960.
48. Earl Mazo, Columbia–OH (Ed Edwin interview).
49. Harris Wofford to JFK, March 26, 1962, POF, Box 67, JFKL.
50. Roberts, *First Rough Draft,* p. 194.
51. Rand Report RM–2683, POF, Box 64, JFKL.
52. *NYT,* December 7, 1960.
53. Eisenhower Memorandum, December 6, 1961, DDRS (80) 451F.
54. Charles Spalding, JFKL–OH (John F. Stewart interview); Robert F. Kennedy, JFKL–OH (Anthony Lewis interview).
55. Robert F. Kennedy, JFKL–OH (Arthur M. Schlesinger, Jr., interview).
56. John Sharon, Columbia–OH (John Luter interview).
57. Eisenhower Memorandum, December 6, 1961, DDRS (80) 451F.
58. Jacqueline Kennedy to Kenneth Galbraith, January 6, 1961, Box 76, Galbraith Papers, JFKL.
59. *NYT,* December 20, 1960.
60. *Boston Globe,* December 10, 21, 1960; *NYT,* December 21, 1960.
61. *NYT,* December 19, 20, 1960.
62. Walter W. Heller, "Recollections of Early Meetings with Kennedy," January 12, 1964, Heller private papers.
63. Walter W. Heller, interview, June 18, 1980.
64. Council of Economic Advisers, JFKL–OH (Joseph Pechman interview).
65. Brooks Hays, JFKL–OH (Warren Cikins interview).
66. William L. Batt, Jr., JFKL–OH (Larry Hackman interview).
67. *NYT,* January 2, 1961.
68. Fairlie, *Kennedy Promise,* p. 153.
69. Mark I. Gelfand, *A Nation of Cities* (New York: Oxford University Press, 1975), p. 311; Robert C. Weaver, interview, July 24, 1981.
70. Robert C. Weaver, interview, July 24, 1981.
71. *NYT,* January 6, 7, 1961; Robert C. Weaver, interview, July 24, 1981; Philip Klutznick, JFKL–OH (Dennis J. O'Brien interview).
72. Gelfand, *Nation of Cities,* p. 312.
73. Schlesinger, *Thousand Days,* p. 162.
74. *NYT,* January 10, 1961.
75. George Kennan, JFKL–OH (Louis Fischer interview).
76. *NYT,* January 11, 1961.
77. Ibid.
78. Clark Clifford, JFKL–OH (Larry Hackman interview).
79. Clark Clifford to JFK, January 24, 1961, Box 129, POF, JFKL; Laos Situation Reports, December 30, 1960, January 2, 3, 4, 1961, DDRS (80) 49B, 49C, 50A–50C.
80. Sorensen, *Kennedy,* p. 649.
81. Hugh Sidey, *John F. Kennedy, President* (New York: Atheneum, 1964), pp. 37–38.
82. *NYT,* January 20, 1961.
83. Ibid., January 21, 1961.
84. William Walton, interview, January 15, 1981.

Chapter 4

1. Chalmers Roberts, Memorandum, March 27, 1962, Roberts Private Papers.
2. Confidential source; Walt W. Rostow, JFKL–OH (Richard Neustadt interview).
3. POF, Box 130, JFKL.

4. Charles Bartlett, JFKL–OH (Fred Holborn interview).
5. Fred Dutton to JFK, January 27, 1961, POF, Box 63, JFKL.
6. *NYT*, March 19, 1961, sec. IV, p. 1.
7. Salinger, *With Kennedy*, p. 63.
8. *Boston Globe*, January 22, 1961.
9. Roy Wilkins, JFKL–OH (Thomas Baker interview); Schlesinger, *Thousand Days*, p. 932.
10. JFK to Chester Bowles, January 26, 1961, Bowles Papers, Box 297, Yale; Roger Jones, JFKL–OH (John F. Stewart interview).
11. *NYT*, January 22, 1961.
12. Lawrence F. O'Brien, *No Final Victories* (Garden City, N.Y.: Doubleday, 1974), p. 107; Alfred Steinberg, *Sam Johnson's Boy* (New York: Macmillan, 1968), p. 550.
13. *NYT*, January 26, 1961.
14. *Boston Globe*, January 21, 1961.
15. Kennedy, *Public Papers . . . 1961*, pp. 10–11.
16. Ibid., p. 27.
17. Ibid., pp. 19–28.
18. Fred Dutton, JFKL–OH (Charles T. Morrissey interview).
19. Douglas Dillon in Stein and Plimpton, *American Journey*, p. 150.
20. Roger Hilsman, JFKL–OH (Paige E. Mulhollan interview).
21. Carl Kaysen, comments at JFKL Symposium, January 24, 1981.
22. *NYT*, March 19, 1961.
23. Walt W. Rostow, JFKL–OH (Richard Neustadt interview).
24. Alfred Kazin, "The President and Other Intellectuals," *American Scholar*, Autumn 1961, p. 509.
25. John Kenneth Galbraith to JFK, February 2, 1961, POF, Box 29, JFKL.
26. John Kenneth Galbraith, *Ambassador's Journal* (Boston: Houghton Mifflin, 1969), p. 23.
27. Roger Hilsman, JFKL–OH (Dennis J. O'Brien interview); I. N. Destler, *President, Bureaucrats, and Foreign Policy: The Politics of Organizational Reform* (Princeton, N.J.: Princeton University Press, 1972), p. 99.
28. Chalmers Roberts, Memorandum, April 7, 1961, Roberts Personal Papers.
29. Salinger, *With Kennedy*, pp. 117–118.
30. George H. Gallup, ed., *The Gallup Poll: Public Opinion, 1935–1971* (4 vols; New York: Random House, 1972), v. 3, pp. 1,703, 1,708, 1,727.
31. Theodore C. Sorensen, JFKL–OH (Carl Kaysen interview).
32. David E. Bell, JFKL–OH (Robert Turner interview).
33. Walter W. Heller, interview, June 18, 1980.
34. Walter W. Heller, *New Dimensions of Political Economy* (Cambridge: Harvard University Press, 1966), p. 26.
35. Walt W. Rostow, JFKL–OH (Richard Neustadt interview).
36. Robert B. Anderson, interview, August 12, 1981.
37. Roswell Gilpatric, JFKL–OH (Dennis J. O'Brien interview).
38. Walt W. Rostow, JFKL–OH (Richard Neustadt interview).
39. Walter W. Heller, interview, June 18, 1980.
40. Fred Dutton, JFKL–OH (Charles T. Morrissey interview); Hobart Rowen, "Kennedy's Economists," *Harper's*, September 1961, p. 30.
41. *NYT*, February 17, 1961.
42. Chalmers Roberts, Memorandum, April 7, 1961, Roberts Personal Papers.
43. Rowen, "Kennedy's Economists," p. 31.
44. Schlesinger, *Thousand Days*, p. 170.
45. Council of Economic Advisers, JFKL (Joseph Pechman interview).
46. Council of Economic Advisers (CEA) Memorandum for the President, February 16,

1961, Heller Papers, Box 19, JFKL; *Washington Star,* February 20, 1961; White House Appointment Books, February 17, 1961.

47. Walter W. Heller to Fred Dutton, Heller Papers, Box 19, JFKL.

48. Walter W. Heller to James Tobin and Kermit Gordon, February 20, 1961, Heller Personal Papers.

49. Walter W. Heller to JFK, February 24, 1961, Heller Papers, Box 5, JFKL.

50. Lawrence F. O'Brien to Theodore C. Sorensen and JFK, April 10, 1962, Box 58, Sorensen Papers, JFKL.

51. Kennedy, *Public Papers . . . 1961,* pp. 290–303.

52. Hobart Rowen, *The Free Enterprisers* (New York: Putnam, 1964), p. 50.

53. Cf. Heller's handwritten notes of the meeting of April 14, 1961, and "Proposals for a Second-Stage Economic Program," as drafted by Kermit Gordon for the CEA, Robert C. Turner for the Bureau of the Budget, and Lee White for the White House, April 17, 1961, Heller Papers, Box 21, JFKL.

54. James Tobin, *The New Economics, One Decade Older* (Princeton, N.J.: Princeton University Press, 1974), p. 13.

55. Kennedy, *Public Papers . . . 1961,* p. 87.

56. *NYT,* April 9, 1961, sec. IV, p. 2.

57. Walter W. Heller to JFK, May 10, 1961, Heller Papers, Box 5, JFKL.

58. Typescript, "Proposals for a Second-Stage Economic Program," April 17, 1961, Heller Papers, Box 21, JFKL.

59. Arthur Goldberg to Theodore C. Sorensen, April 19, 1961, Heller Papers, Box 21, JFKL.

60. Typescript, "Proposals for a Second-Stage Economic Program," April 17, 1961, Heller Papers, Box 21, JFKL.

61. *NYT,* January 25, 1961.

62. Walter W. Heller to JFK, March 24, 1961, Heller Papers, Box 5, JFKL.

63. Rowen, "Kennedy's Economists," p. 28.

64. Kennedy, *Public Papers . . . 1961,* p. 310.

65. McGeorge Bundy to JFK, March 30, 1961, POF, Box 62, JFKL.

66. *NYT,* March 26, 1961.

67. James L. Sundquist, *Politics and Policy: The Eisenhower, Kennedy, and Johnson Years* (Washington, D. C.: The Brookings Institution, 1968), p. 85.

68. George H. Gallup, ed., *The Poll: Public Opinion, 1935–1971,* 4 vols. (New York: Random House, 1972), v. 3, pp. 1,703 and 1,717.

69. *NYT,* March 12, 1961, sec. IV, p. 2.

70. Kennedy, *Public Papers . . . 1961,* p. 172.

71. Thomas Mann, JFKL–OH (Larry Hackman interview).

72. *Newsweek,* March 13, 1961, p. 32.

73. Lou Harris and Associates, Confidential Study #1012, March 22, 1961, POF, Box 63a, JFKL; Gallup, *The Poll,* v. 3, p. 1,711.

74. Walter W. Heller, interview, June 18, 1980.

75. Adolf A. Berle, *Navigating the Rapids, 1918–1971* (New York: Harcourt, Brace, Jovanovich, 1973), p. 740; Frederick Collins, "The Mind of John F. Kennedy," *Nation,* May 8, 1961, p. 17.

Chapter 5

1. Joan Meyers, ed., *John Fitzgerald Kennedy: As We Remember Him* (New York: Atheneum, 1965), p. 124; Lincoln, *Twelve Years,* p. 52.

2. Salinger, *With Kennedy,* p. 71.

3. Eugene M. Zuckert, JFKL–OH (Lawrence McQuade interview).

4. *NYT,* February 2, 1961.
5. Ibid., February 12, 1961.
6. John F. Davis, *The Bouviers: Portrait of an American Family* (New York: Farrar, Straus & Giroux, 1969), pp. 345–346.
7. Jacqueline Kennedy to Adlai Stevenson, July 24, 1961, Stevenson Papers, Box 832, Princeton.
8. Davis, *Bouviers,* p. 346.
9. Letitia Baldrige to Evelyn Lincoln, October 27, 1961, POF, Box 62, JFKL.
10. Mary Barelli Gallagher, *My Life with Jacqueline Kennedy* (New York: McKay, 1969), p. 145; Lincoln, *Twelve Years,* pp. 241, 335.
11. Salinger, *With Kennedy,* p. 90.
12. Lincoln, *Twelve Years,* pp. 298–299.
13. Jacqueline Kennedy to Lawrence F. O'Brien, January 23, 1963, Lincoln Dictation File, Box 62, POF, JFKL.
14. Typescript, Gridiron Dinner Comments, March 11, 1961, Sorensen Papers, Box 61, JFKL.
15. Gallagher, *My Life,* p. 122; *NYT,* February 22 and April 6, 1961; Salinger, *With Kennedy,* p. 87.
16. Wilma Hollness, JFKL–OH (Nancy Tuckerman and Pamela Turnure interview); *NYT,* February 5, 1961.
17. *NYT,* February 11, 1961.
18. Ibid., February 13, 1961; White House Appointment Books, JFKL.
19. Birmingham, *Onassis,* p. 97.
20. Gail Cameron, *Rose: A Biography of Rose Fitzgerald Kennedy* (New York: Putnam, 1971), p. 187.
21. Ibid., p. 189.
22. William Walton, interview, January 15, 1981.
23. Parmet, *Jack,* p. 118.
24. Rita Dallas and Jeanira Ratcliffe, *The Kennedy Case* (New York: Putnam, 1973), pp. 48–49.
25. Cameron, *Rose,* pp. 181, 187.
26. Dallas and Ratcliffe, *Kennedy Case,* p. 64.
27. William Walton, interview, January 15, 1981.
28. Gallagher, *My Life,* p. 76.
29. J. B. West, *Upstairs at the White House* (New York: Warner Paperback Library, 1974), p. 260.
30. William Walton, interview, January 15, 1981.
31. Press Panel, JFKL–OH (Fred Holborn interview).
32. Edwin Bayley, JFKL–OH (Larry Hackman interview).
33. Elizabeth Carpenter, LBJL–OH (Joe B. Frantz interview).
34. Chester Bowles to JFK, January 19, 1962, Bowles Papers, Box 297, Yale.
35. Frank Thompson, Jr., interview, May 11, 1977.
36. Gallagher, *My Life,* pp. 213, 223.
37. Confidential interview, March 10, 1981.
38. Pierre Salinger, JFKL–OH (Theodore H. White interview).
39. Salinger, *With Kennedy,* p. 87.
40. Birmingham, *Onassis,* pp. 100–101.
41. Dallas and Ratcliffe, *Kennedy Case,* p. 77; Traphes Bryant (with F. S. Leighton), *Dog Days at the White House* (New York: Macmillan, 1975), p. 13.
42. William Walton, interview, January 15, 1981.
43. Joseph Alsop, interview, July 26, 1977.
44. Edwin Bayley, JFKL–OH (Larry Hackman interview).
45. *Time,* December 29, 1975, p. 12.
46. F. M. Kater to Robert F. Kennedy, October 19, 1961, FBI Papers.

47. Laura Bergquist, interview, May 15, 1979.
48. Memorandum, J. Edgar Hoover, November 22, 1961, FBI Files.
49. H.W.G. to J. Edgar Hoover, March 30, 1962, FBI Files.
50. Bradlee, *Conversations,* p. 45.
51. Clark Clifford, JFKL–OH (Larry Hackman interview).
52. Fletcher Knebel, interview, May 15, 1979.
53. Clark Clifford, JFKL–OH (Larry Hackman, interview).
54. Bradlee, *Conversations,* p. 48; Memorandum, J. Edgar Hoover, November 22, 1961, FBI Files.
55. Bradlee, *Conversations,* p. 47.
56. Clark Clifford, JFKL–OH (Larry Hackman interview).
57. Fletcher Knebel, interview, May 15, 1979.
58. *Time,* September 28, 1962, p. 38.
59. *NYT,* April 4, 24, 1964.
60. Charles Spalding, JFKL–OH (John F. Stewart interview).
61. David J. Garrow, *The FBI and Martin Luther King, Jr.* (New York: W. W. Norton, 1981), p. 61.
62. *New York Journal American,* June 29, 1963.
63. C. A. Evans to J. Edgar Hoover, July 3, 1963, and attached unsigned memorandum, FBI Files.
64. G. Robert Blakey and Richard N. Billings, *The Plot to Kill the President* (New York: Times Books, 1981), p. 379; Judith Exner, *My Story* (New York: Grove Press, 1977), p. 86.
65. FBI Report, March 29, 1960, and Station Area Chief, Los Angeles (94–558) to J. Edgar Hoover, April 1, 1960, FBI Files.
66. M. A. Jones to Cartha DeLoach, July 13, 1960, and FBI Report, March 29, 1960, FBI Files.
67. O'Donnell and Powers, *"Johnny,"* p. 18.
68. Sally Quinn, "Judith Campbell Exner," *Washington Post,* June 24, 1977, pp. B-1 and B-3.
69. Exner, *My Story,* p. 231n.
70. Kenneth P. O'Donnell, interview, December 4, 1976.
71. Exner, *My Story,* p. 230.
72. White House Appointment Books, JFKL.
73. Galbraith, *Ambassador's Journal,* p. 135.
74. Dr. Janet Travell, JFKL–OH (Theodore C. Sorensen interview); White House Appointment Books, JFKL.
75. Dr. George Burkley, JFKL–OH (William McHugh interview); Dr. Hans Kraus, interview, December 8, 1980.
76. Chester V. Clifton, interview, October 1, 1981; Dr. George Burkley, JFKL–OH (William McHugh interview); Dr. Janet Travell, JFKL–OH (Theodore C. Sorensen interview).
77. Exner, *My Story,* pp. 221, 244–245.
78. Janet Travell, "Basis for the Multiple Uses of Local Block of Somatic Trigger Areas," *Mississippi Valley Medical Journal,* January 1949, pp. 13–21; Janet Travell, "The Myofascial Genesis of Pain," *Postgraduate Medicine,* May 1952, pp. 425–434.
79. Janet Travell, interview, December 10, 1980.
80. Hans Kraus, interview, December 8, 1980.
81. *NYT,* December 4, 1972.
82. Dr. George Burkley, JFKL–OH (William McHugh interview).
83. George Burkley, interview, January 12, 1981.
84. Janet Travell, interview, December 10, 1981.
85. Chester V. Clifton, interview, October 1, 1981.
86. Hans Kraus, interview, December 8, 1980.

87. George Burkley, LBJL–OH (T. Harrison Baker interview).
88. George Burkley, interview, January 12, 1981; Hans Kraus, interview, December 8, 1980.
89. Travell, *Office Hours*, p. 397.
90. Janet Travell, interview, December 10, 1980.
91. Hans Kraus, interviews, December 8, 1980, and October 27, 1981; George Burkley, interview, January 12, 1981, and George Burkley, LBJL–OH (T. Harrison Baker interview); Janet Travell, interview, December 10, 1980.
92. George Burkley, interview, January 12, 1981.
93. W. R. Smedberg III to George Burkley, June 14, 1963, POF, Box 67, JFKL.
94. *NYT*, July 19, 1963.
95. Janet Travell, interview, December 10, 1980.
96. George Burkley, JFKL–OH (William McHugh interview).
97. Chester V. Clifton, interview, October 1, 1981.
98. Whalen, *Founding Father*, pp. 479–480; Janet Travell, JFKL–OH (Theodore C. Sorensen interview); *NYT*, December 20 and 21, 1961.
99. Dallas and Ratcliffe, *Kennedy Case*, pp. 27–28, 217.
100. Robert F. Kennedy, JFKL–OH (John Bartlow Martin interview).
101. William Walton, interview, January 15, 1981; Charles Lewin, JFKL–OH (Ed Martin interview).
102. Ed Reid, *The Grim Reapers* (Chicago: Henry Regnery, 1969), pp. 183, 294–295.
103. Ibid., p. 287.
104. Robert F. Kennedy, *The Enemy Within* (New York: Harper & Row, 1960), p. 252.
105. U.S. Congress, Senate, *Alleged Assassination Plots Involving Foreign Leaders*, 94th Cong., 1st sess., Report #94–465 (Washington, D.C.: U. S. Government Printing Office, 1975), pp. 129–130. Hereafter cited as *Assassination Report*; Blakey and Billings, *Plot*, p. 59.
106. Kenneth P. O'Donnell, interview, December 4, 1976.
107. Blakey and Billings, *Plot*, p. 381.
108. *Assassination Report*, pp. 130–131.
109. Ibid., p. 130n.
110. Ibid., pp. 131–133.
111. Ibid., p. 133n.
112. Kennedy, *Public Papers . . . 1962*, p. 401.
113. DDRS (81) 71A.
114. Kennedy, *Public Papers . . . 1962*, p. 347.
115. Ibid., p. 387.
116. Gallup, *The Poll*, v. 3, pp. 1,759 and 1,762.
117. Charles Bartlett, JFKL–OH (Fred Holborn interview).
118. Ibid.
119. Robert F. Kennedy, JFKL–OH (John Bartlow Martin interview).
120. Gallup, *The Poll*, v. 3, p. 1,834.

Chapter 6

1. Robert F. Kennedy, JFKL–OH (John Bartlow Martin interview).
2. *Harper's*, February 1962, p. 14.
3. Kennedy, *Public Papers . . . 1962*, p. 259.
4. Ibid., p. 266.
5. *New York Herald Tribune*, March 24, 1957.
6. *New Republic*, January 8, 1962, p. 2.
7. John F. Kennedy, *The Strategy of Peace* (New York: Harper and Bros., 1960), p. 105.
8. McGeorge Bundy, interview, April 9, 1981.

9. Dwight D. Eisenhower, "Notes on a Luncheon Meeting with Kennedy," April 22, 1961, DDRS (81) 124B.
10. The Senator Gravel Edition, *The Pentagon Papers,* 5 vols. (Boston: Beacon Press, 1971), v. 2, p. 33.
11. Kennedy, *Public Papers . . . 1962,* p. 582.
12. Charles Stevenson, *The End of Nowhere: American Policy Toward Laos Since 1954* (Boston: Beacon Press, 1972), p. 240.
13. Dwight D. Eisenhower, *Waging Peace, 1956–1961* (Garden City, N.Y.: Doubleday, 1965), p. 607.
14. Gravel, *Pentagon Papers,* v. 5, p. 252; Roger Hilsman, *To Move a Nation* (Garden City, N.Y.: Doubleday, 1967), pp. 111–112; Schlesinger, *Thousand Days,* p. 325.
15. Stevenson, *End of Nowhere,* p. 111.
16. Gravel, *Pentagon Papers,* v. 5, p. 259.
17. Bernard B. Fall, *Anatomy of a Crisis* (Garden City, N.Y.: Doubleday, 1969), p. 199.
18. Joint Chiefs of Staff, Laos Situation Reports, December 30, 1960, and January 2–4, 1961, DDRS (80), 49B, 49C, 50A–50C.
19. Edward G. Lansdale, Columbia–OH, (Major Alnwich interview).
20. Sorensen, *Kennedy,* p. 649.
21. *NYT,* January 23, 1961.
22. Joint Chiefs of Staff, Laos Situation Report, January 7, 1961, DDRS (80) 52A.
23. Schlesinger, *Thousand Days,* p. 339.
24. Sorensen, *Kennedy,* p. 644.
25. Robert F. Kennedy, JFKL–OH (John Bartlow Martin interview).
26. Ibid.
27. Schlesinger, *Thousand Days,* p. 332.
28. George C. Herring, *America's Longest War,* (New York: John Wiley & Sons, 1979), p. 77.
29. Douglas S. Blaufarb, *The Counterinsurgency Era* (New York: Free Press, 1977), p. 18.
30. Chester V. Clifton, interview, October 1, 1981.
31. Gravel, *Pentagon Papers,* v. 2, p. 19.
32. Ibid., pp. 7, 26; Herring, *America's Longest War,* p. 76.
33. JFK to McGeorge Bundy, February 5, 1961, Lincoln Dictation File, Box 62, POF, JFKL.
34. DDRS (81) 84B.
35. Walt W. Rostow, JFKL–OH (Richard Neustadt interview).
36. Walt W. Rostow to Theodore C. Sorensen, March 16, 1961, NSF, Box 324, JFKL.
37. Edward G. Lansdale, Columbia–OH (Major Alnwich interview).
38. U.S., Congress, Senate, *Final Report of the Select Committee to Study Government Operations with Respect to Intelligence Activities,* 94th Cong., 2d sess., Report 94–755 (Washington, D.C.: U.S. Government Printing Office, A76), p.52. Hereinafter cited as *Church Committee.*
39. Michael Forrestal, interview, February 17, 1981.
40. Kennedy, *Public Papers . . . 1961,* p. 16.
41. Ibid., p. 154.
42. Stevenson, *End of Nowhere,* pp. 134–135, 138–139.
43. Sorensen, *Kennedy,* p. 643.
44. Stevenson, *End of Nowhere,* p. 141.
45. Roswell Gilpatric, JFKL–OH (Dennis O'Brien interview).
46. Eugene Zuckert, JFKL–OH (Lawrence McQuade interview); Walt W. Rostow, JFKL–OH (Richard Neustadt interview).
47. Eugene Zuckert, JFKL–OH (Lawrence McQuade interview).
48. Schlesinger, *Thousand Days,* p. 338; Charles J. V. Murphy, "Cuba: The Record Set Straight," *Fortune,* September 1961, p. 95.
49. Murphy, "Cuba," p. 96; Richard Bissell, interview, December 21, 1981.
50. John Kenneth Galbraith to JFK, May 10, 1961, POF, Box 29, JFKL.

51. Gravel, *Pentagon Papers,* v. 5, p. 261; *NYT,* March 19, 1961, sec. IV, p. 2.
52. Kennedy, *Public Papers . . . 1961,* p. 215.
53. J. William Fulbright to JFK, March 24, 1961, Fulbright Papers, Series 1, Box 1, University of Arkansas.
54. Schlesinger, *Thousand Days,* pp. 333–334; Arthur Dommen, *Conflict in Laos* (New York: Praeger Publishers, 1964), pp. 189–191; Warren I. Cohen, *Dean Rusk* (Totowa, N.J.: Cooper Square Publishers, 1980), p. 128; Stevenson, *End of Nowhere,* p. 146; *NYT,* March 26, 1961, sec. IV, p. 1.
55. Stevenson, *End of Nowhere,* p. 147; Schlesinger, *Thousand Days,* p. 334.
56. Stevenson, *End of Nowhere,* p. 148; *NYT,* March 30, 1961.
57. Schlesinger, *Thousand Days,* p. 334.
58. Chester V. Clifton, interview, October 1, 1961.
59. Harold Macmillan, *At the End of the Day, 1961–1963* (New York: Harper & Row, 1973), p. 238.
60. Chalmers Roberts, Memorandum of Background Briefing by President Kennedy, April 7, 1961, Roberts Personal Papers; cf. Roberts, *First Rough Draft,* pp. 192–193.
61. Kennedy, *Public Papers . . . 1961,* pp. 228–229; Stevenson, *End of Nowhere,* p. 147.
62. *NYT,* April 21, 1961; Kennedy, *Public Papers . . . 1961,* p. 260.
63. Chalmers Roberts, Memorandum, April 7, 1961, Roberts Personal Papers.
64. Robert F. Kennedy, JFKL–OH (Arthur M. Schlesinger, Jr., interview).
65. Schlesinger, *Robert Kennedy,* p. 385.
66. Joseph Alsop, interview, July 26, 1977.
67. Harold Macmillan to Dwight D. Eisenhower, April 9, 1961, POF, JFKL, Box 129.
68. Galbraith, *Ambassador's Journal,* pp. 89–90.
69. John Kenneth Galbraith, *A Life in Our Times* (Boston: Houghton Mifflin, 1981), p. 466.
70. Arthur Krock, Memorandum, Krock Papers (Black Notebook III), Box 1, Princeton.
71. John McCone to Arthur Krock, April 26, 1961, Krock Papers, Box 40, Princeton.
72. *National Review,* April 22, 1961, p. 248.
73. *NYT,* April 21, 1961.
74. Howard L. Burris to Lyndon B. Johnson, April 28, 1961, Vice-Presidential Security File, Box 5, LBJL.
75. CHMAAG to CINCPAC, April 26, 1961, Vice-Presidential Security File, Box 4, LBJL.
76. Winthrop Brown to Dean Rusk, April 26, 1961, Vice-Presidential Security File, Box 4, LBJL.
77. Gravel, *Pentagon Papers,* v. 2, p. 42.
78. Richard Bissell, interview, December 21, 1981.
79. Robert F. Kennedy, JFKL–OH (John Bartlow Martin interview).
80. U. Alexis Johnson, JFKL–OH (William H. Brubeck interview).
81. Robert F. Kennedy, JFKL–OH (John Bartlow Martin interview).
82. U. Alexis Johnson, JFKL–OH (William H. Brubeck interview).
83. Roswell Gilpatric, JFKL–OH (Dennis J. O'Brien interview).
84. DDRS (78) 147A; Report of NSC Meeting, April 27, 1961, NSF, Box 313, JFKL.
85. Roswell Gilpatric, JFKL–OH (Dennis J. O'Brien interview).
86. William Colby, *Honorable Men: My Life in the CIA* (New York: Simon and Schuster, 1978), p. 194.
87. Theodore C. Sorensen to JFK, April 28, 1961, Sorensen Papers, Box 34, JFKL.
88. U. Alexis Johnson, JFKL–OH (William H. Brubeck interview).
89. Galbraith, *Ambassador's Journal,* p. 93, and *A Life in Our Times,* p. 467.
90. DDRS (80) 300B; *NYT,* April 29, 1961.
91. Cohen, *Rusk,* p. 129; Gravel, *Pentagon Papers,* v. 5, p. 261.
92. Dean Rusk to JFK, May 1, 1961, DDRS (80) 300C.
93. Galbraith, *Ambassador's Journal,* p. 95.

94. *NYT,* May 1, 1961.
95. Report of NSC Meeting, NSF, Box 313, JFKL.
96. Kennedy, *Public Papers* . . . *1962,* p. 568.
97. Dean Rusk to JFK, May 1, 1961, DDRS (80) 300C.
98. Gravel, *Pentagon Papers,* v. 2, pp. 2–3.
99. Report of NSC Meeting, NSF, Box 313, JFKL.
100. Kennedy, *Public Papers* . . . *1961,* pp. 354, 356.
101. Howard L. Burris to Lyndon B. Johnson, April 28, 1961, Vice-Presidential Security File, Box 5, LBJL.
102. Hubert Humphrey, Memorandum, May 13, 1961, Humphrey Papers, Box 185, Minnesota Historical Society.
103. Gravel, *Pentagon Papers,* v. 2, p. 644.
104. DDRS (80) 373A, June 19, 1962.
105. Gravel, *Pentagon Papers,* v. 2, p. 646.
106. Colby, *Honorable Men,* p. 194.
107. *Church Committee,* pp. 147, 156.
108. John McCone to JFK, n.d., NSF, Countries, Vietnam, v. 14, LBJL.
109. Thomas Powers, *The Man Who Kept the Secrets: Richard Helms and the CIA* (New York: Pocket Books, 1981), p. 226; Colby, *Honorable Men,* p. 194; Wise and Ross, *Invisible Government,* p. 163.
110. David Nunnerly, *President Kennedy and Britain* (London: The Bodley Head, 1972), pp. 45–46.
111. *NYT,* June 4, 12, 13, 19, 1961.
112. Herring, *America's Longest War,* pp. 78–79.

Chapter 7

1. Kennedy, *Public Papers* . . . *1961,* pp. 312–313; Schlesinger, *Thousand Days,* p. 290.
2. Sorensen, *Kennedy,* p. 297.
3. *NYT,* February 11, 1961.
4. Ibid., February 15, 1961.
5. Jerome Levinson and Juan de Onis, *The Alliance that Lost Its Way* (Chicago: Quadrangle Books, 1970), p. 60; Berle, *Navigating the Rapids,* p. 737.
6. Sorensen, *Kennedy,* p. 306.
7. Leonard Mosley, *Dulles* (New York: Dial Press/James Wade, 1978), p. 468.
8. Richard Bissell, interview, December 21, 1981.
9. Wyden, *Bay of Pigs,* p. 165.
10. McGeorge Bundy, interview, April 9, 1981.
11. Mosley, *Dulles,* p. 473n.
12. Philip W. Bonsal, "Cuba, Castro and the United States," *Foreign Affairs,* January 1967, p. 267.
13. Ibid.; Eisenhower, *Waging Peace,* p. 613.
14. Report to the Inter-American Peace Committee, August 1, 1960, White House Office, International Series, Box 4, Cuba (5), Eisenhower Library, DDRS (81) 191B.
15. Sorensen, *Kennedy,* p. 298.
16. Irving L. Janis, *Victims of Groupthink* (Boston: Houghton Mifflin, 1972), p. 36.
17. Robert Amory, Jr., JFKL–OH (Joseph O'Connor interview).
18. Richard Bissell, interview, December 21, 1981.
19. Wyden, *Bay of Pigs,* p. 124.
20. *Church Committee,* pp. 121–123; Wyden, *Bay of Pigs,* pp. 43, 109–110; David C. Martin, *Wilderness of Mirrors* (New York: Harper & Row, 1980), pp. 121–122.

21. Richard Bissell, interview, December 21, 1981.
22. Theodore C. Sorensen, JFKL–OH (Carl Kaysen interview).
23. Martin, *Stevenson and the World,* p. 624.
24. Chester Bowles, *Promises to Keep* (New York: Harper & Row, 1971), pp. 327–330; cf. Chester Bowles to Dean Rusk, March 31, 1961, and to JFK, April 14, 1961, Bowles Papers, Box 297, Yale.
25. Schlesinger, *Thousand Days,* pp. 245–246, 255.
26. Arthur M. Schlesinger, Jr., to JFK, March 15, 1961, DDRS (77) 250D; Schlesinger to JFK, March 31, 1961, Box 5, JFKL.
27. Arthur M. Schlesinger, Jr., to Tracy Barnes, March 29, 1961, DDRS (77) 250E.
28. Arthur M. Schlesinger, Jr., to JFK, April 10, 1961, POF, Box 65, JFKL.
29. Dean Acheson, JFKL–OH (Lucius Battle interview).
30. DDRS (77) 11A; Arthur M. Schlesinger, Jr., to JFK, March 20, 1961, POF, Box 65, JFKL.
31. Turner Catledge, *My Life and The Times* (New York: Harper & Row, 1971), pp. 261–265.
32. Maxwell Taylor, *Swords and Plowshares* (New York: W. W. Norton, 1972), p. 188.
33. Richard Bissell, JFKL–OH (Joseph E. O'Connor interview).
34. Cuba Study Group, Memo #3, NSF, Box 61, JFKL.
35. Wyden, *Bay of Pigs,* p. 139n; Richard Bissell, interview, December 21, 1981.
36. Richard Bissell, interview, December 21, 1981.
37. Cuba Study Group, Memo #1, June 13, 1961, p. 11, NSF, Box 61, JFKL.
38. Ibid.
39. CIA Weekly Report, April 6, 1961, DDRS (77) 11C.
40. Schlesinger, *Thousand Days,* p. 267.
41. Kennedy, *Public Papers . . . 1961,* pp. 258–259.
42. Schlesinger, *Thousand Days,* p. 266.
43. Kennedy, *Public Papers . . . 1961,* pp. 276–277, 279.
44. Bowles, *Promises,* p. 329.
45. *NYT,* April 16, 1961.
46. Ibid.
47. Dean Rusk to Adlai Stevenson, April 12, 1961, Schlesinger Papers, Box 5, JFKL.
48. Richard Bissell, interview, December 21, 1981.
49. Schlesinger, *Robert Kennedy,* p. 448.
50. Richard Bissell, interview, December 21, 1981.
51. Wyden, *Bay of Pigs,* pp. 197–200.
52. Ibid., p. 170.
53. Richard Bissell, telephone conversation, December 22, 1981.
54. Schlesinger, *Robert Kennedy,* p. 448.
55. Wyden, *Bay of Pigs,* pp. 205–206.
56. *NYT,* April 18, 1961.
57. Martin, *Stevenson and the World,* p. 628.
58. Wyden, *Bay of Pigs,* p. 264.
59. DDRS (77) 266B; *NYT,* April 18, 1961.
60. DDRS (77) 266B.
61. Martin, *Stevenson and the World,* p. 629.
62. Wyden, *Bay of Pigs,* p. 236.
63. Ibid., pp. 267, 271.
64. Ibid., p. 271.
65. Schlesinger, *Thousand Days,* p. 275.
66. Wyden, *Bay of Pigs,* p. 289.
67. *NYT,* April 19, 1961.
68. Tad Szulc and Karl E. Meyer, *The Cuban Invasion* (New York: Ballantine Books, 1962), p. 86; Wyden, *Bay of Pigs,* p. 116.
69. Hugh Thomas, *Cuba: The Pursuit of Freedom* (New York: Harper & Row, 1971), p. 1,283.

70. Schlesinger, *Thousand Days,* p. 278.
71. Wyden, *Bay of Pigs,* p. 303n.
72. Ibid., p. 292; Arthur M. Schlesinger, Jr., to JFK, April 19, 1961, POF, Box 65, JFKL; Blakey and Billings, *Plot,* pp. 158–159; Schlesinger, *Thousand Days,* p. 284.
73. J. William Fulbright, JFKL–OH (Pat Hopt interview).
74. *NYT,* April 20, 1961.
75. Ibid., April 21, 1961.
76. Chester Bowles, JFKL–OH (Robert Brooks interview).
77. Fred Dutton, JFKL–OH (Charles T. Morrissey interview).
78. Chester Bowles to JFK, April 20, 1961, Bowles Papers, Box 297, Yale.
79. Bowles, *Promises,* p. 332.
80. DDRS (81) 124B.
81. Ibid.
82. Ibid.
83. *NYT,* April 23, 1961.
84. Charles Spalding, JFKL–OH (John F. Stewart interview).
85. *NYT,* May 2, 1961.
86. Memorandum, June 5, 1961, Eisenhower Post-Presidential Papers, Box 10, Eisenhower Library.
87. *NYT,* April 21, 1961; Kennedy, *Public Papers . . . 1961,* p. 306.
88. *NYT,* April 26, 1961.
89. Nixon, *RN,* pp. 234–235.
90. *NYT,* April 21, 26, 1961.
91. Ibid., April 26, 1961.
92. O'Donnell and Powers, *"Johnny,"* p. 14.
93. Schlesinger, *Thousand Days,* p. 339; Sorensen, *Kennedy,* p. 641; William Manchester, *American Caesar* (Boston: Little, Brown, 1978), pp. 696, 744.
94. Krock, Private Memorandum, Krock Papers (Black Notebook III), Box 1, Princeton.
95. Kennedy, Notes of Conversation, April 28, 1961, POF, Box 31, JFKL.
96. Gallup, *The Poll,* v. 3, p. 1,717.

Chapter 8

1. Dean Rusk, "The President," *Foreign Affairs,* April 1960, pp. 360–361.
2. Sorensen, *Kennedy,* p. 542.
3. *NYT,* June 9, 1961; Dr. George Burkley, JFKL–OH (William McHugh interview).
4. Chester V. Clifton and Cecil Stoughton, *Memories* (New York: W. W. Norton, 1980), p. 7.
5. *NYT,* December 4, 1972.
6. Kennedy, *Public Papers . . . 1961,* p. 406.
7. Sorensen, *Kennedy,* p. 584.
8. Jack M. Schick, *The Berlin Crisis, 1958–1962* (Philadelphia: University of Pennsylvania Press, 1971), pp. 12–14, 31.
9. Ibid., p. 143.
10. Kennedy, *Strategy of Peace,* p. 212.
11. Adam B. Ulam, *Expansion and Coexistence* (New York and Washington: Praeger Publishers, 1968), pp. 630–631; Robert M. Slusser, *The Berlin Crisis of 1961* (Baltimore: Johns Hopkins University Press, 1973), pp. 16–17, 20.
12. Schick, *Berlin,* p. 140.
13. J. William Fulbright, JFKL–OH (Pat Hopt interview).
14. Martin J. Hillenbrand, JFKL–OH (Paul R. Sweet interview).
15. Schlesinger, *Thousand Days,* pp. 380–381; *NYT,* June 1, 1961.
16. Arthur M. Schlesinger, Jr., to JFK, April 6, 1961, Box 5, Schlesinger Papers, JFKL.

17. Paul Nitze, JFKL–OH (Dorothy Fosdick interview).
18. Fred Holborn, interview, March 10, 1981; Abram Chayes, JFKL–OH (Eugene Gordon interview).
19. Wofford, *Kennedys and Kings*, p. 125.
20. Kennedy, *Public Papers . . . 1961*, p. 417.
21. Schlesinger, *Thousand Days*, p. 349.
22. *NYT*, June 7, 1961.
23. Ibid., June 15, 1961.
24. Charles Bohlen, *Witness to History, 1929–1969* (New York: W. W. Norton, 1973), p. 480.
25. Abram Chayes, JFKL–OH (Eugene Gordon interview).
26. *NYT*, June 3, 1961.
27. Ibid.
28. Ibid., June 6, 1961.
29. Richard J. Walton, *Cold War and Counterrevolution* (New York: Viking Press, 1972), p. 171.
30. Paul Nitze, JFKL–OH (Dorothy Fosdick interview); *NYT*, June 1, 1961; Bohlen, *Witness*, pp. 479–480.
31. Bohlen, *Witness*, p. 480.
32. Thomas Finletter, JFKL–OH (Philip J. Farley interview).
33. Charles de Gaulle, *Memoirs of Hope: Renewal and Endeavor* (New York: Simon and Schuster, 1971), p. 258.
34. Walter Lippmann, JFKL–OH (Elizabeth Farmer interview).
35. Sir Alec Douglas-Home, JFKL–OH (statement issued on March 17, 1965).
36. David Ormsby-Gore to Robert F. Kennedy, October 18, 1961, RFK Personal Correspondence, Box 3, JFKL.
37. Kennedy, *Public Papers . . . 1961*, p. 224.
38. *NYT*, June 5, 6, 1961.
39. As quoted in Walton, *Cold War*, p. 81.
40. *NYT*, June 5, 1961.
41. Peter Lisagor, JFKL–OH (Ronald Grele interview).
42. Schlesinger, *Thousand Days*, p. 374.
43. Strobe Talbott, ed., *Khrushchev Remembers: The Last Testament* (Boston: Little, Brown, 1974), p. 497.
44. Charles Bohlen, JFKL–OH (Arthur Schlesinger, Jr., interview).
45. Talbott, ed., *Khrushchev*, p. 495.
46. Bohlen, *Witness*, p. 481.
47. Sorensen, *Kennedy*, p. 545.
48. *NYT*, June 12, 1961.
49. McGeorge Bundy to JFK, June 9, 1961, POF, Box 62, JFKL; *NYT*, June 5, 6, 1961.
50. *NYT*, June 4, 1961.
51. Mike Mansfield, JFKL–OH (Seth Tillman interview).
52. Kennedy, *Public Papers . . . 1961*, pp. 443–445.
53. Slusser, *Berlin Crisis*, pp. 7, 10–17.
54. J. William Fulbright, JFKL–OH (Pat Hopt interview).
55. Robert F. Kennedy, JFKL–OH (John Bartlow Martin interview).
56. Kennedy, *Public Papers . . . 1961*, p. 476.
57. Schlesinger, *Thousand Days*, p. 381.
58. NSC Memorandum, June 29, 1961, NSF, Box 313, JFKL, and Berlin Papers for Hyannis Port, July 14–16, 1961, NSF, Box 313, JFKL.
59. Slusser, *Berlin Crisis*, p. 20.
60. Cohen, *Rusk*, pp. 139–140.
61. Berle, *Navigating the Rapids*, p. 750.

62. Theodore C. Sorensen, JFKL-OH (Carl Kaysen interview).
63. Sorensen, *Kennedy*, p. 587.
64. Chester Bowles to Dean Rusk, July 7, 1961, Bowles Papers, Box 297, Yale.
65. Robert F. Kennedy, JFKL-OH (John Bartlow Martin interview).
66. Martin J. Hillenbrand, JFKL-OH (Paul R. Sweet interview).
67. Chester V. Clifton, interview, October 1, 1981; Paul Nitze, JFKL-OH (Dorothy Fosdick interview).
68. Patterson, "Bearing the Burden," p. 206.
69. Paul Nitze, JFKL-OH (Dorothy Fosdick interview).
70. *NYT*, September 25, 1961.
71. Stewart Alsop, "Kennedy's Grand Strategy," *Saturday Evening Post*, March 31, 1962, p. 14.
72. Arthur M. Schlesinger, Jr., to McGeorge Bundy, July 18, 1961, DDRS (78) 301A.
73. Michael Mandelbaum, *The Nuclear Question* (New York: Cambridge University Press, 1979), p. 94.
74. Kennedy, *Public Papers . . . 1961*, pp. 533–540; White House Press Release, July 26, 1961.
75. Letitia Baldrige to JFK, July 27, 1961, POF, Box 62, JFKL.
76. JFK to Eleanor Roosevelt, July 28, 1961, Eleanor Roosevelt Papers, Box 4473, FDRL.
77. JFK to Richard Russell, August 2, 1962, POF, Box 122, JFKL.
78. *New Republic*, January 15, 1962, pp. 19–24.
79. Harry Truman to JFK, August 1, 1961, POF, Box 33, JFKL.
80. J. William Fulbright to JFK, July 26, 1961, Fulbright Papers, Series 1, Box 1, University of Arkansas.
81. Gallup, *The Poll*, v. 3, p. 1,729.
82. Chester V. Clifton, interview, October 1, 1981.
83. Martin J. Hillenbrand, JFKL-OH (Paul R. Sweet interview).
84. Lucius Clay to Dean Rusk, January 17, 1962, POF, Special Correspondence, JFKL.
85. Theodore C. Sorensen, JFKL-OH (Carl Kaysen interview).
86. Sorensen, *Kennedy*, p. 594.
87. Robert Amory, Jr., JFKL-OH (Joseph O'Connor interview).
88. Roberts, *First Rough Draft*, pp. 200–201.
89. Lyndon B. Johnson to JFK, August 31, 1961, Vice-Presidential Security Files, Box 7, LBJL.
90. Carl Kaysen, interview, January 19, 1981.
91. Sorensen, *Kennedy*, p. 619.
92. Chalmers Roberts, Memorandum, February 28, 1966, Roberts Personal Papers.
93. Gallup, *The Poll*, v. 3, p. 1,759.
94. Robert F. Kennedy, JFKL-OH (John Bartlow Martin interview).
95. Kennedy, *Public Papers . . . 1961*, p. 587.
96. Glenn T. Seaborg, *Kennedy, Khrushchev, and the Test Ban* (Berkeley: University of California Press, 1981), p. 88.
97. Kennedy, *Public Papers . . . 1961*, p. 584; Kennedy, *Public Papers . . . 1962*, p. 187.

Chapter 9

1. Chester Bowles to JFK, December 1, 1962, POF, Box 128, JFKL.
2. Harris Wofford to JFK, July 17, 1961, Box 128, JFKL.
3. Abram Chayes, JFKL-OH (Eugene Gordon interview).
4. Sorensen, *Kennedy*, p. 288.
5. Chester Bowles to JFK, Bowles Papers, Box 297, Yale.

6. U. Alexis Johnson, JFKL–OH (William H. Brubeck interview).
7. Bowles, *Promises,* p. 353.
8. Schlesinger, *Thousand Days,* p. 441.
9. Robert F. Kennedy, JFKL–OH (John Bartlow Martin interview).
10. Robert F. Kennedy, JFKL–OH (John Bartlow Martin interview).
11. Bowles, *Promises,* pp. 352–359; Chester Bowles, JFKL–OH (Robert Brooks interview).
12. Kenneth Dameron, "President Kennedy and Congress: Process and Politics," unpublished Ph.D. dissertation, Harvard University, 1975, p. 164.
13. Ibid., p. 173.
14. Confidential source.
15. Richard Russell to Robert E. Bruce, Jr., n.d., Russell Papers, Box I. C. 3, Russell Library, University of Georgia.
16. *Congressional Quarterly,* November 14, 1962, and January 17, 1964.
17. Lewis J. Paper, *The Promise and the Performance* (New York: Crown Publishers, 1975), p. 331.
18. Wilbur Mills, interview, March 10, 1981; Charles U. Daly, JFKL–OH (Charles T. Morrissey interview).
19. Wilbur Mills, interview, March 10, 1981.
20. Ibid.
21. Allen Ellender, JFKL–OH (Larry Hackman interview).
22. Hale Boggs, JFKL–OH (Charles T. Morrissey interview).
23. Leverett Saltonstall, JFKL–OH (Dennis J. Lynch interview).
24. J. William Fulbright, JFKL–OH (Pat Hopt interview).
25. Charles U. Daly, JFKL–OH (Charles T. Morrissey interview).
26. Edwin Bayley, JFKL–OH (Larry Hackman interview).
27. Fred Holborn, interview, March 10, 1981.
28. Morgan, *Kerr,* p. vii.
29. Ibid., p. 223.
30. Robert F. Kennedy, JFKL–OH (Anthony Lewis and John Bartlow Martin interviews).
31. Morgan, *Kerr,* p. 222.
32. Edwin Bayley, JFKL–OH (Larry Hackman interview).
33. White House Appointment Book, JFKL.
34. Edwin Bayley, JFKL–OH (Larry Hackman interview).
35. Morgan, *Kerr,* p. 222.
36. Schlesinger, *Robert Kennedy,* p. 512n.
37. Kennedy, *Public Papers . . . 1962,* p. 573.
38. Ibid., p. 635.
39. Chalmers Roberts, Memorandum, October 11, 1962, Roberts Personal Papers.
40. Lyndon B. Johnson to JFK, August 21, 1961, DDRS (78) 301B.
41. Schlesinger, *Robert Kennedy,* p. 462.
42. Kennedy, *Public Papers . . . 1962,* p. 535.
43. Schlesinger, *Robert Kennedy,* p. 467.
44. Robert F. Kennedy, JFKL–OH (John Bartlow Martin interview).
45. Kennedy, *Public Papers . . . 1962,* p. 641.
46. James Killian, interview, June 12, 1980.
47. Clark Clifford, JFKL–OH (Larry Hackman interview).
48. James Killian, interview, June 12, 1980, and Richard Bissell, interview, March 5, 1982.
49. Clark Clifford, interview, April 18, 1980; Robert F. Kennedy, JFKL–OH (John Bartlow Martin interview).
50. Roger Hilsman, JFKL–OH (Dennis J. O'Brien interview).
51. Edwin Bayley, JFKL–OH (Larry Hackman interview); Theodore C. Sorensen, interview, May 17, 1977; Robert Amory, Jr., JFKL–OH (Joseph O'Connor interview).
52. Edwin Bayley, JFKL–OH (Larry Hackman interview).
53. DDRS (78) 442A, May 10, 1961.

54. Circular Instructions to Ambassadors, April 16, 1962, NSF, Box 373, JFKL.
55. NASM 162, June 19, 1962, DDRS (80) 373A.
56. U. Alexis Johnson, JFKL–OH (William H. Brubeck interview).
57. Blaufarb, *Counterinsurgency,* p. 54.
58. *Assassination Report,* pp. 146–147.
59. Robert F. Kennedy, JFKL–OH (John Bartlow Martin interview).
60. Schlesinger, *Robert Kennedy,* p. 497.
61. *Assassination Report,* pp. 149–152; Richard Bissell, interview, March 5, 1982.
62. Cord Meyer, *Facing Reality: From World Federalism to the CIA* (New York: Harper & Row, 1980), p. 218.
63. *Assassination Report,* p. 132.
64. Ibid., pp. 138–139.
65. George Smathers, JFKL–OH (Don Wilson interview).
66. Roswell Gilpatric, JFKL–OH (Dennis J. O'Brien interview).
67. *Assassination Report,* p. 148.
68. Ibid., pp. 157–158.
69. Berle, *Navigating the Rapids,* pp. 741, 743.
70. Mike Mansfield to JFK, May 1, 1961, Vice-Presidential Security Files, Box 4, LBJL.
71. Paul B. Fay, Jr., *The Pleasure of His Company* (New York: Harper & Row, 1966), pp. 174–175.
72. David Detzer, *The Brink: Cuban Missile Crisis, 1962* (New York: Thomas Y. Crowell, 1979), pp. 136–137.
73. Graham T. Allison, *Essence of Decision: Explaining the Cuban Missile Crisis* (Boston: Little, Brown, 1971), p. 141.
74. Roswell Gilpatric, JFKL–OH (Dennis J. O'Brien interview).
75. *Assassination Report,* p. 140.
76. Ibid., p. 144.
77. Ibid., p. 150.
78. Powers, *Man Who Kept the Secrets,* p. 171.
79. *Assassination Report,* p. 141.
80. Ibid., pp. 150–151, 156, 160.
81. Powers, *Man Who Kept the Secrets,* p. 178.
82. Schlesinger, *Robert Kennedy,* p. 478.
83. *Assassination Report,* p. 143.
84. Ibid., p. 144.
85. Ibid., p. 145.
86. Ibid., p. 144.
87. Powers, *Man Who Kept the Secrets,* p. 178.
88. Blakey and Billings, *Plot,* p. 60.
89. Robert F. Kennedy, JFKL–OH (John Bartlow Martin interview).
90. *Assassination Report,* p. 162.
91. Powers, *Man Who Kept the Secrets,* p. 196.
92. Department of State, *Bulletin,* Oct. 14, 1963, p. 579.
93. Schlesinger to Goodwin, April 12, 1961, Schlesinger Papers, Box 11, JFKL.
94. Bowles to Rusk, Feb. 8, 1962, Bowles Papers, Box 301, Yale.
95. Stephansky to Rusk, March 14, 1962, Schlesinger Papers, Box 1, JFKL.
96. Daniel M. Braddock to Rusk, April 23, 1962, Schlesinger Papers, Box 1, JFKL.
97. George Ball to ARA Diplomatic Posts, May 4, 1962, Schlesinger Papers, Box 1, JFKL.
98. Kennedy, *Public Papers . . . 1962,* p. 521.
99. Department of State, *Bulletin,* Oct. 14, 1963, p. 580.
100. Levinson and De Onis, *Alliance,* p. 14.
101. Lucius D. Battle to Walt W. Rostow, April 18, 1961, NSF, Box 205, and Robert W. Komer to JFK, January 19, 1963, NSF, Box 314, JFKL.

102. George McGhee, JFKL–OH (Martin J. Hillenbrand interview).
103. Roberts, *First Rough Draft*, p. 203.
104. George McGhee, JFKL–OH (Martin J. Hillenbrand interview).
105. Cohen, *Rusk*, p. 209.
106. Joseph E. Johnson, interview, April 13, 1981; Robert F. Kennedy, JFKL–OH (John Bartlow Martin interview).
107. Dean Rusk, interview, April 27, 1981.
108. Phillips Talbot, interview, May 6, 1981.
109. David P. Forsythe, *United Nations Peacemaking* (Baltimore: Johns Hopkins University Press, 1972), p. 124.
110. *NYT*, April 18, 21, 1961.
111. Joseph E. Johnson, interview, April 13, 1981.
112. Kennedy, *Statements and Speeches*, p. 1,135.
113. Philip M. Klutznick, JFKL–OH (Dennis J. O'Brien interview).
114. *NYT*, June 25, 1961.
115. JFK to McGeorge Bundy, July 10, 1961, POF, Box 62, JFKL.
116. Myer Feldman, JFKL–OH (John F. Stewart interview).
117. As quoted in Joseph E. Johnson, *Arab vs. Israeli: A Persistent Challenge to Americans* (Harriman, N.Y.: Arden House, 1963), p. 12.
118. Joseph E. Johnson, interview, April 13, 1981; Myer Feldman, JFKL–OH (John F. Stewart interview).
119. Dean Rusk, interview, April 27, 1981.
120. *NYT*, May 13, 1962.
121. Joseph E. Johnson, interview, April 13, 1981.
122. Myer Feldman, JFKL–OH (John F. Stewart interview).
123. Telegrams, Armin Meyer to Dean Rusk, September 25, 28, 1962; Summary of Foreign Radio and Press Reaction to the U.S. Decision to Sell Missiles to Israel, n.d., NSF, Box 119, JFKL.
124. Telegrams, Dean Rusk to Myer Feldman, August 10, 1962, and Dean Rusk to David Bruce, August 17, 1962, NSF, Box 118, JFKL.
125. John Badeau, JFKL–OH (Dennis O'Brien interview).
126. William Macomber, JFKL–OH (Dennis J. O'Brien interview).
127. Phillips Talbot, interview, May 6, 1981.
128. Robert Komer, telephone conversation, April 11, 1981.
129. John Badeau, JFKL–OH (Dennis J. O'Brien interview).
130. Memorandum for the President, August 17, 1962, NSF, Box 118, JFKL.
131. Myer Feldman to Dean Rusk, August 20, 1962, NSF, Box 118, JFKL.
132. Dean Rusk to John S. Badeau, August 21, 1962, NSF, Box 118, JFKL.
133. Myer Feldman to Dean Rusk, August 21, 1962, NSF, Box 118, JFKL.
134. *NYT*, October 4, 1962, and November 13, 1962.
135. Joseph E. Johnson, interview, April 13, 1981; Myer Feldman, JFKL–OH (John F. Stewart interview).
136. *NYT*, February 1, 1963.
137. Dean Rusk, interview, April 27, 1981.
138. State Department, Memorandum of Conversation, December 27, 1962, NSF, Box 119, JFKL.
139. Walworth Barbour to Dean Rusk, January 22, 1963, NSF, Box 119, JFKL.

Chapter 10

1. Roger Blough, interview, April 7, 1981.
2. Charles Bartlett, JFKL–OH (Fred Holborn interview).

3. Arthur J. Goldberg, interview, March 10, 1981; Dorothy Goldberg, *A Private View of a Public Life* (New York: Charter House, 1975), p. 112.
4. Bradlee, *Conversations,* p. 77.
5. Grant McConnell, *Steel and the Presidency* (New York: W. W. Norton, 1963), p. 106.
6. Bradlee, *Conversations,* pp. 81–82.
7. McConnell, *Steel,* p. 98.
8. Ibid., p. 90; Schlesinger, *Robert Kennedy,* p. 404.
9. Kennedy, *Public Papers . . . 1962,* p. 376.
10. Paper, *Promise and Performance,* p. 326.
11. Charles U. Daly, JFKL–OH (Charles T. Morrissey interview).
12. Kennedy, *Public Papers . . . 1962,* pp. 344–345.
13. Ibid., p. 433.
14. Robert F. Kennedy, JFKL–OH (John Bartlow Martin interview).
15. Rowen, *Free Enterprisers,* pp. 130–131.
16. Robert A. Lovett, JFKL–OH (Dorothy Fosdick interview).
17. Sorensen, *Kennedy,* pp. 421–424.
18. *Washington Post,* June 2, 1962.
19. Walter W. Heller, "Notes on JFK's Yale Commencement Speech," Heller Papers, Box 4, JFKL; Heller, interview, June 18, 1980.
20. Ibid.
21. Kennedy, *Public Papers . . . 1962,* p. 473.
22. Ibid., p. 472.
23. Ibid.
24. Ibid., pp. 471–475.
25. Research Institute Report, June 30, 1962, Sorensen Papers, Box 29, JFKL.
26. Theodore C. Sorensen, "Talking Paper for Cabinet Meeting, July 26, 1962," Sorensen Papers, Box 29, JFKL.
27. Walter W. Heller to JFK, August 9, 1962, Sorensen Papers, Box 40, JFKL.
28. Gallup, *The Poll,* v. 3, p. 1,780.
29. Transcript of Remarks, June 4, 1962, Sorensen Papers, Box 29, JFKL.
30. White House Appointment Books, JFKL.
31. Luther Hodges to Theodore C. Sorensen, July 19, 1962, Sorensen Papers, Box 29, JFKL.
32. Theodore C. Sorensen, "Talking Paper for Cabinet Meeting of July 26, 1962," Sorensen Papers, Box 29, JFKL.
33. Felix Frankfurter, JFKL–OH (Charles McLaughlin interview) and summary of conversation, July 26, 1962.
34. Walter W. Heller to JFK, July 14, 1962, Heller Papers, Box 5, JFKL.
35. Theodore C. Sorensen to JFK, July 12, 1962, Sorensen Papers, Box 40, JFKL.
36. Gardner Ackley, Memorandum for the Files, July 26, 1962, Heller Papers, Box 6, JFKL.
37. Walter W. Heller to JFK, August 9, 1962, Sorensen Papers, Box 40, JFKL.
38. Kennedy, *Public Papers . . . 1962,* pp. 615–616.
39. Ibid., pp. 877–879.
40. Herbert Stein, *The Fiscal Revolution in America* (Chicago: University of Chicago Press, 1969), p. 421.
41. Sorensen, *Kennedy,* p. 430.
42. Seymour E. Harris, *Economics of the Kennedy Years and a Look Ahead* (New York: Harper & Row, 1964), p. 73; Kennedy, *Public Papers . . . 1963,* pp. 73–92.
43. Bernard D. Nossiter, *The Mythmakers* (Boston: Little, Brown, 1964), p. 36.
44. Felix Frankfurter, JFKL–OH (Charles McLaughlin interview).
45. Walter W. Heller to JFK, October 17, 1962, Heller Papers, Box 5, JFKL.
46. Charles Bartlett, JFKL–OH (Fred Holborn interview).
47. Robert F. Kennedy, JFKL–OH (John Bartlow Martin interview).

Chapter 11

1. Kirk H. Porter and Donald Bruce Johnson, *National Party Platforms, 1840–1960* (Urbana: University of Illinois Press, 1961), pp. 599–600.
2. Hart, "Kennedy, Congress, and Civil Rights," pp. 168–169.
3. Carl M. Brauer, *John F. Kennedy and the Second Reconstruction* (New York: Columbia University Press, 1977), p. 153.
4. George Smathers, interview, April 13, 1977.
5. Roy Wilkins, JFKL–OH (Thomas Baker interview).
6. Mike Mansfield, JFKL–OH (Seth Tillman interview).
7. Harvard Sitkoff, *The Struggle for Black Equality, 1954–1980* (New York: Hill & Wang, 1981), p. 106.
8. Hale Boggs, JFKL–OH (Charles T. Morrissey interview).
9. Sitkoff, *Struggle,* p. 113.
10. Burke Marshall, JFKL–OH (Louis Oberdorfer interview).
11. Cf. Sitkoff, *Struggle,* pp. 101–103.
12. Transcript of Telephone Conversation, Robert F. Kennedy and George E. Cruit, May 15, 1961, RFK Correspondence, Box 12, JFKL.
13. Burke Marshall, JFKL–OH (Louis Oberdorfer interview).
14. Victor S. Navasky, *Kennedy Justice* (New York: Atheneum, 1971), p. 21.
15. Burke Marshall, JFKL–OH (Louis Oberdorfer interview).
16. Kennedy, *Public Papers . . . 1961,* p. 391.
17. Robert F. Kennedy, Memorandum of Telephone Conversation, May 20, 1961, RFK Personal Correspondence, Box 12, JFKL.
18. Sitkoff, *Struggle,* pp. 107–108.
19. Schlesinger, *Robert Kennedy,* p. 295.
20. Navasky, *Kennedy Justice,* p. 21.
21. Joseph Dolan to Robert F. Kennedy, May 26, 1961, RFK Personal Correspondence, Box 12, JFKL.
22. Navasky, *Kennedy Justice,* p. 21.
23. *NYT,* June 6, 1961.
24. Wofford, *Kennedys and Kings,* pp. 157–158.
25. Harris Wofford to JFK, June 6, 1961, POF, Box 67, JFKL.
26. Sitkoff, *Struggle,* p. 114.
27. Navasky, *Kennedy Justice,* pp. 20–21.
28. Schlesinger, *Thousand Days,* p. 935; Steven F. Lawson, *Black Ballots: Voting Rights in the South, 1944–1969* (New York: Columbia University Press, 1976), pp. 283, 290, 342.
29. Brauer, *Second Reconstruction,* p. 69.
30. Robert C. Weaver, JFKL–OH (Daniel P. Moynihan interview).
31. Brauer, *Second Reconstruction,* p. 79.
32. Robert C. Weaver, JFKL–OH (Daniel P. Moynihan interview).
33. Schlesinger, *Robert Kennedy,* p. 315.
34. Joseph Rauh, Jr., JFKL–OH (Charles T. Morrissey interview).
35. Wofford, *Kennedys and Kings,* p. 136.
36. *NYT,* February 13, 24, 1961.
37. Hart, "Kennedy, Congress, and Civil Rights," p. 171.
38. Ibid., p. 172.
39. Kennedy, *Public Papers . . . 1962,* pp. 382–383.
40. Brauer, *Second Reconstruction,* pp. 135–137; *NYT,* May 10, 11, 13, 15, 16, 17, 1962; Burke Marshall, JFKL–OH (Anthony Lewis interview).
41. Brauer, *Second Reconstruction,* p. 143.
42. Nicholas Katzenbach to Byron White, October 20, 1961, Sorensen Papers, Box 30, JFKL.
43. Brauer, *Second Reconstruction,* p. 85.

44. Lee White to JFK, November 13, 1961, Sorensen Papers, Box 30, JFKL.
45. Theodore Hesburgh, JFKL–OH (Joseph O'Connor interview).
46. Burke Marshall, JFKL–OH (Anthony Lewis interview).
47. Ibid.
48. Gallup, *The Poll,* v. 3, p. 1,742.
49. *Washington Post,* December 11, 1961.
50. Kennedy, *Public Papers . . . 1962,* p. 21.
51. Ibid., p. 544.
52. Sitkoff, *Struggle,* p. 125.
53. Brauer, *Second Reconstruction,* p. 173.
54. Kennedy, *Public Papers . . . 1961,* pp. 592–593.
55. Brauer, *Second Reconstruction,* p. 175.
56. Cf. Walter Lord, *The Past That Would Not Die* (New York: Harper & Row, 1965), *passim;* Schlesinger, *Robert Kennedy,* pp. 317–326.
57. Schlesinger, *Robert Kennedy,* pp. 317–318.
58. Robert F. Kennedy, JFKL–OH (Anthony Lewis interview).
59. Theodore C. Sorensen to JFK, September 28, 1962, Sorensen Papers, Box 30, JFKL.
60. Kenneth P. O'Donnell, interview, December 4, 1976.
61. Log of Presidential Recordings, JFKL.
62. Schlesinger, *Robert Kennedy,* p. 326.
63. Ibid., p. 321.
64. Kennedy, *Public Papers . . . 1962,* pp. 726–728.
65. Schlesinger, *Robert Kennedy,* p. 324.
66. Hart, "Kennedy, Congress, and Civil Rights," p. 175; Brauer, *Second Reconstruction,* pp. 206–207.
67. Sorensen, *Kennedy,* p. 282; Kennedy, *Public Papers . . . 1962,* p. 832.
68. Joseph Rauh, Jr., to JFK, December 7, 1962, Humphrey Papers, Box 241, Minnesota Historical Society.
69. Brauer, *Second Reconstruction,* p. 220.
70. Kennedy, *Public Papers . . . 1963,* p. 10.
71. Brauer, *Second Reconstruction,* p. 220.
72. Kennedy, *Public Papers . . . 1963,* pp. 221–230.
73. Brauer, *Second Reconstruction,* pp. 221–222.
74. Ibid., p. 224.
75. Sitkoff, *Struggle,* p. 139; Schlesinger, *Robert Kennedy,* p. 329; Brauer, *Second Reconstruction,* p. 239.
76. Schlesinger, *Robert Kennedy,* p. 329.
77. Burke Marshall, JFKL–OH (Louis Oberdorfer interview).
78. *Wall Street Journal,* May 16, 1963.
79. Burke Marshall, JFKL–OH (Louis Oberdorfer interview).
80. *Wall Street Journal,* May 16, 1963.
81. Kennedy, *Public Papers . . . 1963,* pp. 397–398.
82. Schlesinger, *Robert Kennedy,* pp. 338–340.
83. Burke Marshall, JFKL–OH (Louis Oberdorfer interview).
84. Schlesinger, *Robert Kennedy,* pp. 340–342.
85. Robert F. Kennedy, JFKL–OH (Anthony Lewis interview).
86. Theodore C. Sorensen, JFKL–OH (Carl Kaysen interview).
87. Schlesinger, *Robert Kennedy,* pp. 330–335.
88. Transcript of Telephone Conversation, Lyndon B. Johnson and Theodore C. Sorensen, June 3, 1963, LBJL.
89. Ibid.
90. Kennedy, *Public Papers . . . 1963,* pp. 469–470.
91. Brauer, *Second Reconstruction,* p. 265.
92. Sitkoff, *Struggle,* p. 151.

93. Earl Blaik, JFKL-OH (Charles T. Morrissey interview).
94. Ibid.
95. Gallup, *The Poll*, v. 3, pp. 1,823–1,828.
96. Ibid., pp. 1,835, 1,841, 1,850, 1,851.
97. Ibid., pp. 1,833–1,834.
98. Burke Marshall, JFKL-OH (Louis Oberdorfer interview); Brauer, *Second Reconstruction*, pp. 275–276.
99. William Connell to Hubert H. Humphrey, June 26, 1963, Humphrey Papers, Box 593, Minnesota Historical Society.
100. JFK to Dwight D. Eisenhower, June 10, 1963, Sorensen Papers, Box 30, JFKL; Brauer, *Second Reconstruction*, p. 269.
101. Ibid.; Evans and Novak, *Lyndon B. Johnson*, p. 377.
102. Brauer, *Second Reconstruction*, p. 272.
103. Theodore C. Sorensen, JFKL-OH (Carl Kaysen interview).
104. Richard Russell to William Knowland, June 24, 1963, Russell Papers, Box I. J. 10, Russell Library, University of Georgia.
105. Frank Boykin to Harry Byrd, et al., June 25, 1963, Byrd Papers, Box 265, University of Virginia; Robertson to Virginius Dabney, June 1, 1963, Robertson Papers, College of William and Mary.
106. H. L. Hunt to Harry Byrd, July 11, 1963, Byrd Papers, Box 270, University of Virginia.
107. *Washington Post*, July 21, 1963.
108. Transcript of Remarks, July 24, 1963, Johnson Papers, Civil Rights, Box 6, JFKL.
109. Lewis, *King*, ch. 8.
110. White House Appointment Books, JFKL.
111. Hart, "Kennedy, Congress, and Civil Rights," p. 174.
112. Schlesinger, *Thousand Days*, p. 978.
113. Fay, *Pleasure*, p. 240.

Chapter 12

1. Detzer, *Brink*, p. 179.
2. Sorensen, *Kennedy*, p. 693.
3. Detzer, *Brink*, p. 229.
4. Richard Neustadt to Theodore C. Sorensen, October 27, 1962, Sorensen Papers, Box 36, JFKL.
5. Ibid., p. 177.
6. Schlesinger, *Thousand Days*, p. 817.
7. Ibid., p. 797.
8. Theodore C. Sorensen, JFKL-OH (Carl Kaysen interview).
9. Elie Abel, *The Missile Crisis* (New York: Bantam Books, 1966), p. 38.
10. Dean Acheson, JFKL-OH (Lucius Battle interview).
11. Walt W. Rostow to JFK, December 29, 1962, POF, Box 65, JFKL.
12. Allison, *Essence*, p. 117.
13. Ibid., p. 50.
14. Herbert S. Dinnerstein, *The Making of a Missile Crisis, October 1962* (Baltimore: Johns Hopkins University Press, 1976), pp. 155–156.
15. Roswell Gilpatric, JFKL-OH (Dennis J. O'Brien interview).
16. Schlesinger, *Robert Kennedy*, pp. 503–504.
17. Detzer, *Brink*, pp. 40–41.
18. Abel, *Missile Crisis*, p. 8.
19. Mandelbaum, *Nuclear Question*, p. 135.

20. Robert F. Kennedy, JFKL–OH (John Bartlow Martin interview).
21. Sorensen, *Kennedy,* p. 667.
22. Robert F. Kennedy, *Thirteen Days* (New York: W. W. Norton, 1969), p. 27.
23. Abram Chayes, *The Cuban Missile Crisis* (New York: Oxford University Press, 1974), p. 11; Kennedy, *Thirteen Days,* p. 28.
24. Chester Bowles to JFK, October 15, 1962, Bowles Papers, Box 297, Yale; Averell Harriman, Columbia–OH (Edward W. Barrett interview).
25. Schlesinger, *Robert Kennedy,* p. 528; Talbott, ed., *Khrushchev Remembers,* p. 511.
26. Talbott, ed., *Khrushchev Remembers,* p. 511.
27. Roberts, *First Rough Draft,* p. 211.
28. Robert Amory, Jr., JFKL–OH (Joseph O'Connor interview).
29. Kennedy, *Public Papers . . . 1962,* p. 652.
30. Roberts, *First Rough Draft,* p. 203.
31. Chayes, *Cuban Missile Crisis,* pp. 10–11; Detzer, *Brink,* p. 67.
32. Kennedy, *Public Papers . . . 1962,* p. 675.
33. Arthur Krock, Confidential Memorandum, n.d., Krock Papers, Box 1 (Black Notebook III), Seeley G. Mudd Library, Princeton.
34. John McCone, LBJL–OH (Joe B. Frantz interview).
35. Allison, *Essence,* p. 190; Detzer, *Brink,* p. 63.
36. Detzer, *Brink,* p. 80.
37. Howard L. Burris to Lyndon B. Johnson, October 3, 1962, Vice-Presidential Security File, Box 6, LBJL.
38. Howard L. Burris to Lyndon B. Johnson, October 3, 1962, Vice-Presidential Security File, Box 6, LBJL.
39. Edwin Martin, JFKL–OH (Lee Miller interview); Chayes, *Cuban Missile Crisis,* p. 13.
40. O'Donnell and Powers, *"Johnny,"* p. 310.
41. Schlesinger, *Robert Kennedy,* p. 506.
42. Edwin Martin, JFKL–OH (Lee Miller interview).
43. Roswell Gilpatric, JFKL–OH (Dennis J. O'Brien interview).
44. Edwin Martin, JFKL–OH (Lee Miller interview).
45. Roberts, *First Rough Draft,* p. 204; Chalmers Roberts, Memorandum, October 16, 1962, Roberts Personal Papers.
46. Elie Abel, JFKL–OH (Dennis J. O'Brien interview).
47. U.S. Intelligence Board Report, October 16, 1962, NSF Files, Box 313, JFKL.
48. Schlesinger, *Thousand Days,* p. 805.
49. Detzer, *Brink,* p. 129.
50. Kennedy, *Thirteen Days,* p. 31.
51. Schlesinger, *Robert Kennedy,* p. 508.
52. Detzer, *Brink,* pp. 164–168.
53. Henry M. Pachter, *Collision Course: The Cuban Missile Crisis and Coexistence* (New York: Praeger Publishers, 1963), p. 42.
54. Sorensen, *Kennedy,* p. 692.
55. Schlesinger, *Robert Kennedy,* pp. 509–510.
56. Pachter, *Collision Course,* p. 31.
57. Kennedy, *Thirteen Days,* p. 47.
58. Sorensen, *Kennedy,* p. 693.
59. O'Brien, *No Final Victories,* p. 141.
60. Kennedy, *Thirteen Days,* pp. 47–48.
61. Edwin Martin, JFKL–OH (Lee Miller interview).
62. NSC Meeting #505, Record of Actions, October 20, 1962, Vice-Presidential Security File, Box 8, LBJL.
63. Martin, *Stevenson and the World,* p. 723; Adlai Stevenson to Arthur M. Schlesinger, Jr., n.d., NSF Files, JFKL.

64. Martin, *Stevenson and the World*, p. 723; Schlesinger, *Thousand Days*, p. 808.
65. Theodore C. Sorensen, JFKL–OH (Carl Kaysen interview).
66. Robert F. Kennedy, JFKL–OH (Arthur M. Schlesinger, Jr., interview); Abel, *Missile Crisis*, p. 137.
67. Detzer, *Brink*, pp. 161–162; Schlesinger, *Thousand Days*, p. 810.
68. Martin, *Stevenson and the World*, p. 724.
69. Schlesinger, *Robert Kennedy*, p. 511.
70. Sorensen, *Kennedy*, p. 698.
71. Earl T. Leonard, Russell Library–OH (Hugh Gordon Cates interview).
72. Kennedy, *Thirteen Days*, pp. 53–55.
73. Dean Rusk and J. William Fulbright, Russell Library–OH (Hugh Gordon Cates interview).
74. Kennedy, *Thirteen Days*, p. 67.
75. Ibid., p. 52; Pachter, *Collision Course*, p. 32; Edwin Martin, JFKL–OH (Lee Miller interview).
76. Kennedy, *Public Papers . . . 1962*, pp. 806–809.
77. Kennedy, *Thirteen Days*, pp. 55–56.
78. Loretta Connelly to Evelyn Lincoln, October 23, 1962, POF, Box 28, JFKL.
79. Ross Barnett to Robert F. Kennedy, October 23, 1962, RFK Personal Correspondence, Box 9, JFKL.
80. Detzer, *Brink*, p. 192.
81. Schlesinger, *Robert Kennedy*, p. 514.
82. Martin, *Stevenson and the World*, pp. 726–728.
83. Kennedy, *Thirteen Days*, pp. 60–62.
84. Ibid., pp. 69–70.
85. Ibid., p. 82.
86. Chayes, *Cuban Missile Crisis*, p. 84.
87. *NYT*, October 26, 1962; Martin, *Stevenson and the World*, pp. 733–734.
88. Detzer, *Brink*, p. 227.
89. Detzer, *Brink*, pp. 236–237; Schlesinger, *Thousand Days*, p. 827.
90. Detzer, *Brink*, pp. 237, 239.
91. Walt W. Rostow, JFKL–OH (Richard Neustadt interview).
92. Barton J. Bernstein, "The Cuban Missile Crisis: Trading the Jupiters in Turkey?" *Political Science Quarterly*, Spring 1980, pp. 97–125.
93. Research Memorandum to Dean Rusk, October 27, 1962, NSF, Box 36, JFKL.
94. George McGhee, JFKL–OH (Martin J. Hillenbrand interview).
95. NSC Executive Committee Record of Action, October 27, 1962, Vice-Presidential Security Files, Box 8, LBJL.
96. Kennedy, *Thirteen Days*, p. 98.
97. Detzer, *Brink*, p. 258.
98. Chayes, *Cuban Missile Crisis*, p. 100.
99. Schlesinger, *Thousand Days*, p. 825.
100. Pachter, *Collision Course*, pp. 67–68.
101. Foy Kohler to Dean Rusk, October 28, 1962, Vice-Presidential Security Files, Box 8, LBJL.
102. Kennedy, *Thirteen Days*, pp. 202–203.
103. Ibid., pp. 108–109.
104. Ibid., p. 207.
105. Dwight D. Eisenhower, Memorandum of Telephone Conversation, October 29, 1962, Post-Presidential Papers, 1961–69, Box 10, DDEL.
106. Dean Acheson to JFK, October 29, 1962, POF, Box 27, JFKL.
107. *Assassination Report*, p. 170.
108. Richard Bissell, interview, March 5, 1982.
109. *Assassination Report*, p. 171.

110. Memorandum, Bureau of Intelligence and Research, April 23, 1963, NSF, Box 315, JFKL.
111. Schlesinger, *Robert Kennedy*, p. 551.
112. *Assassination Report*, pp. 173–174.
113. William Attwood, interview, September 11, 1980.

Chapter 13

1. Laura Bergquist, interview, May 15, 1979.
2. Lord Longford, *Kennedy* (London: Weidenfeld and Nicolson, 1976), p. 204.
3. Fletcher Knebel, interview, May 15, 1979.
4. Clem Norton, JFKL–OH (William Mahoney interview).
5. Bryant and Leighton, *Dog Days*, p. 70.
6. Stein and Plimpton, *American Journey*, p. 186.
7. Press Panel Interview, JFKL–OH (Fred Holborn interview).
8. Pierre Salinger, JFKL–OH (Theodore H. White interview).
9. Steel, *Lippmann*, p. 538.
10. Charles Roberts, Columbia–OH (David Berliner interview).
11. Walter Lippmann, JFKL–OH (Elizabeth Farmer interview).
12. Steel, *Lippmann*, p. 538.
13. Walter Lippmann, JFKL–OH (Elizabeth Farmer interview).
14. *Time*, December 29, 1975, p. 11.
15. Ibid., pp. 11–12.
16. Barbara Ward Jackson, JFKL–OH (Walt W. and Elspeth Rostow interview).
17. Parmet, *Jack*, p. 174.
18. Confidential interview, July 25, 1977.
19. William Attwood, interview, September 11, 1980.
20. Meyer, *Facing Reality*, p. 142.
21. Kennedy, *Public Papers . . . 1963*, pp. 704–707.
22. Phillip Nobile and Ron Rosenbaum, "The Curious Aftermath of JFK's Best and Brightest Affair," *New Times*, July 9, 1976, p. 25.
23. Ibid., p. 31.
24. *Newsweek*, March 1, 1976, p. 32.
25. Cf. Nobile and Rosenbaum, "Curious Aftermath," p. 31.
26. Confidential source.
27. Kenneth P. O'Donnell, interview, December 4, 1976.
28. Robert F. Kennedy, JFKL–OH (John Bartlow Martin interview).
29. William Walton, interview, January 15, 1981.
30. Ben Bradlee, interview, May 13, 1977.
31. George Smathers, JFKL–OH (Don Wilson interview).
32. William Walton, interview, January 15, 1981.
33. Dean Rusk, interview, April 27, 1981.
34. Kennedy, *Public Papers . . . 1962*, p. 889.
35. Kennedy, *Thirteen Days*, p. 208.
36. Walt W. Rostow, *The Diffusion of Power* (New York: Macmillan, 1972), p. 178.
37. Seaborg, *Kennedy*, p. 176.
38. Sorensen, *Kennedy*, pp. 725–726.
39. Walt W. Rostow, JFKL–OH (Richard Neustadt interview).
40. Rostow, *Diffusion of Power*, p. 179.
41. McGeorge Bundy to JFK, January 21, 1963, NSF, Box 314, JFKL.
42. Seaborg, *Kennedy*, p. 182.
43. Adrian Fisher, JFKL–OH (Frank Sieverts interview).

44. Seaborg, *Kennedy*, pp. 180–181.
45. Richard Russell to Mrs. Thomas M. Shaw, March 18, 1963, Russell Papers, Box IX. I. 6, Russell Papers, Russell Library, University of Georgia.
46. Thomas Dodd to Adrian Fisher, March 29, 1963, Ibid.
47. Seaborg, *Kennedy*, p. 192.
48. Ibid., p. 193.
49. Ibid., p. 180.
50. Kennedy, *Public Papers* . . . *1963*, pp. 459–464.
51. Seaborg, *Kennedy*, pp. 206–207.
52. Schlesinger, *Thousand Days*, p. 904.
53. John S. D. Eisenhower, Memorandum of Conference, July 24, 1963, Post-Presidential Papers, 1961–69, Box 10, Eisenhower Library.
54. Seaborg, *Kennedy*, p. 259.
55. *Congress and the Nation, 1945–1964* (Washington, D.C.: Congressional Quarterly Service, 1965), p. 134.
56. Kennedy, *Public Papers* . . . *1963*, pp. 622–624.
57. Edward Teller to Jeffrey Cohelan, July 19, 1963, Humphrey Papers, Box 593, Minnesota Historical Society.
58. Sorensen, *Kennedy*, p. 739.
59. William Connell to Kenneth P. O'Donnell, August 6, 1963, Humphrey Papers, Box 593, Minnesota Historical Society.
60. Sorensen, *Kennedy*, p. 739.
61. *Congress and the Nation*, p. 92a.
62. Schlesinger, *Thousand Days*, p. 913.
63. O'Donnell and Powers, *"Johnny,"* p. 379; Kennedy, *Public Papers* . . . *1963*, pp. 724–726.
64. Cf. Walton, *Cold War*, p. 155.
65. Sorensen, *Kennedy*, p. 740.
66. Richard D. Mahoney, "The Kennedy Policy in the Congo, 1961–1963," unpublished Ph.D. dissertation, Johns Hopkins University School of Advanced International Studies, Washington, D.C. 1979, p. 178.
67. Ibid., pp. 145–146, 292–293.
68. Ibid., p. 302.
69. Stephen R. Weissman, *American Policy in the Congo, 1960–1964* (Ithaca: Cornell University Press, 1974), p. 169.
70. Mahoney, "Kennedy Policy," pp. 338–339.
71. Ibid., p. 331.
72. Ibid., p. 339.
73. Ulam, *Expansion and Coexistence*, p. 642.
74. George McGhee, JFKL–OH (Martin J. Hillenbrand interview).
75. Memorandum for the Record, November 1, 1962, DDRS (80) 212B.
76. Curtis LeMay to Robert McNamara, December 11, 1962, DDRS (80) 144B.
77. Office of National Estimates Draft Memorandum, December 11, 1962, DDRS (78) 6C.
78. Memorandum of Meeting, NSC, December 17, 1962, Vice-Presidential Security File, Box 8, LBJL.
79. Madeleine G. Kalb, *The Congo Cables* (New York: Macmillan, 1982), p. 366.
80. Carl Kaysen to George Ball, January 2, 1963, DDRS (80), 213B.
81. Mahoney, "Kennedy Policy," pp. 453–454; Kalb, *Congo Cables*, pp. 366–371.
82. JFK to George McGhee, January 21, 1963, George McGhee Personal Papers.
83. Edmund Gullion, JFKL–OH (Samuel E. Belk interview).
84. Edmund Gullion, interview, August 18, 1980.
85. Richard J. Walton, *The Remnants of Power* (New York: Coward-McCann, 1968), p. 83.

86. Briefing Books, June 1963, Vice-Presidential Security File, Box 3, LBJL.
87. O'Donnell and Powers, *"Johnny,"* pp. 359–360; Kennedy, *Public Papers . . . 1963,* pp. 505–511.
88. O'Donnell and Powers, *"Johnny,"* p. 360.
89. Ibid., p. 360.
90. Kennedy, *Public Papers . . . 1963,* pp. 524–525.
91. O'Donnell and Powers, *"Johnny,"* p. 360.
92. Ibid., p. 363.
93. Ibid., p. 371.
94. Ibid., p. 373.

Chapter 14

1. O'Donnell and Powers, *"Johnny,"* p. 378; cf. Travell, *Office Hours,* p. 421; Lincoln, *Twelve Years,* pp. 349–354; Gallagher, *My Life,* pp. 283–289.
2. Herring, *America's Longest War,* p. 92.
3. Walt W. Rostow, JFK Symposium Remarks, Los Angeles, California, November 14, 1980.
4. Gravel, *Pentagon Papers,* v. 2, pp. 690–691.
5. Ibid., p. 691.
6. Herring, *America's Longest War,* p. 90.
7. Memorandum, Chalmers Roberts, August 30, 1961, Roberts Personal Papers.
8. Kennedy, *Public Papers . . . 1963,* p. 659.
9. Michael Forrestal, interview, February 17, 1981; Roger Hilsman, JFKL–OH (Dennis J. O'Brien interview).
10. Gravel, *Pentagon Papers,* v. 2, pp. 717–725.
11. Herring, *America's Longest War,* p. 94.
12. O'Donnell and Powers, *"Johnny,"* p. 16.
13. Herring, *America's Longest War,* p. 96.
14. Cohen, *Rusk,* p. 189.
15. Robert F. Kennedy, JFKL–OH (John Bartlow Martin interview).
16. Geoffrey Warner, "The United States and the Fall of Diem," *Australian Outlook,* 28 (December 1974), p. 247.
17. Henry Cabot Lodge, Jr., JFKL–OH (Charles Bartlett interview).
18. Herring, *America's Longest War,* p. 97.
19. Ibid., p. 103; Robert F. Kennedy, JFKL–OH (John Bartlow Martin interview).
20. Warner, "Fall of Diem," pp. 249–250.
21. Gravel, *Pentagon Papers,* v. 2, pp. 734–735.
22. Roswell Gilpatric, JFKL–OH (Dennis J. O'Brien interview).
23. Taylor, *Swords,* p. 293.
24. Michael Forrestal, interview, February 17, 1981.
25. Hilsman, *To Move a Nation,* p. 489.
26. Warner, "Fall of Diem," p. 252.
27. Robert F. Kennedy, JFKL–OH (John Bartlow Martin interview).
28. Taylor, *Swords,* p. 293.
29. David Halberstam, *The Best and the Brightest* (New York: Random House, 1972), p. 264; Gravel, *Pentagon Papers,* v. 2, pp. 728–739.
30. Warner, "Fall of Diem," p. 255.
31. Kennedy, *Public Papers . . . 1963,* p. 652.
32. Hilsman, *To Move a Nation,* p. 500.
33. Gravel, *Pentagon Papers,* v. 2, pp. 245–246.
34. *Washington Post,* September 18, 1963.

35. Gravel, *Pentagon Papers*, v. 2, pp. 750–751, 752–753.
36. Roswell Gilpatric, JFKL–OH (Dennis J. O'Brien interview); Sorensen, *Kennedy*, p. 659.
37. Geoffrey Warner, "The Death of Diem," *Australian Outlook* (April 1975), pp. 12–13; Roger Hilsman, JFKL–OH (Dennis J. O'Brien interview).
38. CIA Chronological Report, October 23, 1963, DDRS (78) 142A.
39. Henry Cabot Lodge, Jr., JFKL–OH (Charles Bartlett interview).
40. Warner, "Death of Diem," p. 14.
41. Gravel, *Pentagon Papers*, v. 2, p. 789.
42. Warner, "Death of Diem," pp. 15–16.
43. Taylor, *Swords*, p. 301.
44. George Smathers, JFKL–OH (Don Wilson interview).
45. Michael Forrestal, interview, February 17, 1981.
46. Blair Clark, interview, July 20, 1977.
47. Michael Forrestal, interview, February 15, 1981.
48. Torbert Macdonald, Jr., interview, August 6, 1979.
49. Phyllis Macdonald, interview, August 9, 1979.
50. Confidential interview, July 25, 1977.
51. Ibid.
52. O'Donnell and Powers, *"Johnny,"* p. 382.
53. Chester V. Clifton, interview, October 1, 1981.
54. Theodore C. Sorensen, JFKL–OH (Carl Kaysen interview).
55. Kennedy, *Public Papers . . . 1963*, p. 892.
56. Dean Rusk, interview, April 27, 1981.
57. Kenneth P. O'Donnell, interview, December 4, 1976.
58. Robert F. Kennedy, JFKL–OH (John Bartlow Martin interview).
59. Lincoln, *My Twelve Years*, p. 337.
60. Bradlee, *Conversations*, p. 206.
61. *NYT*, September 18, 1963.
62. Janet Travell, interview, December 10, 1980.
63. Kennedy, *Public Papers . . . 1963*, p. 695; *NYT*, September 21, 1963.
64. Kitty Kelley, *Jackie Oh!* (New York: Lyle Stuart, 1978), p. 196.
65. *NYT*, October 29, 1963.
66. Kelley, *Jackie Oh!*, pp. 196–197.
67. Birmingham, *Onassis*, p. 112.
68. Ibid.; Kelley, *Jackie Oh!*, p. 197.
69. *NYT*, October 5–15, 1963.
70. Birmingham, *Onassis*, p. 113.
71. *NYT*, October 18, 1963.
72. Gallagher, *My Life*, p. 297.
73. Brauer, *Second Reconstruction*, p. 271.
74. Ibid., p. 268.
75. *Congress and the Nation*, p. 1,633.
76. O'Donnell and Powers, *"Johnny,"* p. 39.
77. Martin, *Stevenson and the World*, p. 774.
78. Adlai Stevenson to Agnes Meyer, November 1, 1963, Stevenson Papers, Box 864, Princeton.
79. Adlai Stevenson to Kenneth O'Donnell, November 4, 1963, Stevenson Papers, Box 862, Princeton.
80. Brauer, *Second Reconstruction*, pp. 308–309.
81. Hale Boggs, JFKL–OH (Charles T. Morrissey interview).
82. U.S., Congress, House, *Hearings Before the Select Committee on Assassinations*, 13 vols. (Washington, D.C.: U.S. Government Printing Office, 1979), v. 1, p. 31. Hereafter cited as *Stokes Committee*.
83. *NYT*, November 22, 1963; William Manchester, *The Death of a President* (New York: Harper & Row, 1967), pp. 73–75; Kennedy, *Public Papers . . . 1963*, pp. 882–883.

84. *NYT,* November 22, 1963.
85. Ibid., November 23, 1963.
86. Kennedy, *Public Papers* . . . *1963,* pp. 888–889; *Stokes Committee,* pp. 37–38.
87. *Stokes Committee,* p. 36.
88. Ibid., p. 37.
89. Ibid., p. 38.
90. Ibid., p. 37.
91. Ibid.
92. Ibid., p. 39.
93. Ibid., p. 40.
94. *NYT,* November 23, 1963.
95. Ibid.
96. U.S. Information Agency, "Assassination and Transition," December 2, 1963, Humphrey Papers, Box 240, Minnesota Historical Society.
97. Gallup, *The Poll,* v. 2, p. 1,854.
98. *Report of the Warren Commission on the Assassination of President Kennedy* (New York: McGraw-Hill, 1964), p. 41.
99. David S. Lifton, *Best Evidence* (New York: Macmillan, 1980), p. 692.
100. Anthony Summers, *Conspiracy* (New York: McGraw-Hill, 1980), pp. 277–279.
101. *NYT,* December 30, 1978, and June 3, 1979; *Stokes Committee,* pp. 161, 179, 180.
102. *NYT,* December 2, 1980.
103. Ibid., October 5, 1981.
104. *Stokes Committee,* pp. 744–795.
105. DeLloyd J. Gurth and David R. Wrone, *The Assassination of John F. Kennedy* (Westport, Conn.: Greenwood Press, 1980).
106. David W. Belin, "The Case Against a Conspiracy," *New York Times Magazine,* July 15, 1979, p. 73.
107. *Boston Globe,* March 31, 1981.

Index